The Role of the Public Sector in Building Social and Economic Resilience

Alina Hyz
Editor

The Role of the Public Sector in Building Social and Economic Resilience

A Public Finance Approach

palgrave
macmillan

Editor
Alina Hyz
Department of Accounting & Finance
University of West Attica
Athens, Greece

ISBN 978-3-031-67701-4 ISBN 978-3-031-67702-1 (eBook)
https://doi.org/10.1007/978-3-031-67702-1

This Palgrave Macmillan imprint is published by the registered company Springer Nature Switzerland AG
The registered company address is: Gewerbestrasse 11, 6330 Cham, Switzerland

Acknowledgments

The idea to write this book arose during my time as director of the postgraduate program "Public Economics and Policy" at the University of West Attica in Athens, Greece. This program has always enjoyed great popularity. During conversations with colleagues and students, it became clear that there is a lack of books that combine theory with practice and focus on the role of the public sector in ensuring social and economic stability and resilience.

I would like to express my gratitude to everyone who contributed to the creation of this book; to all those who supported me through discussions, conversations, reflections, criticism and who never doubted the necessity of its creation. Warm words of appreciation are due to my colleagues, students, lecturers and staff members. I would also like to thank everyone who, with their insightful questions, often demonstrating considerable professional experience, verified the theses presented in individual chapters in this book.

The main goal of this book is to convince those not yet fully convinced, uncertain and searching that the public sector plays a very important role in creating and maintaining economic and social resilience.

I would also like to thank everyone at Palgrave Macmillan for enabling me to publish this book and for their collaboration and technical support.

Contents

Notes on Contributors

Andreas Alexopoulos is an Associate Professor in the Dept. of Accounting & Finance at School of Administrative, Economic and Social Sciences, University of West Attica (UniWA), Athens, Greece. He serves as a Lecturer in the postgraduate program of Public Economics and Policy at UniWA since 2014. He also collaborates with various other postgraduate programs. He has participated in a number of National and EU Projects. He has extensive experience in local development projects, having worked as a consultant from 2003 to 2017 for various local authorities. His research interests primarily revolve around local and regional development, local government, social innovation, strategic planning, digital transformation, participatory processes and organizational reforms.

Vassiliki-Maria Balla is Assistant Professor of Accounting in Department of Tourism Management at University of Patras. She holds a BA in Accounting from Technological Educational Institution of Chalkida, a B.Sc. in Economics from University of Piraeus, an M.Sc. in Audit and Applied Accounting from National and Kapodistrian University of Athens and an M.Sc. in Banking and Finance from Athens University of Economics and Business. She holds a Ph.D. in Accounting and Corporate Governance from Technical University of Crete. Furthermore, she holds an Advanced Diploma in Accounting and Business from ACCA. Her research areas of interest are accounting, audit and finance.

Panagiotis Ballas is the Director of Tax and Customs Academy of the Independent Authority for Public Revenue in Greece. He holds a Ph.D. in Innovative Services Marketing Strategy, an M.Sc. in Internal Auditing and Management, an EMSc in Accounting and Financial Management, and a First Degree on Economics. He is a Postdoctoral Researcher in the Department of Accounting and Finance in the University of West Attica, Greece and his research interest is innovation strategy in public administration. He is a Fellow of the Higher Education Academy.

Dimitrios Charamis is currently an Assistant Professor of the Accounting and Finance Department at the University of West Attica. He holds a Ph.D. in Accounting and Auditing, and his research interests are mainly focused on Accounting and Accounting Information Systems, Auditing, Internal Auditing and Corporate Governance. His academic research and scientific studies have been published to internationally recognize academic journals and presented to national and international conferences and professional associations.

Ioannis Chatzopoulos holds a Ph.D. in Economics from the Democritus University of Thrace, a B.A. in Accounting & Finance, from the University of Teesside and an M.A. in Finance & Investment from the University of Exeter. He is currently appointed as permanent employee at the Decentralized Administration of Macedonia—Thrace (Regional Unit of Rodopi) in the field of Administrative Financial Personnel. He has also worked as Freelance Financial Advisor and at the Research Committee of the Democritus University of Thrace (DUTH) in the Departments of Programming and Development, and Monitoring.

George A. Georgiou is acting Director General of Financial Audits within the Ministry of National Economy and Finance, and Chairman of the Audit Coordination Committee. He holds a Ph.D. in the field of financial planning from Strathclyde University, Scotland, UK. He is a Certified Government Audit Professional, Certified Internal Control Auditor and Certified Fraud Examiner. He has served in various posts in the European Institutions as an expert on E U Budget and Internal Audit within the European Defense Agency. His recently book on Performance audit has been published by Papazisis Editions.

Dimitris Giakoulas is a political scientist specializing in international and European studies and macroeconomics. He is an Adjunct Lecturer in International Political Economy at the Department of Political Sciences of the Aristotle University of Thessaloniki, Greece. He is also a Research Associate at the Institute of Small Enterprises of the Hellenic Confederation of Professionals, Craftsmen & Merchants (IME GSEVEE). He holds a Ph.D. from the University of Athens on the determinants of Foreign Direct Investment. His research interests focus on FDI and multinational enterprises, macroeconomics, economic and policy analysis, and European and international political economy.

Grigorios Gikas is a Professor of Financial System at the Department of Business Administration of the University of West Attica, Greece and Adjunct Professor, Hellenic Open University, Postgraduate Program in Banking. He has been a President of the Technological Educational Institute of Epirus, Greece from 2005 till 2013, Dean of the Faculty of Accounting (2001–2003). He taught at the University of Lodz, Warsaw, Gdansk, Ioannina, TEI of Mesologgi and TEI of Patras. He has over 50 publications in refereed journals, international conference papers (full-text review) and articles in economic newspapers and journals.

Apostolis Gkikas is a consultant at the Financial Accounting Advisory Services Industry in Greece, Ernst & Young (E&Y). He holds an M.Sc. degree in Banking and a Master of Business Administration (MBA) from the University of Athens (NKUA). He studied Statistics and Actuarial Science at the University of Piraeus, School of Finance and Statistics. He has participated in numerous seminars and conferences. Currently, he is a Ph.D. candidate at the University of West Attica, Athens, Greece.

Stavroula Grigoriadou is civil servant at the Ministry of Economy and Finance, in the Directorate of Budget and Financial Reporting and Ph.D. candidate at the Department of Accounting and Finance of the University of West Attica. Her research interests are in the public sector and administration, focusing on strategic planning and administrative reforms.

Alina Hyz is Professor of Financial Management and Head of the Department of Accounting and Finance at the University of West Attica, Athens, Greece, where she also serves as the Director of the Postgraduate Programme in Public Economics and Policy. She studied economics at the University of Lodz, Poland and holds a Ph.D. in Business Administration from the same university. She has received invitations and given speeches at various universities and institutions, as well as at international conferences. She is an author of several international publications. She was a Robert Schuman Fellow at the European Parliament, Directorate-General for Research, Luxembourg. Her research interests are focused on business analysis, budgeting and financial economics.

Yiorgos Ioannidis studied Economics at the Department of Economic and Regional Development (Panteion University), completed his post-graduate studies in urban planning at the Department of Architecture of the National Technical University of Athens, in philosophy and methodology of science at the Department of Methodology, History and Philosophy of Science of the National and Kapodistrian University of Athens and was awarded a Ph.D. in Economics at the Department of Economics of the University of Crete, Greece. He has worked as a research associate at the Institute of Small Business of the GSEVEE and as a researcher at the Economic & Social Developments Observatory of the Institute of Labour of the GSEE. From March 2015 to June 2019, he was Special Secretary for the Management of Sectoral Operational Programmes of the European Social Fund (NSRF 2014–2020) at the Ministry of Economy and Development, and member of the research department of the Research Department of the Hellenic Fiscal Council (2019–2024). Today he is Principal Researcher at the Centre for Planning and Economic Research (KEPE). His research interests focus on political economy, economic policy, employment policy, experimental economics and public policy evaluation.

Christos Kallandranis is currently Assistant Professor in Finance at the University of West Attica in Greece. He has also taught at Regent's University London in the UK, at Marconi University in Rome Italy, at the Hellenic Open University and at University of Patras. He holds a Ph.D. in Economics from the University of Patras and an M.Sc. in Finance & Economics from the Manchester Business School. He has published extensively in reputable international academic journals such as Journal of Economic Behavior and Organization, Journal of Common Markets, Finance Research Letters etc.

Andreas Kontos is a Ph.D. candidate at Democritus University of Thrace, Greece, in the Department of Economics. He holds B.Sc. in Economics and an M.B.A. from the same institution. He is also a project partner for the Region of East Macedonia and Thrace in the framework of the "Smart Marketing Strategies for Tourism in Cross Border Area- SMS-CBA", under the program Interreg Greece Bulgaria and Researcher for the Democritus University of Thrace for the project "Machine Learning Investment Readiness."

George Makavelos is an Executive Officer of e-National Security Fund Administration (e-EFKA), Athens, Greece, with main duties of providing instructions and issuing circulars related to the interpretation of insurance legislation, regarding mainly the inspection process. He is also a member of the e-EFKA cooperation team with the European Labor Authority (ELA). He is a graduate of International and European Studies Department of Panteion University and holds a Master's Degree in Public Economics and Policy, from the Department of Accounting & Finance, University of West Attica, Athens, Greece. His research interests are mainly focused on strategic planning, organizational reforms in public sector, participatory processes, digital transformation.

Mario Nicoliello is a Researcher in Business Economics at the Department of Economics and Management of the University of Brescia, Italy. He holds a Ph.D. in Business Economics. He worked as a research fellow at the Department of Economics and Management of the University of Pisa, Italy. He also worked at the Department of Economics and Management at the University of Genoa, Italy.

Panagiotis Papadeas is a former President of the Hellenic Accounting and Auditing Standards Oversight Board (2017–2022) and Professor Emeritus (University of West Attica, Greece). He currently teaches Accounting at the Hellenic Open University. His published scientific work investigates epistemological problems of research in Accounting, such as the problem of generalization or what emerges from the case studies and field research in Accounting, the subjectivity of IAS, the finances of Universities, the comparison of the simple and double entry system, in combination with the Accounting Framework and the IPSAS for the General Government, but also the contribution of intangible assets to the development of export trade, while introducing the terms "Tax Leverage," "IASBasel" (the contribution of losses to the capital adequacy of banks), "Neurofinancial Accounting" and "Pale Green Bonds" in scientific journals and conferences.

Anastasios Pappas has received a Bachelor's degree in Business Administration from the University of the Aegean, an M.Sc. in International Banking and Finance from the University of Southampton (UK) and a Ph.D. degree in Macroeconomics from the University of the Aegean. He has worked as an economist in the private and public sector. Currently, he holds the position of the Head of the Research Department of the Hellenic Fiscal Council. He has taught various courses at the University of Aegean and at the National and Kapodistrian University of Athens at undergraduate and postgraduate level. His research work has been presented in international academic conferences and published in peer-reviewed international academic journals. His research interests cover topics concern, inter alia, Macroeconomic, Fiscal and Monetary Policy, Economic Forecasting, Financial Crises and Capital Mobility.

Argyro Paraskeva has a degree in Business Administration and she recently received her master's degree in public economics and policy from the University of West Attica, Greece. Her current field placement is in the Ministry of Development, with interest in the future of the urban communities in terms of sustainability and resilience where innovation's role is vital. She is interested in the development of an urban pattern that can be adaptable to the changing climatic conditions.

George Petrakos is Professor of Quantitative Methods and Information Systems at Panteion University of Social and Political Sciences, Department of Public Administration and the Director General of the Research Institute for Tourism (RIT) in Athens, Greece. He obtained his diploma in Mathematics from the University of Athens (1988). In 1990 he completed his M.Sc. in Applied Statistics and Information Systems from The George Washington Univ., Wash. D.C., USA. In 1993 he was awarded with an honored Ph.D. degree in Statistics from the University of Wyoming, USA. His main areas of interest are Applied Statistics, Econometrics, Survey Methodology, Sampling, Data Management, Quality and Analysis.

Konstantinos Rontos was Professor of Social Demography and Statistics at the Department of Sociology at the University of the Aegean (Greece) up to 2022. He was, also, appointed Head of the aforementioned Department. He was statistician in the National Statistical Service of Greece (1981–2005), where he served as a Director. He has been Post-Doctoral Visiting Fellow at the London School of Economics and Political Science. He has participated in 59 research programs and he is the author of over 300 publications (books, collective volumes, monographs, research articles) on issues, such as migration, employment, institutional economics, regional and urban analysis, demographic analysis, statistics and information systems.

Maria Rodosthenous (Ph.D., M.Sc., M.A., B.Sc.) is Professor of Accounting in the Department of Accounting and Finance, at the University of West Attica. She had served as Head and Deputy Head of the department and she has a special interest in implementing the International Accounting Standards (IAS) through integrated information systems. Her scientific research has been published in many peer-reviewed academic journals.

Evangelos Roumeliotis (Ph.D.(c), M.Sc., B.Sc.) is Special Technical Teaching and Laboratory Staff of Accounting Information Systems (AIS) and Ph.D. candidate in Management Accounting of the Accounting and Finance Department, at the University of West Attica. His research interests include the implementation of management accounting principles in public hospitals, health economics and the International Public Sector Accounting Standards (IPSAS).

Alexandros Sahinidis is a Professor of Management and Entrepreneurship in the Department of Business Administration at the University of West Attica. He studied in the USA, where he earned his B.B.A. from Baruch College of the City University of New York, his M.B.A. from Long Island University (New York), and completed the coursework of the Ph.D. program of Rutgers University (Newark, New Jersey). He received his Doctoral Degree from University of Piraeus (Greece). His research interests include Organizational Culture, Entrepreneurship, Motivation, Leadership, Corporate Social Responsibility, etc. He published in international and local refereed journals and presented his work in a number of scientific conferences. He has taught in several Academic Institutions in Greece and abroad, in seminars for executives as well as lower employees of numerous companies, private and public ones.

Ioannis Salmon is Associate Professor of Business Administration at the University of West Attica. He received his doctorate from the National and Kapodistrian University of Athens in Change Management and Human Resource Development. His research activities focus on Information and Communication Technologies (ICT)-enabled change management, computer-aided human resource development and digital knowledge representation management for strategic business. He has worked for many years in the private and public sectors in Human Resource Management and Finance. He is the author and co-author of articles in prestigious international journals and conference proceedings. He has participated in a number of European and national research programs. He teaches courses in Leadership and Change Management, Human Resource Management and Development, Business Ethics, and Knowledge Management and Learning Organizations. At the same time, he has been teaching postgraduate programs at the National and Kapodistrian University of Athens and the University of West Attica.

Anastasios Sepetis is an Assistant Professor in the Department of Business Administration at the University of West Attica. He served as President and CEO in different hospitals in Greece and as General Manager and Senior Consultant in big companies and organizations. He has also served as senior social policy consultant on behalf of national administrations and International Organizations, while he is a key expert in EU and national projects in the fields of Sustainable and Environmental Policy, Sustainable Stock Market, Sustainable and Social Responsibility Investment, Corporate Social Responsibility, Sustainable Education, Social Enterprise Sustainable Public Governance, Sustainable Employment, Social Protection, Environmental and Sustainable Health Care. He holds a certification authority for Environmental and Social Risk Analysis (ESRA) after collaborating with the United Nations Environment Programme Finance Initiative and IEMA Certifications for Environmental Management System (ISO 14001, EMAS). Moreover, he is an Auditor for ISO 9001:2008. His main research interests focus on Sustainable management and capital market finance, ESG evaluation, cooperation management, sustainable health, social protection, Sustainable Education and Employment policies; he is author and co-author of over thirty papers and has published in international edited books and journals.

Evanthia Skliopidou is employed at the Court of First Instance of Athens and has more than twenty years of professional experience in different departments. She is a graduate of Aristotle University of Thessaloniki and holds an M.A. in Social Sciences from Cardiff University of Wales and an M.Sc. in Public Economics and Policy from University of West Attica. She is currently a member of the working Group of the Greek Justice Ministry on a test run of a "Backlog Reduction Tool" to be implemented at the Courts of First Instance of Athens and Thessaloniki for the civil procedure, assisted by an EU program, the "24EL13-Supporting the reduction of backlog" (CEPEJ, TSI). Ms Skliopidou is a member of the OPED (Association for Justice Reform) as Head of the open working group "Forensic Psychiatry and Forensic Psychology". She has published in an international scientific journal.

Anastasios Tsamis, Professor Emeritus, Panteion University of Social and Political Sciences, Greece, Professor in Financial Accounting and Banking (1976–2016). Graduate in Economics (Athens Economic University) and Political Studies (Panteion University) with postgraduate studies in Accounting and Finance (Lancaster University, UK). Senior manager in Emporiki Bank Group (1986–2010) as Chief Compliance officer, Organization mgr., Design and Strategic Marketing mgr and Accounting Policies and Applications mgr. Member of the board of directors of mutual funds and investment subsidiaries of Emporiki Bank and CFO and CEO of the Bulgarian Investment Bank subsidiary of EBRD. Participation in working groups of the Hellenic Bank Association, General Secretary of the Hellenic Finance and Accounting Association (HAFA). Chairman of the Exams and Exemptions committees of the Greek certified public accountants. Academic interest expressed with papers in international journals and participation in congresses and conferences covering the areas of Financial Analysis, Corporate Governance, Accounting and Audit standards.

Ioannis Vavouras is Professor Emeritus of Economic Policy at Panteion University of Social and Political Sciences, Department of Public Administration, Athens, Greece. He was elected three times as Head of the Department of Public Administration and twice as Rector of Panteion University. He was also elected as the first Director of the Governance and Sustainable Development Centre of the Department of Public Administration. His main fields of research are: Economic Policy, Institutional Economics, Economic Governance, Macroeconomic Analysis, Public Sector Economics and Economics of Integration. He has more than 200 scientific publications. He is a referee in a large number of international journals.

Chara Vavoura is Assistant Professor of International Economic Theory and Policy at Panteion University of Social and Political Sciences, Department of Public Administration, Athens, Greece. She was educated at the Athens University of Economics and Business (B.A. and M.Sc.

Econ.), at the University of Oxford (MPhil Econ.) and at the University of Nottingham (Ph.D. Econ.). During the period 2019–2023 she was appointed a Postdoctoral Research Fellow at the Department of Economics, National and Kapodistrian University of Athens. Her research interests and published works are in the fields of: International Trade, Game Theory and Industrial Organisation, Economic Policy, and International Macroeconomics.

List of Figures

List of Tables

CHAPTER 1

Introduction: Navigating the Landscape of Social and Economic Resilience

Alina Hyz

1.1 Understanding the Modern Landscape

Various factors such as economic, health, environmental, and social crises, rapid technological advancements with unpredictable consequences, globalization, and the looming climate crisis are shaping the modern landscape. Resilience, in this context, signifies society and the economy's capacity to not only withstand but also adapt and thrive in the face of diverse challenges. It can be argued that a resilient system minimizes the cumulative loss of well-being. The higher the level of resilience, the lower the losses incurred when faced with inevitable shocks that every economy is prone to experience. In other words, resilience is a condition and a catalyst for prosperity.

The main aim of this book is to examine the public sector's role in building resilience across two key dimensions: static, characterized by its

A. Hyz (✉)
Department of Accounting and Finance, University of West Attica, Athens, Greece
e-mail: alinahyz@uniwa.gr

A. Hyz (ed.), *The Role of the Public Sector in Building Social and Economic Resilience*,
https://doi.org/10.1007/978-3-031-67702-1_1

ability to absorb emerging shocks, and dynamic, concerning its capability to anticipate and adapt to evolving circumstances.

The experiences of recent years, particularly during the economic crisis and pandemic, indicate that most economies are not prepared for new conditions where uncertainty plays a fundamental role. As a result, the social trust in public institutions has been on a steady decline. This prompts us to consider what measures should be taken to avert the repetition of past mistakes. What reforms are required within the public sector to enhance our resilience against crises, irrespective of their origins? The high price societies pay for the aftermath of these crises and the inability to effectively manage them underscores the flawed political decisions made in previous decades. This has led to increasing economic instability, soaring social costs, exacerbation of social inequality, and a heightened vulnerability to damaging recessions. Therefore, we must critically assess the weaknesses within the public sector and the prerequisites for building robust infrastructure, fiscal systems, social safety nets, green infrastructure, education, human resources, and more, to ensure that the next crisis does not lead to catastrophic outcomes for both society and the economy.

1.2 Strategies for Building Systematic Resilience

This book aims to shed light on the public sector's role in building a system that can foresee, absorb, recover from, and adapt to a wide array of systemic threats. It is crucial to recognize that social and economic resilience hinges on systematic resilience. So far, resilience has been pursued through interventions involving capital flows. However, this approach is often very costly, time-consuming, and frequently insufficient. It sometimes results in actions that improve one component of the system but have adverse consequences for other components. Therefore, the public sector must create conditions that foster social and economic resilience in various areas, including employment and the labor market, infrastructure, environmental protection, the implementation of pro-environmental policies, crisis management, innovation, education, social security, and public health.

The contributors of this book try to identify the main opportunities and challenges, necessary prerequisites, and key constraints while outlining the future directions for development, under the assumption that achieving resilience may be the primary driving force for global growth.

Despite significant progress made by researchers, there remains a need for a comprehensive approach in the new post-crisis and post-pandemic environment. Economic analysis demands new models that can fully address this evolving reality. While the apparent simplicity of the subject, in reality, things are by no means simple, and we are far from positive knowledge and comprehensive policy proposals that can be supported with relative certainty.

Although the book does not offer an integrative approach to the above issues, its contribution is to present the individual elements of a resilient system, thereby laying the foundations for its construction. Many of the chapters in this collected issue are based on the example of Greece. Greece presents a unique and compelling case study due to its recent economic challenges and subsequent efforts to rebuild and reform its public sector. The country's experiences offer valuable insights into the complexities and nuances of managing economic and social resilience in the face of adversity. By delving deeply into the Greek context, the book can draw out specific lessons and strategies that apply to a broader global audience facing similar challenges. The country's financial struggles and the measures taken to address them offer a real-world illustration of the intricacies involved in financing a public sector during times of crisis. These lessons, when carefully analyzed and presented, can serve as a practical guide for policymakers, researchers, and practitioners worldwide. Furthermore, by concentrating on Greece, the book can contribute to the existing literature by offering a detailed and comprehensive exploration of a specific case rather than providing a broad overview that may lack depth. This in-depth analysis can serve as a foundation for comparative studies, allowing readers to draw parallels between Greece and their contexts. In addition to the compelling nature of Greece as a case study, it is essential to highlight the contributors involved in this project. The contributors to this book are esteemed individuals with extensive experience and expertise in ministries and high-top institutions of public life. These individuals have played pivotal roles in shaping the discourse surrounding the Greek economy, both in its historical context and with an eye toward the future. Their wealth of knowledge and practical insights significantly enrich the content of the book, providing a unique and authoritative perspective that goes beyond mere academic exploration. By including contributors deeply entrenched in the public life of Greece, the book becomes a reservoir of firsthand experiences, lessons learned, and forward-looking strategies from those actively involved in addressing economic challenges. Their contributions ensure that the book is not only a theoretical examination but a practical guide informed by real-world decision-makers who have navigated the complexities of the public sector. Moreover, these contributors bring a level of credibility and relevance to the discussion that resonates with policymakers, researchers, and practitioners globally. Their insights transcend the specifics of the Greek context, offering universally applicable principles and practices for building resilience in the public sector.

1.3 Perspective from Contributors

The book consists of sixteen chapters. The first chapter is introductory and aims to try to understand and effectively deal with the multi-faceted challenges and dynamics shaping the modern world, especially concerning efforts to build social and economic resilience. The remaining chapters, described briefly below, deal with broad issues that create the puzzle of the public sector's impact on social and economic resilience from the perspective of public finances.

George Petrakos, Konstantinos Rontos, Chara Vavoura, and Ioannis Vavouras (Chapter 2: The Detrimental Impact of Political Budget Cycles on the Greek Economy) examine, using the example of the Greek economy, the existence of electoral (political) fiscal or budget cycles. These cycles are characterized by an increase in public expenditures, mainly via social transfers, during the years of parliamentary elections. Social transfers as a form of non-productive public expenditures reduce productive public expenditures. The research leads to the conclusion that it is necessary to control pre-election expenditure on consumption. According to the authors, limiting political budget cycles can lead to improved public finances as well as to the stabilization of the country's economy by moderating economic cycles. The current situation indicates the low quality of political institutions and insufficient control mechanisms related to the low effectiveness of the system of governance. In conclusion, the authors point to the fact that without a reform of the country's governance system, it is impossible to eliminate the phenomenon of political budget cycles and control its destabilizing impact on overall economic activity.

Panagiotis Papadeas and Anastasios Tsamis (Chapter 3: Cash Flow Statements for General Government of Greece from 2025: Answers to Long-Term Queries) point to the benefits resulting from the adaptation to the standards and methodology of the European System Accounts, expected in the case of Greece in 2025. According to the authors, internal audit anti-corruption programs will be re-evaluated, while the level of accountability and transparency in the management of public assets will be strengthened. However, the question remains why the introduction of this system has been so delayed. According to the authors, comparable accounting information obtained through the use of the cash flow statement will concern significant percentages of employment, consumption, and accumulation. The authors broadly describe measurable benefits that solve/answer many questions faced by the economy. The new system will also create better financing conditions for the Recovery and Resilience Fund. The analysis creates an opportunity, on the one hand, to identify problems related to the quality of policy and information over the last years and to explore new perspectives for the future.

Marco Nicoliello discusses the organization and financing of the Olympic Games (Chapter 4: Reducing the Use of Public Funds in Olympic Bids: An Approach to Agenda 2020) and their dependence on public funds. Although investments in infrastructure, including sports, have a positive impact on public health, tourism development, etc., the allocation and management of public funds raises questions about responsibility, effectiveness, and equality. Governments invest in sports facilities to provide venues for sporting competitions, recreational activities, and community events. Analyzing the IOC's efforts to reduce reliance on public funds for Olympic bids, Mario Nicoliello's research shows that these efforts have been largely successful. Agenda 2020 and Agenda 2020+5 create a framework that promotes greater economic stability and minimizes the financial burden on host cities. The author points out that in the future it is necessary to monitor the effectiveness of these initiatives in order, on the one hand, to guarantee public support for such important initiatives and, on the other hand, to ensure that these initiatives do not have a negative impact on public finances.

In their chapter, Yiorgos Ioannidis, Dimitris Giakoulas, and Anastasios Pappas (Chapter 5: The Role of Public Sector Wage Rates in the Determination of Labor Share) discuss the issue of the functional distribution of income in the euro area countries and they try to investigate whether wages civil servants behave procyclically or countercyclically and whether there are common trends across country groups. Their analysis shows that the labor share (LS) indicator, first of all, calculated for the entire economy, seems to have returned to pre-crisis levels. Researchers note that in the first years of the crisis, the LS increased sharply due to the delayed adjustment of the wage level to the economic environment, then it decreased significantly, but after the improvement of economic conditions it began to increase again. Interestingly, according to the results, the effects of the economic crisis on LS (and capital, respectively) were neutral, which resulted solely from the importance of public sector employment and, consequently, public sector wage expenditure. On the contrary, the decline in the private sector labor share was more pronounced and the LS remained lower than in the pre-crisis period. In this respect, public sector employment plays a significant role in supporting labor force participation (and consequently reducing inequalities), especially in the context of the crisis. At the same time, research shows that when the economy is performing poorly, increasing public sector wage rates can reduce this output gap. In this respect, government spending on wages has a significant impact on economic growth. These results apply to all European Union countries.

Georgios Georgiou (Chapter 6: Building Resilience in the Public Sector Through Risk Assessment, Activity-Based Budgeting, and Performance Audit) identifies two main elements influencing resilience: risk perception and performance-based budgeting and audit. He sees risk as an opportunity for change, and results are the driving force behind sound financial management. In this chapter, the author presents the important elements and techniques required to assess risk and maximize the added value of public sector activities. The study examines main methodologies such as the CAF model, resilience benchmarking, performance budgeting, financial accounting, and performance auditing. The considerations contained in the article lead to important conclusions, such as: (a) building capacity in the field of reporting and accountability can strengthen the transparency of public authorities, (b) risk monitoring and reporting may have a significant potential impact on the activities of central administration, (c) the use of powers regulatory, procurement and tax measures to influence sustainability, natural resources and resilience, (d) efforts to document training and guidance on various resilience-related activities through ongoing best practices across the EU, (e) knowledge and guidance on performance management and evaluation for decision-making, and (f) use results and internal audit to assess the effective use of funds and establish an effective management process.

The subject of Stavroula Grigoriadou's considerations (Chapter 7: Public Budgeting: The Amoeba of Public Policies) is the public budget, its history, and its evolution. The author points out that crises should be treated as an opportunity to search for and reflect on the policies available within public budgeting. Grigoriadou proposes establishing a reference framework for reallocating budgetary resources to better respond to threats or crises. Using a systemic approach, according to which emerging, numerous, and diverse challenges are not limited to one country, the author emphasizes the need to adopt accrual and performance budgets, with constant changes in their formulation and implementation. Referring in some way to the considerations of Georgos Georgiou, the researcher emphasizes new forms of participatory budgeting that increase the active participation of citizens, as well as the need to define the public budget in a simpler, more flexible, communicative, and democratic way. Referring to the Greek philosopher, Heraclitus, the author concludes her considerations by pointing out that the environmental needs require the budget to constantly adapt and change like an amoeba as a result of the adoption of new public policies and the use of a strategic approach to its creation.

Apostolis Gkikas, Ioannis Salmon, Alexandros Sahinidis, and Anastasios Sepetis (Chapter 8: Greening Human Capital: A Catalyst for Organizational and Environmental Resilience) raise the important problem of human resources management. They analyze the new concept of managing people, the so-called green human resources management (GHRM). The purpose of this chapter is the conceptual analysis of the impact of GHRM on organizational and environmental resistance. The authors analyze the main causes and ways to make human resources green, and the benefits resulting from the adaptation of human resources to the environmental goals of organizations. The authors in an efficient way connect this problem with a new approach to measuring the activities of the organization under ESG. The article contains function analysis in the process of green human management, as well as a case study describing the training and development of employees. Analysis of this chapter gives clear guidelines regarding the concept of green management and its influence on the involvement of the human factor in the dissemination of environmental values in the organization and outside of it. This contributes to the sustainable development of individual companies, but also the economy as a whole.

Panagiotis Ballas and Vassiliki-Maria Balla (Chapter 9: Enhancing Social and Economic Resilience in a Changing World: The Strategic Role of Continuous Training and Capacity Building in Modern Tax and

Customs Administrations) seek to explain the role of tax and customs administration qualifications to achieve economic and social resilience in a changing environment. The description of changes taking place in the modern world provides a background for analyzing the role of tax and customs administration. The authors concluded that as the world continues to face ongoing challenges, the strategic importance of these administrations in promoting resilience will only increase. Using examples from various countries, the authors broadly analyze tax systems and their impact on economic activity, including investment decisions, consumption patterns, and resource allocation. Additionally, effective tax administration promotes tax compliance, improves revenue collection, and increases public confidence in government institutions. The main conclusions arising from the considerations regarding training initiatives and capacity building of tax and customs administration are as follows: (a) focus on soft skills in addition to technical expertise, (b) combine learning approaches that offer flexibility to meet diverse learning styles, (c) use knowledge exchange platforms to facilitate mutual learning and share best practices, and (d) incorporate the latest research and best practices shared by administrations. By adopting a learning organization approach, tax and customs administrations can become more flexible and better equipped to deal with these challenges.

Ioannis Chatzopoulos, Andreas Kontos, and Christos Kallandranis (Chapter 10: Development of State Infrastructure with the Involvement of the Private Sector) discuss the infrastructure and investment puzzle. Public–private partnerships in Greece started in 1993, however, the first projects were completed in 2002. The authors present a short outline of the creation of legislation related to PPPs, analyze the first projects implemented by PPPs, and also important advantages resulting from the cooperation between the public and private sectors. These advantages are particularly clear in the case of indebted countries, but also those struggling with problems of delays in the implementation of state projects and investments due to bureaucracy, long procedures, and high costs often related to corruption in public sectors. The sectors that attracted the most funding in the case of Greece were the transport industry because it was rather underdeveloped in the previous decades, education, telecommunications, and energy/environment. Most of them were financed from European funds. The comparison with other countries shows that Greece has achieved some significant results, but there is still much to do.

The next chapter by Andreas Alexopoulos and Evanthia Skliopidou (Chapter 11: A Methodology for Measuring Job Satisfaction in the Public Sector) examines the problem of the human factor and its role in economic and social resilience. The chapter presents research results on job satisfaction and its impact on efficiency, productivity, and economy in the public sector. Even though the research concerns only one public organization, it shows interesting results. The results indicate that salary has the lowest average satisfaction score with the lowest variance, indicating a high level of dissatisfaction with the salary among the employees. Further results indicate no differences in wages in the study group. Worryingly, low levels of satisfaction are also observed in training and mobility, which indicates that the employees perceive that there are low career development opportunities. In an era of change and the need for quick assimilation, low satisfaction with the training and mobility offered may result in low organizational effectiveness. People participating in the research indicate that factors such as leadership, supervision, and interpersonal relationships correlate most with the achieved job satisfaction.

Alina Hyz and Grigorios Gikas (Chapter 12: Fortifying Economic Foundations: Cybersecurity Imperatives for a Resilient Financial System) debate cybersecurity. They indicate that with the ongoing development of technology and digitization, threats in cyberspace are increasing. The authors analyze changes in the way of working and everyday functioning observed in recent years mainly as a result of the so-called fourth industrial revolution. Even though in this new reality it is difficult to understand what the effect and what is the cause and whether this new reality technology makes us live differently, faster, exposing us and the systems we create to attacks, or whether we, by living faster, provoke changes in technology and thus create opportunities for attacks. The truth, however, is that IT systems collect data that is extremely valuable and therefore attractive to attacks. This is what brings the issue of cybersecurity to the forefront. Current financial systems, which are so important for economic stability, are most exposed to the risk of cyberattacks. The authors delve into the tactics used by malicious actors, from advanced cyberattacks to ransomware incidents, assessing their impact on economic resilience. The chapter provides strategic recommendations for policymakers, financial institutions, and cybersecurity professionals. The authors promote a proactive approach based on strengthening synergies between the public sector and the financial system in the face of evolving cyber threats.

Argyro Paraskeva (Chapter 13: Innovation Districts as a Model of Sustainable Urban Economic Development) analyzes the creation of innovation districts as a model for future urban development and the role of the public sector in this evolution. The considerations take place within the framework of the global urbanization trend. This shift toward cities requires a reassessment of urban development models, emphasizing sustainability and resilience. In response to this need, innovation districts have been created to support collaboration and entrepreneurship on a global scale to address urban challenges. The phenomenon of urbanization is driven by historical events such as the Industrial Revolution, which led to the rapid concentration of population in urban areas. Despite fluctuations such as deindustrialization and economic crises, manufacturing remains crucial, now supported by technology in the Fourth Industrial Revolution (4IR). Demographic changes, especially aging populations in developed countries, are intensifying competition for talents that are key to the sustainable development of urban areas. Globalization facilitates the exchange of knowledge, driving innovation and economic growth primarily in urban centers. Over the past two decades, innovation districts have spread around the world, where different institutions come together to stimulate innovation-based economies. These districts repurpose urban spaces by connecting universities, businesses, and research centers to support economic growth through innovation. The chapter analyzes two main areas of innovation and the role of innovation districts in the economic development of cities, with particular emphasis on the innovative districts of Athens. The chapter considers topics such as the relationship between innovation, urban sustainability and resilience, and the involvement of public administration in supporting innovation-based urban development. Examining the sustainability of innovation districts in the medium and long term highlights the importance of coordination among stakeholders, including governments, businesses, and citizens. The author advocates the integration of environmental, social, and governance (ESG) criteria to ensure the holistic development of urban areas.

Andreas Alexopoulos and George Makavelos (Chapter 14: The Implementation of Strategic Planning in Public Organizations in Greece: The Case of e-EFKA) consider the problem of strategic planning in public organizations. In a period of intense changes, both economic, technological, environmental, and geopolitical, the authors emphasize the fact that the importance of strategic planning in modern organizations is crucial. The need for planning also in public organizations is consistent to achieve sustainable development and resilience. Many public organizations also in Greece have attempted over the last decades to undertake a broad-based reform of their structure and operations, which is mainly based on the principles of New Public Management (NPM), including the practice of strategic planning. The article is based on research conducted at the Electronic National Social Insurance Fund (e-EFKA), the central entity providing insurance services in Greece. The authors focus their considerations on the factors influencing the formulation and implementation of a strategic plan. The results of their research, valuable from the point of view of the purpose of the book, indicate that factors such as a centralized management system, lack of participatory processes, lack of appropriate planning culture, trust deficits between political leaders and employees, and lack of specialist knowledge hinder the successful implementation of strategic planning in practice. If the results of these studies could be generalized, it would be necessary to conclude that a lot remains to be done in the public sector so that the institutions of this sector can effectively influence the resilience of the economic systems within which they operate and which they shape.

Finally, Maria Rodosthenus, Evaggelos Roumeliotis, and Dimitris Charamis (Chapter 15: Impact of Cost Accounting Models on Estimations in Adult Intensive Care Units (ICUs) and on Reimbursement System: A Case Study of a Public Hospital During the Covid-19 Pandemic) present research on the financing of the healthcare system. As the authors emphasize in the introduction, global health expenditure, as a percentage of Gross Domestic Product (GDP), exceeded 10% after the outbreak of the Covid-19 pandemic. The chapter contains a case study of the finances of intensive care units (ICU) in Greek public hospitals and shows significant discrepancies between the actual cost of services as well as hospital costs and national reimbursement rates. This discrepancy has caused a significant shortage and highlights the need for a more flexible and dynamic costing system in Greek public hospitals. The study recommends adopting a robust accounting system that allows costs to be monitored and adjusted in real time. Such a system would provide a more accurate reflection of reimbursement rates for actual costs incurred, thereby improving financial stability and resource allocation. This is particularly important in the context of extraordinary health crises such as the Covid-19 pandemic, where cost structures can change rapidly and unpredictably. The broader implications of this study suggest that proper cost estimation and management are essential to the efficiency of healthcare systems around the world.

The last chapter (Chapter 16: Conclusions: Mapping of the Course Forward) contains a general perspective and lessons, resulting from the theoretical and practical considerations contained in the book. Through the synthesis of conclusions from individual chapters, we create a new landscape in which resilience becomes synonymous with economic and social progress.

CHAPTER 2

The Detrimental Impact of Political Budget Cycles on the Greek Economy

George Petrakos, Konstantinos Rontos, Chara Vavoura, and Ioannis Vavouras

2.1 Introduction

Over the last fifty years, and specifically during the post-1974 period, known as the "Third Hellenic Republic," Greece has been characterized by a long-term trend of increasing total real GDP.[1] This long-term trend was reversed in three sub-periods: first, during the period of the global financial crisis that triggered an economic crisis (2008–2009); second, during the period of the great Greek recession or the period of the Greek fiscal crisis (2010–2016); third, during the initial stage of the COVID-19

[1] See European Commission, AMECO database, AMECO Online, GDP at constant prices (OVGD) (Version 2023-11-15).

G. Petrakos
Department of Public Administration, Panteion University of Social and Political Sciences, Athens, Greece

Research Institute for Tourism (RIT), Athens, Greece

A. Hyz (ed.), *The Role of the Public Sector in Building Social and Economic Resilience*,
https://doi.org/10.1007/978-3-031-67702-1_2

pandemic (2020).[2] The evolution of the real GDP of Greece during the period 1974–2023 is presented in Fig. 2.1, from which we can observe the three aforementioned sub-periods, during which the long-run trend was reversed.[3]

Moving on to Fig. 2.2, where we present the evolution of the actual budget balance in Greece during the period 1974–2022, we observe that the years of general or parliamentary elections in Greece, that are marked with an asterisk (*), are generally associated with jumps in public sector deficits.[4] The issue under consideration is whether these jumps can be attributed to the phenomenon of political budget cycles and, if so, to what extent the Greek trend GDP has been shaped by these cycles.

The remainder of the paper is organized as follows: Section 2.2 briefly presents the relevant theoretical and empirical literature. Section 2.3

G. Petrakos
e-mail: petrakos@panteion.gr

K. Rontos
Department of Sociology, University of the Aegean, Mytilene, Greece
e-mail: K.Rontos@soc.aegean.gr

C. Vavoura
Department of Public Administration, Panteion University, Athens, Greece
e-mail: ch.vavoura@panteion.gr

I. Vavouras (✉)
Panteion University of Social and Political Sciences, Athens, Greece
e-mail: vavouras@panteion.gr

[2] After the activation of the "general escape clause" of the Stability and Growth Pact (SGP), that allows EU member states to take budgetary measures to adequately address a severe economic slowdown and temporarily deviate from the adjustment path to achieve the medium-term budgetary objective specified by the SGP, the economies of the EU member states started to recover in 2021. See the communication from the Commission to the Council on the activation of the general escape clause of the Stability and Growth Pact, Brussels, 20.3.2020, COM(2020) 123 final.

[3] During these sub-periods, in addition to the sharp decrease in total production, there was also a significant increase in unemployment, which was a direct consequence of production cuts. For an estimation of the effects of the early stages of Greek economic crisis on employment, see among others in Frangos et al. (2012).

[4] Note that in Fig. 2.2 the positive sign (+) means deficit, while the negative sign (−) means surplus. By the term public sector in this paper, we mean the general government following the Eurostat definition.

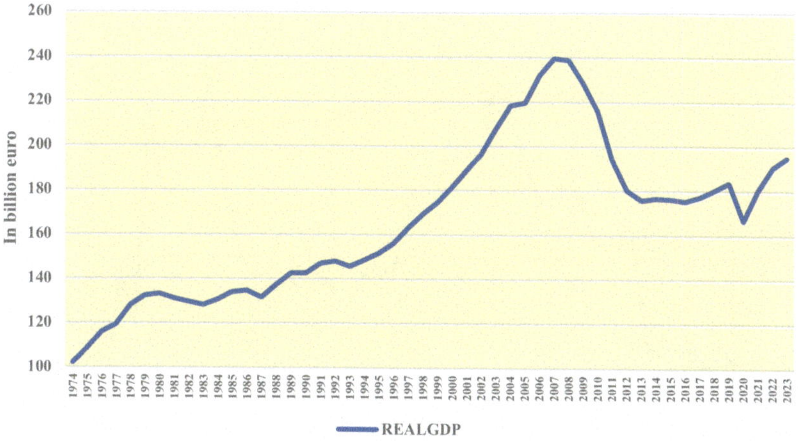

Fig. 2.1 The evolution of the total real GDP of Greece during the period 1974–2023 (*Note* REALGDP = total real GDP in billion euro). *Source* European Commission, AMECO database, AMECO Online, GDP at constant prices [OVGD] [Version 2023-11-15]

presents the data and methodology of our research and provides a discussion of our results. Section 2.4 concludes.

2.2 Literature Review

Political budget cycles or electoral fiscal cycles occur when political parties in power exercise the following pattern of governance during electoral periods: in the pre-election period they pursue an expansionary fiscal policy, that is public spending increases and/or tax cuts, that result in budget deficit increases.[5] This opportunistic behavior is followed, in the post-election period, by a contractionary or restrictive fiscal policy, that is public spending reductions and/or tax increases, that result in budget deficit reductions. These budget cycles are not caused by accident as a result of an inefficient or inconsistent economic policy or even by policy failures related to the way in which the governance of the country is exercised. On the contrary, they are deliberately caused in the context

[5] We have found that political budget cycles in Greece mainly emerge via public spending increases (Petrakos et al., 2022a).

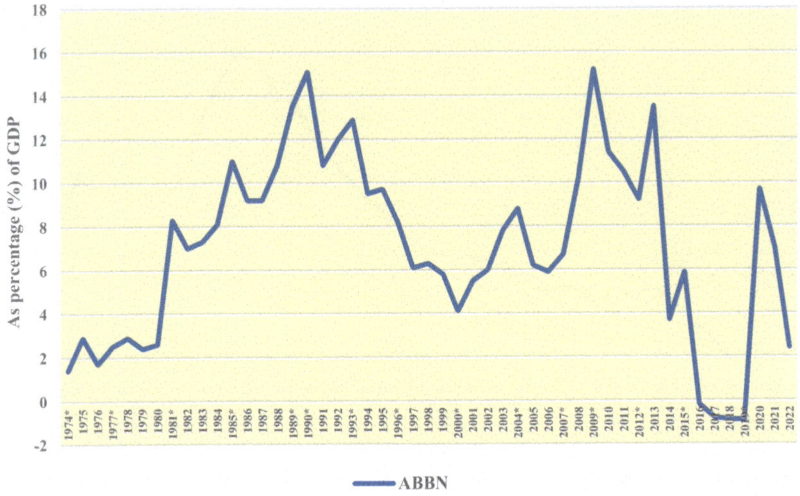

Fig. 2.2 The evolution of the actual budget balance in Greece during the period 1974–2022 (*Notes* (1) ABBN = actual budget balance. (2) The positive sign [+] means deficit while the negative sign [−] means surplus. (3) The years of parliamentary elections are marked with an asterisk [*]. *Source* Eurostat, General government net lending/net borrowing)

of governments' opportunistic efforts to maximize their "voting function," that is their re-election chances, by providing to the electorate the false impression that the political parties or party in power follow(s) an effective and efficient economic policy, that maximizes social welfare. As a result, the electorate forms the false impression that its well-being has recently significantly improved. This illusion is formed either because the electorate has a "myopic perspective," that is voters only remember the recent policy measures affecting their welfare, or because the politicians in power exploit their temporary "information advantage" caused by the asymmetry of information that exists between them and the electorate.[6]

The empirical evidence regarding the frequency and the intensity of political budget cycles in various countries is rather mixed. Some studies

[6] See mainly Downs (1957), Nordhaus (1975), MacRae (1977), Tufte (1978), Rogoff and Sibert (1988), and Persson and Tabellini (2000).

support the existence of this phenomenon[7] while others do not.[8] Philips (2016), using meta-regression analysis of 88 studies on political budget cycles between 2000 and 2015 found statistically significant, yet substantively small, increases in government expenditure and public debt and reductions in government revenues and fiscal balance around elections (Petrakos et al., 2022a).

Based on the findings of the existing empirical research, the recourse to the phenomenon of political budget cycles to maximize or at least increase the chances of re-election of incumbent politicians is questionable. According to several relevant empirical studies, political business cycles increase the chances of re-election (Aidt et al., 2011; Akhmedov & Zhuravskaya, 2004; de Haan & Klomp, 2013). This, in fact, is the prevailing perception. However, others document that cycles have no statistically significant effect. The latter usually prevails in countries characterized by high levels of social and political development,[9] where voters see through the motives of those who resort to such opportunistic behavior and "punish" them in the polls by voting against them (Brender & Drazen, 2008).[10]

We must note that the phenomenon of political budget cycles has been the subject of extensive empirical research. The results of this research suggest that, in general, the ability of political parties in power to create cycles decreases with the following (Petrakos et al., 2021a). First, as the level of economic and social development of the country under consideration increases (Block, 2002; Shi & Svensson, 2006). Second, as the quality of the country's institutions improves and the transparency of its political process increases (de Haan & Klomp, 2013; Persson & Tabellini,

[7] See mainly Schuknecht (1996), Alesina et al. (1997), Mink and de Haan (2006), Alt and Lassen (2006), Brender and Drazen (2007), Benito et al. (2013), Chortareas et al. (2016), Eibl and Lynge-Mangueira (2017), Bohn (2019), Gootjes et al. (2021), Petrakos et al. (2021c, 2022b, 2023a), and Nguyen and Tran (2023).

[8] See de Haan and Sturm (1994), Andrikopoulos et al. (2004), Chang (2008), and Klomp and de Haan (2012).

[9] The quality of governance is directly related to the level of economic development. For an analysis of the causality between governance and growth in the case of Greece, see Petrakos et al. (2023b).

[10] What's more, political budget cycles occur mainly in conditions of uncertainty regarding the election outcomes, given that if governments are very confident of their re-election, they have little or no incentive to resort to them (Alt & Rose, 2007; Hanusch & Magleby, 2014; Schultz, 1995).

2005). Third, as the quality and the duration or the maturity of democracy in the specific country are increasing (Brender & Drazen, 2005; Shi & Svensson, 2003).

The quality of the country's institutions and especially the existence of effective checks and balances for controlling the fiscal decisions of governments seem to be the single most effective means of limiting the extent or the size of electoral fiscal cycles in a country, as the existing institutions mainly determine the choices of voters and shape the incentives and opportunities, as well as the constraints of political parties in power to resort to electoral fiscal cycles in order not to lose the governance of the country (Chang, 2008; Streb & Torrens, 2013).

Finally, the degree of media freedom is considered to be an important factor affecting electoral fiscal cycles, as the absence of free press significantly limits citizens' information (Ademmer & Dreher, 2016; Alt & Lassen, 2006; Veiga et al., 2017). To sum up, the phenomenon of electoral fiscal cycles is more evident in developing economies (Brender & Drazen, 2005; Nguyen & Tran, 2023; Shi & Svensson, 2006). In developed economies it is either non-existent or at least very limited (Andrikopoulos et al., 2004).

The present paper focuses on the case of Greece which seems to be a remarkable deviation from the general rule. Despite being a developed economy, it exhibits the basic social and political characteristics of a developing one. For instance, Greece is infamous for its high levels of corruption and the failure of its regulatory framework. These characteristics, which are prevalent in the literature, are attributed to the fact that the country's social setting has been largely built on corruption and clientelistic politics (Manolas et al., 2010). Focusing on political fiscal cycles, we have estimated that, over the recent decades, their magnitude has been considerable (Petrakos et al., 2021a; Vavoura et al., 2019). This empirical outcome could be attributed mainly to the low quality of the country's institutions (Afonso et al., 2015; Trantidis, 2016),[11] as well as to the fact that its governments more often than not pursue clientelist policies and resort to populism in order to be kept in power, regardless of the effects of their policies (Christodoulakis, 2019; Mitsopoulos & Pelagidis, 2011).

[11] See World Bank, Worldwide Governance Indicators, for the low values of the county's estimated governance indicators (databank.worldbank.org/Source/Worldwide-governance-indicators).

The first objective of the present empirical work is to confirm the existence of electoral fiscal cycles in the case of Greece during the whole period of the Third Hellenic Republic, that is throughout the years 1974–2022, for which data are available. For this purpose, we specify an empirical model in which the actual budget balance is used as dependent variable, expressed as a percentage of GDP. Our primary aim is, therefore, to quantify the possible effects of electoral cycles on actual budget balance in Greece during the post-1974 period. The second objective of this research paper is to explore the hypothesis whether general or national elections affect the country's GDP and, to what extent their effects have been stabilizing or destabilizing for the aggregate economy.

2.3 Data, Methodology and Empirical Results

As it has already been noted, our empirical analysis has two main objectives: firstly, to establish the existence of the phenomenon of politico-economic cycles and in particular of political budget cycles throughout the period of the Third Hellenic Republic, that is during the period 1974–2022, for which the required data set is available, using as dependent variable the general government actual budget balance. We must note at this point that, in earlier empirical research papers, we established the existence of politico-economic cycles in Greece during some parts of the above period.[12] Secondly, to ascertain the possible existence of a statistically significant relationship between general or national elections and real GDP in the case of Greece during the whole period of the "Third Hellenic Republic."

We must note that during the years of the COVID-19 pandemic, immediately followed by the Russian-Ukrainian War, fiscal deficits increased significantly in Greece, as well as in all the other EU member states, in order to deal with the consequences of these events. Especially in the year 2020 the actual budget deficit in Greece soared to 9.7% of GDP, while real GDP decreased by a very high rate of 9.3%. Therefore, in the period after the year 2020, other factors external to the country affected the country's GDP as well as its budget balances. The investigation of these factors is outside the scope of this empirical research, mainly due to the insufficiency of the required data and the small number of the

[12] See Vavoura et al. (2019) and Petrakos et al. (2021a, 2021b, 2022a, 2023a).

existing annual observations. In order to avoid the exceptional effects of the year 2020, we run our empirical model using a second data set, that is by omitting the data series of the year 2020.

To achieve the objectives of our research, we construct two empirical models, that is Model 1 that includes all the annual observations of the period 1974–2022 and Model 2 from which the data referring to the year 2020 are omitted. In both models we use the following dependent and explanatory variables:

A. Dependent Variable:

(1) *The actual budget balance (ABBN) of general government as percent of GDP*, as it is defined and measured by Eurostat. It is the general government net lending (+)/net borrowing (−),[13] while general government according to European System of Accounts (ESA 2010) covers the consolidated general government sector and its subsectors.[14] We consider the actual budget balance as percent of GDP and not its value in absolute monetary terms, that is in millions of euros, mainly for three important reasons: first, because the percentage expression of the general government net lending/net borrowing provides a more reliable indicator of the relative magnitude of the actual budget balance; second, because the percentage term removes the long-term effects of inflation on fiscal aggregates, including the actual budget balance; third, because the critical fiscal policy condition of the EU member states in order to avoid entering the Excessive Deficit Procedure (EDP) of the Stability and Growth Pact (SGP) is not to breach the fiscal criterion that their actual budget deficit (in this case net borrowing) does not exceed the 3% of their corresponding GDP. We must note that the EDP is established in the Treaty on the Functioning of the European Union (TFEU) and it is specified in the SGP.

B. Explanatory Variables:

(2) *The one-year lag of actual budget balance (ABBN-1) of general government as percent of GDP*, since the public balance is "compounded"

[13] The minus (−) sign corresponds to deficit while the plus (+) sign to surplus. Eurostat, Government finance statistics (GFS), Government deficit and debt (gov_10dd), metadata, Government deficit/surplus, debt and associated data (https://doi.org/10.2908/gov_10dd_edpt). General government.

[14] Eurostat, Government deficit and debt (gov_10dd), metadata, as well as, European Commission (2013).

in the sense that the budget deficit (or surplus) of the previous year affects, to some extent of course, the deficit (or surplus) of the current year. In effect, the one-year lag of the dependent variable is used to allow for any existing slow adjustment process and persistence of actual budget balance, capturing the autoregressive, AR(1), component of the actual budget balance of the series (Petrakos et al., 2021a).

(3) *The growth rate of real total GDP (TYGR)* as it is estimated by the Eurostat. Real GDP is measured at market prices and in chain-linked volumes and it is the final result of the production activity of resident producer units.[15]

(4) *The change in the growth rate of total real GDP (DTYGR)*, i.e., the difference between the growth rate of total real GDP of the current year and the previous one, i.e., $DTYGR_i = TYGR_i - TYGR_{i-1}$. This variable is introduced as it might not be so much the rates of change in total real GDP that cause pressures for expansionary fiscal policy, as the variations or fluctuations of these rates from year to year.

(5) *The balance of trade or net trade as percent of GDP (EXP-IMP)*, estimated as the difference between exports of goods and services as percent of GDP (EXP) and imports of goods and services as percent of GDP (IMP), as they are both estimated by the World Bank (World Development Indicators). We must note that according to the World Bank methodology, exports of goods and services represent the value of all goods and other market services provided to the rest of the world while imports of goods and services represent the value of all goods and other market services received from the rest of the world.[16] Both, EXP and IMP, are measured as transactions in goods and services between residents and non-residents.

(6) *Election (ELE)*, a binary variable taking the value of 1 in the years of the period 1974–2022 in which parliamentary or (general) national elections were held in Greece and 0 otherwise. During the period 1974–2022 Greece had 15 years during which parliamentary elections were held.

According to the arguments presented above, we run two models: Model 1 where the data of the year 2020 are included and Model 2 where the data of the year 2020 are excluded and the results are following.

[15] Eurostat, annual national accounts (nama10), metadata, GDP and main components (output, expenditure and income). Unit of measure: chain-linked volumes, percentage change on previous period (https://doi.org/10.2908/nama_10_gdp).

[16] World Bank national accounts data, NE.EXP.GNFS.ZS and NE.IMP.GNFS.ZS.

Table 2.1 illustrates the coefficient estimation and testing for the statistically significant variables of Model 1, while in Table 2.2 two quality indices the coefficient of determination and the standard deviation of the residual are presented.

Table 2.3 is the Analysis of Variance table for Model 1 containing the contribution of each variable of the model to the total variability, while in Table 2.4 the outliers of Model 1 are presented.

Tables 2.5, 2.6, 2.7, and 2.8 summarize the same analysis and results for Model 2.

Table 2.1 Regression coefficients of Model 1

Term	*Coef*	*SE coef*	*T-value*	*P-value*	*VIF*
Constant	0.435	0.993	0.44	0.664	
ABBN-1	0.5700	0.0872	6.53	0.000	1.18
TYGR	0.3520	0.0949	3.71	0.001	1.16
EXP-IMP	0.483	0.129	3.75	0.001	1.23
ELE 1	−1.314	0.746	−1.76	0.085	1.02

Table 2.2 Summary of Model 1

S	*R-sq*	*R-sq(adj)*	*R-sq(pred)*
2.38004	70.62%	67.95%	60.29%

Table 2.3 Analysis of variance of Model 1

Source	*DF*	*Adj SS*	*Adj MS*	*F-value*	*P-value*
Regression	4	599.22	149.806	26.45	0.000
ABBN-1	1	241.78	241.781	42.68	0.000
TYGR	1	77.88	77.885	13.75	0.001
EXP-IMP	1	79.50	79.500	14.03	0.001
ELE	1	17.55	17.550	3.10	0.085
Error	44	249.24	5.665		
Total	48	848.47			

Table 2.4 Fits and diagnostics of unusual observations of Model 1

Obs	*ABBN*	*Fit*	*Resid*	*Std Resid*	
41	−13.500	−6.898	−6.602	−2.94	R
48	−9.700	−6.048	−3.652	−1.95	X

Note R = Large residual; X = Unusual X

Table 2.5 Regression coefficients of Model 2

Term	*Coef*	*SE coef*	*T-value*	*P-value*	*VIF*
Constant	0.806	0.978	0.82	0.415	
ABBN-1	0.6596	0.0953	6.92	0.000	1.39
TYGR	0.230	0.110	2.10	0.042	1.40
EXP-IMP	0.397	0.132	3.01	0.004	1.37
ELE 1	−1.646	0.740	−2.22	0.031	1.07

Table 2.6 Summary of Model 2

S	*R-sq*	*R-sq(adj)*	*R-sq(pred)*
2.30110	72.93%	70.41%	64.49%

Table 2.7 Analysis of variance of Model 2

Source	*DF*	*Adj SS*	*Adj MS*	*F-value*	*P-value*
Regression	4	613.46	153.365	28.96	0.000
ABBN-1	1	253.50	253.500	47.87	0.000
TYGR	1	23.26	23.257	4.39	0.042
EXP-IMP	1	47.92	47.923	9.05	0.004
ELE	1	26.18	26.184	4.94	0.031
Error	43	227.69	5.295		
Total	47	841.15			

Table 2.8 Fits and diagnostics of unusual observations of Model 2

Obs	*ABBN*	*Fit*	*Resid*	*Std Resid*	
41	−13.500	−6.830	−6.670	−3.07	R
42	−3.700	−8.579	4.879	2.45	R

Note R = Large residual

Table 2.9 Analysis of means of Model 1

ELE	*N*	*Mean*	*StDev*	*95% CI*
0	34	0.635	4.691	(−0.838, 2.109)
1	15	−1.620	3.060	(−3.839, 0.599)

Note Pooled StDev = 4.27108

Table 2.10 Analysis of means of Model 2

ELE	*N*	*Mean*	*StDev*	*95% CI*
0	33	0.994	4.265	(−0.386, 2.374)
1	15	−1.620	3.060	(−3.666, 0.426)

Note Pooled StDev = 3.93718

2.3.1 *Analysis of Means for DTYGR*

In order to investigate possible differences in the mean of DTYGR between the two ELE groups, we test the hypothesis H_0: $\mu_1 - \mu_2 = 0$ against H_1: $\mu_1 - \mu_2 \neq 0$, where $\mu_1 = E(DTYGR|ELE = 0)$ και $\mu_2 = E(DTYGR|ELE = 1)$. H_0 is rejected at $\alpha = 0.05$ and the differencesin the means of TYGR are presented in Table 2.9 for Model 1 and in Table 2.10 for Model 2, and it is further illustrated by Interval Plots in Figs. 2.3 and 2.4.

2.3.2 *Discussion of Empirical Results*

The coefficient of determination (R^2) scores above 70% for both models indicating overall goodness of fit. More specifically, the R^2 value of Model 1 equals to 70.62%, while the R^2 value of Model 2 equals to 72.33%.

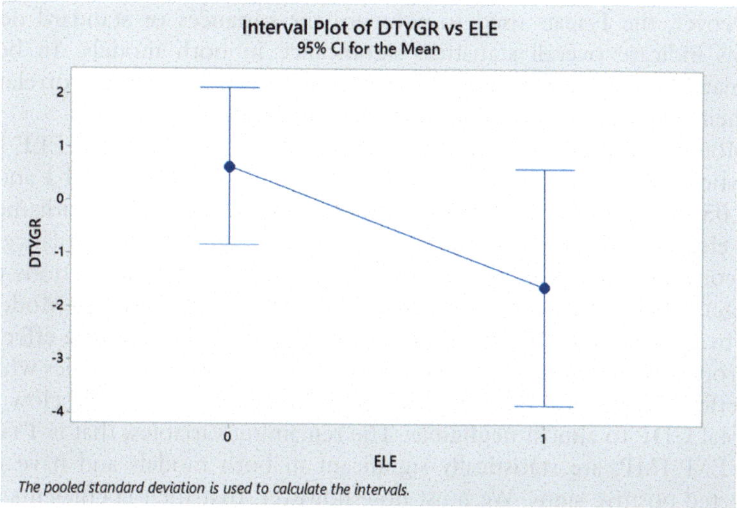

Fig. 2.3 Interval plot of DTYGR vs. ELE in Model 1

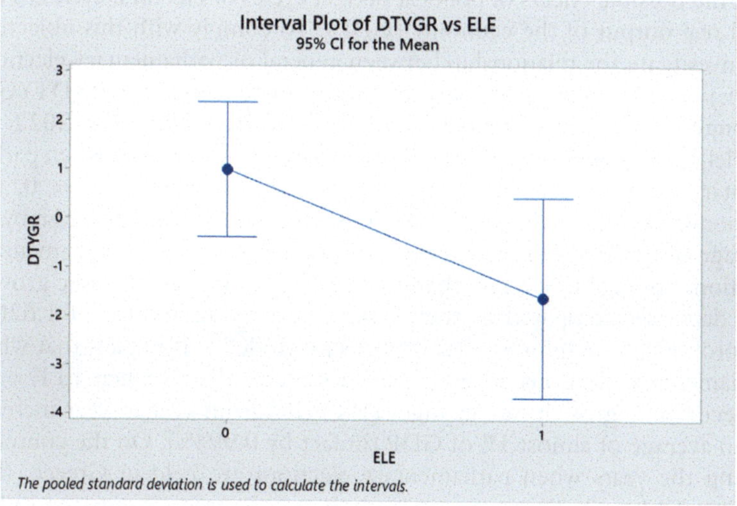

Fig. 2.4 Interval plot of DTYGR vs. ELE in Model 2

Moreover, the F-tests used to compare the variances or standard deviations indicate overall statistical significance in both models. In both estimated models, actual budget balances appear to be strongly correlated to their one-year lagged values, especially in Model 2.

More importantly, however, in both models it turns out that ELE is a statistically significant binary variable, at level $\alpha = 0.1$ for Model 1 and $\alpha = 0.05$ for Model 2. In other words, the years of general or parliamentary elections in Greece significantly affect the actual budget balance of the corresponding year. In the years of general or national elections the budget deficit increases by more than 1.3% of GDP according to Model 1 and by 1.646% of GDP according to Model 2. This destabilizing effect is disproportionately higher in relation to other developed economies where the effects of political budget cycles on output range from well below 1% of total GDP to almost negligible. The remaining variables, that is TYGR and EXP-IMP, are statistically significant in both models and have the expected positive signs. We must note however, that their coefficients are higher in Model 1.

Moving on to the second objective of the paper, which is to investigate the possible effects of political budget cycles or electoral cycles to the total real output of the economy (GDP). To comply with this objective, we investigate the relationship between general or parliamentary elections (ELE) and the change in the growth rate of total real GDP (DTYGR) throughout the period of the Third Hellenic Republic 1974–2022. In Model 1, the analysis of means indicates that during the years when parliamentary elections are not held in Greece, that is when ELE = 0, the economic growth rate changes (DTYGR) from year-to-year increase by an average of 0.635%. On the contrary, during the years when parliamentary elections are held in Greece, that is when ELE = 1, the economic growth rate decreases compared to the previous year by an average of 1.620%. Accordingly, something similar happens in Model 2. It implies that when parliamentary elections are not held in Greece, that is when ELE = 0, the economic growth rate changes (DTYGR) from year-to-year increase by an average of almost 1% of GDP (in fact by 0.994%). On the contrary, during the years when parliamentary elections are held in Greece, that is when ELE = 1, the economic growth rate decreases compared to the previous year by an average of 1.620%. As it has been stated, during the period 1974–2022 we have 15 years of parliamentary elections, that is a large number. It is therefore beyond any doubt that the electoral cycles in Greece are associated with serious destabilizing consequences on total real economic output. The descriptive and inductive measures of the variables DTYGR | ELE = 0 and DTYGR | ELE = 1 (separately) are presented in Tables 2.9 and 2.10, while the corresponding confidence intervals at 95% (95% CI) are presented in Figs. 2.3 and 2.4.

2.4 Summary and Conclusions

According to our empirical analysis presented and discussed in the previous section of the paper, Greece is characterized by the existence of large electoral budget or fiscal cycles, which are not characteristic of developed economies, but, rather, have only been observed in certain developing countries. Moreover, these political budget cycles affect the Greek total real GDP in a destabilizing way. This phenomenon is mainly due to the fact that during the years of parliamentary elections in Greece, public expenditures increase, especially in the form of social transfers. Social transfers are considered by the existing theory a form of "non-productive" public expenditure that does not contribute to the increase of the total output of the economy. On the contrary, "non-productive" public expenditure displaces productive public expenditure. We have shown that the opportunistic political and economic behaviors in Greece arise on the part of elected politicians in power via manipulation of public expenditure rather than through the handling of public revenue (Petrakos et al., 2022a).

This finding implies that in the case of Greece, future fiscal rules aiming at suppressing political budget cycles should primarily aim to control pre-election collective consumption expenditures instead of regulating direct and indirect taxes. In line with the above arguments, it is of critical importance to restrict political budget cycles in Greece for two main reasons: first, in order to improve the country's public finances and comply with the commitments arising from the restrictions set by the SGP; second, in order to stabilize the country's economy by moderating and not strengthening economic cycles. This in fact is the essence of the stabilizing role of the state, which in the case of Greece seems to be violated or at least ignored.

Finally, we must not fail to point out that the existence of such large political budget cycles in Greece during the last fifty years could be considered as a very strong indication that the country is associated with certain political and social characteristics which are observed only in economically developing countries, such as low-quality political institutions and insufficient control mechanisms or ineffective checks and balances (Petrakos et al., 2021a). All these characteristics are mainly the outcomes of a low quality and low effectiveness of the system of governance. Consequently, the effective control of political budget cycles in Greece presupposes the significant improvement of the country's system of governance. Without reforming the country's governance system, the phenomenon of political budget cycles cannot be eradicated and its destabilizing effects on the overall economic activity cannot be controlled.

References

Ademmer, E., & Dreher, F. (2016). Constraining political budget cycles: Media strength and fiscal institutions in the enlarged EU. *Journal of Common Market Studies, 54*(2), 508–524.

Aidt, T. S., Veiga, F. J., & Gonçalves Veiga, L. (2011). Election results and opportunistic policies: A new test of the rational political business cycle model. *Public Choice, 148*(1–2), 21–44.

Afonso, A., Zartaloudis, S., & Papadopoulos, Y. (2015). How party linkages shape austerity politics: Clientelism and fiscal adjustment in Greece and Portugal during the eurozone crisis. *Journal of European Public Policy, 22*(3), 315–334.

Akhmedov, A., & Zhuravskaya, E. (2004). Opportunistic political cycles: Test in a young democracy setting. *Quarterly Journal of Economics, 119*(4), 1301–1338.

Alesina, A., Cohen, G. D., & Roubini, N. (1997). *Political cycles and the macroeconomy*. The MIT Press.

Alt, J. E., & Lassen, D. D. (2006). Transparency, political polarization, and political budget cycles in OECD countries. *American Journal of Political Science, 50*(3), 530–550.

Alt, J. E., & Rose, S. S. (2007). Context-conditional political business cycles. In S. C. Stokes & C. Boix (Eds.), *Oxford handbook of comparative politics* (pp. 845–867). Oxford University Press.

Andrikopoulos, A., Loizides, I., & Prodromidis, K. (2004). Fiscal policy and political business cycles in the EU. *European Journal of Political Economy, 20*(1), 125–152.

Benito, B., Bastida, F., & Vicente, C. (2013). Creating room for manoeuvre: A strategy to generate political budget cycles under fiscal rules. *Kyklos, 66*(4), 467–496.

Block, S. A. (2002). Political business cycles, democratization, and economic reform: The case of Africa. *Journal of Development Economics, 67*(1), 205–228.

Bohn, F. (2019). Political budget cycles, incumbency advantage, and propaganda. *Economics and Politics, 31*(1), 43–70.

Brender, A., & Drazen, A. (2005). Political budget cycles in new versus established democracies. *Journal of Monetary Economics, 52*(7), 1271–1295.

Brender, A., & Drazen, A. (2007). Electoral fiscal policy in new, old, and fragile democracies. *Comparative Economic Studies, 49*(3), 446–466.

Brender, A., & Drazen, A. (2008). How do budget deficits and economic growth affect reelection prospects? Evidence from a large panel of countries. *American Economic Review, 98*(5), 2203–2220.

Chang, C. C. (2008). Electoral incentives and budgetary spending: Rethinking the role of political institutions. *Journal of Politics, 70*(4), 1086–1097.

Chortareas, G., Logothetis, V. E., & Papandreou, A. A. (2016). Political budget cycles and reelection prospects in Greece's municipalities. *European Journal of Political Economy, 43*, 1–13.

Christodoulakis, N. (2019, May). *Greece and the euro area: The cost of weak institutions* (CGK working paper no. 2019-05). The Fletcher School, Tufts University.

de Haan, J., & Klomp, J. (2013). Political budget cycles and election outcomes. *Public Choice, 157*(1/2), 245–267.

de Haan, J., & Sturm, J.-E. (1994). Political and institutional determinants of fiscal policy in the European Community. *Public Choice, 80*, 157–172.

Downs, A. (1957). *An economic theory of democracy*. Harper & Row.

Eibl, F., & Lynge-Mangueira, H. (2017). Electoral confidence and political budget cycles in non-OECD countries. *Studies in Comparative International Development, 52*(1), 45–63.

European Commission. (2013). Eurostat, *European system of accounts (ESA 2010)*. Luxembourg.

Frangos, C. C., Fragkos, C. C., & Hyz, A. (2012). On the Greek economic crisis of 2009–2012: Fundamental causes and effects; Future prospects for Greece and Eurozone. *Acta Universitatis Lodziensis, Folia Oeconomica, 273*, 99–115.

Gootjes, B., de Haan, J., & Jong-A-Pin, R. (2021). Do fiscal rules constrain political budget cycles? *Public Choice, 188*, 1–30.

Hanusch, M., & Magleby, D. B. (2014). Popularity, polarization, and political budget cycles. *Public Choice, 159*(3–4), 457–467.

Klomp, J., & de Haan, J. (2012). Political budget cycles and election outcomes. *Public Choice, 157*(1–2), 245–267.

MacRae, D. C. (1977). A political model of the business cycle. *Journal of Political Economy, 82*(2), 239–263.

Manolas, G., Sfakianakis, G., Syrmali, M.-E., & Vavouras, I. (2010). Institutions, quality of governance and economic growth: The case of Greece. *Statistical Review, 6*(1–2), 15–34.

Mink, M., & de Haan, M. (2006). Are there political budget cycles in the Euro Area? *European Union Politics, 7*(2), 191–211.

Mitsopoulos, M., & Pelagidis, T. (2011). *Understanding the crisis in Greece: From boom to bust*. Palgrave Macmillan.

Nguyen, T. C., & Tran, T. L. (2023). The political budget cycles in emerging and developing countries. *Journal of Economics and Development, 25*(3), 205–225.

Nordhaus, W. D. (1975). The political business cycle. *Review of Economic Studies, 42*(2), 169–190.

Persson, T., & Tabellini, G. (2000). *Political economics: Explaining economic policy*. The MIT Press.

Persson, T., & Tabellini, G. (2005). *The economic effects of constitutions*. The MIT Press.

Petrakos, G., Rontos, K., Salvati, L., Vavoura, C., & Vavouras, I. (2022a). Toward a political budget cycle? Unveiling long-term latent paths in Greece. *Quality & Quantity*. Published online on November 2nd, 2021, at https://doi.org/10.1007/s11135-021-01260-1

Petrakos, G., Rontos, K., Salvati, L., Vavoura, C., & Vavouras, I. (2022b, August). Domestic vs. external economic sectors and the political process: Insights from Greece. *Economies, 10*(8). https://doi.org/10.3390/economies10080198. Reprinted in *Recent topics in economic research: Feature papers for celebrating the 10th anniversary of Economies* (R. Fendel, R. Czudaj, & Anwar, S., Eds.). MDPI, Basel, Switzerland, March, 2023, pp. 157–169.

Petrakos, G., Rontos, K., Salvati, L., Vavoura, C., & Vavouras, I. (2023a, February). The impact of economic, political, and institutional factors on budget balances of the heavily indebted European countries. *Journal of Urban and Regional Analysis, 15*(1), 81–103, https://doi.org/10.37043/JURA.2023.151.4

Petrakos, G., Sfakianakis, G., Vavoura, C., & Vavouras, I. (2023b, December). An empirical investigation of the interactions between governance and economic growth in the case of Greece. *Theoretical Economics Letters, 13*(7), 1684–1697. https://doi.org/10.4236/tel.2023.137097

Petrakos, G., Rontos, K., Vavoura, C., & Vavouras, I. (2021a). The destabilizing effects of political budget cycles: The case of Greece. In N. Tsounis & A. Vlachvei (Eds.), *Advances in quantitative economic research, 2021 International Conference on Applied Economics (ICOAE)*. Springer Proceedings in Business and Economics, 2022 (pp. 129–141). Springer. https://doi.org/10.1007/978-3-030-98179-2_3

Petrakos, G., Rontos, K., Vavoura, C., & Vavouras, I. (2021b). The mechanism of political budget cycles in Greece. In N. Tsounis & A. Vlachei (Eds.), *Advances in longitudinal data methods in applied economic research, 2020 International Conference on Applied Economics (ICOAE 2020)*, Springer Proceedings in Business and Economics (pp. 123–133). Springer.

Petrakos, G., Rontos, K., Vavoura, C., Salvati, L., & Vavouras, I. (2021c). Political budget cycles and the effects of the Excessive Deficit Procedure: The case of Greece. *Regional Statistics, 11*(2), 1–20.

Philips, A. Q. (2016). Seeing the forest through the trees: A meta-analysis of political budget cycles. *Public Choice, 168*(3–4), 313–341.

Rogoff, K., & Sibert, A. (1988). Elections and macro-economic policy cycles. *Review of Economic Studies, 55*(1), 1–16.

Schuknecht, L. (1996). Political business cycle and fiscal policies in developing countries. *Kyklos, 49*(2), 155–170.

Schultz, K. A. (1995). The politics of the political business cycle. *British Journal of Political Science, 25*(1), 79–99.

Shi, M., & Svensson, J. (2003). Political budget cycles: A review of recent developments. *Nordic Journal of Political Economy, 29*(1), 69–76.

Shi, M., & Svensson, J. (2006). Political budget cycles: Do they differ across countries and why? *Journal of Public Economics, 90*(8–9), 1367–1389.

Streb, J. M., & Torrens, G. (2013). Making rules credible: Divided government and political budget cycles. *Public Choice, 156*(3–4), 703–722.

Trantidis, A. (2016). *Clientelism and economic policy: Greece and the crisis*. Advances in European Politics (Book 126). Routledge.

Tufte, E. (1978). *Political control of the economy*. Princeton University Press.

Vavoura, C., Vavouras, I., Rontos, K., & Petrakos, G. (2019). Electoral cycles and public deficits in Greece. In *Social sciences today: Dilemmas and perspectives beyond the crisis*. Conference Proceedings, scientific edition N. Nagopoulos, Mytilene, pp. 30–741 (in Greek).

Veiga, F. J., Gonçalves Veiga, L., & Morozumi, A. (2017). Political budget cycles and media freedom. *Electoral Studies, 45*, 88–99.

CHAPTER 3

Cash Flow Statements for General Government of Greece from 2025: Answers to Long-Term Queries

Panagiotis Papadeas and Anastasios Tsamis

3.1 Introduction

Greece has launched key reforms under its recovery and resilience plan that are aimed at resolving long-standing issues, such as (i) streamlining the allocation of responsibilities between the different levels of government; (ii) introducing strategic workforce planning; (iii) modernising hiring procedures; (iv) reskilling and upskilling the workforce in the public sector; and (v) introducing a reward system for public entities and civil servants.

P. Papadeas (✉)
University of West Attica, Athens, Greece
e-mail: panapapa@uniwa.gr

A. Tsamis
Panteion University of Social and Political Sciences, Athens, Greece
e-mail: atsamis@panteion.gr

A. Hyz (ed.), *The Role of the Public Sector in Building Social and Economic Resilience*,
https://doi.org/10.1007/978-3-031-67702-1_3

Over the past 4 years, Greece's performance in the open government data indicator has deteriorated and now ranks among the bottom 20% of countries, as shown in Fig. 3.1. Against this backdrop, the recovery and resilience plan targets the completion of the data governance strategy by the 4th quarter of 2025 (European Commission, 2023a).

In order to achieve the aforementioned target plan, Greece has to implement European Public Sector Accounting Standards (EPSAS), which have been formulated based on the International Public Sector Accounting Standards (IPSASs). These standards yield significant benefits of achieving consistent and comparable financial information across jurisdictions. Both IPSASs and EPSAS are dealing with financial reporting under the cash basis of accounting and the accrual basis of accounting (Papadeas & Cohen, 2018).

The objective of the International Accounting Standards Board (IASB) is to serve the public interest by developing high-quality accounting standards and to enhance the quality of transparency of public sector financial

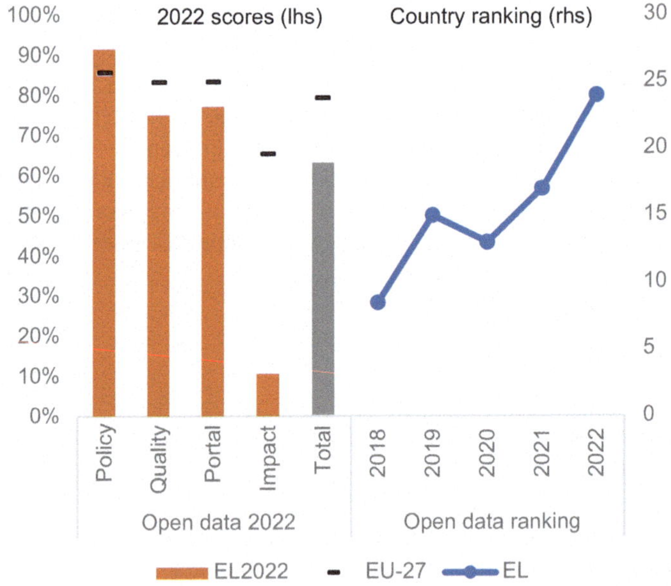

Fig. 3.1 Open government data maturity indicator: 2022 scores (% of the total maximum score) (lhs); country ranking, overall score (rhs)

reporting by providing better information for public sector financial management and decision-making (Papadeas, 2006).

The International Public Sector Accounting Standards Board (IPSASB) supports the convergence of international and national public sector accounting standards and the convergence of accounting and statistical bases of financial reporting.

The following text refers the transition from National to European Accounts (Sect. 3.2), the Government Accounts of Greece (Sect. 3.3), National Accounts and Business Accounts: practical issues (Sect. 3.4), Correlations and Coefficients of Public Sector in Greece (Sect. 3.5) and ends to the Conclusions (Sect. 3.6).

3.2 From National to European Accounts

European accounts are not equal to the sum of the national accounts of the Member States after conversion to a common currency. The accounts of resident European institutions need to be added. The scope of the concept of residence changes when one steps from the national accounts of Member States to European accounts (European System of Accounts—ESA 2010, 2014).

In the national accounts of the Member States, a foreign direct investment enterprise may have investors which are residents of another Member State of the European Union/the euro area. The corresponding reinvested earnings are not recorded as such in European accounts. Besides, special purpose entities may need to be reclassified in the same institutional sector as their parent company when the latter is resident of another Member State. Finally, cross-border economic flows and financial stocks between European countries need to be reclassified. These differences are presented in Figs. 3.2 and 3.3, assuming, for the sake of simplicity, a European area composed of only two Member States: A and B. Flows and stocks involving residents and non-residents are schematically displayed with arrows of Member States to European accounts. The ways in which the reinvested earnings of foreign direct investment enterprises or special purpose entities are treated are good examples in this context. In the national accounts of the Member States, a foreign direct investment enterprise may have investors which are residents of another Member State of the European Union/the euro area. The corresponding reinvested earnings are not recorded as such in European accounts. Besides, special purpose entities may need to be reclassified in the same institutional sector as their parent company when the latter is resident of another Member State. Finally, cross-border economic flows and financial stocks between European countries need to be reclassified.

According to European System of Accounts (European System of Accounts—ESA 2010, 2014), when the national accounts of countries A and B are aggregated, the aggregated rest of the world accounts record intra-flows between countries A and B, and with other countries and European institutions.

The European Union/euro area is considered as a single entity: the accounts of European institutions/the European Central Bank are included and only transactions of resident units with third countries are recorded in the rest of the world accounts.

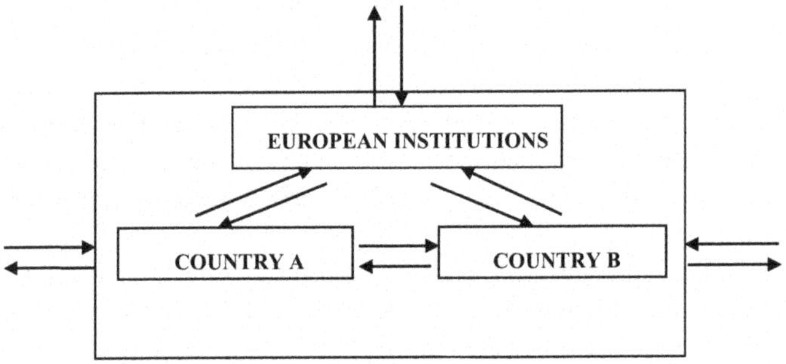

Fig. 3.2 Intra-flows between 2 countries

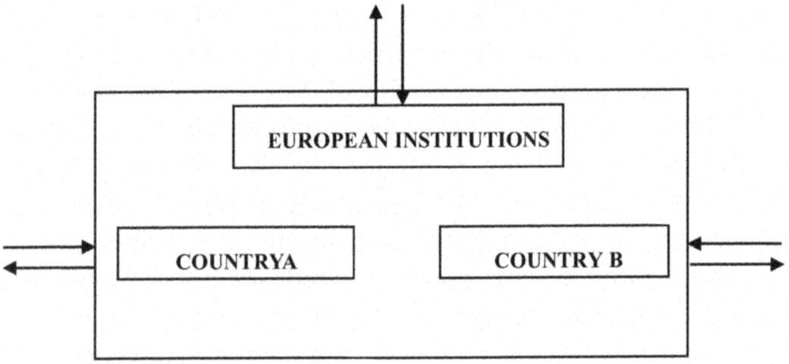

Fig. 3.3 Transactions with third countries

In European accounts, financial balance sheets can be compiled using a similar treatment as for transactions:

- The financial balance sheets of the Member States are complemented by stocks of assets held and liabilities assumed by European institutions which are resident of the European Union/euro area.
- Stocks of financial assets of a resident of the European Union/euro area held by another resident (intra-stocks) are withdrawn from the national rest of the world accounts.
- Imbalances created by the mismatch between intra-stocks of financial assets and the corresponding liabilities are allocated to the different sectors through balancing.

3.3 The Government Accounts for Greece

The activities of government are presented separately from those of the rest of the economy because the powers, motivation and functions of government are different from those of other sectors. This section presents General Government sector accounts that are going to be applied in a short period of time and give an integrated picture of government economic activities: revenue, expenditure, deficit/surplus, financing, other economic flows and balance sheet.

As part of the accounting system, entities shall keep the Chart of Accounts for recording revenues, gains, expenses, losses, accumulated surpluses/deficits, equity items, assets, liabilities and provisions (Table 3.1). The accounting system shall provide the maximum analysis of the accounts and all information regarding their movement (Papadeas, 2007).

The accounts in the Chart of Accounts are developed at least to the fifth level of analysis (with a few exceptions), while the first digit signifies the group of accounts (Greek Law 4772/2021, article 31, 2021; Greek Law 4964/2022, article 123, 2022). The second and third levels of analysis classify into further categories the level preceding them, depending on their nature and the required level of aggregation of information, mainly in accordance with standards set by the European System of Accounts (ESA), and the Government Finance Statistics (GFS). The fifth level of the Chart of Accounts further analyses the fourth one and they are both developed into double-digit accounts (01-99).

Table 3.1 Chart of Accounts

Group 1 Revenue	*Group 2 Expenditure*	*Group 3 Tangible assets, intangible assets and inventories*	*Group 4 Financial and relevant assets*	*Group 5 Financial and relevant liabilities*	*Group 6 Provisions*	*Group 7 Depreciation/ Amortization and other flows*	*Group 8 Equity accounts*
1.1 Taxes	2.1 Compensation of employees	3.1 Fixed assets	4.1 Special Drawing Rights—SDR	5.1 Financial and relevant liabilities recognition	6.1 Provision for pensions	7.1 Profits and losses from the data availability	8.1 Capital
1.2 Social contributions	2.2 Social benefits	3.2 Inventories	4.2 Cash and deposits	5.2 Initial recognition of financial and relevant liabilities	6.2 Provision for expenditure	7.2 Profits and losses of fair value	8.2 Fair value reserves
1.3 Transfers	2.3 Transfers	3.3 Valuables	4.3 Debt securities	5.3 Accounts update	6.3 Provision for fixed assets	7.3 Profits and losses of exchange differences	8.3 Accumulative deficit/ surplus
1.4 Sales of goods and services	2.4 Purchases of goods and services		4.4 Loans	5.4 Subsequent measurement of financial and relevant liabilities		7.4 Financial exposure/safety	8.4 Minority Options
1.5 Other current revenue	2.5 Subsidies		4.5 Equity and investment fund shares			7.5 Destructive losses	
	2.6 Interest			5.6 Reserves earmarked for insurance and pensions		7.6 Other impairments	

Group 1 Revenue	*Group 2 Expenditure*	*Group 3 Tangible assets, intangible assets and inventories*	*Group 4 Financial and relevant assets*	*Group 5 Financial and relevant liabilities*	*Group 6 Provisions*	*Group 7 Depreciation/ Amortization and other flows*	*Group 8 Equity accounts*
	2.7 Other current expenditure			5.7 Financial derivatives		7.7 Uncompensated seizures	
	2.8 Depreciation		4.8 Receivables	5.8 Liabilities		7.8 Other flows	
	2.9 Credits to be allocated		4.9 Advances and other receivables	5.9 Advances received and other liabilities			

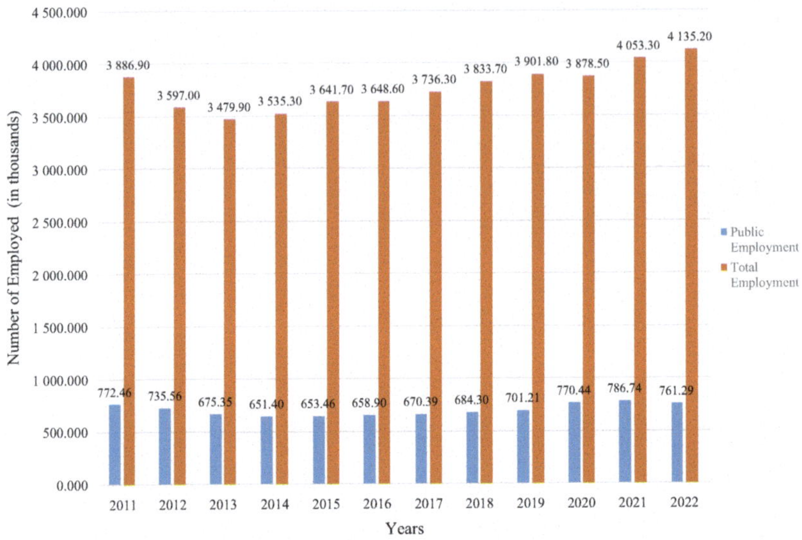

Fig. 3.4 Public and Total Employment in Greece for the period 2011–2022

The contribution of this accounting framework to the comparability of financial information for the Greek economy can also be quantified with the participation of the public sector in the total number of employed as depicted in Fig. 3.4.

3.4 National Accounts and Business Accounts: Practical Issues

For national accountants to be able to use business accounts on a large scale and not just in individual cases, certain conditions must be met (Papadeas, 2005).

The first is access to businesses' accounts. Usually, the publication of accounts is mandatory for large enterprises. Databases of such accounts are set up by private or public bodies, and it is important that national accountants be able to access them. For large enterprises, it is generally possible to obtain accounts directly from them.

The second condition is a minimum degree of standardization of the accounting documents published by enterprises, since this is a necessary condition for computerized processing. A high level of standardization is often associated with the existence of a body collecting accounts from enterprises in a standardized form. Collection may be organized on a voluntary basis, as in the case of the body running a financial statements centre which performs analyses for its members, or it may be made mandatory by law, as is the case where the collecting body is the tax authority. In both cases, national accountants are to request access to the databases, respecting the confidentiality policies that apply.

Of the financial statements, Cash Flow Statements are of greatest research interest in the public sector.

These statements include cash flows deriving from the General Government of Greece operating activities and the activities related to financing and investment transactions. We should notice the importance of the difference between the income statement and the cash flow statement, i.e. the income statement includes only transactions that create income and expenses to determine the result of the accounting period, while the cash flow statement includes transactions that involve changes in assets and liabilities.

Specifically, the cash flow statement in Greece will be linked to the General Government's accounting plan. Figure 3.5 depicts the interconnections of operating activities.

The cash flow statement, which includes only the General Government operating activities, shows only a part of the revenues and payments of the accounting period. Revenues are related to increases in cash or receivable accounts, increasing the working capital. When revenues are higher than expenses, operating cash flow will increase.

Referring to the calculation of the actual cash flows we should also note the correspondence of investment activities with the accounting framework of Greece. These are investments in fixed assets.

To calculate the real cash flow referred to the investments in fixed assets, the net fixed assets should be increased by depreciations of the accounting period and then be deducted of the previous accounting period.

Statements of sources and uses of capital describe the sources of fixed capital, which is invested in fixed assets and other non-current assets. Figure 3.6 depicts the interconnections of investment activities.

Finally, the correspondence between the financing activities and the chart of accounts in Greece can help the analyst to understand how management meets capital needs, which source of capital is selected in

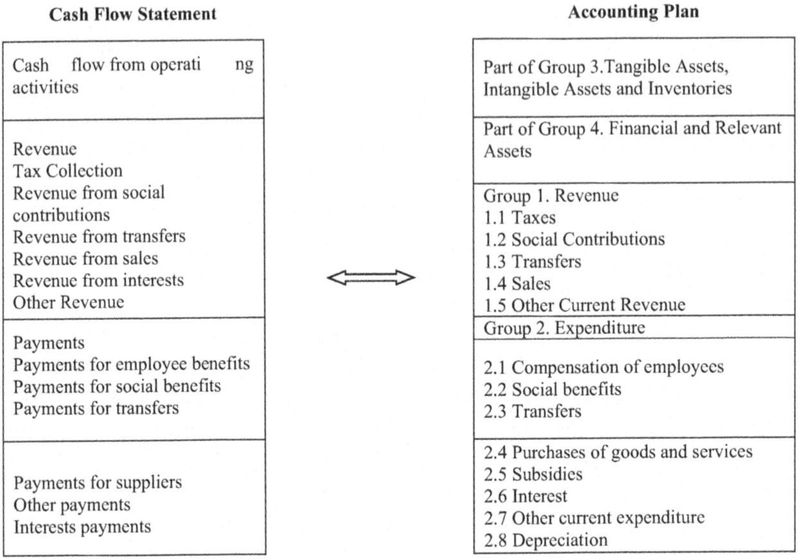

Fig. 3.5 Interconnections of Operating Activities with the General Government's accounting plan

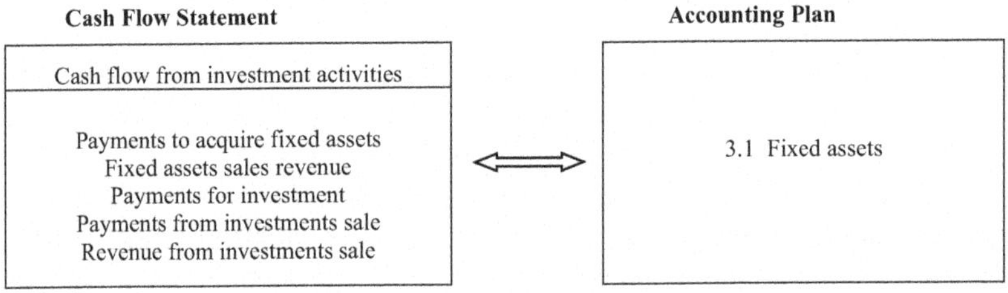

Fig. 3.6 Interconnections of Investment Activities with the General Government's accounting plan

order to raise additional funds and how by much liabilities have decreased. This type of analysis also shows how the profits of General Government of Greece are distributed diachronically, and how the capital is invested. The statement can provide information about the size and the structure of each source of capital. Figure 3.7 depicts the interconnections of financing activities.

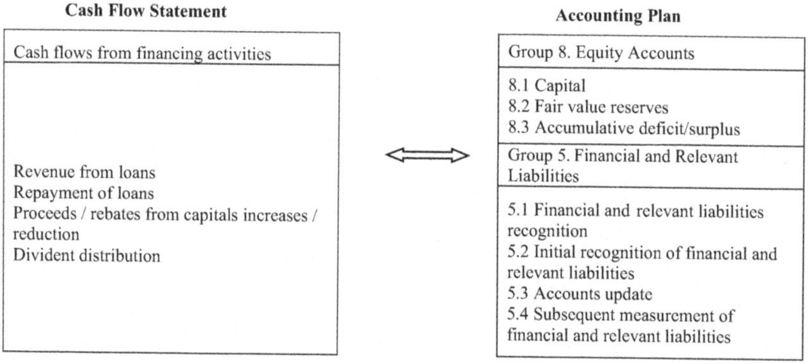

Fig. 3.7 Interconnections of Financing Activities with the General Government's accounting plan

The income from investments is considered as operating cash flow because it derives from investments or financing activities. There are specific cash flows related to operating activities, that are considered investment or financing cash flows. Examples of these cash flows are cash inflows from assets' sales. Profits or losses from debt repayments that are considered financing cash flows are also considered investment or financing cash flows.

3.5 Correlations and Coefficients of Public Sector in Greece

Apart from the quantitative criterion of employee participation, the correlation between the participation of the public sector in gross capital formation and consumption in Greece (monetary values) is of interest in order to approach the possible contribution of chart of accounts to the Greek economy (European Commission, 2023b).

Figure 3.8 shows the curve of the percentage of public gross capital formation increasing from the year 2011 to the year 2017 where it is at its peak. Thereafter, there seems to be a gradual decline until the year 2022. Also, it can be seen that the share of public employees in all years ranges from about 18% to 20%.

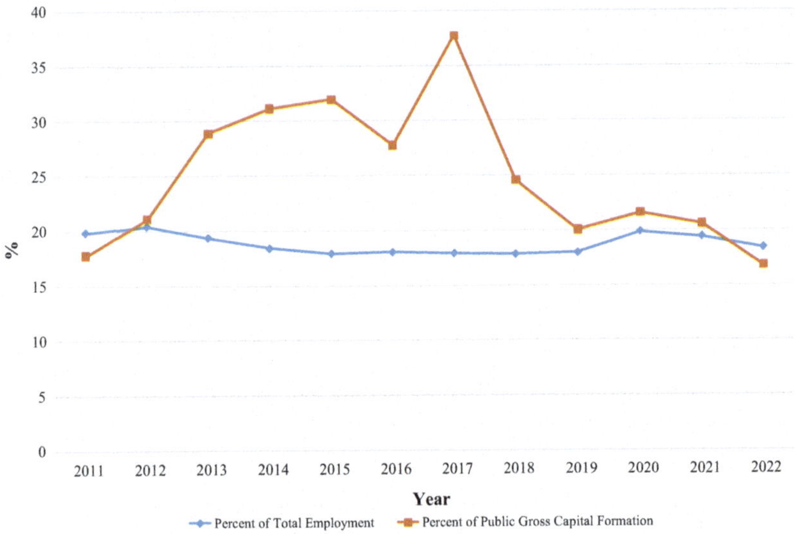

Fig. 3.8 Participation of the Public Sector in the Total Gross Capital Formation and in the Total Employment of Greece

Moreover, it is interesting to correlate the participation of the public sector in the Total Gross Capital Formation and in the Total Consumption of Greece.

Figure 3.9 shows the curve of the public gross capital formation, which holds as stated above, while for the consumption rate curve, it seems to remain constant at about 22% with minimal fluctuations. Table 3.2 depicts the correlations between the quantitative variables Waged Employment in Greek Public Sector, Total Waged employment in Greece, Public Consumption, Total Consumption and Total Gross Capital Formation.

Table 3.2 shows that the variable Waged Employment in Greek Public Sector has a strong correlation with the variables Total Waged employment in Greece and Public Consumption (0.735 and 0.798 respectively). Furthermore, the variable Total Waged employment in Greece has a strong correlation with the variable Total Gross Capital Formation (0.798), while the same is true for the variables Public Consumption and Total Consumption (0.869) (The Correlation Coefficient (r), 2021). The estimation of Total Waged Employment in Greece using the Waged

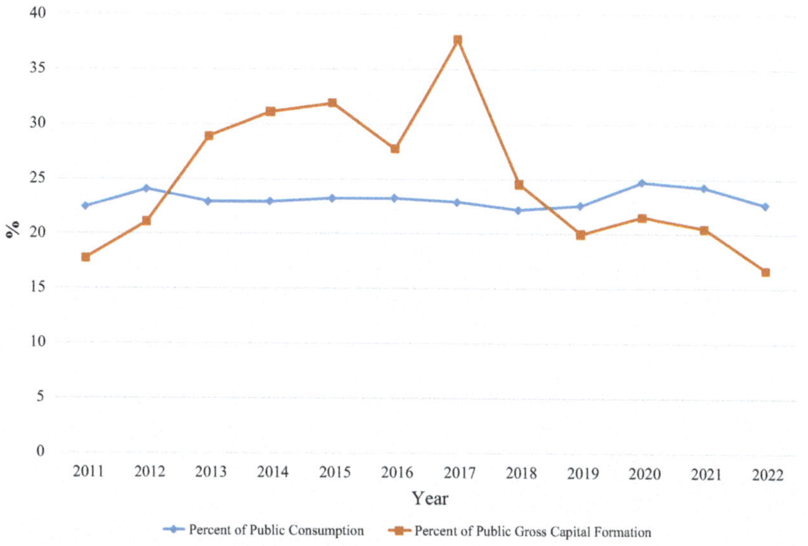

Fig. 3.9 Participation of the public sector in the Total Gross Capital Formation and in the Total Consumption of Greece

Employment in the Greek Public Sector as independent variable yields the results that are shown in Tables 3.3 and 3.4 and in Fig. 3.10.

The linear model above explains the 54% of the variability of Total Waged Employment in Greece and can be used to estimate Total Waged Employment in Greece (2011–2022) if we know Waged Employment in Greek Public Sector (The Correlation Coefficient (r), 2021).

3.6 Conclusions

According to the above, from 2025 onwards the General Government of Greece will be fully aligned to the standards and the methodology of the European System Accounts. The internal audit programmes for corruption tackling will be reassessed, while the levels of accountability and transparency in public assets management will be strengthened.

Specifically, the comparable accounting information through the application of the cash flow statement concerns significant percentages of employment, consumption and capital formation and provides the following five benefits that are likely to respond to long-term queries for

Table 3.2 Correlations between the quantitative variables Waged Employment in Public Sector, Total Waged Employment, Public Consumption, Total Consumption and Total Gross Capital Formation, years 2011–2022

		Waged Employment in Greek Public Sector	*Total Waged employment in Greece*	*Public Consumption*	*Total Consumption*	*Total Gross Capital Formation*
Waged Employment in Greek Public Sector	Pearson Correlation	1	,735**	,798**	,577*	,659*
	Sig. (2-tailed)		0.006473557	0.001867957	0.049584282	0.019762834
	N	12	12	12	12	12
Total Waged Employment in Greece	Pearson Correlation	,735**	1	0.422112837	0.4090429	,798**
	Sig. (2-tailed)	0.006473557		0.171661422	0.186728301	0.001844811
	N	12	12	12	12	12
Public Consumption	Pearson Correlation	,798**	0.422112837	1	,869**	,639*
	Sig. (2-tailed)	0.001867957	0.171661422		0.000242006	0.025167894
	N	12	12	12	12	12
Total Consumption	Pearson Correlation	,577*	0.4090429	,869**	1	,657*
	Sig. (2-tailed)	0.049584282	0.186728301	0.000242006		0.020333865
	N	12	12	12	12	12
Total Gross Capital Formation	Pearson Correlation	,659*	,798**	,639*	,657*	1
	Sig. (2-tailed)	0.019762834	0.001844811	0.025167894	0.020333865	
	N	12	12	12	12	12

**Correlation is significant at the 0.01 level (2-tailed)
*Correlation is significant at the 0.05 level (2-tailed)

Table 3.3 Coefficients (2011–2022)

Model		*Unstandardized Coefficients*		*Standardized Coefficients*	t	*Sig.*
		B	*Std. Error*	*Beta*		
1	(Constant)	1712,749	603,959		2,836	,018
	Employment Greek Public Sector	2,907	,848	,735	3,427	,006

a. Dependent Variable: Total Waged Employment in Greece

Table 3.4 Model summary (2011–2022)

Model	R	R *Square*	*Adjusted* R *Square*	*Std. Error of the Estimate*
1	,735a	,540	,494	145,6668

a. Predictors: (Constant), Waged Employment Greek Public Sector
Total Waged_Employment in Greece = 1712.749 + 2.907 · Waged_Employment in Greek Public Sector

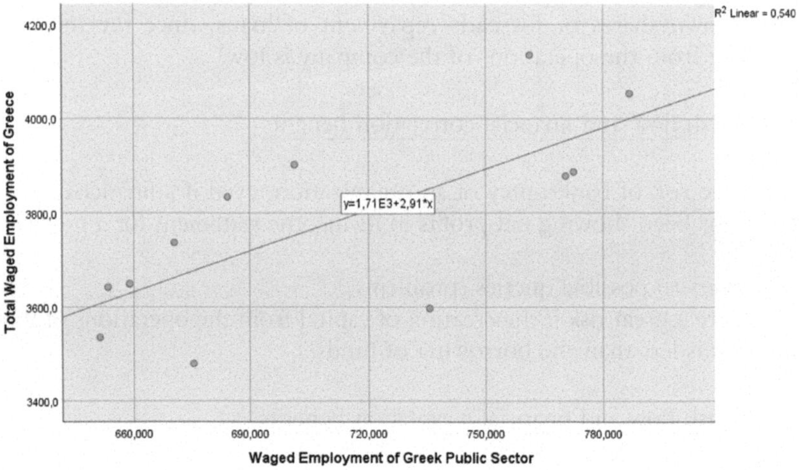

Fig. 3.10 Linear regression of Total Waged Employment and Waged Employment in Public Sector in Greece

the Greek economy (Papadeas & Cohen, 2018) to investigate improved funding conditions from the Recovery and Resilience Fund up to 2027.

(a) <u>Cash flow and financial correlation benefits</u>

Information about cash resources and sources, but also the account balance at the end of the financial year.

Answers to possible queries (problems):

Why is working capital lower than the company's needs? The unusual increases in receivables and stocks show any liquidity problems?

(b) <u>Cash flow and financial correlation benefits</u>

Information on borrowing, repayment, dividend payments and other cash distributions of an organization.

Answers to possible queries (problems):

How does the General Government manage to fund its new assets: by self-financing, borrowing or issuing new shares? Instead of exaggerating capital increases to expand it, should it take advantage of low interest rate borrowing? Why are large amounts paid for dividends, or for the redemption of own shares or for early repayment of loans, since the internal financing from the operations of the company is low?

(c) <u>Cash flow and financial correlation benefits</u>

Assess the risk of bankruptcy of an organization, even if a financial institution has been showing net profits in its income statement for a number of years.

Answers to possible queries (problems):

Is there a great risk if the creation of capital from the operations of the company is less than the borrowing of funds?

(d) <u>Cash flow and financial correlation benefits</u>

Information on the availability of net cash flows that can support the General Government's investment plan.

Answers to possible queries (problems):

Have the facilities of the business been renewed and, if so, by what means? Why was there plenty of cash to buy land?

(e) Cash flow and financial correlation benefits

Information to potential stock market investors about the ability of a business to generate net cash inflows and thus to support both its unimpeded operation and future developmental goals and objectives.

Answers to possible queries (problems):

Have the funding methods changed? Does the ever decreasing self-funding indicate any future funding problems?

References

European Commission. (2023a, May 24). *2023 Country Report—Greece.* Commission Staff Working Document.

European Commission. (2023b). *Eurostat.* https://ec.europa.eu/eurostat. Accessed 7 April 2024.

European System of Accounts—ESA 2010. (2014). European Commission.

Greek Law 4772/2021, article 31. (2021). *General Government Accounting Framework (GGAF).* Government Gazette Issue A17/05.02.2021.

Greek Law 4964/2022, article 123. (2022). *Entry of GGAF into force.* Government Gazette Issue A150/30.07.2022.

Papadeas, P. (2005). Tax provisions for listed EU companies and subjectivity—The case of Greek companies. *Journal of Finance & Informatics, 1*(1).

Papadeas, P. (2006). Comparable financial information and decision making for the public sector. *The Southeuropean Review of Business Finance and Accounting, 4*(2).

Papadeas, P. (2007). Validity and theoretical contribution of accounting research. *Archives of Economic History, XIX*(1).

Papadeas, P., & Cohen, S. (2018, December 14–15). *Expected implementation of IPSAS: Challenges and Benefits for the General Government entities.* Paper presented at the 17th Conference of the Hellenic Financial Accounting Association 2018 (in Greek).

The Correlation Coefficient (r). (2021). https://sphweb.bumc.bu.edu/otlt/MPH-Modules/PH717-QuantCore/PH717-Module9-Correlation-Regression/PH717-Module9-Correlation-Regression4.html. Accessed 7 April 2024.

CHAPTER 4

Reducing Public Funds Reliance in Olympic Bids: The Agenda 2020 Approach

Mario Nicoliello

4.1 Introduction

The hosting of the Olympic Games has long been regarded as a prestigious opportunity for Countries around the world (Gold & Gold, 2024), but the process has been fraught with financial challenges and host cities have faced significant costs and a heavy reliance on public funds (Preuss, 2024). Recognising the need for change, the International Olympic Committee (IOC) introduced Agenda 2020, a visionary blueprint to transform the way the Olympics are hosted and ensuring their long-term sustainability (IOC, 2014).

Olympic Agenda 2020 and its subsequent iteration Agenda 2020+5 represent a bold commitment by the IOC to enhance the economic viability and social responsibility to host the Olympic Games. They are founded on the principles of sustainability, collaboration and transparency,

M. Nicoliello (✉)
Department of Economics and Management, University of Brescia, Brescia, Italy
e-mail: mario.nicoliello@unibs.it

A. Hyz (ed.), *The Role of the Public Sector in Building Social and Economic Resilience*,
https://doi.org/10.1007/978-3-031-67702-1_4

with the overarching goal to reduce the reliance on public funds and maximise benefits for host cities and their residents (IOC, 2021).

This chapter aims to explore the key principles and strategies outlined in Agenda 2020 and Agenda 2020+5, with a specific focus on their potential to reduce the reliance on public funds in Olympic bids. Examining the evolution of the bidding process, the promotion of sustainable practices and the encouragement of collaborative efforts between regions and cities, we aim to provide insights into the future of Olympics.

Through a systematic analysis of the IOC's initiatives and their impact on the bidding process, we will demonstrate how Agenda 2020 offers a more economically viable and socially responsible framework for the Games, prioritising existing infrastructure, streamlining the bidding process and fostering collaboration to create a legacy of sustainable development and financial stability.

In the subsequent sections of this chapter, we will investigate into the key principles of Agenda 2020, explore their implementation through four case studies (Paris 2024 Summer Games, Milan-Cortina 2026 Winter Games, Los Angeles 2028 Summer Games and Brisbane 2032 Summer Games) and analyse their potential to reduce the reliance on public funds in Olympic bids. With this analysis, we contribute to the ongoing dialogue surrounding the future of Olympics and financial responsibility in shaping it. Specifically, we aim to explore the key principles and strategies outlined in Agenda 2020 and Agenda 2020+5, focusing on their potential to enhance the sustainability and economic viability.

The chapter will continue with a section dedicated to the literature review focused on four elements: public financing in the sports sector, the dependence on public money, the Olympic Games and the two documents from which this research starts: the Olympic Agenda 2020 and the Agenda Olympic 2020+5.

The methodology section will introduce the documentary analysis carried out both on the IOC documents and on the bid proposal of the four cases. The results of the investigation will be reported in the results section and subsequently discussed. In particular, we found that the key points able to reduce the financial burden on host cities consist in prioritising existing infrastructure, streamlining the bidding process and promoting collaborative efforts. The implications of the research are to inform policymakers, stakeholders and host cities about the benefits to adopt a more sustainable and financially responsible approach for the Olympics.

4.2 Literature Review

4.2.1 Public Funding in the Sports Sector

The use of public funds in the sports sector is a topic of significant interest and debate among policymakers, scholars and practitioners, because investment in infrastructure, events and programmes play a vital role in community cohesion, economic development and national identity, but the allocation and management of public funds raise questions about accountability, efficiency and equity (Chappelet, 2012).

Public funds serve as a critical source of support for sports infrastructure development, facility maintenance and event hosting (Dickson et al., 2011). Governments invest in sports facilities such as stadiums, arenas and training centres to provide venues for athletic competitions, recreational activities and community events (Groothuis et al., 2004).

Sports facilities provide opportunities for physical activity and recreation, contributing to improved public health outcomes and reduced healthcare costs (Siegfried & Zimbalist, 2006), while sports events and programmes stimulate economic activity, generate tourism revenue and create jobs in sectors such as hospitality, transportation and retail (Kučera et al., 2023).

Unfortunately, public funds for sports infrastructure and events benefit wealthy individuals, sports organisations and corporations at the expense of taxpayers and public services (Otarbaevich & Dlimbetovich, 2021). The long-term financial sustainability of sports facilities and events financed by public funds may be uncertain, leading to concerns about cost overruns, underutilisation and maintenance expenses (Andreff & Szymanski, 2006). The decision-making processes governing the allocation of public funds for sports projects are often opaque, lacking in public consultation and oversight and the financial arrangements between governments, sports organisations and private entities may lack transparency, raising concerns about potential conflicts of interest and corruption (Essex & Chalkley, 2004).

Governments may allocate public funds to cover infrastructure upgrades and temporary facilities required for hosting these events (Gratton et al., 2015). While such investments aim to showcase the host city's capabilities and attract tourists, they also entail considerable financial risks and long-term implications for public finances (Kasimati, 2015).

Research indicates that public funding can yield economic benefits through increased tourism, job creation and infrastructure development

(Baade & Matheson, 2016; Preuss, 2024; Scandizzo & Pierleoni, 2018). However, the costs associated with hosting mega-events may outweigh the benefits, particularly if public funds are diverted from essential services or if there is a lack of post-event utilisation plans for sports facilities (Brookes & Wiggan, 2009; Downward et al., 2019).

In addition to infrastructure and event hosting, public funds support sports programmes aimed at fostering athletic development, promoting social inclusion and nurturing talent, since governments may allocate resources to fund grassroots sports initiatives, school sports programmes and elite athlete training centres (Rebeggiani, 2006), or to increase sports participation among marginalised communities (Sutin, 2011).

Public-private partnerships (PPPs) have emerged as a promising approach to reduce public funds reliance in sports infrastructure projects (Riess, 1998), augmenting cost-effectiveness, innovation and risk management in sports infrastructure projects and reducing the need for extensive public funding (Alakshendra, 2016).

Engaging local communities and stakeholders in the planning, design and implementation of sports projects can help reduce public funds reliance (Andreff & Szymanski, 2006), since community-based initiatives, such as volunteer programmes, crowdfunding campaigns and corporate sponsorships, can complement public funding and enhance the viability of sports projects (Lowther et al., 2016). Participatory planning and co-design methodologies empower stakeholders to contribute ideas, resources and expertise, nurturing a sense of ownership and stewardship over sports facilities and programmes (Kasale et al., 2018).

4.2.2 Olympic Games

The Olympic Games represent one of the world's most significant sport events, bringing together athletes from around the globe to compete in a spirit of friendship, excellence and fair play. The Olympic Games have a rich history dating back to ancient Greece, where they were held as part of religious festivals. The modern Olympic Games were revived in 1896 by Pierre de Coubertin, to promote international understanding and peace. Since then, the Olympic Games have grown into a global phenomenon, with millions of athletes and spectators participating in both the Summer and Winter Games (Gold & Gold, 2024).

The Olympic Games have a significant socio-economic impact on host cities and countries, generating both opportunities and challenges for local communities (Könecke & de Nooij, 2017; Preuss, 2024).

Hosting the Olympic Games can provide a boost to the local economy through increased tourism, spending and investment, because the Games attract millions of visitors from around the world, leading to higher hotel occupancy rates, restaurant revenues and retail sales. Moreover, infrastructure projects such as stadiums, transportation networks and urban redevelopment initiatives create jobs and stimulate economic activity in host cities.

The economic benefits are accompanied by significant costs and risks (Kassens-Noor, 2012).

In recent years, there has been increasing attention to the environmental sustainability of the Olympic Games, with efforts to minimise the ecological footprint of the event and promote sustainable practices (IOC, 2014, 2021). The International Olympic Committee (IOC) has made commitments to promote environmental sustainability in the Olympic Games, including environmental considerations into the bidding process, implementing sustainable procurement practices and offsetting carbon emissions associated with the event. Moreover, host cities are encouraged to prioritise green building design, renewable energy sources and waste reduction measures in the construction and operation of Olympic venues and infrastructure (Li & Jago, 2013; Zimbalist, 2015).

Agenda 2020 and its subsequent iteration, Agenda 2020+5, represent pivotal initiatives introduced by the IOC to address the challenges and opportunities associated with hosting the Olympic Games. They outline a comprehensive set of principles and strategies aimed at enhancing the sustainability, economic viability and legacy of the Games, while also reducing the reliance on public funds (Nicoliello, 2021).

Agenda 2020, launched in 2014, served as a catalyst for change within the Olympic movement. It identified key areas for reform and proposed innovative solutions to address the evolving needs of host cities and the broader Olympic community. Central to Agenda 2020 is the concept of sustainability, encompassing environmental, social and economic considerations.

Building on the successes and lessons learned from Agenda 2020, the IOC introduced Agenda 2020+5 in 2021. This updated framework reaffirms the IOC's commitment to sustainability and innovation while also addressing emerging challenges and opportunities in the Olympic landscape. Agenda 2020+5 builds upon the core principles of its predecessor, with a renewed focus on legacy, transparency and accountability in the entire process (Nicoliello, 2021).

Both frameworks accentuate the concept of existing facilities to minimise the need for costly new construction. Agenda 2020 and Agenda 2020+5 encourage collaborative efforts between regions, countries and even multiple cities in hosting the Olympic Games. Sharing resources, expertise and infrastructure, host cities spread the financial responsibility and maximise the benefits for the broader community (Matheson, 2013).

4.3 Methodology

Content analysis is a research method widely used in social sciences, communication studies and other disciplines to systematically analyse and interpret textual, visual or audiovisual data (Neuendorf, 2002). The content analysis process typically begins with the selection of a sample of texts or media artefacts relevant to the research question or topic of interest, after that researchers systematically analyse the content of each text to identify key themes, topics or patterns (Krippendorff, 2018).

Content analysis can be conducted using qualitative, quantitative or mixed methods approaches. Qualitative content analysis focuses on the interpretation and meaning of textual data, while quantitative content analysis involves the use of statistical techniques to quantify and analyse patterns within the data (Neuendorf, 2002).

Applying content analysis to case studies (Yin, 1984), in the first part of the research we analysed all the documents published on the IOC website in the Olympic Agenda section. In particular, in these documents, all available in PDF format, we searched the expressions "Reducing Public Funds" and "Olympic Bids", in line with the research aims, so as to identify the areas of the IOC documents with these issues.

As result we have identified four areas in which the two themes are addressed: prioritising existing infrastructure; streaming the bidding process; promoting collaborative efforts; commitment to sustainability and transparency.

In the second part of the research, we investigated the bid documents of four locations, those relating to the editions of the Olympic Games assigned after the Agenda 2020: Paris 2024, Milan-Cortina 2026, Los Angeles 2028 and Brisbane 2032. We found the documents, in pdf format, in the Olympic Library online and we searched within them the four previously identified areas.

4.4 The analysis

4.4.1 IOC's Documents

With the documentary investigation of Agenda 2020 and Agenda 2020+5, we retrieved the topics "Reducing Public Funds" and "Olympic Bids" in four areas:

- prioritising existing infrastructure;
- streaming the bidding process;
- promoting collaborative efforts;
- commitment to sustainability and transparency.

4.4.1.1 Prioritising Existing Infrastructure

In the field of the Olympics, the notion of prioritising existing infrastructure has emerged as a pivotal strategy inside the Olympic Agenda 2020. Central to this approach is the recognition that many potential host cities already possess a wealth of resources and facilities that could be repurposed to accommodate the needs of the Games. Leveraging the existing assets, host cities sidestep the financial pitfalls associated with large-scale construction projects while simultaneously minimising the environmental impact of the Games. At its core, prioritising existing infrastructure aligns with the principles of sustainability and responsible stewardship outlined in both Agenda 2020 and Agenda 2020+5. Rather than succumbing to the temptation of grandiose development schemes, host cities are encouraged to adopt a more pragmatic approach that takes full advantage of the resources at their disposal, reducing the financial burden on host cities and ensuring that Olympic investments yield tangible benefits for local communities long after the Games have concluded. However, while the benefits of prioritising existing infrastructure are undeniable, the approach is not without its challenges, in primis the need for careful planning and coordination to ensure that existing venues and facilities meet the requirements of Olympic events. In some cases, upgrades or modifications may be necessary to bring these facilities up to international standards, introducing additional costs and logistical complexities for host cities to navigate.

4.4.1.2 Streamlining the Bidding Process

Agenda 2020 and Agenda 2020+5 place a strong emphasis on streamlining the bidding process for potential host cities. Historically, the bidding process for the Olympic Games has been characterised by complexity, bureaucracy and high costs. Recognising the need for reform, the IOC has introduced measures to simplify the process, making it more accessible and cost-effective for interested cities. Rather than adhering to rigid timelines and requirements, potential host cities are encouraged to tailor their bids to suit their unique circumstances and priorities, considering the option to propose alternative venues, dates and formats.

Agenda 2020 underlines the reduction of the financial burden implementing cost-saving measures and providing financial support and assistance where needed, for example offering technical expertise and guidance to potential host cities, as well as providing financial incentives and guarantees to offset the costs.

Agenda 2020+5 aims to make the bidding process more transparent and accessible to the public, allowing for greater scrutiny and oversight of the decision-making process, therefore detailed information about the bidding process, evaluation criteria and selection criteria are published, as well as opportunities for public input and feedback are provided.

4.4.1.3 Promoting Collaborative Efforts

Agenda 2020 and Agenda 2020+5 highlight efforts between regions, countries and even multiple cities. The collaborative approach represents a departure from the traditional model of single-city hosting and acknowledges the benefits of shared responsibility.

Pooling resources and sharing costs, host cities mitigate the financial risks and challenges associated with hosting large-scale sporting events. The collaborative financing model reduces the strain on individual cities, promoting solidarity and mutual support among participating regions or nations.

According to Olympic Agenda 2020 promoting collaborative efforts can help address the challenges of urban development and infrastructure investment in host cities. Bringing together multiple stakeholders, including government agencies, private sector entities and civil society organisations, host cities develop integrated solutions that address the diverse needs and priorities of their communities. The approach to urban development enhances the quality of life for residents and creates a more resilient and sustainable urban environment for future generations.

Following Olympic Agenda 2020+5, promoting collaborative efforts can contribute to the promotion of social inclusion and diversity in host cities. The promotion of collaborative efforts represents a multifaceted approach to Olympic hosting that extends beyond the confines of the Games themselves, since the IOC can create a more sustainable, equitable and inclusive Olympic experience that benefits all stakeholders.

4.4.1.4 Commitment to Sustainability and Transparency

Embedded within the ethos of Agenda 2020 and Agenda 2020+5 is a steadfast commitment to sustainability and transparency, principles that form the bedrock of the IOC's vision for the future of Olympic hosting, reflecting a recognition of the imperative to minimise environmental impact and ensure accountability in decision-making processes. Sustainability extends beyond environmental considerations to encompass social and economic dimensions as well, because IOC wishes to promote social inclusion, diversity and economic development in host cities, ensuring that the benefits of hosting the Games are shared equitably among all members of the community.

Agenda 2020 aims to boost transparency in the Olympic bidding and organising process providing greater access to information, ensuring public scrutiny of decision-making processes and promoting open dialogue and engagement with stakeholders. Transparency extends beyond the bidding and organising process to encompass broader issues of governance, finance and operations within the Olympic movement. Agenda 2020+5 calls for a great improvement in the management of Olympic funds, in the allocation of resources and in the conduct of IOC officials and members.

4.4.2 The Cases

4.4.2.1 Paris 2024 Olympic Games

Paris 2024 aimed to prioritise existing infrastructure, showcasing iconic venues like the Stade de France in St. Denis (the venue for the athletics and the closing ceremony) and the Roland Garros stadium (the venue for tennis and boxing). The bid highlighted refurbishing and repurposing existing facilities to minimise costs and environmental impact: e.g. the choice to use the Grand Palais or the Arena in Bercy, two historical sport venues of the French capital, or to use temporary structure to host urban sports in Place de la Concorde or aquatics in Defense Arena and to widespread competitions along the Ile de France Region: St. Quentin for track cycling, Vaires sur Marne for rowing and canoe, Le Borget for climbing, Guyancourt for golf, Elancourt for MTB, Colombes for Hockey, Nanterre for swimming and waterpolo.

Paris 2024 advocated for a streamlined bidding process, focusing on transparency, accountability and efficiency. The bid proposed reforms to simplify bid requirements and provide enhanced support for candidate cities. For the first time in the history the IOC decided, following the Agenda 2020, to assign two consecutive editions of the Games in the same time. Therefore in September 2027, during the Session in Lima, both Paris and Los Angeles obtained the Games.

The Paris bid underscored collaboration between government agencies, sports organisations and local communities in order to save public money. It proposed partnerships with neighbouring regions to share resources and distribute economic benefits equitably. Very significative was the choice to host the surf in Tahiti, in the Pacific Ocean, or to involve other cities, such as Lille for handball and basketball, Chateauroux for shooting, Marseille for sailing.

Paris 2024 demonstrated a strong commitment to sustainability, with plans to minimise carbon emissions, reduce waste and promote renewable energy sources. Another absolutely innovations are the choice to open the marathon for all runners (20.024 amateurs will run the 42 K after the elite athletes) and the decision to host the opening ceremony alongside the Seine river.

4.4.2.2 Milan-Cortina 2026 Olympic Winter Games

Milan-Cortina 2026 showcased the region's extensive existing infrastructure, leveraging ski resorts, ice arenas and sporting venues. The bid prioritised venues with proven track records and proposed temporary structures to minimise the need for permanent construction. It is the first time that two cities appear in the official name of the Games. In order to use the 90% of existing venues the competitions widespread in two Regions (Lombardy and Veneto) and two Provinces (Trento and Bozen). Only two new venues will build: the ice hockey arena in Milan and the sliding centre for bob, luge and skeleton in Cortina. Italy will exploit historic places for winter sport like Bormio (men's alpine skiing), Val di

Fiemme (Nordic skiing), Antholz (biathlon), Cortina (womens' alpine skiing and curling) and Assago Forum in Milan (figure skating and short track speed skating). Ice hockey and speed skating will use temporary venues in the exhibition area in Milan, while the opening ceremony will be in San Siro Stadium in Milan, the medal plaza in Piazza del Duomo in Milan and the closing ceremony in the iconic Arena in Verona.

The Milan-Cortina masterplan highlighted Italy's commitment to uphold Olympic values and proposed measures to streamline the bidding process and reduce bureaucracy. Milan-Cortina 2026 was the last edition of Olympic Games assigned with the traditional path: first the bid from the potential organisers, after the election process from the IOC Session. In the final vote Milan-Cortina (Mi-Co) defeated the Swedish couple Stockholm-Aare.

In the governance of Mi-Co 2026 there are the National Government, the two majors, the two regional governors and the two county's presidents. It is a unique opportunity to put together all the level of public bodies, to create a new way to manage the Games.

Milan-Cortina bid prioritised sustainability and environmental stewardship, proposing measures to minimise the Games' ecological footprint and promote green practices. In 2023 they launched a specific Sustainability Strategy, stressing transparency and integrity in all aspects of Games planning and delivery.

4.4.2.3 Los Angeles 2028 Olympic Games

Like Paris (1904, 1924 and 2024) also Los Angeles will host in 2028 the Summer editions of the Olympics for the third time, after 1932 and 1984.

They obtained the Games eleven years in advance, therefore with a long timeline to set up an impressive strategy to deliver the competition in a proper way, totally in line with the recommendations of Olympic Agenda 2020 and 2020+5.

The strategy leveraged the city's extensive sports infrastructure, including iconic venues like the LA Memorial Coliseum (athletics, becoming the first stadium to host three Olympiads), the Staples Center (basketball), the Rose Bowl (football) and the Sofi Stadium (archery). The bid underlined no new venues construction (first time in the history of the Games), focusing instead on upgrading existing facilities (Crypto Arena) and utilising university campuses for accommodation: the athlete village will be situated in the UCLA campus, the media village in the USC campus.

The Los Angeles bid championed a simplified and cost-effective bidding process, leveraging the city's proven track record as a host city. Another innovative idea will be the splitting of the opening ceremonies in two arenas, one segment in Memorial Coliseum and another one in Sofi Stadium.

Los Angeles 2028 proposed public-private partnerships to fund infrastructure upgrades, ensuring a legacy of economic development and social inclusion. Doing so, for example, the venues for canoeing slalom was identified far away in Oklahoma.

The LA bid placed a high priority on sustainability and transparency, incorporating green building practices, renewable energy technologies and resource-efficient design principles into Games infrastructure.

Great news also inside the program of the Games, with the new entry of five sports: the debut of flag football and squash as optional events proposed by the organising committee, joined by the return of baseball/softball, cricket (since 1900) and lacrosse (for since 1908). After the debut in 2020 as optional events, skateboarding, sport climbing and surfing have been promoted to the core events, while boxing had been provisionally removed and modern pentathlon will employ a new format, replacing horse jumping with obstacle course racing.

4.4.2.4 Brisbane 2032 Olympic Games

Brisbane was the first city appointed after the reform of the assigned process decided in 2019. There was no electing process from the Session, but the decision took place in July 2021 after a long-term discussion between IOC Host Commission and the city.

Brisbane 2032 proposed a decentralised approach to venue planning, leveraging existing infrastructure across multiple cities in Queensland. The bid underlined venues with existing or planned future use beyond the Games, ensuring a legacy of sustainable development and community benefit. Maximising the use of existing facilities, Brisbane 2032 aimed to deliver a cost-effective and legacy-driven Games.

In the map or the Games there are 19 venues in Brisbane (13 existing, 4 new—for aquatics, basketball, boxing and canoe slalom) and 2 temporaries. In the Gold Coast region there are 7 venues (5 existing and 2 temporaries), in the Sunshine coast there are 4 venues (existing, 1 new and 1 temporary), in other cities 4 venues, already existing.

The Brisbane bid embraced sustainability as a core principle, with plans to deliver a carbon–neutral Games and leave a positive environmental legacy.

4.4.2.5 A Comparison Among the Cases

The analysis provides insights into how each Olympic Games bid addressed the key aspects of Agenda 2020 and 2020+5.

For prioritising existing infrastructure, Paris 2024 highlighted refurbishing and repurposing existing facilities to minimise costs and environmental impact, leveraging iconic venues. Milan-Cortina 2026 showcased extensive existing infrastructure, prioritising venues with proven track records and proposing temporary structures. Los Angeles 2028 utilised the city's extensive sports infrastructure, focusing on upgrading existing facilities and utilising university campuses, Brisbane 2032 proposed a decentralised approach to venue planning, leveraging existing infrastructure across multiple cities in Queensland.

Regarding the process, Paris 2024 advocated for a streamlined bidding process, focusing on transparency, accountability and efficiency, Milan-Cortina 2026 stressed a transparent and inclusive bidding process, proposing measures to reduce bureaucracy, Los Angeles 2028 championed a simplified and cost-effective bidding process, emphasising clarity, consistency and flexibility, Brisbane 2032 advocated for a collaborative and transparent bidding process, engaging stakeholders at all levels of government and the community.

Concerning the collaboration, Paris stressed collaboration between government agencies, sports organisations and local communities, proposing partnerships with neighbouring regions, Milan-Cortina highlighted collaboration between the cities of Milan and Cortina, as well as regional and national governments, proposing joint planning and investment strategies, Los Angeles underscored collaboration between the city government, private sector partners and community stakeholders, proposing public-private partnerships, Brisbane showcased collaboration between multiple cities and regions in Queensland, proposing a coordinated approach to venue planning and transportation infrastructure.

In terms of sustainability, the French organisers demonstrated a strong commitment to sustainability, with plans to minimise carbon emissions, reduce waste and promote renewable energy sources, accenting transparency and accountability; the Italian case prioritised sustainability and environmental stewardship, proposing measures to minimise the Games' ecological footprint and promote green practices, stressing transparency and integrity; the American proposal placed a high priority on sustainability and transparency, incorporating green building practices and renewable energy technologies into Games infrastructure, emphasising open communication and independent oversight; the Australian edition embraced sustainability as a core principle, with plans to deliver a carbon-neutral Games and leave a positive environmental legacy, emphasising transparency and ethical conduct.

Each Olympic Games bid had its unique approach and priorities, but all the cases demonstrated a commitment to reduce public funds reliance.

4.5 Discussion

Despite the challenges, the four case studies serve as compelling evidence of feasibility and effectiveness of prioritising existing infrastructure in Olympic bids. Showcasing the successful integration of pre-existing venues and facilities into the fabric of the Games, they underscore the potential for cities to host world-class sporting events without resorting to extravagant construction projects. They also demonstrate the enduring legacy that can be achieved when Olympic investments are aligned with the broader development goals and priorities of host cities and their residents (Kassens-Noor, 2012).

Looking ahead, the prioritisation of existing infrastructure is likely to remain a central tenet of Olympics for years to come. As host cities continue to grapple with the economic, environmental and social challenges, the wisdom of this approach becomes increasingly apparent (Li & Jago, 2013). The lessons learned from past experiences will continue to inform future bids, shaping the evolution of Olympic hosting and ensuring that the Games remain a beacon of excellence, unity and inspiration for generations to come (Winand et al., 2012; Zimbalist, 2015).

Agenda 2020 and Agenda 2020+5 aim to attract a wider range of potential host cities and ensure that the Games remain financially sustainable and socially responsible. Through these reforms, the IOC seeks to foster greater competition and innovation in Olympic bidding, ultimately enhancing the overall quality and integrity of the Games for athletes, spectators and host cities alike (Nicoliello, 2021). Leveraging the strengths and resources of multiple cities or regions, host cities offer a diverse range of venues, cultural experiences and attractions to athletes, spectators and visitors in order to enrich the Olympic experience and reinforce the Games' role as a global celebration of sport, culture and friendship (Preuss, 2024).

Promoting collaborative efforts aligns with the principles of sustainability and responsible stewardship outlined in Agenda 2020 and Agenda 2020+5, maximising the use of existing infrastructure and resources across multiple host cities and minimising the need for new encouraging regions, countries and cities to work together towards a common goal, the IOC aims to create a more sustainable experience for all stakeholders (Chappelet, 2012).

The IOC's commitment to sustainability and transparency reflects its recognition of the need to address pressing global challenges and uphold the values of accountability, responsibility and integrity. Through its actions and initiatives, the IOC aims to demonstrate leadership in promoting sustainable development, environmental stewardship and ethical governance, while also inspiring positive change and innovation within the world of sport and beyond (Scandizzo & Pierleoni, 2018).

Paris 2024 and Milan-Cortina 2026 prioritised refurbishing and repurposing existing facilities, while Los Angeles 2028 accentuated upgrading existing venues and utilising university campuses. Brisbane 2032 proposed a decentralised approach to venue planning, maximising the use of existing infrastructure across multiple cities.

Paris 2024 advocated for a simplified bidding process, resulting in the unprecedented decision by the IOC to award both the 2024 and 2028 Games simultaneously. Milan-Cortina 2026 underlined transparency and inclusivity in the bidding process, while Los Angeles 2028 championed a cost-effective approach, leveraging the city's proven track record as a host city. Brisbane 2032 introduced a new model of bid selection, with the city appointed directly by the IOC following discussions with the Host Commission.

Paris 2024 and Milan-Cortina 2026 proposed partnerships with neighbouring regions and cities to share resources and distribute economic benefits equitably, Los Angeles 2028 collaborations between the city government, private sector partners and community stakeholders, while Brisbane 2032 showed collaboration between multiple cities and regions in Queensland. The cases provide valuable insights for future Olympic

Games bids, stressing the need for innovative approaches that prioritise long-term sustainability and community benefits (Kasale et al., 2018; Könecke & de Nooij, 2017).

4.6 Conclusion

The analysis identified key themes, patterns and trends related to the IOC's efforts to reduce the reliance on public funds in Olympic bids for both Summer and Winter Games. Across the documents analysed, we found numerous references about prioritising existing infrastructure, minimising the need for new construction and promoting collaborative efforts between regions, countries and cities to reduce the financial burden on host cities and ensure the long-term sustainability of the Games (Kasale et al., 2018).

Our analysis revealed a shift towards a more flexible and dynamic approach to Olympic bidding and hosting (Nicoliello, 2021). Rather than adhering to rigid timelines and requirements, potential host cities are encouraged to tailor their bids to suit their unique circumstances and priorities, therefore from one side the flexibility allows for greater innovation and creativity in Olympic hosting, from the other side it reduces the financial and logistical barriers for potential host cities (Preuss, 2024).

The documents analysed highlighted to provide clear and transparent information to potential host cities, ensuring that they understand the requirements and expectations of hosting the Games. Additionally, the IOC has taken steps to increase transparency in the evaluation and selection of host cities, allowing for greater public scrutiny and oversight of the decision-making process. The results revealed a growing trend towards collaboration and partnership in Olympic bidding and hosting. Rather than competing against each other, potential host cities are encouraged to work together to share resources, spread costs and maximise the benefits of hosting the Games.

Summing up, the research suggests that the IOC's efforts to reduce the reliance on public funds in Olympic bids have been largely successful. With the Agenda 2020 and the Agenda 2020+5, the IOC has created a framework that fosters greater economic stability and minimises financial burdens on host cities. Moving forward, it will be important for the IOC to continue to monitor and evaluate the effectiveness of these initiatives, ensuring that they remain responsive to the evolving needs and challenges of Olympic bidding and hosting.

The study primarily relies on publicly available information and documents provided by the IOC and the respective bidding committees. These sources offer valuable insights into the bidding and hosting processes, but they may not provide a complete picture of the decision-making processes and challenges faced by the bidding cities. The analysis does not take into account potential discrepancies between the proposed plans and the actual implementation of the Games, therefore it is possible that unforeseen challenges or changes in circumstances may have influenced the execution of the bids, which are not captured in the analysis. Future studies could explore the long-term impacts of the process on host cities, including their economic, social and environmental legacies, or the alternative models for Olympic bidding, including collaborative approaches that involve multiple cities or regions. Continued research and development in the field of Olympics are essential to ensure that future Games are delivered in a manner that maximises the benefits for host cities and communities while minimising the financial and environmental costs.

References

Primary Sources

Brisbane 2032 Summer Olympic Games Bid Proposal.
IOC (2014), Olympic Agenda 2020, Lausanne.
IOC (2021), Olympic Agenda 2020+5, Lausanne.
Los Angeles 2028 Summer Olympic Games Bid Proposal.
Milan Cortina 2026 Winter Olympic Games Bid Proposal.
Paris 2024 Summer Olympic Games Bid Proposal.

Secondary Sources

Alakshendra, A. (2016). How are we funding professional sports stadiums? An Overview. *Managerial Finance, 42*(9), 885–890.

Andreff, W., & Szymanski, S. (2006). *Handbook on the economics of sport* (1st ed.). Edward Elgar.

Baade, R. A., & Matheson, V. A. (2016). Going for the gold: The economics of the Olympics. *Journal of Economic Perspectives, 30*(2), 201–218.

Brookes, S., & Wiggan, J. (2009). Reflecting the public value of sport. *Public Management Review, 11*(4), 401–420.

Chappelet, J. L. (2012). Mega sporting event legacies: A multifaceted concept. *Papeles de Europa, 25*, 76–86.

Dickson, T. J., Benson, A. M., & Blackman, D. A. (2011). Developing a framework for evaluating Olympic and Paralympic legacies. *Journal of Sport & Tourism, 16*(4), 285–302.
Downward, P., Frick, B., Humphreys, B. R., Pawlowski, T., Ruseski, J. E., & Soebbing, B. P. (2019). *The SAGE handbook of sports economics* (1st ed.). SAGE Publications.
Essex, S., & Chalkley, B. (2004). Mega-sporting events in urban and regional policy: A history of the Winter Olympics. *Planning Perspectives, 19*(2), 201–204.
Gold, J., & Gold, M. M. (Eds.). (2024). *Olympic cities: City agendas, planning, and the world's games, 1896–2020* (4th ed.). Routledge.
Gratton, C., Preuss, H., & Liu, D. (2015). Economic and legacy to cities from hosting mega sport events: A case study of Beijing 2008. In R. Holt & D. Ruta (Eds.), *Routledge handbook of sport and legacy: Meeting the challenge of major sports events* (pp. 46–58). Routledge.
Groothuis, P. A., Johnson, B. K., & Whitehead, J. C. (2004). Public funding of professional sports stadiums: Public choice or civic pride? *Eastern Economic Journal, 30*(4), 515–526.
Kasale, L. L., Winand, M., & Robinson, L. (2018). Performance management of national sports organisations: A holistic theoretical model. *Sport, Business and Management: An International Journal, 8*(5), 469–491.
Kasimati, E. (2015). Post-Olympic use of the Olympic venues: The case of Greece. *Athens Journal of Sports, 2*(3), 167–184.
Kassens-Noor, E. (2012). *Planning Olympic legacies: Transport dreams and urban realities*. Routledge.
Könecke, T., & de Nooij, M. (2017). The IOC and Olympic bids from democracies and authoritarian regimes—A socioeconomic analysis and strategic insights. *Current Issues in Sport Science, 2*, 009.
Krippendorff, K. (2018). *Content analysis: An introduction to its methodology* (4th ed.). Sage Publications.
Kučera, J., Zimková, E., Nemec, J., & Nemec, M. (2023). A comparative analysis of the efficiency of public funding policies for sports in the European Union. *Cogent Social Sciences, 9*(2), 2280335.
Li, S., & Jago, L. (2013). Evaluating economic impacts of major sports events—A meta analysis of the key trends. *Current Issues in Tourism, 16*(6), 591–611.
Lowther, M., Digenaro, S., Borgogni, A., & Lowther, A. P. (2016). Exploring and establishing a framework for effective governance in European grassroots sports organisations. *Journal of Applied Sport Management, 8*(1), 80–110.
Matheson, V. (2013). Assessing the infrastructure impact of mega-events in emerging economies. In G. K. Ingram & K. L. Brandt (Eds.), *Infrastructure and land policies* (pp. 215–232). Lincoln Land Institute.
Neuendorf, K. A. (2002). *The content analysis guidebook*. Sage Publications.

Nicoliello, M. (2021, June). The new agenda 2020+5 and the future challenges for the olympic movement. *Athens Journal of Sports, 8*(2), 121–140.

Otarbaevich, A. A., & Dlimbetovich, B. T. (2021). The impact of sports on human life and health. *International Journal of Academic Pedagogical Research, 5*(6/2021), 45–47.

Preuss, H. (2024). Olympic finance. In J. Gold & M. M. Gold (Eds.), *Olympic cities: City agendas, planning, and the world's games, 1896–2020* (4th ed.). Routledge.

Rebeggiani, L. (2006). Public vs. private spending for sports facilities—The case of Germany 2006. *Public Finance and Management, 6*(3), 395–435.

Riess, S. A. (1998). Historical perspectives on sports and public policy. *Policy Studies Review, 15*(1), 3–15.

Scandizzo, P. L., & Pierleoni, M. R. (2018). Assessing the Olympic Games: The economic impact and beyond. *Journal of Economic Surveys, 32*(3), 649–682.

Siegfried, J., & Zimbalist, A. (2006). The economic impact of sports facilities, teams and mega-events. *The Australian Economic Review, 39*(4), 420–427.

Sutin, S. E. (2011). Reducing reliance on public funding: The place where creativity and practicality converge. In S. E. Sutin, D. Derrico, R. L. Raby, & E. J. Valeau (Eds.), *Increasing effectiveness of the community college financial model*. Palgrave Macmillan.

Winand, M., Zintz, T., Scheerder, J., & Dolles, H. (2012). A financial management tool for sport federations. *Sport, Business and Management: An International Journal, 2*(3), 225–240.

Yin, R. K. (1984). *Case study research: Design and methods*. Sage Publications.

Zimbalist, A. S. (2015). *Circus Maximus: The economic gamble behind hosting the Olympics and the World Cup*. Brookings Institution Press.

CHAPTER 5

The Role of Public Sector Wage Rates in the Determination of Labour Share

Yiorgos Ioannidis, Dimitris Giakoulas, and Anastasios Pappas

5.1 Introduction

The distribution of national income between labour and capital (i.e. the functional distribution of income) has been studied from the beginning of modern economic theory and according to Ricardo's famous phrase, it constitutes the "principal problem of Political Economy" (Ricardo, 1911 [1817]). However, initial interest in the topic gradually waned after a series of empirical studies on the functional distribution of income over the long term in the USA (Johnson, 1954) and the UK (Bowley,

Y. Ioannidis (✉)
Centre for Planning and Economic Research (KEPE), Athens, Greece
e-mail: ioannidis@kepe.gr

D. Giakoulas
Aristotle University of Thessaloniki, Thessaloniki, Greece

Small Enterprises Institute (IME GSEVEE), Athens, Greece

A. Pappas
National and Kapodistrian University of Athens, Athens, Greece

A. Hyz (ed.), *The Role of the Public Sector in Building Social and Economic Resilience*,
https://doi.org/10.1007/978-3-031-67702-1_5

1920, 1937). These studies led to the formation of a widely shared belief that the share of labour remains stable over the long term (indicatively see Keynes, 1939; Kaldor, 1961). This assumption, despite the objections raised from time to time (indicatively Kuznets, 1959; Solow, 1958), remained dominant for several decades (Gollin, 2008) and acquired its most formal expression in the Cobb–Douglas production function (1928) which also assumes a stable distribution of income.

However, from the mid-1990s, early-2000s onwards a growing body of studies has challenged the hypothesis of the long-run constant functional distribution of income. Piketty's Capital in the twenty-first century (Piketty, 2013) gave further impetus to the debate and resulted in a multiplication of the number of relevant studies. It is characteristic that Giovannoni (2014) records seventeen similar studies conducted by international organizations like the UN, the ILO, the IMF, the US Central Bank, the OECD, the ECB, the EC and the Bank for International Settlements. A common finding of most of these studies is that the labour share, in the advanced economies, increased during the 1960s and the 1970s, but from the 1980s onwards began to decline at an accelerating rate. For example, the OECD estimated that during the period 1990–2009 the labour share shrank from 66.1% to 61.7% in 26 out of the 30 developed economies it examined (OECD, 2012). Likewise, Karabarbounis and Neiman (2014a) found that during the period 1975–2012 the labour share decreased in 42 out of the 59 countries and in 10 out of the 12 industries examined.[1] The renewed interest in the labour share was initially related to the debate on economic inequalities (indicatively Glyn, 2009; Ryan, 1996) but it is also linked to other aspects of economic and fiscal policy like the inflation rate (de Serres et al., 2002), potential GDP (Christodoulakis & Axioglou, 2017), the level of household consumption (Onaran & Galanis, 2013), the growth rate of the national (Charpe et al., 2019, Lavoie & Stockhammer, 2012) and the global economy (Onaran & Galanis, 2013).

[1] Similar conclusions can be found also in numerous other studies (indicatively European Commission 2007; Guerriero 2019; ILO 2012; Rodriguez & Jayadev 2010).

5.2 Labour Share, Income Inequalities and Public Sector Employment

A high labour share in an economy usually means that the income is more evenly distributed. This happens because, as Glyn (2009), Piketty (2014), Schlenker and Schmid (2015), and Milanovic (2017) argue, the capital income, conversely to the labour income, tends to be more unevenly distributed and in this respect, a rise in the labour income share against the capital income share should reduce inequality.

Several studies have indeed found evidence of a negative relation between the labour share and income inequality. Milanovic (2017) examines the relationship between capital share and inequalities through the lens of three types of economic systems. The socialist, where income is distributed equally, the classical capitalist where workers draw their entire income from their work and capitalist from their capital and the new capitalist where workers and capitalists draw their income from both work and capital, respectively. He asserts that in a socialist system, a rising capital income does not affect inequalities while in the new capitalism in contrast, it causes inequalities to increase. Finally, in the classic capitalism, a rising capital income share increases inequalities but only when the share of capitalists becomes very high. Erauskin (2020) examined the relationship between the labour share and income inequality, by using panel data for 62 developed and developing countries from 1990 to 2015. His findings suggest that a low labour share is related to higher inequalities rates, expressed with the Gini index. He also stressed that public policies should pursue the increase in participation in the labour markets and the strengthening of the human capital of the poorest to further decrease income inequalities. Bises et al. (2023) investigate the relation between functional and personal income distribution. They use panel data from 33 OECD countries from 2000 to 2017 and their findings suggest that an increase in labour share reduces the correlation between market and disposable income inequality. Sergi et al. (2023) examine the impact of the government's economic growth, labour share and income inequality, analysing data from 11 post-soviet countries from 2000 to 2020. Their findings suggest that increased labour shares might decrease income inequalities, but for this to happen, the existence of an effective and democratic government that will further alleviate inequalities through government spending is crucial.

Income inequalities have negative impacts on societies. They tend to create social and political unrest which increases political and economic instability that harms investments and economic growth (Alesina & Perotti, 1996). High levels of inequalities reduce the ability of households to maintain their health and human capital with a negative impact on economic growth (Autor & Dorn, 2013; Corak, 2013). Furthermore, low-income people tend to give birth to many children but do not have the needed resources to allocate to their education in contrary with higher income people. In this respect, inequality might lead to a downward spiral that will create more inequalities (De la Croix & Doepke, 2003). Several studies have identified a negative relation between income inequalities and growth (Alesina & Rodrik, 1994; Braun et al., 2019; Breunig & Majeed, 2020); Knowles, 2005; Panizza, 2002).

Governments can use public sector employment as a fiscal and social policy tool to restrain unemployment in times of recession, divert resources to less advantaged regions and also boost demand (Caponi, 2017). Public sector wages tend to be more homogenous between a country's regions and thus contribute to minimizing regional inequalities (Caponi, 2014). Additionally, public sector wages tend to be more rigid and, in this respect, in times of recession when wages in the private sector are more downward elastic, public sector employment acts countercyclical (Quadrini & Trigari, 2007).

On the other hand, employment in the public sector has been often accused of crowding out workers from the private sector since wages and working conditions in the public sector are usually more attractive, especially for low-skilled employees and even in some cases reducing productivity when it diverts resources to less productive sectors (Gomes, 2015). However, several studies show that the correlation between public sector and private sector jobs might even be positive (Lamo et al., 2013).

The public sector's compensations tend to be higher than the private sector on average and thus bridge the income inequalities of the labour share compared to the capital share. De Castro et al. (2013) investigate the wage differentials between the public and the private sector in all the economies of the EU, using data from the European Structure of Earnings Survey, from 2006 and 2010. Their findings suggest that employees in the public sector have averagely higher wages than employees in the private sector in most EU countries apart from some eastern European and Nordic countries and France.

Additionally, public sector employment tends to reduce inequalities between employees within its sector. For example, Ghinetti and Lucifora (2008) examine the distribution of wages between the public and the private sector using microdata from France, Italy and the UK and find that wage differentials among high and low-skilled public sector workers are lower than in the private sector, respectively. Additionally (Meurs & Ponthieux, 2008) investigate gender-specific wage differentials in the public and the private sector of eight EU countries in order to assess what will be the impact of privatizations of public services. Their results indicate that gender wage gap in the public sector is smaller than in the private sector.

5.3 Factors Causing Changes in the Labour Share

The labour share (LS) is a fraction where the numerator is the labour compensation and the denominator is an indicator of the economy's income (such as the national income, the gross domestic product or the gross value added). Therefore, the LS will change if the terms of the fraction move in the same direction but in a non-proportional manner or if they move in the opposite direction. It follows that the LS will decline if wage growth falls short of labour productivity growth. In general, any factor putting pressure on wages (like international competition, the relocation of production to other countries, the reduced bargaining power of trade unions, fiscal adjustment programmes and so on) is expected to have a negative impact on LS. The above interpretation has been adopted by several studies to explain the observed decline in the LS during recent decades.[2]

Restrictive fiscal policies can also result in a lower LS. For example, Ball et al. (2013) found that the fiscal consolidation programmes that were implemented in 17 OECD countries during the period 1978–2009 resulted in a reduction of the LS by around 0.8% of GDP and an increase in inequality. Similarly, market liberalization policies tend to reduce the

[2] In this sense, it has been argued that the decline in the labour share can be attributed to wage pressures (Dimova, 2019; Rodrik, 1999) which may result from the globalization (Harrison, 2002), by diminishing the bargaining power of trade unions (European Commission, 2007; Ellis & Smith, 2010; Epstein & Burke, 2001; Furceri et al., 2013) or from a combination of the above factors (Jayadev, 2007).

LS. For example, Azmat et al. (2011) estimated that around a fifth of the reduction in the LS in Britain and France was due to the decrease in employment caused by the privatization of networks. On the other hand, Pak and Schwellnus (2019) argue that the LS in the most competitive markets tends to be higher due to the intensity of competition which reduces profit margins.

Another factor that can cause changes in LS is changes in the sectoral structure of the economy. Even if the LS remain stable inside individual sectors, the strengthening of capital-intensive sectors vis-à-vis labour-intensive sectors would lead to a reduction in the LS (and vice versa). Similarly, changes in the LS may be due to a change in the structure of employment. A reduction in the number of self-employed and an increase in the number of employees would increase the LS. Several researchers have argued that the decline of the LS in developed economies is due to this very reason, namely the gradual strengthening of capital-intensive sectors such as the financial sector and the parallel decline of labour-intensive sectors like manufacturing.[3] If that is the case, this means that a restrictive wage policy will have less effect on boosting employment than expected (de Serres et al., 2002).

In addition, the LS may decline as a result of changes relating to technology, since the adoption of technologies that substitute labour with capital will result in a reduction in the LS, an interpretation that has been adopted by several researchers.[4] Nonetheless, in a highly quoted study, Karabarbounis and Neiman (2014a) examined 50 countries for the period 1975–2012 and found that more than 90% of the negative change in the LS can be attributed to changes within industrial sectors and only 10% to changes in the sectoral structure of the economy. In this case, the reduction of LS is not a cyclical but a structural phenomenon (Guscina, 2006) the interpretation of which must be sought in the changing structure of the economy.

[3] Indicatively see Ripatti and Vilmunen (2001), Bentolila and Saint-Paul (2003), and Guscina (2006).

[4] Indicatively see Poterba (1997), Bentolila and Saint-Paul (2003), Arpaia et al. (2009), Driver and Muñoz-Bugarin (2010), Raurich et al. (2012), and Hutchinson and Persyn (2012).

5.4 Measuring the Labour Share

Calculating the LS requires some assumptions regarding the numerator and in the denominator of the fraction.[5] As far as the denominator is concerned, the main question concerns whether it is preferable to use GDP or GVA or domestic income. Using GDP has the advantage of calculating an easily understood index (the LS as a percentage of GDP).[6] However, most studies subtract from GDP the indirect taxes and taxes on production (minus subsidies) because indirect taxes and taxes on production do not constitute any type of return of capital or labour (Gollin, 2002; Guerriero, 2012; Izyumov & Vahaly, 2015). There is, also, a question of whether gross or net values should be used, i.e. whether or not to deduct capital depreciation. In this case, instead of GDP, one can use Net Domestic Product or Domestic Income (Bridgman, 2017; Rognlie, 2015).[7] Some researchers argue that when capital depreciation is deducted the findings call into question the argument that the LS is declining. Others, like Karabarbounis and Neiman (2014b), argue that using net instead of gross values does not affect the trend for the LS because gross and net values change in an almost parallel way (this argument is confirmed and by our study). In any case, both approaches have been extensively implemented. The famous references made by Keynes (1939) and Kaldor (1957) were to net values, on the other hand, most recent studies use gross values (take, for example, Glyn, 2009; Karabarbounis & Neiman, 2014a; Piketty & Zucman, 2014).

As far as the numerator is concerned, the most important issue concerns the income of the self-employed. This category comprises three distinct groups: employers, self-employed persons working for their own account, and unpaid assistants in family businesses. For simplification purposes, we shall refer to these three groups as the "self-employed", meaning all the non-salaried working population. The self-employed are

[5] All calculations use current prices.

[6] The gross value added at current prices (UVG0) includes fixed capital consumption and is equal to the value of the product minus the intermediate consumption at purchaser's prices (https://ec.europa.eu/economy_finance/ameco/HelpHtml/uvg0.html).

[7] The net domestic product at market prices (UVND) is equivalent to the national income at current market prices (UVND) and is given by the formula: UVND = UVGD–UKCT, where UVGD is the gross domestic product at current market prices and UKCT is the consumption of fixed capital at current prices (https://ec.europa.eu/economy_finance/ameco/HelpHtml/uvnd.html).

a extensive category which ranges from small farmers to craftsmen of all kinds, owners of small businesses who may employ staff but also contribute themselves with personal work, high-profile scientific professions like doctors, lawyers and engineers, and many others. Also, in recent years, due to the liberalization and personalization of industrial relations (OECD, 2019), this category includes a large number of persons who may appear typically to be self-employed but in essence, provide dependent work. According to National Accounts, the income of all the above working persons is classified as "mixed-income", i.e. as income derived partly from work and partly from capital returns. So treating mixed-income solely as capital return would result in an underestimation of the LS and the level of this underestimation will depend on the extent of these forms of work in the employment structure.[8] If we do not adjust labour compensation by the volume of self-employment, i.e. if we accept that labour income equals the compensation of paid to employees only, what we will be calculating is the unadjusted labour share. Although this approach has been used (Daudey & Garcia-Peñalosa, 2007, Jayedev, 2007, Rodrik, 1999) the results are not satisfactory because it implies that all self-employed income is capital return.

Alternatively, we can adjust labour income (compensation of employees) for the income of the self-employed to derive the so-called adjusted labour share. That is to accept that part of the mixed-income constitutes some form of "salary" corresponding to the personal work provided by the self-employed. In this case, the question concerns the adjustment methodology which should be used. If mixed-income is distinctly reflected in the National Accounts, one option is to treat it entirely as salary income (Kravis, 1959). This solution will work in economies where the average wage of a self-employed person is lower than that of an employee and where the self-employed do not use large amounts of capital (i.e. land). Nevertheless, this is hardly the case for modern economies. A great number of self-employed persons use significant amounts of capital and/or land (Gollin, 2002), while the distinction between the self-employed who earn less than the average salary-earner and those who earn more is quite a difficult task, often demanding largely arbitrary assumptions to be made.

[8] Some researchers have even argued that if we treat part of the self-employed income as equivalent to salary income the labour share remains constant over the long run (Bernanke & Gürkaynak 2001; Gollin 2002).

Another option is to treat two-thirds of the mixed-income as salary income and the remaining third as capital income. The method was proposed by Johnson (1954) and has been used in several studies (indicatively Guscina, 2006; Izyumov & Vahaly, 2015; Krueger, 1999). The problem here, apart from the justification for the use of two-thirds (why not 1/4 or 1/2?), is that this methodology fails to capture changes in the nature of self-employment, changes that may be significant when we examine long time series. The latter problem also arises in the third option, which is to assume that the mixed-income composition is analogous to that of the corporate sector of the economy (Atkinson, 1983; Izyumov & Vahaly, 2015; Rognlie, 2015; Ryan, 1996).

A widespread method is to adjust labour income on the assumption that the average hourly earnings of the self-employed are equal to the average hourly earnings of the employees. For greater reliability, we could assume that a self-employed person receives a "salary-income" equal to the average hourly earnings of an employee in the same sector (Arpaia et al., 2009; Bagnoli, 2009; Feinstein, 1968; Gollin, 2002; Guerriero, 2012; de Serres et al., 2002) This methodology is used by the OECD, the EU KLEMS project (Stehrer et al., 2019), and by the AMECO database.[9] Even better—but not always possible due to lack of data—is to assume that the average hourly earnings of a self-employed person equal the average hourly earnings of an employee of the same age, gender and educational level in the same sector (Jorgenson et al., 2010; Young, 1995). The advantage of this solution is that it requires easily accessible data and that it is based on reasonable assumptions. The biggest problem is that it can give "peculiar" results if self-employment constitutes a large proportion of total employment and/or if the average earnings of the self-employed are lower than that of salary earners. Combining these two factors can lead to estimates of the LS that exceed 1. In this study, we had to address a similar problem.

Finally, questions arise on how to deal with the public sector. The public sector affects both the denominator and the numerator of the LS fraction because the gross value added (GVA) of the public sector equals

[9] The adjusted wage share in total economy (ALCD0) as a percentage of GDP at market prices is given by the formula: ALCD0 = [(UWCD: NWTD): (UVGD: NETD)] × 100, where UWCD is the compensation of employees, NWTD is the number of employees, NETD is the total employment and UVGD is the GDP at current market prices (https://ec.europa.eu/economy_finance/ameco/HelpHtml/alcd0.html).

civil servants' salaries. As a result, the inclusion of the public sector in the LS tends to result in it being overestimated (ILO & OECD, 2015; Rognlie, 2015). A clean-cut solution, bypassing the problem, is the one adopted by Karabarbounis and Neiman (2014a) who, to minimize the effects of self-employment and of the public sector, focus on the LS in the corporate sector only. This approach has the advantage of clarity and does not require extended adjustments that might have an impact on the outcome of the estimation. On the other hand, this methodology by definition provides us with the functional distribution of income in the corporate sector only. Therefore, in countries where large corporations are not the dominant form of production organization and/or form of employment, estimation of the LS in the corporate sector does not tell us much about the situation in the total economy. It does not give us the big picture but only a small fraction of it.

Taking account of the above, we have chosen a solution that considers the available data and that can be extended to other countries to obtain comparative results.

First, we calculate the LS as a percentage of National Income to get a better picture of the functional distribution of income between wages and profits. To do so, we subtract fixed capital consumption from the denominator of the fraction. The algebraic expression of the formula is:

$$LS = \frac{\mathrm{CoE} * \frac{\mathrm{EMPL}}{\mathrm{EMPE}}}{\mathrm{NI}(= \mathrm{GVA} - \mathrm{CoFC})} \tag{5.1}$$

where CoE is the compensation of employees, EMPL is the volume of employment, EMPE is the number of employees and NI is national income at current factor cost and CoFC is the consumption of fixed capital. In other words, we assumed that the average earnings of a self-employed person equal the average compensation of employees in the economy.

Secondly, we calculate the LS in the private economy also as a percentage of Domestic Income. To do so some additional adjustments are required. First, the compensation of civil servants is deducted from the denominator, implying that the gross value added of the public sector is equal to the compensation of civil servants. Secondly, we deducted the compensation of civil servants from the numerator, and finally, we deducted the number of employees by the number of civil servants. In other words, we assumed that the average wage of public servants is the same in all of the sectors and that all civil servants are salary earners. Consequently, the LS in the private economy was assessed based on the formula:

$$LS^{pr} = \frac{CoE^{pr} * \frac{EMPL^{pr}}{EMPE^{pr}}}{NI^{pr}(= GVA^{pr} - CoFC^{pr})} \tag{5.2}$$

Where

$$CoE_i^{pr} = CoE_i - CoE_i^{publ}, \tag{5.3}$$

$$EMPL_i^{pr} = EMPL_i - EMPL_i^{publ}, \tag{5.4}$$

$$EMPE_i^{pr} = EMPE_i - EMPL_i^{publ}, \tag{5.5}$$

$$GVA_i^{pr} = GVA_i - CoE_i^{publ}, \tag{5.6}$$

$$CoE_i^{publ} = y_i CoE^{publ}. \tag{5.7}$$

Finally, our calculations on EU exclude some countries due to lack of data on public employment. These countries are Bulgaria, Croatia, Cyprus, Malta and Romania.

5.5 The Impact of Public Sector in the Labour Share in EU and Greece

When examining the private sector in a crisis context, it is reasonable to assume that employers will try to limit profit losses by lowering wages. On the other hand, as far as government is concerned, it is reasonable to assume that, due to the high political costs involved, the reduction of public sector employee's wages is not dictated by any reason other than the obligation to cut total public expenditure due to the requirements of the fiscal adjustment programmes (Memorandums). Therefore, to assess the real impact of the crisis on the distribution of income between wages and profits we need to look at the LS in the private sector. Moreover, to have a clear picture we should deduct capital depreciation from the capital income, meaning that we have to calculate the LS as a percentage of domestic income.

Figure 5.1 shows our calculations for the Labour Share in the Private Sector expressed as a percentage of National Income produced by the Private Sector (as defined in Eq. 5.2) for Greece and EU, respectively. There are two main points steaming from Fig. 5.1.

First, the economic crisis resulted at a significant decrease of the Labour Share in Greece. More specifically, in Greece, the Labour Share peaked just after the onset of the debt crisis (in 2010 it rose by 4.6 percentage point at 64.0% compared to 59.4% at 2008). This temporary rise was due to a relative rigidity of wages from 2008 to 2010. In particular the average annual wages in Greece continued to rise by 2.7 in 2008 and 5.7 in 2009 and only fell by −3.3% in 2010 (Bertonati et al., 2018). In the contrary there has been a decrease of 9.6% of the national income produced by the private sector from 2008 to 2010. Nevertheless, after 2010 the Labour Share started to fall and collapsed after 2012 at 55.8% in 2015 i.e. a diminish of 13.2 percentage points. In other words, in the private sector labour income during the crisis has decreased much more compared to the decrease in profits. As to the causes of these changes, the decline in LS is almost exclusively due to the reduction in wages and a

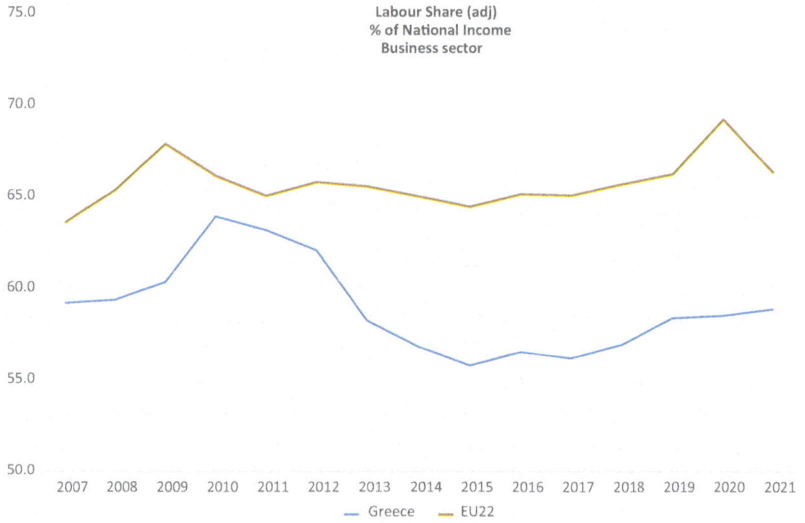

Fig. 5.1 Labour share (adj) % of National Income Business sector (*Source* Own calculations based on Eurostat data)

consequent significant reduction in unit labour cost since unit labour cost moves in parallel with the LS. Therefore, in the case of Greece during the recession, other factors such as changes in the structure of the economy or labour substitution by capital should be excluded. Finally, due to the betterment of the general economic condition and the fall of unemployment seen after 2017, the Labour Share in Greece started to rise again reaching 58.9% of National Income in 2021, which is still one percentage point lower compared to the pre-crisis level. On the contrary during the same period, the Labour Share in EU remained relatively stable at around 64%–65%.

Secondly, the Labour Share in Greece not only is lower than the EU average but during the period under examination there was a significant divergence compared to the rest of the EU. As seen in Fig. 5.2, while before the crises (2007–2008) the Labour Share in Greece was about 4.5 to 6.0 percentage points lower than in the EU, the gap was widened between 8.7 and 10.7 percentage points during the 2015–2021. It has to be noted that the divergence happen during a time were the Labour Share in Greece started to pick up. In that aspect there is a crisis-legacy accompanying the labour market in Greece.

Up until now, the discussion focused on the Labour Share in the private sector but now we can incorporate the public sector to track down its effect on the labour share. In Fig. 5.3, we portray the Labour Share of the total economy i.e. including the public sector for Greece and EU respectively and expressed as a percentage of the National Income (of the total economy). For better understanding, we have added the values of the Labour Share in the private sector discussed above. The continuous lines represent the Labour Share of the total economy (i.e. including the private and the public sector) while the dotted lines represent the Labour Share of the Private Sector alone (as in the Fig. 5.1).

Three main points arise from Fig. 5.3. Firstly, we see the positive impact of the compensation of employees of the public sector in increasing the Labour Share in both Greece and in EU. Unsurprisingly, the calculation of LS in the private sector produces lower values than in the case of the total economy due to the assumption that the public sector's GVA is equal to the compensation of civil servants. In any case, taking into account that a lower Labour Share is accompanied by higher income disparities this means a positive effect of public wages on lowering income inequality.

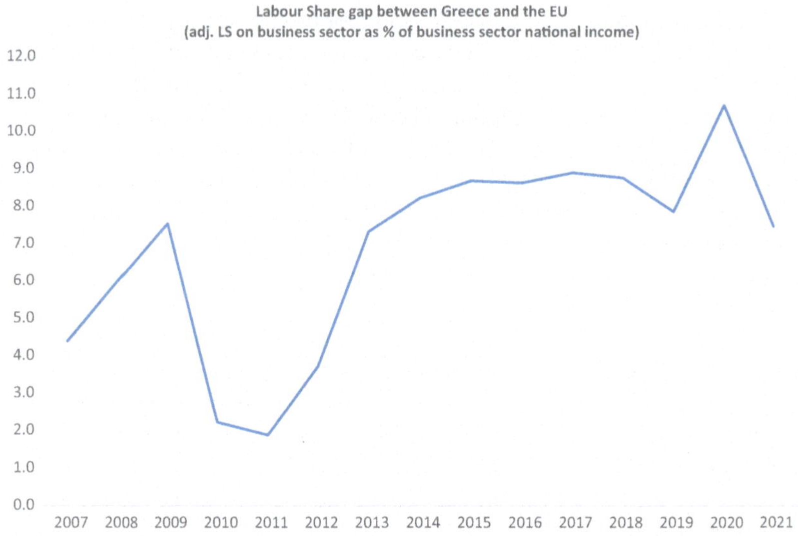

Fig. 5.2 Labour share gap between Greece and the EU (adj. LS on business sector as % of business sector national income) (*Source* Own calculations based on Eurostat data)

Secondly, public sector wage expenditure has a positive impact on bridging the gap between Greece and the EU. In specific, the gap between the Labour Share of Greece and the EU decreased by at least 50% (the lowest). This means that the general government's compensations in Greece have a greater impact on the total Labour Share of the country in comparison with the EU. The contribution of employment in the public sector in Greece in its labour share especially during the crisis period is comprehensively described by Christopoulou and Monastiriotis (2016) who investigate the public–private wage duality in Greece during the crisis. Their findings suggest that there was a notable difference in the adjustment of wages between the public and private sectors. Public sector monthly regular wages took a longer time to adjust and only saw significant decreases after 2011, while the private sector wages were affected more rapidly and to a greater extent, even before significant deregulation measures were implemented.

Looking deeper into our case, we investigate which countries have the lowest and the highest gap between the Labour Share of the total

Fig. 5.3 Labour share (adj) % of National Income Business sector & total economy (*Source* Own calculations based on Eurostat data)

economy and the private sector respectively (Fig. 5.4). We see that all the countries have a positive gap meaning that the labour share in the total economy is higher than in the private sector alone. In other words, the compensation of the general government's employees has a positive impact on the labour share of all the countries. Greece has by far the biggest gap of all countries (12.4 percentage points), followed by the Czech Republic and Hungary (10.0 and 9.6 percentage points respectively). On the other side, the countries with the lowest gap are Germany (5.5 percentage points), Luxembourg (6.2 percentage points) and the Netherlands (6.5 percentage points). It seems that countries of the periphery that were hit more severely by the economic crisis have the biggest gaps compared to core industrial countries.

Finally, there are strong indications that the public sector's wages act in an anti-cyclical manner. To make this point clearer we calculate the ratio of public wages into the total Labour Share (Fig. 5.5). As we see, the importance of public wage expenditure (in Greece) is strengthened during

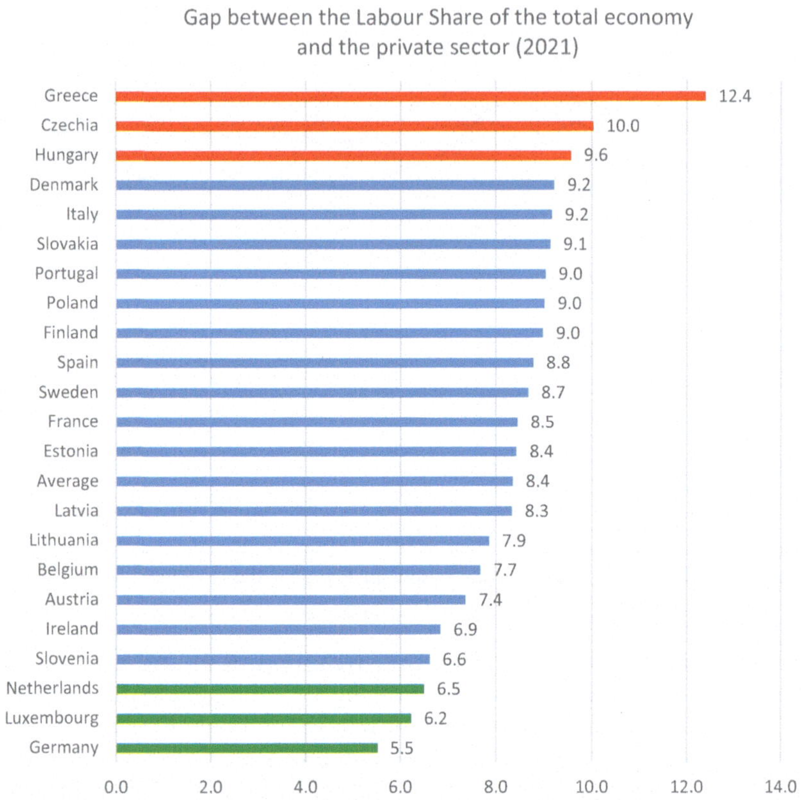

Fig. 5.4 Gap between the labour share of the total economy and the private sector (2021) (*Source* Own calculations based on Eurostat data)

the recession years (2009–2015) and then recedes when the economy returns into positive growth rates. The subject of the next section is to test econometrically this hypothesis.

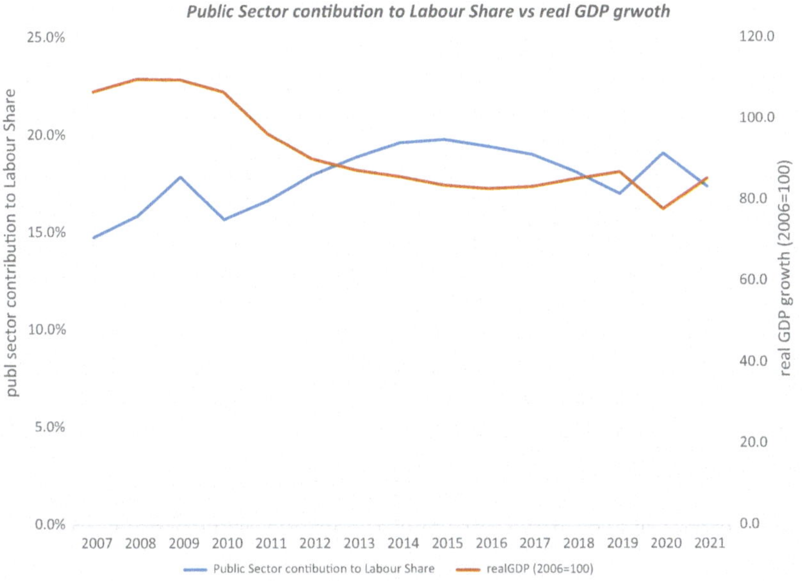

Fig. 5.5 Public sector contribution to labour share vs real GDP growth (*Source* Own calculations based on Eurostat data)

5.6 Government Expenditure on Wages and Economic Resilience

We now focus on the compensation of General Government (GG) employees and its stabilization effect on the Output Gap. In particular, we estimate the following model:

$$\text{OP\_Gap}_{i,t} = \beta_0 + \beta_1 \times \text{Comp}_{i,t} + \beta_2 \times X_{i,t} + \delta_i + \gamma_t + \varepsilon_{i,t} \quad (5.8)$$

where $OP\_Gap_{i,t}$ is the Output Gap as a percentage of the potential output, $\text{Comp}_{i,t}$ is the yearly rate of change of the compensation of employees for general government of country i in year t, respectively, $X_{i,t}$ is a vector of country characteristics associated in the literature with GDP growth[10] (Barro, 1991; Eggoh & Khan, 2014; Klenow & Rodriguez-Clare, 1997; Rodrik et al., 2004; Ross & Renelt, 1992; Polin & Zhu, 2006; Sala-I-Martin, 1997a; 1997b). These variables include investments as a share of GDP (Inv), the openness of the economy (Open) measured by the sum of exports and imports as a share of GDP, long-term interest rates (Ltir), public debt as a share of GDP (Debt) and government effectiveness (Gov). Our dataset encompasses 27 EU member countries, covering the years 2000 to 2021. The data is sourced from Eurostat, except for the index of government effectiveness, for which we obtained data from the World Bank database.

Furthermore, to explore possible nonlinearities between the rate of change of compensation for General Government (GG) employees and the change in the output gap, we introduce the quadratic term of our variable of interest, the compensation of GG employees (Comp Squared), into our model (1).[11]

$$\begin{aligned} \text{OP\_Gap}_{i,t} = \beta_0 + \beta_1 \times \text{Comp}_{i,t} + \beta_2 \times \text{Comp Squared}_{i,t} \\ + \beta_3 \times X_{i,t} + \delta_i + \gamma_t + \varepsilon_{i,t} \end{aligned} \tag{5.9}$$

The results presented in Table 5.1 suggest that the variables Ltir, Open and Debt exhibit non-stationarity in their levels. Therefore, these variables were incorporated into our regressions after applying the first difference (Table 5.1). Moreover, in order to focus exclusively on the Greek

[10] We assume that variables that are being found as determinants of GDP growth may also explain the variation of output gap.

[11] By introducing nonlinearity into our model through the inclusion of the squared compensation term, we estimate regression equations as second-degree polynomials. This approach enables us to capture changes in slopes that are contingent on variations in the independent variable. Consequently, the slope of the estimating equation can vary in response to fluctuations in the rate of change of the compensation of General Government (GG) employees, facilitating the identification of turning points in the relationship between the output gap and the aforementioned rate of change. To limit the possibility of spurious regressions, we use fixed effects in our linear and non-linear models to control for unobserved individual heterogeneity. Additionally, panel unit root tests are employed using both common and individual unit root processes to assess the stationarity of variables and mitigate the risk of spurious findings in the context of non-stationary time series. We employed two-unit root tests, namely the Levin, Lin & Chu test (Levin et al., 2002) for common unit root processes and the Im, Pesaran and Shin test (Im et al., 2003) for individual unit root processes.

economy, we estimate the following time-series models:

$$\text{OP\_Gap}_t = \beta_0 + \beta_1 \times \text{Comp}_t + \beta_2 \times X_t + \varepsilon_t \tag{5.10}$$

$$\text{OP\_Gap}_t = \beta_0 + \beta_1 \times \text{Comp}_t + \beta_2 \times \text{Comp Squared}_t + \beta_3 \times X_t + \varepsilon_t. \tag{5.11}$$

To further investigate the stabilization properties of the compensation of GG employees, we conduct two different logistic regressions. The first binary logit model uses a dependent variable that is an indicator equal to one for a negative output gap and zero otherwise. A positive (negative) coefficient indicates a higher (lower) likelihood of a negative output gap, and vice versa.

$$\text{P}(\text{OP\_Gap}_{i,t} = 1) = \frac{1}{e\beta_o + \beta_1 \times \text{comp}_{i,t} + \beta_2 \times X_{i,t} + \varepsilon_{i,t}} \tag{5.12}$$

The second binary logit model uses a dependent variable that is an indicator equal to one for a recession, computed as a GDP real growth rate lower than zero, and zero otherwise. A positive (negative) coefficient indicates a higher (lower) likelihood of a recession.

$$\text{P}(\text{Recession}_{i,t} = 1) = \frac{1}{e\beta_o + \beta_1 \times \text{comp}_{i,t} + \beta_2 \times X_{i,t} + \varepsilon_{i,t}} \tag{5.13}$$

Thus, these logit regressions allow us to investigate whether the rate of change of compensation for GG employees contributes to the stabilization of the economy by either reducing the likelihood of a negative output gap or lowering the probability of a recession occurrence. The dataset and the variables remain the same as in the panel regressions.

Finally, we reran the previous logit regressions exclusively for the Greek economy to determine whether our results are also applicable to Greece.[12]

$$\text{P}(\text{OP\_ GAP}_t = 1) = \frac{1}{e\beta_o + \beta_1 \times \text{comp}_t + \beta_2 \times X_t + \varepsilon_t} \tag{5.14}$$

[12] As we have, only 21 yearly observations the results from the logit regressions particularly for Greece are considered only as indicative. For the same reason we run the logit regressions for Greece without control variables due to the limited degree of freedom.

$$P(\text{Recession}_t = 1) = \frac{1}{e\beta_o + \beta_1 \times \text{comp}_t + \beta_2 \times X_t + \varepsilon_t} \tag{5.15}$$

The panel regression results (Table 5.2 in the Annex) demonstrate a positive association between the growth rate of GG employees' compensation and the output gap (Model 1). This suggests that, in general, there is a specific rate of change in the compensation of GG employees that propels the economy higher, either reducing the negative output gap or increasing the positive output gap.[13] This implies that above a certain rate of change in the compensation of GG employees, the effect on the output gap turns negative. However, upon calculating the particular turning point,[14] we observe that this is quite high, averaging 0.31. This means that only after a 31% rate of change per year in the compensation of GG employees does the effect on the output gap become negative (Table 5.2 in the Annex). The results remained unchanged when considering only the Greek economy (Models (3) and (4) and Table 5.3 in the Annex).

Furthermore, the results from the logit regressions, considering the negative output gap as the dependent binary variable, are presented in Table 5.4 (in the Annex). Our variable of interest, the rate of growth of the compensation of GG employees, proves to be highly significant and has a negative sign in all specifications (1–5). This means that, on average, higher compensation for GG employees is associated with a decreased likelihood of observing a negative output gap.[15] These findings align with our earlier results, indicating that an increase in GG employees' compensation generally boosts the economy (Table 5.4 in the Annex). Our earlier findings are confirmed when considering an observable variable like GDP

[13] These results hold across all different specifications of Model 1 (Specifications 1 to 5). The positive relationship persists even after running the non-linear form of the panel regression (Model 2). The squared form of our variable of interest proves to be statistically significant and carries a negative sign (Specifications 6 to 10).

[14] The formula is: Turning point = – ((compensation coefficient)/(2*(compensation-squared coefficient)).

[15] As mentioned before, these results hold after controlling for other factors that may affect the output gap, such as investments, openness of the economy, monetary policy (long-term interest rates), fiscal condition (public debt to GDP) and the effectiveness of the government.

growth rate, as opposed to the non-observable output gap.[16] The results lead to the same conclusion: higher compensation for GG employees is associated with a reduced likelihood of observing a negative real GDP growth rate. In other words, higher compensation for GG employees is connected to a lower chance of a recessionary episode occurring and vice versa (Table 5.5 in the Annex). By following the same procedure and focusing solely on the Greek economy, the earlier results remain unchanged (Table 5.6 in the Annex). On average, higher compensation for GG employees is linked to a decreased likelihood for both negative output gap and recession in the Greek economy (Table 5.6 in the Annex).[17]

5.7 Conclusions

To sum up, our analysis shows that the LS, when calculated for the total economy, appears to have returned to pre-crisis levels. In the early years of the crisis, the LS increased sharply due to the delayed adjustment of the level of wages to the economic environment. Subsequently, the LS declined significantly but after the improvement in economic conditions, it began to rise again. As a result, the LS reached pre-crisis levels in 2018. Therefore, our analysis shows that, despite short-term fluctuations, the losses of labour were proportional to the losses of capital. On this basis, the effects of the economic crisis on the LS (and capital respectively) were neutral. However, this neutrality is solely due to the importance of the public employment and consequently the public sector's wage expenditure. When we exclude the public sector from our calculations and calculate the LS in the private sector we get a different picture. The labour share's decline was more pronounced, and the LS remained lower than in the pre-crisis period. In that aspect the public sector employment plays a significant role in supporting labour share (consequently restrict inequalities) especially in a crisis context.

Secondly, our panel regression results demonstrate a positive association between the growth rate of general government employees'

[16] In this logistic regression, the dependent variable equals one when the yearly growth rate falls below zero, signalling a recession.

[17] Due to the limited dataset of only 21 yearly observations for Greece, we run the logit regressions without control variables. Including controls would substantially reduce the degrees of freedom and may compromise the robustness of our analysis.

compensation and the output gap. When the economy is underperforming i.e. when an output gap is present an increase in the public wage-rates can reduce the gap (this applies for both European level and Greece). In theory, we cannot exclude a crowding out effect, but according to our calculations this effect appears only in the case of an 31% annual increase in the wages of public servants. In that aspect government wage expenditure entails a significant growth enchasing impact.

Finally, our analysis shows that a higher compensation for government employees is associated with a reduced likelihood of observing a negative real GDP growth rate, that is higher compensation for government employees is connected to a lower chance of a recessionary episode occurring and vice versa. This finding also applies for Greece and European Union. In that sense, a higher public expenditure on wages shields the economy from recession episodes.

Annex

See Tables 5.1, 5.2, 5.3, 5.4, 5.5, and 5.6.

Table 5.1 Tests for unit roots (levels)

Variables	*Common unit root process*[a]	*Individual unit root process*[b]	*Common unit root process*[a]	*Individual unit root process*[b]
	Levels		1st difference	
OP_Gap	−5.255***	−6.584***	–	–
Compensation	−5.186***	−5.012***	–	–
Ltir	−0.489	2.566	−11.339***	−9.302***
Inv	−3.085***	−2.769***	–	–
Open	−1.248	1.820	−12.37***	−12.07***
Debt	−0.973	1.228	−3.092***	−5.039***
Gov	−2.049**	−1.403*	–	–

Notes

[a]Refers to Levin, Lin and Chu test. Levin et al. (2002)

[b]Refers to Im, Pesaran and Shin test. Im et al. (2003)

[c]***, ** and * implies that the null hypothesis of a unit root is rejected at a 1%, 5% and 10% level, respectively. The probabilities computed assuming asymptotic normality

[d]Values refer to *t*-statistics

Table 5.2 Model results—panel regressions for 27 EU economies (baseline and non-linear)

Dependent: OP_ Gap	*(1)*	*(2)*	*(3)*	*(4)*	*(5)*	*(6)*	*(7)*	*(8)*	*(9)*	*(10)*
Constant	−1.584***	−6.855***	−6.608***	−6.192***	−10.47***	−1.817***	−6.393***	−6.592***	−5.933***	−9.928***
	(0.199)	(1.844)	(1.894)	(1.861)	(2.112)	(0.101)	(1.737)	(1.881)	(1.766)	(2.120)
Compensation	22.261***	17.093***	20.10***	16.03***	19.79***	34.48***	27.32***	27.69***	25.36***	25.24***
	(3.783)	(3.366)	(3.065)	(3.292)	(2.442)	(2.477)	(2.855)	(3.227)	(2.789)	(3.154)
Inv		0.254***	0.239***	0.232***	0.249***		0.223***	0.235***	0.209***	0.241***
		(0.084)	(0.087)	(0.084)	(0.083)		(0.080)	(0.087)	(0.080)	(0.083)
D(Open)		−0.064**	−0.060**	−0.068**	−0.057**		−0.055**	−0.056**	−0.059**	−0.055**
		(0.026)	(0.026)	(0.027)	(0.027)		(0.025)	(0.026)	(0.027)	(0.027)
D(Ltir)			0.085					0.119		
			(0.186)					0.163512		
D(Debt)				−0.089**					−0.069*	
				(0.042)					(0.041)	
Gov					3.274***					2.880***
					(0.478)					(0.545)
Compensation^2						−59.51***	−46.59***	−49.91***	−41.38***	−33.143**
						(9.224)	(7.979)	(13.221)	(7.749)	(11.448)
Observations	567	567	547	567	540	567	597	547	567	540
Countries	27	27	27	27	27	27	27	27	27	27
Adj. *R*-squared	0.602	0.655	0.679	0.666	0.701	0.636	0.675	0.691	0.681	0.706
Redundant Fixed Effects Test (Chi-square)	468.3	405.4	398,4	321.8	419.3	398.3	396.5	393.9	328.3	412.0
Threshold	–	–	–	–	–	0.29	0.29	0.28	0.31	0.38

Notes Panel regressions with country and time fixed effects. Robust standard errors in parentheses. The ***, ** and * denote statistical significance at the 1%, 5% and 10% level, respectively. The D(x) denotes that the particular variable is in first difference. Redundant Fixed Effects tests suggest that including fixed effects to the model contributes significantly to explaining the variation in the dependent variable

Table 5.3 Model results—OLS regressions for Greece (baseline and non-linear)

Dependent: OP_Gap	*(1)*	*(2)*	*(3)*	*(4)*	*(5)*	*(6)*	*(7)*	*(8)*	*(9)*	*(10)*
Constant	−7.469***	−21.151***	−21.32***	−21.17***	−21.284***	−7.769***	−21.664***	−21.926***	−21.805***	−22.188***
	(1.049)	(2.380)	(2.490)	(2.456)	(2.578)	(1.342)	(2.356)	(2.466)	(2.425)	(2.525)
Compensation	84.902***	35.91905**	35.439**	36.919**	35.449**	82.35119***	35.71**	35.036**	39.414**	34.318**
	(14.794)	(13.308)	(13.727)	(15.374)	(14.214)	(16.611)	(13.000)	(13.377)	(15.022)	(13.578)
Inv		0.848***	0.857***	0.844***	0.817***		0.927***	0.943***	0.923***	0.817***
		(0.146)	(0.153)	(0.153)	(0.263)		(0.155)	(0.162)	(0.158)	(0.250)
D(Open)		0.219255*	0.223*	0.229*	0.219*		0.197*	0.202*	0.233*	0.194*
		0.101546	(0.105)	(0.127)	(0.109)		(0.101)	(0.103)	(0.123)	(0.105)
D(Ltir)			−0.059					−0.083		
			(0.165)					(0.162)		
D(Debt)				0.010					0.038	
				(0.071)					(0.072)	
Gov					1.476					5.826
					(7.454)					(7.626)
Compensation^2						70.907	−158.19	−164.802	−176.38	−211.35
						(189.901)	(117.41)	(120.90)	(124.94)	(134.01)
Observations	21	21	21	21	21	21	21	21	21	21
Adj. *R*-squared	0.614	0.866	0.858	0,857	0.849	0.596	0.872	0.865	0.866	0.863
RESET	0.139	3.236	4.067938	3.012	3.159	9.440$^{(F)}$	1.409	2.937	1.041	0.866
White	0.752	0.702	1.478675	1.239	3.676	0.327	0.585	1.443	2.048	0.634
B-G	0.776	0.647	0.821	0.628	0.543	0.691	0.423	0.605	0.246	0.258
Threshold						–	–	–	–	–

Notes The ***, ** and * denote statistical significance at the 1%, 5% and 10% level, respectively. The D(x) denotes that the particular variable is in first difference. The *F*-statistic is presented for stability test (Ramsey, 1969), heteroscedasticity test (White, 1980) and autocorrelation test (Breusch & Godfrey, 1981). (*F*) denotes that test is not passed at the significance level of at least 0.1

Table 5.4 Determinants of the likelihood of negative output gap—27 EU economies—logit estimates

Dependent: Negative Output Gap	*(1)*	*(2)*	*(3)*	*(4)*	*(5)*
Constant	0.800***	2.916***	2.605***	2.656***	2.951
	(0.159)	(0.789)	(0.806)	(0.842)	(0.836)
Compensation	−15.384***	−12.621***	−17.383***	−10.013***	−16.332
	(3.062)	(3.334)	(3.042)	(3.538)	(2.824)
Inv		−0.101***	−0.080**	−0.101**	−0.090
		(0.039)	(0.039)	(0.041)	(0.039)
D(Open)		−0.009	−0.013	0.018	−0.014
		(0.012)	(0.013)	(0.014)	(0.012)
D(Ltir)			−0.273***		
			(0.093)		
D(Debt)				0.163***	
				(0.026)	
Gov					−0.050
					(0.164)
Observations	567	567	547	567	540
Countries	27	27	27	27	27
McFadden R-squared	0.10	0.12	0.14	0.19	0.14
LR statistic	76.88	92.32	107.04	105.72	104.64

Notes The dependent variable is the binary indicator equal to one for negative output gap country-year observations. Positive (negative) coefficients indicate a higher (lower) likelihood of negative output gap. Logit is the equal-correlation logistic model estimated using a generalized estimating equation estimator. Robust standard errors are noted in parentheses: $^{*}p<0.10$, $^{**}p<0.05$, $^{***}p<0.01$

Table 5.5 Determinants of the likelihood of recession (Real GDP growth lower from zero)—27 EU economies—Logit estimates

Dependent: Recession	*(1)*	*(2)*	*(3)*	*(4)*	*(5)*
Constant	−0.972***	0.016	0.059	−1.386	0.246
	(0.134)	(0.795)	(0.798)	(1.161)	(0.779)
Compensation	−13.57***	−24.176***	−24.923***	−14.626***	−25.051***
	(2.916)	(5.214)	(5.607)	(5.437)	(5.419)
Inv		−0.032	−0.029	−0.028	−0.010
		(0.039)	(0.040)	(0.0527)	(0.041)
D(Open)		−0.189***	−0.187***	−0.153***	−0.192***
		(0.030)	(0.031)	(0.027)	(0.031)
D(Ltir)			0.149*		
			(0.090)		
D(Debt)				0.336***	
				(0.065)	
Gov					−0.529**
					(0.237)
Observations	567	567	547	567	540
Countries	27	27	27	27	27
McFadden *R*-squared	0.07	0.28	0.28	0.52	0.29
LR statistic	38.96	149.59	145.28	281.39	150.44

Notes The dependent variable is the binary indicator equal to one for recession (negative real GDP growth) country-year observations. Positive (negative) coefficients indicate a higher (lower) likelihood of recession. Logit is the equal-correlation logistic model estimated using a generalized estimating equation estimator. Robust standard errors are noted in parentheses: $*p<0.10$, $**p<0.05$, $***p<0.01$

Table 5.6 Determinants of the likelihood of negative output gap and recession (Real GDP growth lower from zero)—Greece—Logit estimates

Dependent:	*Negative Output Gap*	*Recession*
Constant	2.328***	0.039
	(0.865)	(0.450)
Compensation	−49.827*	−18.181*
	(29.168)	(9.514)
Observations	21	21
McFadden R-squared	0.54	0.19
LR statistic	15.00	5.45

Notes The dependent variables are (a) the binary indicator equal to one for negative output gap country-year observations. Positive (negative) coefficients indicate a higher (lower) likelihood of negative output gap and (b) the binary indicator equal to one for recession (negative real GDP growth) country-year observations. Positive (negative) coefficients indicate a higher (lower) likelihood of recession. Logit is the equal-correlation logistic model estimated using a generalized estimating equation estimator. Robust standard errors are noted in parentheses: *$p<0.10$, **$p<0.05$, ***$p<0.01$

References

Alesina, A., & Perotti, R. (1996). Income distribution, political instability, and investment. *European Economic Review, 40*(6), 1203–1228.

Alesina A., Rodrik D. (1994). Distributive politics and economic growth. *Quarterly Journal of Economics, 109*(2), 465–490.

Arpaia, A., Prez E., & Pichelmann, K. (2009). *Understanding labour income share dynamics in Europe* (European Economy Economic Papers 379). European Commission.

Atkinson, A. B. (1983). *The economics of inequality*. Clarendon Press.

Autor, D. H., & Dorn, D. (2013). The growth of low-skill service jobs and the polarization of the US Labor market. *American Economic Review, 103*, 1553–1597.

Azmat, G., Manning, A., & Van Reenen, J. (2011). Privatization and the decline of labour's share: International evidence from network industries. *Economica, 79*(315), 470–492.

Bagnoli, P. (2009). Real wages, productivity and the determinants of the labour share: A structural approach OECD report ECO/CPE/WP1(2009)6.

Ball, L., Furceri, D., Leigh, D., & Loungani, P. (2013). *The distributional effects of fiscal consolidation* (IMF Working Paper, WP/13/151, IMF).

Barro, J. R. (1991). Economic growth in a cross section of countries. *The Quarterly Journal of Economics, 106*(2), 407–443.

Bentolila, S., & Saint-Paul, G. (2003). Explaining movements in the labor share. *The B.E. Journal of Macroeconomics, 3*(1), 1–33.

Bernanke, B. S., & Gürkaynak, R. S. (2001). Is growth exogenous? Taking Mankiw, Romer, and Weil Seriously. In B. S. Bernanke & K. Rogoff (Eds.), *NBER Macroeconomics Annual, 16*, 11–57.

Bertonati, C., Brugiavini, A., & Favero, C. (2018). *Nominal wage rigidity in the EU Countries before and after the great recession: Evidence from the WDN surveys* (ECB Working Paper Series No 2159). European Central Bank.

Bises, B., Bloise, F., & Scialà, A. (2023). Labor share as an "automatic stabilizer" of income inequality. *International Tax and Public Finance*. https://doi.org/10.1007/s10797-023-09782-0

Bowley, A. (1920). *The change in the distribution of the national income, 1880–1913*. Clarendon Press.

Bowley, A. (1937). *Wages and income in the United Kingdom since 1860*. Cambridge University Press.

Braun, M., Parro, F., & Valenzuela, P. (2019). Does finance alter the relation between inequality and growth? *Economic Inquiry, 57*(1), 410–428.

Breunig, R., & Majeed, O. (2020). Inequality, poverty, and growth. *International Economics, 161*(C), 83–99.

Breusch, T. S., & Godfrey, L. G. (1981). A review of recent work on testing for autocorrelation in dynamic simultaneous models. In D. Currie, R.

Nobay, & D. Peel, (Eds.), *Macroeconomic analysis: Essays in macroeconomics and econometrics* (pp. 63–105). Croom Helm.

Bridgman, B. (2017). Is labor's loss capital's gain? Gross versus net labor shares. *Macroeconomic Dynamics, 22*(8), 1–18.

Caponi, V. (2014). *Public employment policies and regional unemployment differences* (IZA Discussion Paper No. 8511).

Caponi, V. (2017). *The effects of public sector employment on the economy* (IZA World of Labor (332)).

Charpe, M., Bridji, S., & McAdam, P. (2019). *Labor share and growth in the long run* (Working Paper Series No 2251/March 2019). European Central Bank.

Christodoulakis, N., & Axioglou, C. (2017). Underinvestment and unemployment: The double hazard in the Euro Area. *Applied Economics Quarterly, 63*(1).

Christopoulou, R., & Monastiriotis, V. (2016). Public-private wage duality during the Greek crisis. *Oxford Economic Papers, 68*(1), 174–196. Oxford University Press.

Cobb, C. W., & Douglas, P. H. (1928). A theory of production. *American Economic Review, 18*, 139–165.

European Commission. (2007). The labour income share in the European Union. In *Employment in Europe 2007*. Directorate-General for Employment Social Affairs and Equal Opportunities.

Corak, M. (2013). Income inequality, equality of opportunity, and intergenerational mobility. *Journal of Economic Perspectives, 27*, 79–102.

Daudey, E., & García-Peñalosa, C. (2007). The personal and the factor distributions of income in a cross-section of countries. *Journal of Development Studies, 43*(5), 812–829.

de Castro, F., Salto, M., & Steiner, H. (2013). *The gap between public and private wages: New evidence for the EU* (European Economy—Economic Papers 2008–2015, 508). Directorate General Economic and Financial Affairs (DG ECFIN), European Commission.

De la Croix, D., & Doepke, M. (2003). Inequality and growth: Why differential fertility matters. *American Economic Review, 93*(4), 1091–1113.

de Serres, A., Scarpetta, S., & de la Maisonneuve, C. (2002). *Sectoral shifts in Europe and the United States: How they affect aggregate labour shares and the properties of wage equations* (OECD Economics Department Working Paper No. 326).

Dimova, D. (2019). *The structural determinants of the labor share in Europe* (IMF Working Paper WP/19/67). International Monetary Fund.

Driver, C., & Muñoz-Bugarín, J. (2010). Capital investment and unemployment in Europe: Neutrality or not? *Journal of Macroeconomics, 32*, 492–496.

Eggoh, J. C., & Khan, M. (2014). On the nonlinear relationship between inflation and economic growth .*Research in Economics, 68*.

Ellis, L., & Smith, K. (2010). The global upward trend in the profit share. *Applied Economics Quarterly, 56*(3), 231–255.

Epstein, G., & Burke, S. (2001). *Threat effects and the internationalization of production* (Political Economy Research Institute Working Paper 15). University of Massachusetts.

Erauskin, I. (2020). The labor share and income inequality: Some empirical evidence for the period 1990–2015. *Applied Economic Analysis, 28*(84), 173–195.

Feinstein, C. H. (1968). Changes in the distribution of national income in the United Kingdom since 1860. In J. Marchal & B. Ducros (Eds.), *The distribution of national income*. Macmillan.

Furceri, D., Jaumotte, F., & Loungani, P. (2013). *The distributional effects of capital account liberalization* (IMF Working Paper). Washington.

Ghinetti, P., and Lucifora, C. (2008). Public Sector Pay Gaps and Skill Levels: a Cross-Country Comparison. Working Papers 118, SEMEQ Department—Faculty of Economics—University of Eastern Piedmont.

Giovannoni, O. (2014). *What do we know about the labor share and the profit share? Part I: Theories* (The Levy Economics Institute of Bard College, working paper No. 803)

Glyn, A. (2009). Functional distribution and inequality. In W. Salverda, B. Nolvan, & T. M. Smeeding (Eds.), *The Oxford handbook of economic inequality*. Oxford University Press.

Gollin, D. (2002). Getting income shares right. *Journal of Political Economy, 110*(2), 458–474.

Gollin, D. (2008). *Labour's share of income*. MacMillan.

Gomes, P. M. (2015). Optimal public sector wages. *Economic Journal, 125*(587), 1425–1451.

Guerriero, M. (2012). *The labour share of income around the world. Evidence from a panel dataset* (IDPM, Development Economics and Public Policy Working Paper Series WP No.32/2012).

Guerriero, M. (2019, February). *The labor share of income around the world: evidence from a panel dataset* (Working Paper No. 920). Asian Development Bank Institute.

Guscina, A. (2006). *Effects of globalization on labor's share in national income* (IMF Working Paper, 06/294). Washington: International Monetary Fund.

Harrison, A. (2002). *Has globalization eroded labor's share? Some cross-country evidence* University of California.

Hutchinson J., & Persyn, D. (2012). Globalisation, concentration and footloose Firms: In search of the main cause of the declining labour share. *Review of World Economics, 148*(1).

ILO. (2012). *Global wage report 2012/13: Wages and equitable growth*.

ILO & OECD. (2015, February 26–27). *The labour share in G20 economies*. Report prepared for the G20 Employment Working Group, Antalya, Turkey.
Im, K. S., Pesaran, M. H., & Shin, Y. (2003). Testing for unit roots in heterogeneous panels. *Journal of Econometrics, 115*, 53–74.
International Monetary Fund and World Bank Group. (2015, February 26–27). Report prepared for the G20 Employment Working Group Antalya, Turkey.
Ioannidis, Y. (2020). *The impact of economic crisis on the labour share: The case of Greece, 1995–2018* (Working Paper No 8). Hellenic Fiscal Council [in Greek].
Izyumov, A., & Vahaly, J. (2015). Income shares revisited. *Review of Income and Wealth, 61*(1), 179–188.
Jayadev, A. (2007). Capital account openness and the labour share of income. *Cambridge Journal of Economics, 31*(3), 423–443.
Johnson, D. (1954). The functional distribution of income in the United States, 1850–1952. *Review of Economics and Statistics, 36*, 175–182.
Jorgenson, D. W., Ho, M., & Samuels, J. (2010, August 19–20). *New data on US productivity growth by industry*. WORLD KLEMS Conference.
Kaldor, N. (1961). Capital accumulation and economic growth. In Lutz & Hague (Eds.), *The theory of capital*. Macmillan
Kaldor, N. (1957). A model of economic growth. *Economic Journal, 67*(268), 591–624.
Karabarbounis, L., & Neiman, B. (2014a). The global decline of the labor share. *The Quarterly Journal of Economics, 129*(1), 61–103.
Karabarbounis, L., & Neiman, B. (2014b). *Capital depreciation and labor shares around the world: Measurement and implications* (Working Paper no. 20606). Cambridge, MA: National Bureau of Economic Research.
Keynes, J. M. (1939). Relative movements of real wages and output. *Economic Journal, 49*(193), 34–51.
Klenow, P. J., & Rodriguez-Clare, A. (1997). Economic growth: A review essay. *Journal of Monetary Economics, 40*, 597–617.
Knowles, S. (2005). Inequality and economic growth: The empirical relationship reconsidered in the light of comparable data. *The Journal of Development Studies, 41*(1), 135–139.
Kravis, I. B. (1959). Relative income shares in fact and theory. *The American Economic Review, 49*(5), 917–949.
Krueger, A. (1999). Measuring labor's share. *American Economic Review, 89*(2), 45–51.
Kuznets, S. (1959). Quantitative aspects of the economic growth of nations: IV. Distribution of national income by factor shares. *Economic Development and Cultural Change, 7*(3), 1–100.
Lamo, A., Prez, J. J., & Snchez-Fuentes, A. J. (2013). Crowding-in or crowding-out? Employment in the public and the private sector in the OECD. In A.

R. Bryson (Eds.), *Wages and employment: Economics, structure and gender differences*. Nova Science Publishers.

Lavoie, M., & Stockhammer, E. (2012). *Wage-led Growth: Concept, theories and policies*. International Labour Organization, Conditions of Work and Employment Branch, no. 41, Geneva: ILO.

Levin, A., Lin, C. F., & Chu, C. S. J. (2002). Unit root tests in panel data: Asymptotic and finite-sample properties. *Journal of Econometrics, 108*, 1–24.

Meurs, D., & Ponthieux, S. (2008). Public and private employment and the gender wage gap in 8 European countries. In M. Keune, J. Leschke, & A. Watt (Eds.), *Privatisation and liberalisation of public services in Europe: An analysis of economic and labour market impacts*. ETUI.

Milanovic, B. (2017). Increasing capital income share and its effect on personal income inequality. In H. Boushley, J. B. DeLong, & M. Steinbaum (Eds.), *After Piketty: The agenda for politics and inequality*. Harvard University Press.

OECD. (2012). *Employment Outlook*. OECD.

OECD. (2019). *Negotiating our way up. Collective bargaining in a changing world of work*. OECD.

Onaran, O., & Galanis, G. (2013). Is aggregate demand wage-led or profit-led? A global model. In M. Lavoie & E. Stockhammer (Eds.), *Wage-led growth: An equitable strategy for economic recovery*. Palgrave Macmillan.

Pak, M., & Schwellnus, C. (2019). *Labour share developments over the past two decades: The role of public policies* (Economics Department Working Paper No. 1541, ECO/WKP(2019)10). OECD.

Panizza, U. (2002). Income, inequality and economic growth: Evidence from American data. *Journal of Economic Growth, 7*(1), 25–41.

Piketty, T. (2013). *Le Capital au XXIe siècle*. Seuil.

Piketty, T. (2014). *Capital in the twenty-first century*. Harvard University Press.

Piketty, T., & Zucman, G. (2014). Capital is back: Wealth-income ratios in rich countries 1700–2010. *The Quarterly Journal of Economics, 129*(3), 1255–1310.

Pollin, R., & Zhu, A. (2006). Inflation and economic growth: A cross-country nonlinear analysis. *Journal of Post Keynesian Economics, 28*(4), 593–614.

Poterba, J. (1997). *The rate of return to corporate capital and factor shares: New estimates using revised national income account and capital stock data* (NBER Working Paper No. W6263). Cambridge, Massachusetts: National Bureau of Economic Research.

Quadrini, V., & Trigari, A. (2007). Public employment and the business cycle. *Scandinavian Journal of Economics, 109*(4), 723–742. https://doi.org/10.2307/3488922

Ramsey, J. B. (1969). Tests for specification errors in classical linear least squares regression analysis. *Journal of Royal Statistics Society Series B, 31*(2), 350–371.

Raurich, X., Sala, H., & Sorolla, V. (2012). Factor shares, the price markup, and the elasticity of substitution between capital and labor. *Journal of Macroeconomics, 34*(1), 181–198.

Ricardo, D. (1817). *Principles of political economy and taxation* (1911 ed., p. 43). John Murray.

Ripatti, A., & Vilmunen, J. (2001). *Declining labour share—Evidence of a change in the underlying production technology?* Bank of Finland Discussion Papers (Helsinki).

Rodriguez, F., & Jayadev, A. (2010). *The declining labor share of income*. Human Development Research Paper, Human Development Reports, no. 2010/36.

Rodrik D., Subramanian, Ar., & Trebbi, Fr. (2004). Institutions rule: The primacy of institutions over geography and integration in economic development. *Journal of Economic Growth, 9*, 131–165.

Rodrik, D. (1999). Democracies pay higher wages. *The Quarterly Journal of Economics, 114*(3), 707–738.

Rognlie, M. (2015). *Deciphering the fall and rise in the net capital share: Accumulation or scarcity?* (Brookings Papers on Economic Activity, pp. 1–69).

Ross, L., & Renelt, D. (1992, September). A sensitivity analysis of cross-country growth regressions. *The American Economic Review, 82*(4), 942–963

Ryan, P. (1996). Factor shares and inequality in the UK. *Oxford Review of Economic Policy, 12*(1), 106–126.

Sala-I-Martin, X. X. (1997a, May). I just ran two million regressions. *The American Economic Review, 87*(2), 178–183.

Sala-I-Martin, X. X. (1997b). *I just ran four million regressions* (NBER Working Papers 6252). National Bureau of Economic Research, Inc.

Schlenker, E., & Schmid, K. D. (2015). Capital income shares and income inequality in 16 E.U. member countries. *Empirica, 42*, 241–268.

Sergi, B. S., Balashova, S., & Ratner, S. (2023). The labour share, government expenditure and income inequality of Post-Soviet countries. *Economies, 11*(12), 1–22.

Solow, R. M. (1958). A skeptical note on the constancy of the relative shares. *The American Economic Review, 48*(4), 618–631.

Stehrer, R., Bykova, A., Jäger, K., Reiter, O., & Schwarzhappel, M. (2019). Industry level growth and productivity data with special focus on intangible assets. In Vienna Institute for International Economic Studies Statistical Report. WIIW Statistical Report No. 8. Vienna: Vienna Institute for International Economic Studies.

White, H. (1980). A Heteroskedasticity-Consistent Covariance Matrix Estimator and a Direct Test for Heteroskedasticity. *Econometrica, 48*(4), 817–838. https://doi.org/10.2307/1912934

Young, A. (1995). The tyranny of numbers: Confronting the statistical realities of the East Asian growth experience. *The Quarterly Journal of Economics, 110*(3), 641–680.

CHAPTER 6

Building Resilience in the Public Sector Through Risk Assessment, Activity-Based Budgeting and Performance Audit

George A. Georgiou

6.1 Introduction

Environmental, social, climate and technological factors shape the form of modern societies and public entities. The public resilience refers to the ability of society and the economy to adapt and develop in order to survive and face effectively these challenges. According to bibliography, the higher the level of resilience, the lower the losses caused by shocks and social threats to which every economy is exposed. The public sector plays a crucial role in building social and economic resilience. However, it is worthily noting that this is not an automatic process. It requires from public sector to follow a disciplined systematic approach, firstly how to identify and assess the risks and then how to plan and implement strategic actions to remedy risks and transfer the threats to opportunities.

G. A. Georgiou (✉)
Ministry of Finance, Athens, Greece
e-mail: g.georgiou2@glk.gr

A. Hyz (ed.), *The Role of the Public Sector in Building Social and Economic Resilience*,
https://doi.org/10.1007/978-3-031-67702-1_6

Research on resilience has grown over decades across disciplines such as economics, engineering and social and ecological studies and practice. Resilience as a concept and in practice implies ability of systems, individuals or social groups and societies to deal with, live through or manage changes and austerity fiscal shocks caused by recession or other climate or catastrophic events (Berkes et al., 2000, Kenechukwu, 2016; Lyon, 2014; Tierney & Bruneau, 2007; Woods, 2006. Researchers such as Alemu and Deyganto, 2019; Enofe et al., 2013; Dawuda, 2010; Morteza, 2014; Taiwo et al., 2016; Va Kirima, 2016) found that performance and internal auditing contributes to effective use of public resources in one hand promote public governance.

6.2 Global Risks Which Modern Societies Face and Their Severity to Emerge Resilience

Modern societies are exposed to risks such as pollution, climatic changes, shortage in natural resources, pandemicillnesses, economic exposures, fraud and severe conflicts among States. All these risks form the mosaic of a potential polycrisis consisting of various socioeconomic and environmental factors, which public sector emerging resilience mechanism has to face reacting proactively and ex post to minimize cost and negative effects to societies.

The world is facing nowadays a set of risks. We have seen a return of older risks-inflation, cost of living crises, trade wars, capital outflows from emerging markets, which few of this generation's business leaders and policymakers have experienced. These are being amplified by comparatively new developments in the global risks landscape, including unsustainable levels of debt, a new era of low growth, low global investment, a decline in human development after decades of progress and the growing pressure of climate change impacts. According to the 18th edition of the Global RISKS Report 2023, these conditions are converging to shape a unique, uncertain and turbulent decade to come.

The Global Risks Report 2023 presents the results of the latest Global Risks Perception Survey. It also considers a selection of risks that are likely to be most severe in the long term (10 years) as these are depicted in Fig. 6.1. The report concludes by considering perceptions of the comparative state of preparedness for these risks and highlighting enablers to charting a course to a more resilient world. The report underlines that as an economic era ends, the next will bring more risks of stagnation, divergence and distress.

Enhanced risk identification and foresight can be a key enabler for strategic decision-making, agenda-setting and resilience measures, helping to prioritize areas that would benefit from data collection and monitoring, risk controls and redundancies. The first task of foresight is to identify future developments, risks and opportunities. Another step to enhance risk foresight is to explore dynamics of change to map interconnections between risks. Risks that are most influenced by or exposed to other risks will be the most challenging to mitigate. The mitigation of risks should be part of a strategic plan implemented by performance budgeting, assessed by evaluation and audit.

Fig. 6.1 Global risks ranked by severity and long time (*Source* World Economic Forum Global Risks Perception Survey 2022–2023)

Recent crises have seen an extraordinary level of fiscal intervention to protect individuals and companies from the financial impacts of crises from the COVID-19 pandemic to energy prices.

Strengthening resilience efforts in critical areas in liaison with strategic planning and performance budgeting and audit improves preparedness and effectiveness for a multiplicity of tasks and actions.

6.3 Strengthening the Resilience of Public Administrations After the COVID-19 Crisis Through the Common Assessment Framework (CAF)

The CAF Model is a result of co-operation among the EU Ministers responsible for Public Administration. The CAF Resource Centre at the European Institute of Public Administration (EIPA) is in charge of further development of CAF methodology and coordination of the network of CAF users across Europe. The CAF is offered as an easy-to-use tool to assist public sector organizations to introduce quality management through the comprehensive self-assessment framework (Staes et al., 2016).

The model is based on the premise that excellent results in organizational performance, citizens/customers, people and society are achieved through leadership driving strategy and planning, people, partnerships, resources and processes. It looks at the organization from different angles at the same time; a holistic approach to organization performance analysis. Being a generic tool CAF includes the 9 criteria, 28 sub criteria and the scoring system. The structure of the CAF Model is illustrated on Fig. 6.2.

The CAF aims to be a catalyst for a full improvement process within the organization. The aim is better services for the citizens, because implementing the CAF helps to increase the quality of services for the customers and thus citizens' satisfaction (CAF Report, 2020).

European Commission during the recent pandemic crisis strengthened the resilience of public sector organizations in European Members by collecting and assessing the recent experience of managing the COVID-19 crisis. The project used the EU Common Assessment Framework (CAF) and its network of contact points (at country and organizational level), to gather insights from organizations who have recently used the CAF on their experience in maintaining resilience during the COVID-19 crisis. Through a combination of case studies, workshops and analysis, the

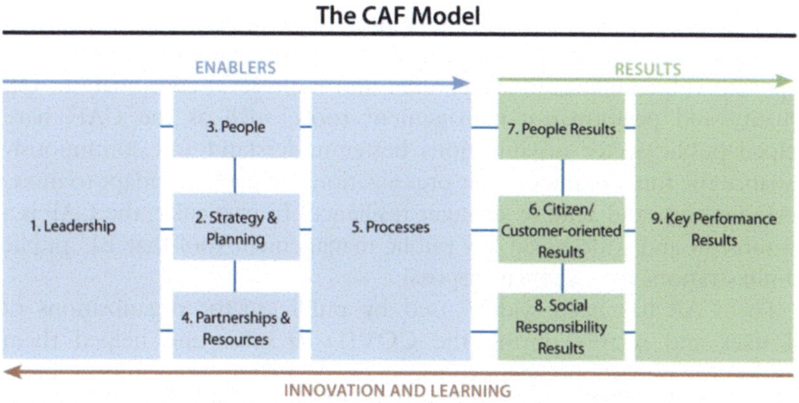

Fig. 6.2 The CAF model (*Source* CAF Report [2020])

project developed new insights into the ways that European public organizations can improve resilience in the face of unforeseen future shocks and challenges.

Indeed, on 28 November 2019, the EUPAN Directors-General in Helsinki unanimously adopted the CAF 2020. Currently, around 4100 organizations use the CAF, and many countries have included the CAF in their administrative reform strategies. CAF 2020 was developed by the European CAF Correspondents Network and the European Institute of Public Administration (EIPA) in an interactive two-year process.

According to the CAF report,[1] CAF is the first European quality management tool specifically tailored for and developed by the public sector itself. It is a general. Simple, assessible and easy-to-use model for all public sector organizations. It deals with all aspects of organizational excellence and drives for continuous improvement.

CAF2020 reinforces the focus on digitization, agility, sustainability, innovation, collaboration (participation) and diversity. As a result, there have been significant changes in each individual sub-criterion and examples. Flexibility and innovation actions incorporated as strategic elements in the organizations's structures and processes and above all in the awareness of the staff is required in order to master the necessary change.

[1] CAF report (2019), The European model for improving public organizations through self-assessment.

Public sector organizations, including CAF users, faced significant obstacles in providing services effectively during the COVID-19 crisis, exposing vulnerabilities in stakeholder and multi-level coordination, OE Quality and performance management tools, such as the CAF, have helped public sector organizations better understand and continuously enhance the functioning of their organizations prepare and adapt to unexpected events, and achieve stronger resilience. In particular, the CAF is a resourceful and widespread key public management tool that EU public administrations have at their disposal.

The CAF has been widely used by public sector organizations of all sizes and sectors during the COVID-19 crisis and helped them cushion the impact and adapt to the crisis. As a continuous improvement framework, the CAF provided users with a better knowledge of the organization acquired during past CAF exercises, a higher capacity to mobilize the organization, and tools to identify and address specific issues and challenges in relation to CAF criteria. CAF users benefited from performance improvement initiatives already started or implemented before the crisis based on CAF implementation plans, for instance on digitalization or remote working. The regular practice of CAF has participated to creating a process of continuous learning and improvement for users, which has helped them react and adapt in a context of an external shock.

Public sector organizations experienced an important impact on strategy and planning with new challenges emerging Strategic planning. This experience obtained, can help public sector organizations identify and define priorities, translate them into strategic and action plans, and ensure that they are implemented in a coordinated and efficient manner. Such strategies might exist at the national/sector level, at the regional level or at the level of the organization depending on the size and the sector. Public sector organizations identified a high impact and adaption on strategy and planning, like on other CAF criteria.

The COVID-19 crisis has entailed important changes in the needs and expectations of citizens and in the strategic priorities of organizations, with a stronger focus on immediate, operational priorities to maintain the delivery and functioning of public organizations, such as digitalization and workforce management.

The OECD has also pointed out to a number of important drivers of resilience in the COVID-19 context drawing lessons from the experiences of governments. These drivers include notably the need to respond at scale and speed to shocks, by building the appropriate innovation capabilities, supporting the development of relevant leadership and skill sets, developing the appropriate infrastructure and addressing cross-cutting priorities, and to enhance transparency and trust, particularly in developing inclusive decision-making and strategic-making processes, maintaining high levels (OECD, 2023).

6.4 Resilience Benchmarking Approaches

Benchmarking is also used to compare inputs, processes, outputs or outcomes. Much of the practitioner literature emphasizes its use to compare intermediate outcomes—very particularly customer satisfaction and perceived service quality. By offering key information the database can help public sector organizations identify suitable bench marking partners.

Resilience encompasses all attributes of the quality of working well in a changing world that includes faults, failures, errors and attacks, Viera, M., et al. (2009). This way, resilience benchmarking merges concepts from performance, dependability and security benchmarking.

The major goal of a resilience benchmarking is to provide a standard workload and metrics for measuring and evaluating the performance of certain social economic and environmental aspects. In addition, resilience benchmarking should provide a flexible framework for performance analysis. To achieve this goal the workload must be designed to meet a number of requirements which are focused on resilience measures and actions.

6.5 The Reforms of Activity-Based Budgeting, Financial Accounting and Performance Audit and Its Contribution to Resilience Operations

Public management movement has enforced this tendency towards more results-oriented use of public resources. Moreover, at the audit and evaluation side, more results-oriented techniques are introduced: audit of efficiency and effectiveness, audit of performance information and policy evaluation. Activity-Based Budgeting, Financial Accounting and Performance Audit are the biggest challenges which public sector used largely activity-based budgeting techniques to plan resilience programmers and actions through objectives and indicators to ensure cross-cutting issues. This would not only increase the institutions' accountability and transparency but also enhance a performance-driven culture.

"Performance measurement is the quantitative representation through measurement of the quality or quantity of input, output, and/or outcome of organizations or programs in its societal context".

"Performance orientation" is one of the most important trajectory to track concerns changes in the way in which performance is measured—the nature of the output and outcome measures and how they are used. This would assist in reviewing the degree to which measures are "churned", either because they must be changed regularly as they inevitably lose their impact over time (Thiel & Leeuw, 2002), or because of a somewhat cynical attempt to maximize the apparent performance improvement (Talbot, 1999).

Chepkorir (2010) noted that internal audit assists an institution to accomplish their objectives by putting in place an orderly, controlled approach to review and enhance the effectiveness of risk management, control and governance processes. The internal audit activity assesses risk exposures with respect to the enterprise's governance, operations and information systems. The internal auditors are supposed to provide recommendations for enhancement in those areas where opportunities or weaknesses are identified.

The three main directions of the budgetary, accounting and audit reforms take into consideration, public resilience needs and demands. They are linked with procedures related to activity-based budgeting, accounting and budget performance, as these are presented in Fig. 6.3. Through procedures envisaged in every element of resilience measure these three dimensions are properly registered in budgetary and accounting terms and assessed with the support of KPIs.

Especially as regards Key Performance Indicators (KPIs) these enable public sector to assess the relationship between inputs, outputs and final results, which is of great importance. Performance evaluation of an organization's risk management system is also essential to assess if the system can effectively respond to crisis and demands of the society which could be incorporated in a plan with strategic context.

As regards audit there is a shift from compliance to performance audit in order to assess all actions including the resilience ones, in three areas of economy, efficiency and effectiveness which consists the 3Es of the sound financial management principle (Georgiou, 2021).

Resilience assessment frameworks must be people-focused. This increases priorities for choosing indicators that reflect the status of the people's well-being (past, present and future) and guides the analysis of the relevance, effectiveness, efficiency, impact and sustainability of their development focused activities; and the relevance/appropriateness, connectedness, coherence, coverage, efficiency, effectiveness and impact of humanitarian action-focused intervention (Kenechukwu, 2016).

Therefore, performance indicators should also reflect quality, reliability and social values rather than hard product or services attributes. This means that public resilience services are not only about efficiency and effectiveness but also about justice, fairness, equity and accountability (Thiel & Leeuw, 2002). Fountain J. E. (2001) notes that the application of private sector techniques, such as performance indicators, cannot replace, indeed may obscure, such political or democratic outcomes of public service provision.

Figure 6.3 presents the three dimensions of reforms related to budgetary, financial and audit essential elements, which could be perfectly adapted to cope resilience measures and actions to plan, (activity-based budgeting) register (accrual accounting) and assess (performance audit) all dimensions.

Public organizations could consider developing strategic planning capabilities to adapt strategic plans and objectives to face urgent needs and cope resilience measures which are essential for responding to crises and key challenges within the society.

6.6 Conclusions and Way Ahead

Public sector organizations need to draw lessons from the past dealing with crisis in order to strengthen their resilience capability to cope future shocks.

The issues of great importance are as follows

1. Build capacity on reporting and accountability so that public entities can enhance transparency and share god practices.
2. Merge resilience with fiscal risks associated with the operations of public entities, which may have a significant potential impact on central government operations. Such risks need to be closely monitored, reported and where possible quantified.

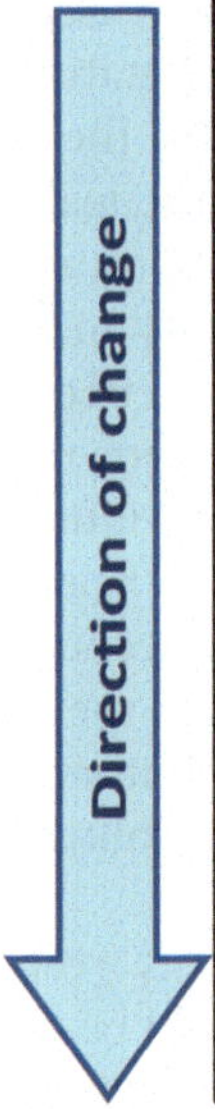

Budget reforms	Accounting reforms	Audit reforms
1. Input-oriented line item budget 2. +some performance information 3. +revised format and content 4. +revised procedures and timing 5. +revised method of charging (accrual basis)	1. Cash-based 2. Double-entry bookkeeping 3. Accrual accounting with extended cost calculation supported by performance measurement system	1. Traditional financial and compliance audit 2. +elements of performance and evaluation 3. Institutionalised financial, compliance and performance auditing

Fig. 6.3 Budgetary, accounting and audit reforms related to resilience process (*Source* Based on Pollitt and Bouckaert [2004])

3. Use regulatory, procurement and taxation powers to affect sustainability, natural resources and resilience that are significant in scope and should be accounted for.
4. Link Key Risk Indicators (KRIs) to Key Performance Indicators (KPIs) in a such way in order public sector to be in the position to assess the relationship between risk and public sector performance and incorporate the mitigation of risks to performance-based budgeting and audit.
5. Continued efforts on training and guidance documentation on various actions related to resilience through best practices on an ongoing basis throughout the EU.
6. Provide to Managers of Public Sector with knowledge and guidance about performance management and evaluation for decision-making.
7. Put the right staff to the right place to perform the tasks and achieve best results.

8. Use performance and internal audit to assess efficient use of funds and establish effective governance process.

Last but not least innovation is strongly related with resilience actions in the public sector and it is ranked among the top priorities. Innovation is linked with the capacity of organizations to adapt to the crisis and find new solutions and models to cope with shocks.

References

Alemu, A., & Deyganto, K. (2019). Assessing the internal audit practice and its role in protecting and effective utilization of public resources: Evidence from sector bureaus in SNNEPS. *Research Journal of Finance and Accounting, 10*(15).

Asaolu, T., Adedokun, S., & Monday, J. (2016). Promoting Good Governance through Internal Audit Function (IAF): The Nigerian Experience. *International Business Research, 9*(5), 196–204. Published by Canadian Center of Science and Education.

Berkes, F., Folke, C., & Colding, J. (2000). *Linking social and ecological systems: Management practices and social mechanisms for building resilience.* Cambridge University Press.

Chepkorir, L. (2010). Roles and challenges of internal auditing in the banking industry in Kenya, MBA Projects.

Dawuda. (2010). *The effectiveness of the internal audit units in the public sector in promoting good corporate governance: The case of the metropolitan, municipal and district assemblies in the northern region of Ghana.*

Enofe, Dr., A., Mgbame, C. J., Osa-Erhabor, V. E., & Ehiorobo, A. J. (2013). The role of internal audit in effective management in public sector. *Research Journal of Finance and Accounting, 5*, 23 (2014). www.iiste.org. ISSN 2222-1697 (Paper) ISSN 2222-2847 (Online).

European Public Administration Network. (2020). Common Assessment Framework (CAF). The European model for improving public organizations through self-assessment.

Fountain, J. E. (2001). Paradoxes of public sector customer service. *Governance, 14*, 55–73.

Georgiou, G. (2021). *Performance audit*. Editions Papazisi.

EU. (2019). Directorate General for Internal Policies of the Union, "Aligning the budget with the Performance-Based Budgeting: Lessons from Member States".

Kenechukwu C. (2016). A participatory self-assessment framework for community resilience monitoring, evaluation, accountability and learning (Community Resilience-MEAL), Onukwube.

Kirima, N. (2016). Factors affecting the performance of the internal audit function in Government Ministries in Kenya: A research project submitted to the Chandaria School of Business in Partial Fulfillment of the Requirement for the Degree of Masters in Business Administration (MBA) United States International University—Africa.

Lyon, C. (2014). Place systems and social resilience: A framework for understanding place in social adaptation, resilience, and transformation. *Society & Natural Resources, 27*(10), 1009–1023.

Morteza, Z. (2014). The effect of audit quality on the performance of listed companies Tehran Stock Exchange: International Letters of Social and Humanistic Sciences Online. 2014-02-08 ISSN: 2300-2697, Vol. 21, pp 36–43 10.18052, www.scipress.com/. ILSHS.21.36 © 2014 SciPress Ltd., Switzerland.

OECD. (2023). *More resilient public administrations after COVID-19, Lessons from using the Common Assessment Framework (CAF) 2020.*

OECD Global Risk Report 2024.

PEFA Assessment Fieldguide, 2018, Volume II, Public Expenditure and Financial Accountability.

Pollitt, C., & Bouckaert, G. (2004). *Public management reform: A comparative analysis*. Oxford University Press.

Quang Huy, P., & Kien Phuc, V. (2022). Insight into the critical success factors of performance—Based budgeting implementation in the public sector for sustainable development in the Covid-19 pandemic. Sustainability 2022, 14.

Rama Lingeswara Satyanarayana Tamineedi. (2018, July). Integrating KRIs and KPIs for effective technology risk management. ISACA, Journal, 4.

Staes, P., Thijs, N., & Claessen, D. (2016). Enhancing social responsibility in public sector through application of the Common Assessment Framework, Research paper for the International Forum on China's Reform and Opening-Up and Poverty Reduction 29.10–2.11.2018, Beijing, China.

Sterk, M., et al. (2007). Budgeting, accounting and auditing for results. Towards integrated financial management, Project: Financial management & performance measurement, Leuven, SBOV 167 p.

Talbot, C. (1999). Public performance—Towards a new model? *Public Administration Committee, 14*(3).

Tierney, K., & Bruneau, M. (2007). *Conceptualizing and measuring resilience: A key to disaster loss reduction.* TR News (250).

Thiel, S., & Leeuw, F. (2002). The performance paradox in the public sector. *Public Performance and Management Review, 25*(3), 267–281.

Viera, M., et al. (2009). *Resilience benchmarking*. Article reference https://doi.org/10.1007/978-3-642-29032-9_14
World Economic Forum. (2023). *The global risks report 2023* (18th ed.).

CHAPTER 7

Public Budgeting: An Amoeba of Public Policies

Stavroula Grigoriadou

7.1 Introduction

It is clear that public budgeting is not a simple concept. It is a discipline section of public administration that is perplexed by its approaches, functions, formation and types. The interlinked nature of the budgetary process includes information on the revenue and expenditure accounts, the system for monitoring these accounts, the procedures followed for drawing up and maintaining the budget, the form of the decisions taken, how they are determined, the role of the government institutions in their formulation and a country's position in relation to its economic, social, political and cultural environment. In other words, public budgeting is a synthesis of all the causal relationships of the items contained in its description. According to the OECD, there is no standard definition that fully explains the concept of a government budget, as the diversity

S. Grigoriadou (✉)
Department of Accounting and Finance,
University of West Attica, Athens, Greece
e-mail: sgrigoriadou@uniwa.gr

A. Hyz (ed.), *The Role of the Public Sector in Building Social and Economic Resilience*,
https://doi.org/10.1007/978-3-031-67702-1_7

and objectives that budgets are called upon to cover are as numerous as the human objectives. This merely explains the shortage of a generally accepted theory that could analyze and predict the events and factors that may shape it (Lacasse, 1996).

Historically, the term "budget" began to be used in Britain to describe the leather bag used by the Chancellor of the Exchequer to carry to Parliament the statement of the government's needs (expenditure) and resources (revenue). Administratively, a budget is a collection of documents that present the financial situation of a country and state the government's future plans. As a public document, it contains a wealth of information about government operations, which varies across countries in scope and form of presentation. The well-known research question that addresses the basic budgeting problem, which is also considered a classic essay was presented in 1940 by V.O. Key and is summarized in the phrase "On what basis will we decide to allocate X dollars to action A instead of action B?" or "How can we compare the prices of dissimilar functions (e.g. education with defence) in order to allocate scarce resources?" (Caiden, 2020).

The development of public budgeting follows the evolution of fundamental human rights and is directly linked to the formation of the state, as it is fully dependent on the prevailing economic, political and social conditions. In essence, it is the notion of a pre-agreed contract between the government leadership and the social groups under its authority. Under this scope, the budgeting community is paying tribute to Aaron Wildavsky for his contribution examining budget as reflection of politics, treating on budgetary procedure, culture, strategy, competition and power. According to Schick (Rubin, 2015), a general characteristic that all types of government budgets share is three basic functions which, although functionally invisible, are separated for technical reasons: planning, management and operational control. Over the years the author has observed that the emphasis has moved from control to management and then to budget planning (Rubin, 2015).

7.2 Functions of Public Budgeting

Budgeting is the art of public state to determine and best assess the allocation of resources, the distribution of goods and services and economic stability. At the operational level, it comprises three elements: (a) a period, as it is repeated at regular intervals; (b) a forecast, as it involves risk by predicting future revenues, which are also the limits of expenditure; (c) an authorization from legislature branch to the executive one to collect revenues and make expenditures. The interdependence of the latter characteristic creates the checks and balances that modern developed societies have established.

As a fiscal policy instrument, public budgeting is divided into three dimensions: (a) legal, (b) accounting, (c) political and (d) audit (Caiden, 2020). In legal terms public budget is a government act, usually in the form of a law. It determines for the budgetary reference period the government revenues and sets limits on government expenditure. It is not an ordinary rule of law, but it is the basis for the production of substantive rules necessary to enable the collection of the revenues referred to in it and the payment of the corresponding expenditures. As a formal document, it is a state tool for planning, authorization and communication.

In accounting terms, the budget describes the government's need to control the size of the state function and the extent of the state's economic activities. The detailed statement of revenue and expenditure accounts provides information to both the executive and the electorate on the sources and nature of revenue, the purpose and manner of expenditure. It highlights the fiscal program of each government and indicates the future financial path of the state for the next period.

In political terms, the budget is an important political act (Lipsmeyer et al., 2023). It is the means of implementing the political program that the ruling party that obtained a majority in the political elections is committed to implementing, expressing a social consensus. It is the majority way of expressing their views on the collection of revenue, through imposition of taxes, duties, etc. and the implementation of expenditure. The political process of decision-making, prioritization and allocation of government appropriations indicates the priority of public policies that the government chooses to implement. The economic weight given to public policies is shown through the allocation of resources and the economic and social policies pursued become apparent.

In auditing terms, the budget limits the executive's operation by restricting and controlling its action on the basis of certain accounting standards. The need for transparency and efficiency through the use of accrual accounting systems promotes the development of performance management, providing qualitative accounting information. It is also an instrument of state intervention to maintain economic balance and avoid major social problems. It acts as a substitute for the market price mechanism, as there is no equivalent in size mechanism for regulating public goods.

Applying the principle of sound financial management, the budget is now based on the concept of performance with feedback through the measurement of the efficiency and effectiveness of public services. Through accountability (Raudla & Douglas, 2022), conclusions are facilitated by providing information and explanations on the achievement of the actions financed (Lacasse, 1996). Transparency is another key concept and defines the flow of available information, such as the amount of funds allocated to each public action (El-Berry & Goeminne, 2021). Any form of resource that is considered public information is available for public scrutiny. In addition, the pursuit of balance and sustainability of public programs has forced governments to undertake extensive revisions of their public spending to fill the resulting budget gaps by squeezing other substitute programs or actions (Rubin, 2015).

Framing public budgeting, due to its complex nature (Sicilia & Steccolini, 2017), cannot be placed in a single perspective, as it involves political, economic and social conditions that constantly influence each other. As an open system, its internal elements play an equally important role. The causal relationships that develop internally between expenditures, revenues, deficits and budget volatility affect the choices that governments have (Lipsmeyer et al., 2023). Governors are asked to choose the public policies that best reflect their countries' values and priorities and constantly balancing them with environmental conditions.

7.3 Economic and Social Resilience

Following the Coronavirus disease (COVID-19), several tests emerged and dominated the literature on resistance. Resilience comes from the Latin word "resilire" and was mainly used in materials science to explain the ability of a material to elastically absorb compressive forces and return to its original shape without being destroyed. Increased uncertainty and the financial crisis have placed great emphasis on how resilience can be achieved in a state. Governments seek resilience to find a way to return to the previous situation when a crisis breaks out. Experts in almost every administrative sector have sought policies that lead to building resilience in order to anticipate and react to shocks.

Resilience refers to the ability of short and long-term infrastructure and the learning process to cope with threats through the interactions of environmental conditions, using internal capacities and adaptation to appropriate conditions to shape these actions and reactions. It includes organizational processes adopted by governments to address crises and vulnerabilities shaped by external and internal shocks. From an engineering perspective, it examines the conditions under which a state can revert to its original form in order to ensure its survival by creating shock-absorbing slack. From an evolutionary perspective, it focuses on the ability to respond to shocks by exploiting a window of opportunity (Cavalieri, 2023), to reorganize quickly by changing strategies and to continue to operate in crisis conditions (Keck & Sakdapolrak, 2013).

Extensive work on resilience has led to several dimensions. When a state has a clear understanding of its environment and is able to manage vulnerabilities (Röhn et al., 2015), the emphasis is on risk prediction and awareness. From another perspective, the emphasis is on the adaptive capacity of states facing disruptions and their response through perseverance, adaptation and transformation to deal with unforeseen shocks.

Economic resilience can be defined as the ability of a country to minimize or withstand the negative effects of shocks to which it may be inherently exposed and to recover or return quickly to potential levels. It includes vulnerability to shocks, shock absorption and recovery capacity (Zamfir et al., 2022). According to international organizations, the first component is influenced by the size of the economy, the degree of openness to the international market, large current account imbalances and negative net international investment positions. In addition, inherent domestic vulnerabilities (e.g. unemployment levels) and financial market characteristics are highly correlated with vulnerability to shocks (Joseph, 2021).

Shock-absorbing capacity requires sound fiscal space with sustainable public and private sector debt, while credit systems and non-performing loans can offset volatility. In addition, factors such as the composition of the labor force, the level of income inequality, poverty and social exclusion are elements that shape the range of this capacity.

The factors affecting the ability to recover from a shock are equally important. The quality of institutions (Lisnyak & Sharipov, 2015) and economic structures that reduce economic volatility, as well as the level of worker safety and labor productivity, affect the duration of a crisis. In addition, the negative impact of population aging testifies to the capacity of the state to recover. Static economic resilience refers to the best use of assets to reduce losses, while dynamic resilience includes the recovery effort and the ability to achieve the new normal (Yuniza et al., 2022).

As a process economic resilience follows a sequential cycle of emergency, stabilization, decline and restructuring (Hu et al., 2022). As a system resilience is path-dependent through adaptation and reorientation, operating under uneven contextual conditions and contingencies. OECD and World Bank have identified vulnerabilities that can lead counties to costly crises, providing indicators, tools and complements to monitor country-specific risks (Hallegatte, 2014; Röhn et al., 2015; Zamfir et al., 2022).

Although various patterns of economic resilience have emerged, such as self-regulation, limited or reactive adaptation, satisfaction from powerless fatalism etc., there is no standardized measure of excellence in practice. It is usually associated with economic vulnerability, which includes various elements of exposure, degree of sensitivity, coping skills, which explain the resulting relationship between the environment and government operations. External shocks can affect various dimensions of vulnerability, such as trade openness, export concentration, reliance on strategic imports, vulnerability to natural disasters, etc (Briguglio, 2016).

While the study of economic resilience emerged from the fiscal gap after the Great Recession of 2008, social resilience emerged as a key element of reducing the negative impacts of natural disasters and the need to revise strategies to anticipate them. Social resilience is commonly referred to as the ability of individuals, communities and social entities to proactively adapt and recover from any unusual and unexpected disturbance. Its capacity consists of coping, adaptive and transformative mechanisms in order to adjust to its environment (Keck & Sakdapolrak, 2013). Coping capacities include the abilities of social actors to respond to risks by overcoming adversity, maintaining the same relationships as before, maintaining a state of equilibrium. Adaptive capacities reflect the ability to reorganize while undergoing change or preventing serious losses. Transformative capacity addresses new paths when previous ones are unbearable.

While social resilience refers to the ability to respond to change, it evolves the concepts of learning (Lim & Won, 2024), social networks, institutions and power relations. In this context, emphasis is placed on cultural capital (Keck & Sakdapolrak, 2013) and people power, which necessitate social learning, participatory decision-making and processes of collective transformation. In addition to notions of capacity, social resilience is understood in terms of its structural and cognitive dimensions. Social structure and mechanisms, as well as social capital and equity are necessarily equally important. Moreover, its key challenges depend on context, specific risks and specific phenomena, so it is studied in a general or given context (Saja et al., 2018).

Social structure may include characteristics of demography, household structure and mobility of people. Social capital refers to social support, cohesion and social networks affecting social resilience. Social values refer to elements of collaboration, community goals shared values, norms and culture, whereas social equity indicates access to basic needs and services, equality in gender and ethnicity and people with specific needs. Despite the difficulty of accurate measurement (Atkinson, 2000), social resilience requires a dynamic, knowledge-driven strategy to build up forces to cope with adversity and implement coping strategies. As it turns out, how to ensure social resilience is not only a technical but also a political issue (Keck & Sakdapolrak, 2013).

7.4 Budget as a Key Tool for Public Policies

Public budgeting is at the heart of government functioning (Raudla & Douglas, 2022). The course of his dependency is based on cognitive or normative patterns of behavior and depends primarily on his past and secondarily on the feedback he receives from his environment. It arose from the need to reduce uncertainty by providing a framework, as a behavioral guide, for human interaction, defining and at the same time delimiting the set of options available. Through budget execution, governments interact with and influence their environment by adopting or imposing a range of public policies (Atkinson, 2000). When state problems or opportunities arise, governments try to respond to these changes through their administrative services that interact and evolve with stakeholders.

The constant interaction through feedback of information, resources and stakeholder influences means that the budget is subject to strong environmental influences. As such, proper budgeting is a key factor in the long-term performance of economies, as it must constantly change and adapt to its environment. The complexity of the information involved leads to multiple findings where actors can play political games, resulting in wrong decisions (adverse selection) or limited information (information asymmetries). The measurement indicators used are often difficult to define in practice, both in terms of their scope and their level.

The importance of the budget is to lead each state to the desired economic and social level by adopting policies to limit losses and implementing the best available options (Dzigbede et al., 2023). Sometimes public officials may not have perfect information and adopt subjective models to draw conclusions that are often wrong. In this case the public budget ends up being something that is not necessarily created to be socially effective. Instead, it is created to serve the interests of those who have the bargaining power to impose new rules.

The prioritization of governments' policy objectives, which is shaped by the domestic and supranational environment, the institutional process established for undertaking public spending (Jo & Rothenberg, 2020), the impact of these decisions on the wealth and behavior of citizens shapes the framework of political decisions on the budget compromising between conflicting criteria (Lootsma et al., 1990). Budget incorporates a complex web of specific relationships, resulting in socio-economic system in the form of the objective and subjective aspects seeking to ensure economic and social resilience capacity.

One of the key factors in maintaining economic and social resilience is the quality of the government institutions involved in a particular economic system (Lisnyak & Sharipov, 2015). The roles and functions performed by the budget institution can monitor the constraints of economic and social groups in order to ensure economic and social resilience. For this reason, almost every public budget establishes specific principles that can guide the activities of economic and social entities in the best possible direction in order to cope with an unknown event. In this way, the negative consequences of a shock are inhibited as much as possible and an atmosphere of security and trust is created between the government and those in power.

Any economic or social crisis challenges the government's ability to fulfill its duties (Yuniza et al., 2022). If resilience has been achieved after a crisis, it means that the right government responses have been taken and that the government has responded in a timely and accurate manner to environmental requirements. Anticipatory capabilities through optimal situational awareness and sensible government solutions are based on the tools available to each state to manage its vulnerabilities and correctly identify economic and social problems before they manifest themselves in the form of shocks. Buffering capacities allow budget holders to absorb the impact of a shock without radical changes and manage vulnerabilities, while adaptive capacities reveal the ability of governments to change their operations without altering the principles, values and culture of governance (Barbera et al., 2017). The ability of a government to implement radical changes and integrate them into its structures and operations betrays its transformative capacities.

Establishing an appropriate budgeting mechanism through efficient forms and methods of financial management, as well as reducing the transaction costs of monitoring a crisis are key factors for the quality of the public budget. In addition, the correct selection and accumulation of information ensure that economic and social phenomena are properly addressed. The regulatory function is also necessary not only to enforce action in the right direction, but also to prevent activities that bring about negative consequences. The identification of priority risk areas and proactive policy changes through governments' public budgets ensure that economic and social protection continues not only after a shock or disaster, but also that recovery ensures the potential of future generations.

Although immediate and rational decisions may be taken, recovery costs that arise after disasters require the immediate use of emergency funds to address the financial losses. However, the ability of governments to respond to an adequate level of risk management is called into question by the budgetary constraints imposed.

7.5 Budgetary Reallocations of Funds

Budgetary trade-offs are the backbone of public budgeting. However, the policy of reallocation or reorientation of government activities has not been extensively studied (Fuchs & Thaler, 2018). Faced with a crisis, a state may postpone or cancel any unnecessary activity, since public finances are finite. Budget priorities can go through a review mechanism and a new set of public policies can be promoted in order for a country to achieve economic and social resilience (Cavalieri, 2023).

The budget review mechanism involves adjusting the budget priorities for certain activities and allocations or delays based on certain criteria. Activities that are no longer considered relevant, such as travel expenses, may give way to, for example, medical equipment or hospital infrastructure. This requires classification into priority and non-priority expenditure with a focus on economic and social protection or recovery. Moreover, reorientation of activities, reallocation of funds and acceleration of urgent issues are at the core of the public budget restructuring strategy (Wang & Scorsone, 2020).

As our era is plagued by a massive upsurge of uncertainty (Romdhane et al., 2022) and systemic correlation factors (Lindbeck & Weibull, 1987), there is a need for concrete policies to ensure that governments allocate properly and are not driven into a political game of resources. The challenges facing a state are to maintain stability when all sectors are under pressure (Raudla & Douglas, 2022). Spending is increasingly difficult to control in an uncertain environment (Yuniza et al., 2022).

In addition, there are a number of gaps that challenge strategic thinking. There is often tight fiscal space, especially in the economically weaker countries. Moreover, there are no clear guidelines or IT mechanisms of this magnitude for the reallocation of resources in the event of a crisis, which leads to the use of the human factor, which increases the likelihood of mismanagement. Additionally, there is neither time nor space to find money from external institutional lenders, as usually crises are systemic and negatively affect all countries.

In the effort to ensure resilience, states should identify a set of tools to ensure that available resources are reallocated promptly and appropriately to best balance exposure and vulnerability. The challenge for policymakers is to plan strategically and in a timely manner, and to implement a resource reallocation act in the event of a crisis. Given the systemic nature of crises, this capacity of states should be based on a framework of synchronized actions aimed at eliminating the crisis and improving their effectiveness (Zamfir et al., 2022).

7.6 Conclusion

In this paper, the case of crises has been treated as an opportunity to search for and reflect on the policies available within public budgeting. To this end, it is proposed to establish a framework of reallocations of budgeting funds with the aim of dealing threats or crisis more competently. The case of the crisis was seen as an opportunity (Cavalieri, 2023) to search and reflect on the policies available in the context of public spending. It is therefore proposed to establish a reference framework for the reallocation of budgetary resources to better respond to threats or crises. The challenges faced are numerous and varied and are usually not systemically limited to a single state.

We propose that the reference framework should include a set of tools that incorporates all current public finance challenges, allowing sufficient room for maneuver in the event of a crisis. Moreover, the adoption of accrual and performance-based budgets, with continuous changes in their formulation and execution, should follow the current scientific trend. New forms of participatory budgeting, enhancing the active participation of citizens, require the definition of the public budget in a simpler, more flexible, communicative and democratic direction.

According to Heraclitus, no one can cross the riverbed twice, as it is constantly changing. This is at the heart of public budgeting, as environmental needs require the budget to constantly adapt and change in the form of an amoeba by adopting new public policies. It is hoped that this document will bring about a change in the way we approach it and make it a more strategic tool.

References

Atkinson, A. (2000). *Increased income inequality in OECD countries and the redistributive impact of the government budget*. Oxford Academic.

Barbera, C., Jones, M., Korac, S., Saliterer, I., & Steccolini, I. (2017). Governmental financial resilience under austerity in Austria, England and Italy: How do local governments cope with financial shocks? *Public Administration, 95*(3), 670–697.

Briguglio, L. P. (2016). Exposure to external shocks and economic resilience of countries: Evidence from global indicators. *Journal of Economic Studies, 43*(6), 1057–1078.

Caiden, N. (2020). *Budgeting, policy, politics: Appreciation of Aaron Wildavsky*. Routledge.

Cavalieri, A. (2023). *Italian budgeting policy: Between punctuations and incrementalism*. Springer Nature.

Dzigbede, K. D., Pathak, R., & Muzata, S. (2023). Budget systems and post-pandemic economic resilience in developing countries. *Journal of Public Budgeting, Accounting & Financial Management, 35*(3), 333–353.

El-Berry, N. A., & Goeminne, S. (2021). Fiscal transparency, fiscal forecasting and budget credibility in developing countries. *Journal of Forecasting, 40*(1), 144–161.

Fuchs, S., & Thaler, T. (Eds.). (2018). *Vulnerability and resilience to natural hazards*. Cambridge University Press.

Hallegatte, S. (2014). *Economic resilience: Definition and measurement* (World Bank Policy Research Working Paper, 6852).

Hu, X., Li, L., & Dong, K. (2022). What matters for regional economic resilience amid COVID-19? Evidence from cities in Northeast China. *Cities, 120*, 103440.

Jo, J., & Rothenberg, L. S. (2020). Budgetary choices and institutional rules: Veto rules and budget volatility. *Economics of Governance, 21*(1), 1–25.

Joseph, R. (2021). The great recession and economic resilience: A longitudinal analysis of low-income households in the United States. *Journal of Social Service Research, 47*(6), 886–897.

Keck, M., & Sakdapolrak, P. (2013). What is social resilience? Lessons learned and ways forward. *Erdkunde*, 5–19.

Lacasse, F. (1996). Budget and policy making: Issues, tensions and solutions. *Development, Budgeting and Policy Making, 8*, 23–52.

Lim, J., & Won, D. (2024). Social resilience and risk society analysis model of the COVID 19 pandemic. *International Journal of Disaster Risk Reduction*, 104329.

Lindbeck, A., & Weibull, J. W. (1987). Balanced-budget redistribution as the outcome of political competition. *Public Choice*, 273–297.

Lipsmeyer, C. S., Philips, A. Q., & Whitten, G. D. (2023). *The politics of budgets: Getting a piece of the pie*. Cambridge University Press.

Lisnyak, S., & Sharipov, I. (2015). Exploring the formal and informal institutions as a key tool for enhancing economic resilience. *CES Working Papers*, *7*(4), 891.

Lootsma, F. A., Mensch, T. C. A., & Vos, F. A. (1990). Multi-criteria analysis and budget reallocation in long-term research planning. *European Journal of Operational Research, 47*(3), 293–305.

Raudla, R., & Douglas, J. W. (2022). Austerity and budget execution: Control versus flexibility. *Journal of Public Budgeting, Accounting & Financial Management, 34*(2), 292–309.

Röhn, O., Sánchez, A. C., Hermansen, M., & Rasmussen, M. (2015). Economic resilience: A new set of vulnerability indicators for OECD countries.

Romdhane, Y. B., Kammoun, S., & Werghi, I. (2022). Economic resilience to the FDI shock during the COVID-19 pandemic: Evidence from Asia. *Journal of Economic and Administrative Sciences*, (ahead-of-print).

Rubin, I. (2015). Past and future budget classics: A research agenda. *Public Administration Review, 75*(1), 25–35.

Saja, A. A., Teo, M., Goonetilleke, A., & Ziyath, A. M. (2018). An inclusive and adaptive framework for measuring social resilience to disasters. *International Journal of Disaster Risk Reduction, 28*, 862–873.

Sicilia, M., & Steccolini, I. (2017). Public budgeting in search for an identity: State of the art and future challenges. *Public Management Review, 19*(7), 905–910.

Wang, S., & Scorsone, E. (2020). Economic resilience after the great recession: An examination of unreserved fund balance in Michigan counties. *Local Government Studies, 46*(5), 716–733.

Yuniza, M. E., Inggarwati, M. P., & Nandita, N. N. D. R. P. (2022, April). Government policy on refocusing activity and re-allocation budget of local government in pandemic and new normal period. In *2nd Riau Annual Meeting on Law and Social Sciences (RAMLAS 2021)* (pp. 75–83). Atlantis Press.

Zamfir, E. M., Balaban, G., & Marinescu, C. (2022). Economic resilience in Central and Eastern European countries. *Theoretical & Applied Economics*, *29*(1).

CHAPTER 8

Greening Human Capital: A Catalyst for Organizational and Environmental Resilience

Apostolis Gkikas, Ioannis Salmon, Alexandros Sahinidis, and Anastasios Sepetis

8.1 Introduction

The literature review indicates that the concept of green human resources (GHR) is relatively new. This concept creates a significant perspective in the development of the theory and practice of management sciences. In modern conditions, environmental and social factors play a key role in the sustainable development of organizations. Green Human Resources Management is embedded in providing a balance between HRM policies, activities and practices with environmental sustainability management (Sharma, 2016).

A. Gkikas (✉) · I. Salmon · A. Sahinidis · A. Sepetis
Department of Business Administration, University of West Attica, Athens, Greece
e-mail: agkikas@uniwa.gr

A. Hyz (ed.), *The Role of the Public Sector in Building Social and Economic Resilience*,
https://doi.org/10.1007/978-3-031-67702-1_8

The concept of green human resources management can be described as the process of greening organizations along with their people (Majeed et al., 2019). In this process, organizations take initiatives to achieve their specific goals related to the human factor but also to participate in the implementation of the broader goal of environmental sustainability.

In the context of green people management, the activities of the human resources department are not limited to managing, developing and retaining employees in the organization but also to recruiting the right people for the right job, training them, retaining and developing them as per requirement and current trends in the industry (Patil & Sarode, 2018). It is hoped there will be changes in organizational culture related to environmental management and this will make employees aware of the use of natural resources more economically and encourage the existence of environmentally friendly products (Nawangsari & Sutawidjaya, 2018).

This chapter aims to conceptually analyse the impact of green human resources or human capital management on organizational and environmental resilience. At this point, the concept of "human resources" so commonly used in the analysis of the subject seems to be inappropriate, drawing attention to the fact that resources are characterized by the ability and tendency to be exhausted. Therefore, the analysis will use the term "capital" alternatively because this concept, unlike resources, has the ability to increase its effectiveness based on investments. Organizational and environmental resilience, in turn, means the ability of an organization to survive, adapt and develop in the face of various challenges, environmental changes and disruptions. This concept includes both the organization's ability to cope with internal difficulties and adapt to changing external conditions. It also includes the ability to quickly respond to problems, adapt to new conditions and quickly return to normal functioning. Ecologically resilient organizations are able to effectively manage the impact of their activities on the environment, adapt to changes in the environment and make sustainable decisions. The ability of an organization to combine both types of resilience, i.e. organizational and environmental, is crucial for long-term success and sustainable development. It covers both operational and strategic aspects, enabling the organization to function effectively in both normal and difficult conditions. In the above context, this chapter tries to explain the emergence of the concept of sustainability and greening, the importance and the meaning of green human resources, what are the reasons for greening and the ways to make human resources functions green. The chapter attempts to embed the concept of green people management in known management theories as well as in the sphere of ethics. Finally, the article contains an analysis of the individual functions of GHRM, with particular emphasis on the function of training and development of employees. The outcomes of this chapter are expected to enrich both theoretical and empirical knowledge regarding how green human resources management can provide environmentally committed employees and diffuse environmental values across the organization. This, in turn, is anticipated to contribute to the sustainability of not only individual businesses but also the whole economy.

8.2 From Sustainable Development to ESG

Climate change is one of the key challenges of our time, causing serious long-term effects worldwide. Climate change includes extreme weather events such as floods, heat waves, hurricanes, droughts and storms, which are intensified by changes in the atmosphere. These natural disasters have direct and indirect effects on everyday life, causing human suffering and upheaval in societies. Continuous climate upheavals and disasters require immediate adaptation and response measures. In this context, climate change requires multi-level solutions and cooperation between governments, societies and businesses.

Throughout history, the world has increasingly begun to understand that everything must be done to ensure that human activity no longer contributes to climate change. Sustainable development is not a synonymous term to environmental protection but rather a new concept of economic growth where trade and foreign policies, economic and fiscal policies, agricultural and industrial policies, all aspire to stimulate such development paths that are economically, ecologically and socially sustainable (Shaikh, 2010). In turn, the term environmental sustainability refers to the responsibility of conserving natural resources and protecting the global ecosystem.

In recent decades, many provisions and treaties have been formulated aimed at sustainable development. The concept of sustainability gained its prominence at the Earth Summit of 1992 and its subsequent Johannesburg Declaration of 2002, Kyoto 1997, Bali 2007, Copenhagen 2009, Paris Agreement 2016 (Alquadah et al., 2021; Naya, 2022). Now the concept is recognized as the international development agenda (Ricketts, 2010). The European Union's climate law includes an obligation that Europe will become the first climate-neutral continent in the world (European_Commission, 2021). In July 2021, a proposal was presented on how to prepare all sectors of the EU economy to meet this challenge. All 27 Member States have committed to transforming the EU into the first climate-neutral continent by 2050. As a starting point for the implementation of the resolutions, it has been proposed to reduce gas emissions by at least 55 per cent by the end of this decade (2030) compared to 1990 levels. The "Fit for 55" legislation package, now fully adopted, sets the stage for the EU to achieve its 2030 climate goals in a fair, cost-effective and competitive way. This package was approved before the very important UN Climate Change Conference COP28. Climate change is the greatest challenge of our time. It is also an opportunity to build a new economic model. The European Green Deal has set out a blueprint for transformational change. This change will bring many benefits—it will create new opportunities not only for innovation and investment and green jobs but also for improving our health and well-being. The EU now has legally binding climate targets covering all key economic sectors. The overall package includes emission reduction targets across many sectors, a target to increase carbon sequestration capacity, an emissions trading system that has been updated to reduce emissions and make pollution pay and to generate investment in the transition ecological, social support for citizens and small businesses (European_Commission, 2021). Actions to improve the state of the environment have been and are undertaken not only by international organizations and governments of individual countries but also by companies themselves. Many ethical and pro-environmental activities are observable. Various technological, normative (e.g. ISO 14001) and social (e.g. Corporate Social Responsibility) solutions are adopted, the concept of Total Quality Environment Management (TQEM) is implemented, the principles of a green supply chain, green investing, financing, etc. are applied (Budgol et al., 2021; Zaid et al., 2019).

The integration of the concept of sustainability in corporate decision-making and overall management led to the formulation of the ESG criteria framework (Amel-Zadeh & Serafeim, 2018; Sciarelli et al., 2021). The framework includes three main categories: environmental criteria related to the protection of the natural environment, social criteria related to social cohesion and cultural impact and corporate governance criteria related to the administrative management of businesses. This means that the previously mentioned categories contain non-financial criteria for assessing the activities of enterprises and organizations aimed at assessing the impact of activities on the environment, social responsibility and corporate governance. This assessment is independent of the financial results achieved. These three criteria are used by investors to assess responsibility and future risk. However, it should be emphasized that these three areas complement each other. For example, the environment influences the local community, and these two factors, in turn, influence governance. Concerning the environment, the main set of criteria under ESG includes indicators which measure the impact of an organization's activities on natural resources, as well as its consequences. Characteristic measures used in the reports are energy management, waste management, water consumption, air pollution, use of renewable energy sources, as well as the use of natural resources for production as well as compliance with ethical aspects (Garcia et al., 2017). The field of social responsibility refers to the quality of relationships and cooperation with employees, customers and the local community. Due to the multidimensional nature of the business activities and the involvement of various stakeholders, there are measures related to employees (fair wages, financial benefits, professional development through education and training, volunteering programs (Kotsandonis & Serafeim, 2020)), customer-related measures, which asses a company's relationship with customers through ethically acceptable and sustainable practices, such as effective communication and post-sale customer satisfaction (Chen & Mussalli, 2020). In addition, an important subcategory is the assessment of a company's approach to social issues such as gender equality, and equal opportunities and response to social issues such as natural disasters (De Lucia et al., 2020). Finally, indicators related to the contribution of companies to the promotion and preservation of the cultural and historical heritage of the region are included, such as support through voluntary actions and sponsorships (Duke, 2015). Social responsibility also includes the company's charitable activities. Finally, governance includes transparency, accountability, stakeholders' rights and staff and executives' compensation system (Khan, 2019). In this way, corporate governance indicators attempt to ensure that the company is managed fairly and transparently while applying ethical principles to the company's strategy and operations.

In 2021, the European Union introduced the Corporate Sustainability Reporting Directive (CSRD), which imposes the obligation to publish annual ESG reports on all company activities. Initially, the reporting obligation covered public interest entities, such as banks, investment funds and insurance companies. From 2024, this obligation applies to companies employing more than 500 employees, as well as companies with annual revenues exceeding EUR 40 million. Over the next few years, the obligation will be extended to additional companies. This obligation does not apply only to European Union countries. It is worth mentioning the Global Reporting Initiative (GRI) and the Sustainability Accounting Standards Board (SASB), which set ESG reporting standards. A company's use of an ESG framework serves two main purposes. First, it helps a company fully understand the consequences of its decisions and actions by providing the opportunity to recognize and offset those impacts. Through the judicious use of ESG metrics, a company can avoid practices that lead to negative impacts, encouraging the development of new, sustainable methods that improve both the efficiency of corporate operations and the wider natural and social environment (Chouaibi et al., 2021). Second, adopting an ESG framework benefits society as a whole by improving a company's image and creating positive impressions in the eyes of stakeholders. This helps to strengthen the company's brand image, creating positive expectations and momentum that can positively affect its sales, profitability and market share (Paolone et al., 2022).

8.3 Environmental Problems and Management Process

Looking at this problem from an interdisciplinary perspective, initially environmental aspects were studied by physicists and environmental protection specialists, then they became problems studied by technologists and finally, they became the subject of management sciences. Of course, each of the mentioned scientific disciplines perceives this problem from a different perspective.

In today's world, most companies set their environmental goals and objectives to not only meet legal requirements but also to improve the company's environmental management. Many of them assume that all eco-innovations should be adopted and incorporated into strategies to improve economic performance. More and more companies are introducing environmental goals into the set of criteria on which the remuneration of management staff depends. However, over the years it has been observed and confirmed by research that frequent investment of financial resources in projects referred to as green may be provoked to pursuit their interests and that some groups of managers are still more interested in meeting the expectations of stakeholders (mainly owners) than in obtaining benefits for the environment, which means that environmental management systems often do not contribute to improving environmental effects. This is probably where the concept of ESG comes from, which obliges companies to take a strategic approach to environmental issues, social responsibility and corporate governance.

From a functional point of view, an enterprise is an organized team of people, and material, financial and intangible resources intended to conduct business activities. Its functioning is based on the implementation of specific processes and functions that are necessary to achieve the assumed goals, such as generating profits, development and providing value to customers and other stakeholders. Within this approach, the main functions of an enterprise are production as a process of producing products or providing services, marketing as activities related to identifying customer needs, creating and promoting products or services, setting prices and distribution, sales as a process of directly offering products or services to customers, conducting negotiations commercial transactions, finalizing transactions and after-sales service, finance including financial planning, cost control, investing, financial risk management and raising capital, research and development (R&D) as activities related to the creation of innovations, new products, technologies and processes, aimed at ensuring long-term enterprise competitiveness and, finally, human resources management (HRM) as the process of recruiting, selecting, training, motivating and evaluating employees, as well as managing employee relations and ensuring compliance with labour law provisions.

The enterprise is therefore a dynamic system that integrates these various functions to operate effectively in a changing market environment and achieve its business goals. The integration of environmental concerns is visible in each of the functions mentioned above. The common denominator here is the human factor. Hence the new concept is addressed to specialists in the field of green human resources management. Environmental problems must occur in every management process, but at the same time concern every human resource management function, so also in selection processes, adaptation, motivation, remuneration or training. No less important is shaping environmental awareness and pro-environmental behaviour. In this way, there has been a change in the view of the role of people managing people in organizations. They must be responsible for developing behaviours that support the environment, especially since these behaviours cannot be limited to the workplace. The very concept of the workplace is already changing. So far, only a small percentage of employees have worked from home. Now, as a result of technological progress, but also unpredictable events such as the pandemic, this situation is changing. Therefore, the development of behaviour also affects and covers a person's private life, not only his professional life.

8.4 The Evolution and Impact of Green Human Resources Management: From Efficiency to Empowerment

The literature on the subject indicates that although green human resources management is a new discipline and a new concept, it is attracting increasing interest among both theoreticians and practitioners. The concept of Green Human Resources Management has its origins in business strategy in the 1990s. It began to gain popularity in the 2000s. Wehrmeyer (1996) is considered to have contributed to the creation of the term green human resources management (GHRM), which is to be understood as systematic and planned adapting traditional human capital management practices to the organization's environmental goals (Wehrmeyer, 1996). Green HR is a key tool in introducing sustainable development in enterprises that strive to achieve the goals set by the green economy. It is a component of sustainable human resources management that takes into account the ecological context as the basis for personnel decisions (Ahmad, 2015; Alghamdi, 2021). The concept of green people management assumes that in the process of building sustainable development of an enterprise, human resources are the most important. The success of the enterprise depends on human resources, i.e. on the actions of employees, their knowledge, skills, their use and awareness of what the green economy strives for (Scheme 8.1).

There are two basic research trends in green human resources management. The first one focuses on individual employees and according to it the main goal of green human resources management becomes employee behaviour. This includes shaping the ecological sensitivity of employees, creating pro-ecological work environments, and ecologically responsible attitudes of employees, which are then transferred to private life (Cherian & Jacob, 2012; Paille et al., 2013; Renwick et al., 2013;

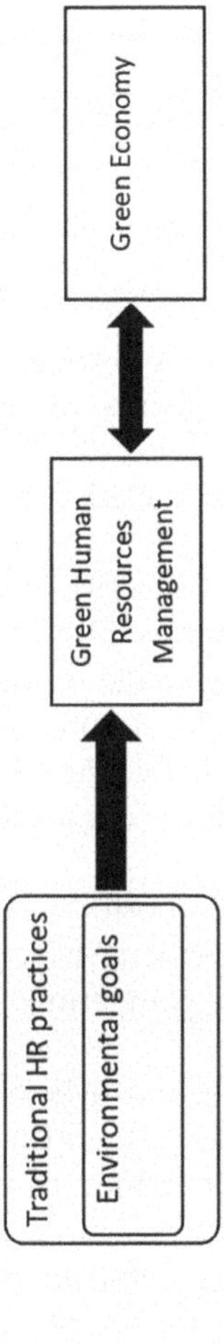

Scheme 8.1 Green human resources management conceptualization

Tomer & Rana, 2020; Zoogah, 2011). However, green human resources management is also of paramount importance in achieving broader goals, such as cost savings, improving corporate social responsibility practices and making companies more attractive in terms of employer branding (Saeed et al., 2019). This is the second trend of research aimed at the organization as a whole. Thus, green management improves, among other things, brand reputation, and the quality of the entire organization, increases stakeholder involvement, and is also an economic solution because it reduces the company's overall costs, as the consumption of water, energy and raw materials becomes lower. Based on more than 250 studies conducted so far and presented in the literature (Ren et al., 2018), green HR contributes to (Jabbour et al., 2013; Tang et al., 2018):

- increased interest of contractors through activities in the area of employer branding, because clients are more interested in cooperation with companies that care about social acceptance and a positive image and build good relationships with the environment (Gonzalez-Benito, 2004).
- increasing consumer loyalty. A modern customer pays attention not only to the quality and features of the product but also to its ecological friendliness and the image of the manufacturer.
- improving relations with the local community. Running a business based on the concept of sustainable development and implementing green solutions makes it possible to gain the support of residents of local communities.
- increased competitiveness. A positive company image improves cooperation with business partners, which may ultimately lead to increased sales and gaining a competitive advantage in the market (Boselie et al., 2001).
- improving the level of the company's organizational culture. By applying the green HR concept, companies achieve a higher level of organizational culture containing new values and behavioural systems.
- shaping a positive image of the company among employees. Thanks to ecological programs and care for the environment, the company's image in the eyes of employees improves. Employees have a better perception of a company that is focused on solving important ecological problems.

- recruiting and retaining talented employees. Employees of companies implementing green HR principles identify to a greater extent with their company and are loyal to it, which means that green organizations have a good chance of retaining the best employees and employing new ones (Bombiak & Marciniuk-Kluska, 2018).
- solving important social problems. Enterprises sensitive to ecological issues not only contribute to publicizing social problems but also to solving them. Companies that take action to protect the environment set a good example for other companies.
- educating society. Companies that implement green HR practices make citizens aware of the importance of issues such as responsibility in economic life and care for the natural environment.
- improving the condition of the natural environment. By implementing ecological programs, companies contribute to reducing the level of pollution and improving the condition of the natural environment. Enterprises also often engage in educational activities aimed at raising citizens' ecological awareness (Majeed et al., 2019).
- providing information about a company operating in the ecological sphere is an important motivating and image factor. Motivating, among other things, to conduct effective social programs (Mishra et al., 2014).
- finally, ecological education at work and developing cooperation are aimed not only at environmental protection but also at the broadly understood well-being of not only the organization but also the employees and the entire society (Norton et al., 2015) (Scheme 8.2).

8.5 Theoretical Foundations and Ethical Considerations

Green Human Resource Management (GHRM) can be considered in relation to various theoretical approaches, which offer frameworks and guidelines for its understanding and implementation. For example, theoretical approaches such as Resources-Based View (RBV), Institutional Theory, Stakeholder Theory, Corporate Social Responsibility, Strategic Human Resources Management, Triple Bottom Line, Sustainable Development Theory, Human Resources Development Theory, Product Life Cycle Theory, Social Exchange Theory, Legitimacy Theory can be mentioned. The network of these theoretical approaches is easily

Scheme 8.2 Impacts of green human resources management (*Source* Authors)

perceived in the scope of research as it was analysed in the previous section.

According to the Resources-Based View (RBV), companies gain a competitive advantage from their internal resources. Within GHRM, employees are perceived as an important and valuable resource, and managing them in an environmentally conscious way can contribute to sustainable development and to gaining a lasting competitive advantage. Institutional Theory, on the other hand, focuses on how organizations adapt to institutional pressures and expectations. GHRM can be seen as a response to social and institutional expectations regarding environmental responsibility. Organizations are adopting green HR practices to align with social norms and expectations.

According to stakeholder theory, companies are not only accountable to their shareholders but also to many other groups who, like shareholders, have a legitimate interest in the company. Stakeholder theory is based on the principle of corporate rights as well as the principle of corporate results. According to the first principle, every business must respect the rights of others. Whereas, according to the second, each company is responsible for the effects of its actions on others. With these two principles in mind, we can define stakeholders as individuals or groups who affect or are affected by a company or whose rights may be violated or should be respected by a company. According to the early conceptions of business management, the sole responsibility of a company is to look after the interests of the owners, i.e. the interest of the shareholders. The evolution of the theory led to the question concerning the integration of the interests of other groups of stakeholders in the operation of the business. This integration comes from the legal approach and the socio-economic approach. Looking at the legal approach we can see that legal obligations do not only exist with employees, customers or suppliers, but also an increasingly dense network of laws and regulations imposed by society that make it a fact that many different stakeholders have certain rights and claims against the company. Indicatively, the introduction of new indicators in the context of the evaluation of companies in three dimensions Environment, Sustainability and Governance (ESG) on the one hand highlights the new needs associated with the complexity of the modern environment and on the other hand creates new claims for management practitioners. Looking at the issue from a socio-economic point of view we can consider a simple case of producing a product that damages the environment that affects not only the environment at a given moment but also has other socio-economic effects, such as the need to restore the negative effects, resulting in a reduction of the financing possibilities of other various activities, possible impact on the health of citizens, increase in expenditure on care and health and decrease in social welfare. Thus a connection is created between the company's goals and society's expectations towards it. Traditional management theory ignored these effects. This development has shifted the focus of interest away from adopting a business strategy that focuses solely on profit, as it is now believed that businesses have a deeper responsibility to stakeholders, often sacrificing a portion of profits for this purpose. Businesses are beginning to realize that without society they cannot be long-term sustainable.

GHRM recognizes and takes into account the interests of various stakeholders, including employees, customers, local communities and the environment. Adopting environmentally friendly HR practices is a way for organizations to meet the expectations and needs of various stakeholders who prioritize sustainability.

GHRM is often perceived as an element of CSR that emphasizes a company's responsibility for its impact on society. Green HR practices contribute to the social and environmental dimensions of CSR. GHRM activities include a commitment to social and environmental responsibility beyond legal requirements, with a particular emphasis on making a positive contribution to the well-being of society. Similarly, GHRM can be assessed within the framework of the ESG approach, as activities within the framework of green people management have an impact on at least the first two elements: the environment and society, as within this framework such company impacts as indirect emissions, risks are analysed and opportunities from climate change, stakeholder involvement, employee training costs, etc. In turn, Social Exchange Theory, according to which employees are likely to show greater commitment and loyalty in relation to ecological issues when they notice that the company rewards ecological behaviour. Similarly, legitimacy theory states that companies adapt their practices to meet social expectations and maintain social acceptance. GHRM can be viewed as a strategic approach to human resource management in which environmental sustainability is integrated with HR policies and practices to enhance the overall strategic goals of the organization. Therefore, as a strategic approach, it must take into account the company's mission within the external environment in which the company operates, but at the same time take into account the internal. The human factor plays a key role in these contexts. It is impossible to ignore the triple bottom line (TBL) in this analysis: The TBL framework takes into account three dimensions of results: economic, social and environmental. GHRM aligns with the environmental dimension of TBL by incorporating ecological considerations into HRM practices. Similarly, GHRM is inextricably linked to the theory of sustainability, which seeks to balance economic, social and environmental considerations to ensure long-term well-being. Sustainable HR practices contribute to the overall sustainability of an organization. GHRM can be seen as an extension of HRD theory, in which organizations invest in developing employee knowledge and skills related to environmental sustainability. The product life cycle theory is also important. This theory is related to the idea that companies go through different stages of the product life cycle. At the maturity stage, adapting to green management can be an important strategic step.

These theoretical approaches offer different interpretations and guidelines for understanding the motivations and outcomes of Green HRM. Consequently, combining GHRM with this theoretical framework helps provide a theoretical foundation for understanding why and how organizations incorporate environmental considerations into their human resource management practices. Perhaps it is important to note here that, as in other management problems, we should not expect ready-made recipes and solutions from research on green people management. Just as each enterprise and organization is a unique system with its own specific core competencies, particularly regarding the human factor, the solutions—i.e., the answer to the question of not what but how—will also differ. These differences depend on the particular moment in which the enterprise or organization finds itself, as well as on its other distinctive characteristics. Therefore, there are no ready-made answers and recipes for management staff. In other words, each manager must develop the most appropriate solutions for himself and the company. The task of scientists in this field is to constantly search for relationships between processes, and analyse and describe these relationships so that managers can choose and adapt these solutions to specific conditions occurring in the enterprise.

Green human resource management (GHRM) is closely linked to ethical considerations as it involves the integration of environmental sustainability principles with human resource practices. The ethical dimensions of GHRM can be explored through various ethical theories and frameworks. Several ethical perspectives relevant to GHRM are environmental ethics, duty-based ethics, but also intergenerational ethics. Thus, GHRM is fundamentally rooted in environmental ethics, which examines the moral relationship between humans and the environment. It involves recognizing the intrinsic value of nature and promoting sustainable practices to protect the environment and for present and future generations. GHRM is committed to the principles of justice and fairness, considering the impact of human resources practices on current and future generations. Ethical considerations may include ensuring that workers are treated fairly, that communities are not negatively impacted, and that ecological resources are used fairly and equitably.

Duty-based ethical frameworks such as deontology emphasize adherence to duties and moral principles. GHRM may be guided by its obligation to protect the environment and promote sustainable practices, even if this requires sacrifices or changes to traditional HR practices. GHRM addresses the long-term environmental and social impacts of human resource practices. Intergenerational ethics involves considering the well-being of future generations and making choices that conserve resources and minimize environmental degradation.

Although normatively it is at the opposite end, we should not forget about utilitarianism, which can be equally useful in these considerations and in this attempt to place GHRM in a theoretical and ethical framework. From a utilitarian point of view, GHRM practices can be judged by their overall utility or happiness produced for society. Adopting environmentally friendly HR practices is seen as contributing to the greater good by promoting ecological sustainability and minimizing environmental damage.

In summary, the ethical dimensions of GHRM include a commitment to environmental sustainability, justice, stakeholder interests and the well-being of present and future generations. Ethical considerations play a key role in guiding the development and implementation of green human resources practices in organizations.

8.6 Green HRM Functions

Green HRM functions include all ecological activities in all processes related to human resources management. They, therefore, include human resources planning, job design and job analysis, green recruitment and selection, green training and development by developing green skills through training and development, green performance management and appraisal, green reward and compensation by motivating environmental protection activities, green empowerment through activities to engage employees in environmental protection and work safety and employee relations issues (Renwick et al., 2013; Yong et al., 2019). These objectives aim to align HR practices with longer-term sustainability goals and contribute to environmental responsibility. The use of the following practices enables the implementation of the above functions: taking into account ecological criteria and ecological competencies in job descriptions, giving preference to candidates with ecological competencies in the recruitment and selection process, conducting pro-ecological training for employees, using ecological criteria in employee evaluation, promoting knowledge sharing, taking initiatives related to ecology and rewarding for their implementation, shaping ecological behaviour among employees.

When analysing the individual functions of GHRM, we can focus on particularly important function training and professional development of employees. Here the role of human resource management starts immediately after the selection of new employees with their familiarization in the new job environment. Beyond the transfer of basic information related to the work they undertake, this process requires the assimilation of the way the employer wants its employees to operate. It is the mix of behaviours, standards and values that the organization requires from its employees. These behaviours, values and generally the culture of the organization obviously in the context of GHRM must include employee awareness of environmental issues and engage them in sustainable practices, eco-friendly practices in the workplace, policies on waste reduction, energy conservation, telecommuting and sustainable commuting options, creation of cross-functional teams focused on identifying and implementing eco-friendly practices, implementation of paperless processes, reduce printing and promote recycling initiatives and so on. Employee familiarization programs can be of different durations and cover many and varied topics using electronic material as well as executive lectures and exercises on topics related to the company's vision and values, the organization's culture, etc. Training in turn refers to the methods employers use to impart necessary skills and abilities to workers. As we mentioned in the previous sections, green human resources management includes the environmental goals of the organization, so the training goals must include the strategic goals of the organization in this dimension. The main thing is to identify the work behaviours that the company will need to implement its strategy, and then the corresponding skills and characteristics that the employees must possess. The next step is to define specific training goals and implement training programs that will impart these skills to employees. Each educational process must include the following stages:

- Analysis: The goal is to identify employee training needs in order to effectively implement pro-ecological initiatives. The steps should include first assessing employee needs by conducting employee surveys and interviews to understand their current knowledge and approach to sustainability and analysing job roles to identify specific training needs related to environmental practices. Secondly, it is necessary to identify gaps by comparing current practices with desired sustainable practices, as well as identifying the gap in knowledge and skills that training should fill. The next step is to define training goals, i.e. setting clear and measurable educational goals (e.g. understanding waste segregation, energy saving practices).

- Design: The goal is to design the structure and content of the training program. The individual stages are a training program covering key areas such as resource management, waste reduction and pollution prevention, training methods such as workshops, e-learning modules and practical exercises, material development such as presentations, manuals, videos and case studies, development of knowledge tests, schedule taking into account the duration and frequency of sessions.
- Development: The aim is to develop training materials and resources. The steps include creating the content for each module, ensuring it is aligned with the training objectives, creating interactive elements including simulations and group discussions, preparing physical and digital resources (e.g. training manuals, setting up the e-learning platform), visual aids and real-life examples to illustrate concepts.
- Implementation: The basic steps are to implement the training program according to a planned schedule, conduct individual training sessions using a combination of in-person workshops, and online modules, engage employees through discussions, and Q&A sessions and encourage a collaborative learning environment, where employees can share experiences and good practices.
- Evaluation: The goal is to evaluate the effectiveness of the training program and make improvements if necessary. The individual stages include: collecting feedback from participants through surveys, interviews and feedback forms, collecting data on training participation and completion rates, assessing performance (changes in employee behaviour and practices through observations and performance indicators, comparison of pre- and post-training assessments to assess knowledge gains), impact analysis (analysis of the impact of training on the company's overall environmental performance). The evaluation should include both qualitative and quantitative results (e.g. waste reduction, and energy savings). Finally, what is called continuous improvement is important, which is the use of feedback and performance data to identify areas for improvement in the training program.

By following this structured approach, employees will be well-equipped with the knowledge and skills needed to effectively contribute to the company's greening initiatives.

8.7 Conclusions

The current economic, political and social situation as well as the effects of the pandemic reinforce the belief that the activities of companies in the area of sustainable development and green human resources management will transform from a demand into an absolute need in the coming years. In this way and in this context, an element of the enterprise's strategy becomes a point of interest for the whole society. Based on many theoretical concepts and ethical approaches, a mechanism for formulating green behaviour of employees can be formulated. The GHRM remains relatively new in organizations due to the lack of documented evidence supporting its functions and practices. There is a need for all organizations, public and private, to implement robust policies and strategies that integrate GHRM into their strategic plans along with adequate management-employee involvement and commitment (Alquadah et al., 2021).

Green Human Resource Management (GHRM) involves integrating ecological practices into all aspects of human resource management, including planning, job design and analysis, recruitment and selection, training and development, performance management, rewards and employee engagement. The primary goal of GHRM is to align HR practices with broader sustainability objectives, contributing to the organization's environmental responsibility and to the building of both organizational and environmental resilience.

The key element of the GHRM is ecological criteria for position descriptions and favouring candidates with green competencies during the recruitment process. This ensures that from the very beginning new employees are prepared to support the objectives of the sustainable development of the organization. Comprehensive training programs are necessary to develop employees' environmental skills and educate them in the field of sustainable practices, such as waste reduction, energy protection and prevention of pollution. Thus, "green human capital" becomes a catalyst for both organizational and environmental resistance. GHRM performance management includes employees' assessment based on ecological criteria, motivating them to engage in sustainable activities. The recognition and reward of green initiatives further strengthen the behaviour responsible for the environment and promote the culture of sustainable development. Strengthening the position of employees is also crucial, encouraging them to actively participate in environmental protection initiatives and sharing knowledge about sustainable development. Such a strategy increases employee involvement, which is crucial for the organization's long-term resistance. Continuous improvement is necessary in GHRM. Regular assessment of the effectiveness of green initiatives and training programs ensures their effective impact. Feedback and performance data are used to introduce continuous improvements, ensuring that the organization's efforts are effective and contribute to the long-term ecological balance. This approach not only increases the effectiveness of ecological activities but also strengthens the organization's ability to adapt and introduce innovations in the face of environmental changes.

To sum up, GHRM integrates sustainable practices with HR functions, adapts organizational activities with environmental goals and promotes the culture of ecological responsibility among employees, but also supports the general strategy of sustainable development of the organization, increasing its immunity and the ability to develop in a changing environment. The above efforts should and will also result in a new assessment of enterprises based on ESG, in which measures based on the enterprises' influences on the environment play crucial roles.

References

Ahmad, S. (2015). Green human resource management: Policies and practices. *Cogent Business & Management, 2*(1), 103–125.

Alghamdi, S. (2021). Effect of green human resources practices on the employee performance and behaviour: A systematic review. *International Journal of Economics, Business and Management Research, 5*(3), 450–464.

Alquadah, M., Yusof, Y., Elayan, M., & Paramita, C. (2021). Green human resources management and organizational environment sustainability during Covid-19 pandemic: A conceptual framework. *Advances in Economic, Business and Management Research, 194*, 158–167.

Amel-Zadeh, A., & Serafeim, G. (2018). Why and how investors use ESG information: Evidence from a global survey. *Financial Analysts Journal, 7*(3), 87–103.

Bombiak, E., & Marciniuk-Kluska, A. (2018). Green human resources management as a tool for the sustainable development of enterprises: Polish young company experience. *Sustainability, 10*, https://doi.org/10.3390/su1006 1739

Boselie, P., Paauwe, J., & Jansen, P. (2001). Human resources management and performance: Lessons from the Netherlands. *The International Journal of Human Resources Management, 12*(7), 1107–1125.

Budgol, M., Goranczewski, B., & Kadzielawski, G. (2021). Systemic support and environmental awareness in a normalised environmental management system consistent with ISO 14001. *Management of Environmental Quality*, 4 May, 949–969.

Chen, M., & Mussalli, G. (2020). An integrated approach to quantitative ESG investing. *Journal of Porfolio Management, 3*(46), 65–74.

Cherian, J., & Jacob, J. (2012). A study of green Hr practices and its effective implementation in the organization: A review. *International Journal of Business and Management, 7*, 26–33.

Chouaibi, S., Chouaibi, J., & Rossi, M. (2021). ESG and corporate financial performance: The mediating role of green innovation. *EuroMed Journal of Business, 6*, 3.

De Lucia, C., Pazienza, P., & Bartlett, M. (2020). Does good ESG lead to better financial performances by firms? Machine learning and logistic regression models of public enterprises in Europe. *Sustainability, 13*(12), 5–31.

Duke, G. (2015). Sustainable private equity investments and ESG due diligence frameworks. In *Responsible investment banking* (pp. 349–358). s.l.:Springer.

European_Commission. (2021). *Delivering the European green deal. On the path to a climate-neutral Europe by 2050*. Brussels, s.n.

Garcia, A., Mendes-DaSilva, W., & Orsato, R. (2017). Sensitive industries produce better ESG performance: Evidence from emerging markets. *Journal of Cleaner Production, 150*, 135–147.

Gonzalez-Benito, J. (2004). Environmental pro-activity and business performance: An empirical analysis. *International Journal of Management Science, 33*, 1–15. https://doi.org/10.1016/j.omega.2004.03.002

Jabbour, C., et al. (2013). Environmental management and operational performance in automotive companies in Brazil: The role of human resources management and lean manufacturing. *Journal of Cleaner Production, 47*, 129–140.

Khan, M. (2019). Corporate governance, ESG, and stock returns around the world. *Financial Analysts Journal, 4*(75), 103–123.

Kotsandonis, S., & Serafeim, G. (2020). Human capital and the future of work: Implications for investors and ESG integration. *Journal of Financial Transformation, 51*, 115–130.

Majeed, S., Khan, A., & Sayeed, R. (2019). Green human resources management practices: A review of literature. *International Human Resources Management Practices; A Review of Literature, IX*(I), 1834–1841.

Mishra, R., Sarkar, S., & Kiranmai, J. (2014). Green HRM: Innovative approach in indian public enterprises. *World Review of Science. Technology and Sustainable Development, 1*(11), 26–42.

Nawangsari, L. C., & Sutawidjaya, A. (2018). How the Green Human Resources Management (GHRM) process can be adopted for the organization business? *Advances in Economics, Business and Management Research, 65*, 463–465.

Naya, P. T. (2022). *Developing tools and evidence to deliver prosperity. The era of Inclusivity: Employees driving green human resources management toward sustainable prosperity* (Working Paper). Institute for Global Prosperity, August, pp. 1–24.

Norton, T., Parker, S., Zacher, H., & AshkanasyN, M. (2015). Employee green behaviour: A theoretical framework, multilevel review, and future research agenda. *Organization & Environment, 28*, 103–125.

Paille, P., Chen, Y., Boiral, O., & Jin, J. (2013). The impact of human resources management on environmental performance: An employee-level study. *Journal of Business Ethics*.

Paolone, F., Cucari, N., Wu, J., & Tiscini, R. (2022). How do ESG pillars impact firms' marketing performance? A configurational analysis in the pharmaceutical sector. *Journal of Business & Industrial Marketing, 37*(8), 1594–1606.

Patil, J., & Sarode, A. (2018). Green human resources management: Role of HR managers to achieve sustainability. *International Journal of Creative Research Thoughts, 6*(1), 527–531.

Ren, S., Tang, G., & Jackson, S. (2018). Green human resource management research in emergence: A review and future directions. *Asia Pacific Journal of Management, 3*(35), 769–803.

Renwick, D., Redman, T., & Maguire, S. (2013). Green human resources management: A review and research agenda. *International Journal of Management Reviews, 15*(1), 1–14.

Ricketts, G. (2010). The roots of sustainability. *Academic Questions, 23*(1), 20–53.

Saeed, B. et al. (2019). Promoting employee's pro-environmental behaviour through green human resources management practices. *Corporate Social Responsibility and Environmental Management, 26*(2), 424–438.

Sciarelli, M., Cosimato, S., Landi, G., & Iandolo, F. (2021). Socially responsible investment strategies for the transition towards sustainable development: The importance of integrating and communicating ESG. *The TQM Journal, 2*(3), 1–18.

Shaikh, M. (2010). Green HRM: A requirement of 21st century. *Journal of Research in Commerce and Management, 1*(10), 120–127.

Sharma, K. (2016). Conceptualization of green HRM and green HRM practices: Commitment to environmental sustainability. *International Journal of Advanced Scientific Research and Management, 1*(8), 74–81.

Tang, G., et al. (2018). Green human resources management practices: scale development and validity. *Asia Pacific Journal of Human Resources, 56*(1), 31–55.

Tomer, S., & Rana, G. (2020). *Green human resources management: A conceptual study*. Proceedings of the international conference on research in management & technovation, pp. 147–150.

Wehrmeyer, W. (1996). *Greening people*. Greenleaf Publishing.

Yong, J., Yusliza, M., & Ramayah, T. (2019). Pathways towards sustainability in manufacturing organizations: Empirical evidence on the role of green human resources management. *Business Strategy and the Environment*, July, 1–18.

Zaid, A., Luo, Y., Zhang, X., & Zhao, J. (2019). The impact of green human resources management and green supply chain management practices on sustainable performance: An Empirical Study. *Journal of Cleaner Production, 204*, 965–979.

Zoogah, D. (2011). The dynamics of Green HRM behaviours: A cognitive social information processing approach. *German Human Resources Management, 25*(2), 117–139.

CHAPTER 9

Enhancing Social and Economic Resilience for a Changing World: The Strategic Role of Continuous Training and Capacity Building in Contemporary Tax and Customs Administrations

Panagiotis Ballas, Alina Hyz, and Vassiliki-Maria Balla

The original version of the chapter has been revised: The chapter contributor name has been updated. A correction to this chapter can be found at https://doi.org/10.1007/978-3-031-67702-1_17

P. Ballas (✉) · A. Hyz
Department of Accounting and Finance, University of West Attica, Athens, Greece
e-mail: pballas@uniwa.gr

A. Hyz
e-mail: alinahyz@uniwa.gr

A. Hyz (ed.), *The Role of the Public Sector in Building Social and Economic Resilience*,
https://doi.org/10.1007/978-3-031-67702-1_9

9.1 Introduction

9.1.1 *Setting the Context: Importance of Social and Economic Resilience in Contemporary Times*

The twenty-first century presents a landscape marked by breakneck globalization, relentless technological advancement, and an unprecedented degree of interconnectedness. Within this context, fostering robust social and economic resilience has become an imperative. Contemporary societies find themselves buffeted by a confluence of challenges. These intricate issues necessitate not only adaptable responses but also the cultivation of a profound capacity for resilience. This chapter serves as a foundational exploration, elucidating the critical importance of social and economic resilience in navigating the labyrinthine complexities and inherent uncertainties that characterize the modern world.

We embark on a foundational exploration of social and economic resilience, establishing a cornerstone for comprehending their critical salience in navigating the complexities and inherent uncertainties that characterize the contemporary global context from the escalating threats posed by climate change to the disruptive forces unleashed by pandemics and economic meltdowns. We stress that these issues are not merely discrete events; they are interconnected threads woven into the very fabric of our globalized society. Effectively navigating this conditions necessitates a nuanced understanding of resilience, encompassing both its social and economic dimensions.

Elucidating Interconnectedness, the chapter delves into a web of interdependencies that bind social, economic, and environmental systems. A robust economy, for example, relies on a healthy and educated workforce—a facet of social well-being. Conversely, social cohesion and stability create fertile ground for economic prosperity. Environmental

---

V.-M. Balla
Department of Tourism Management, University of Patras, Patras, Greece
e-mail: vballa@upatras.gr

P. Ballas
Tax and Customs Academy, Independent Authority for Public Revenue, Athens, Greece

degradation, through factors like climate change, can disrupt agricultural production and supply chains, impacting both economic activity and social stability. This exploration of interconnectedness underscores the holistic nature of resilience—fostering strength in one domain reinforces the resilience of others.

The inherent uncertainties of the modern world demand a proactive approach. While reactive measures may address immediate crises, building a profound capacity for social and economic resilience allows for proactive risk management and adaptation highlighting the pivotal role of resilience. Besides, a proactive approach leads an effective way for managing crises improving the institutional functioning (Hosie, 2006). Resilient societies are better equipped to:

- **Weather Shocks and Disruptions:** Economic downturns, natural disasters, and pandemics can all be mitigated by a society with robust social support systems, diversified economies, and a culture of innovation.
- **Embrace Transformational Change:** The rapid pace of technological advancement necessitates a flexible and adaptable workforce. Resilient societies can foster a culture of lifelong learning and continuous improvement, allowing them to thrive in an ever-evolving landscape.
- **Promote Sustainable Development:** By prioritizing social equity and environmental sustainability, resilient societies create a foundation for long-term well-being.

Elucidating the interconnectedness of social, economic, and environmental systems, we lay the groundwork for a deeper understanding of resilience's critical role in navigating the labyrinthine complexities of the contemporary world.

By delving into the intricate web of interdependencies that bind social, economic, and environmental systems, we illuminate the multifaceted nature of resilience and underscore its profound relevance across diverse societal and economic spheres.

The complexity of contemporary challenges necessitates a multifaceted approach. While adaptable responses are crucial to navigate the ever-shifting sands of issues like climate change and technological disruption, building a profound capacity for resilience is equally essential.

The dynamism of modern challenges demands continual adjustments in strategies and policies including:

- **Technological Innovation:** Investing in cutting-edge solutions for climate change, such as carbon capture or renewable energy advancements, exemplifies this adaptability.
- **Workforce Reskilling:** Equipping our workforce with the skills necessary to thrive in an automation-driven future through targeted training programs or fostering education in emerging fields demonstrates such agility. Fung (2020) concluded that employers can accelerate initiatives such as the Enhanced Training Support while participating in work-study programs to address employees' talent needs.
- **Flexible Economic Frameworks:** Developing adaptable economic policies capable of responding to unforeseen circumstances, allowing for weathering sudden shocks or seizing unexpected opportunities, is a cornerstone of adaptability. Settembre et al. (2021) highlighted the necessity to explore alternative tools that could offer a multidimensional risk perspective promoting a strategic view of risk assessment.

Adaptability needs to be complemented by a robust capability to bounce back from disruptions with minimal lasting damage. A profound capacity for resilience necessitates more than just recovery; it requires building a robust buffer against significant stress:

- **Redundancy and Safety Nets:** Fortifying infrastructure, diversifying supply chains, and establishing social safety nets to support individuals and communities during hardship exemplify building redundancy.
- **Social Cohesion and Community Investment:** Investing in initiatives that foster strong community bonds and social inclusion builds societal resilience by creating support networks during difficult times. Encouraging civic engagement or fostering open communication within communities are such investments.
- **Transformative Learning:** Developing a growth mindset that prioritizes learning and innovation from setbacks allows us to emerge from challenges not just unscathed, but potentially even stronger.

This necessitates a culture of experimentation, open discussion of missteps, and continuous improvement. Schnepfleitner and Ferreira (2021) endorse Mezirow's theory[1] by claiming that educators can perform transformative learning through awareness development and personal and sociocultural appreciation.

By cultivating both adaptability and resilience, societies can transform these intricate challenges from potentially crippling roadblocks into catalysts for progress. We can learn to navigate the ever-evolving landscape, adapt our approaches, and emerge from difficulties not just surviving, but potentially even flourishing.

9.1.2 The Expanding Role of Tax and Customs Administrations as Key Pillars in Promoting Resilience

Tax and Customs administrations play a critical role in fostering social and economic resilience within societies. Their functions transcend mere revenue collection, encompassing broader objectives like ensuring compliance, facilitating trade, and promoting economic stability. In the face of escalating global challenges—economic downturns, natural disasters, and pandemics—the strategic significance of these administrations in bolstering resilience has become increasingly apparent.

First of all, taxation and customs duties are fundamental for generating government revenue, funding public services, and driving economic growth. However, their importance extends beyond these fiscal objectives to encompass the broader goal of promoting resilience and sustainability. Tax administrations are responsible for ensuring compliance with tax laws, fostering a culture of accountability and contributing to the sustainability of public finances. Similarly, Customs administrations facilitate international trade, promote economic integration, and enhance supply chain resilience by ensuring the smooth flow of goods across borders.

Further to the above, Tax and Customs administrations contribute to societal stability by promoting equity, transparency, and social cohesion. Progressively structured tax systems can mitigate income inequality and foster social inclusion by redistributing wealth and funding social

[1] Mezirow's theory (2009) was influenced by conscientization paradigms, consciousness raising and themes from philosophy and psychiatry.

welfare programs. Moreover, transparent and accountable tax systems bolster public trust in government institutions, thereby strengthening social cohesion and political stability. Likewise, efficient customs procedures enhance the predictability of trade transactions, reduce corruption, and promote trust among trading partners, ultimately fostering stability in international relations.

During crises, Tax and Customs administrations play a crucial role in supporting economic recovery efforts. Through the implementation of targeted fiscal measures, such as tax incentives and relief programs, tax administrations can stimulate investment, support businesses, and promote job creation. Customs administrations, in turn, can expedite clearance procedures, facilitate the importation of essential goods, and prevent trade disruptions, thereby accelerating the restoration of economic activity. Furthermore, tax and customs administrations can collaborate with other government agencies and international organizations to coordinate relief efforts, streamline administrative processes, and address emerging challenges.

Tax and Customs administrations contribute to sustainable development by promoting responsible fiscal management, environmental protection, and social progress. By implementing eco-friendly tax policies and incentives, tax administrations can incentivize sustainable practices such as renewable energy production and resource conservation. Customs administrations, on the other hand, can enforce environmental regulations, combat illicit trade in endangered species and hazardous materials, and promote sustainable consumption and production patterns. By aligning their policies and practices with the principles of sustainable development, Tax and Customs administrations can contribute to achieving the United Nations Sustainable Development Goals (SDGs) (United Nations Department of Economic & Social Affairs, 2024).

In summary, Tax and Customs administrations serve as essential pillars in promoting resilience within societies and economies. Their functions extend beyond revenue collection to encompass broader objectives such as ensuring compliance, facilitating trade, and promoting sustainable development. By fostering societal stability, supporting economic recovery, and promoting sustainable development, Tax and Customs administrations play a crucial role in building resilience and creating more inclusive and sustainable societies. As the world continues to face ongoing challenges, the strategic importance of these administrations in promoting resilience will only grow. This underscores the need for proactive measures and collaborative efforts to strengthen their capacities and enhance their contributions to resilience-building efforts.

9.2 The Role of Tax and Customs Administrations in Building Economic Resilience

9.2.1 Examination of How Tax Policies and Administration Strategies Can Influence Economic Stability and Growth

The design and implementation of tax systems directly impact various aspects of economic activity, including investment decisions, consumption patterns, and resource allocation. Furthermore, effective tax administration fosters compliance with tax laws, enhances revenue collection, and bolsters public confidence in government institutions.

It is crucial to acknowledge the ongoing discourse surrounding the optimal design of tax policy for achieving economic stability and growth. Considerations of efficiency, equity, and administrative feasibility all play critical roles in this discussion. One prominent debate centers on the Laffer Curve, a theoretical concept suggesting a tax rate that maximizes government revenue collection. While the Laffer Curve holds some intuitive appeal, its empirical validity remains a subject of ongoing debate among economists. The endless effort for government is to avoid being on the wrong side of the Laffer Curve's peak (Head et al., 2024).

Tax policies can exert a significant influence on economic stability by affecting aggregate demand, investment decisions (e.g. Su et al., 2023), and income distribution. Progressive taxation (e.g. Calabuig & Olcina, 2023), can mitigate income inequality and promote social cohesion by redistributing wealth from high-income earners to low-income individuals through social welfare programs and public services. This can lead to a more stable and inclusive economy, as a broader segment of the population has disposable income to spend and contribute to economic activity. Similarly, countercyclical fiscal policies, such as tax cuts during economic downturns, can stimulate consumption and investment, thereby mitigating the effects of recessions and promoting macroeconomic stability (e.g. Zhou et al., 2023). However, poorly designed tax policies, characterized by excessive burdens or distortionary effects (e.g., high marginal income tax rates that discourage investment or subsidies that distort market prices), can impede economic growth and exacerbate income disparities. This can lead to decreased investment, reduced economic activity, and potentially, social unrest.

Effective tax administration plays a critical role in enhancing revenue collection, reducing tax evasion, and promoting investment and entrepreneurship. By implementing modernization initiatives such as electronic filing systems, data analytics for risk assessment and compliance audits, and improved online communication platforms for taxpayer interactions, tax administrations can streamline administrative processes, improve taxpayer compliance, and reduce administrative costs. This not only increases government revenue but also creates a more predictable and transparent tax environment, fostering confidence among taxpayers and investors. Additionally, collaboration between tax authorities and other government agencies, as well as international cooperation, can enhance tax compliance, combat tax evasion, and facilitate cross-border trade. By ensuring a level playing field and reducing opportunities for tax havens, such collaboration contributes to a more stable and predictable global economic environment.

9.2.2 Insights from Global Examples

The implementation of Value-Added Tax (VAT) systems in emerging economies has helped broaden the tax base, increase revenue collection, and promote fiscal sustainability. This newfound fiscal stability allows governments to invest in infrastructure, education, and other areas crucial for long-term economic growth. Likewise, efforts to simplify tax codes and reduce administrative burdens have led to improved compliance rates and enhanced revenue mobilization in several countries. Additionally, initiatives to enhance taxpayer education and outreach, such as taxpayer assistance programs and online tax filing platforms, have contributed to increased voluntary compliance and improved taxpayer satisfaction. A more informed and engaged citizenry is essential for a well-functioning tax system.

Example 1: An indicative example for the above is the case of Germany and the government decision to temporarily reduce value-added tax (VAT) rate as a policy tool for stimulating economic recovery following the COVID-19 pandemic. In response to the economic downturn, Germany implemented a time-bound decrease in both the standard VAT rate (from 19 to 16%) and the reduced rate (from 7 to 5%). This intervention aimed to bolster consumer spending, mitigate pandemic-induced economic hardship, and accelerate recovery (Fuest et al., 2024; Baudisch and Neuenhirsch, 2023). The policy leverages the concept of demand-side stimulus. By reducing VAT rates, the German government aimed to increase consumer purchasing power, leading to increased demand for goods and services. This, in turn, was expected to:

- **Stimulate Consumer Spending:** Lower VAT translates to lower prices for consumers, incentivizing them to spend more. This increased demand benefits businesses, particularly those in pandemic-affected sectors like retail, hospitality, and tourism.
- **Promote Investment:** The temporary nature of the VAT reduction could encourage consumers to make purchases sooner rather than later, potentially triggering a short-term increase in investment and economic activity.
- **Support Small Businesses:** Lower VAT rates alleviate the financial burden on small businesses, aiding their operational continuity and employee retention during economic difficulties.
- **Enhance Competitiveness:** Reduced VAT rates improve the competitiveness of German goods and services in both domestic and international markets, potentially benefiting the country's export-oriented economy.

Example 2: The Goods and Services Tax (GST), implemented in India in 2017, has become a central pillar of the nation's economic resilience (Deshmukh et al., 2022). This landmark tax reform aimed to unify a previously fragmented indirect tax regime, fostering sustainable economic growth and stability, strengthening fiscal sustainability through increased tax revenue collection and reduced compliance costs. The GST successfully subsumed a multitude of state and central indirect taxes, encompassing previously untaxed sectors and expanding the overall tax net (i.e. broadened tax base). This has led to a significant increase in government revenue, bolstering fiscal sustainability and creating resources for critical public investments in infrastructure, education, and healthcare. Furthermore, the GST leverages a robust digital infrastructure and streamlined procedures to simplify tax administration. This reduces compliance burdens for businesses, discourages tax evasion, and fosters a more efficient collection process. Additionally, the digital system facilitates improved tax revenue predictability, enabling more effective fiscal planning.

What is important to point is that the pre-GST system levied taxes on taxes, leading to a cascading effect that inflated product prices. The GST eliminates this distortion, reducing the overall cost of goods and services. This translates into increased competitiveness for Indian businesses in domestic and international markets, stimulating economic activity. Moreover, GST introduced a unified national market by removing inter-state check posts, streamlining the movement of goods across borders. This reduces transportation costs, improves logistical efficiency, and fosters a more integrated national market, ultimately boosting economic activity eliminating cascading effect.

In addition to the above, the digital nature of the GST system enhances transparency in tax administration. Businesses can easily track their tax filings and payments, fostering trust and improving the overall business environment. This transparency also facilitates better monitoring and detection of potential tax evasion.

Despite its significant benefits, the GST faces ongoing challenges such as ensuring robust compliance among small and medium-sized enterprises (SMEs). Additionally, further simplification of the tax code and addressing potential regressivity concerns remain areas for improvement. Continued efforts to refine the GST system and address these challenges are crucial to maximize its positive impact on India's economic resilience.

9.2.3 *The Strategic Importance of Customs Administrations*

Customs administrations serve as the linchpins of international trade, overseeing the movement of goods across borders while ensuring compliance with regulatory frameworks. In an increasingly interconnected world characterized by globalization, technological advancements, and evolving trade dynamics, customs procedures have undergone significant reevaluation. Modern customs administrations play a pivotal role in facilitating trade, enhancing revenue generation, and promoting economic diversification, ultimately contributing to a nation's economic and social resilience.

Elaborating on trade facilitation, a core function of modern customs administrations is to ensure the smooth flow of goods across borders. This not only promotes economic activity but also contributes directly to social resilience by ensuring the timely delivery of essential goods, particularly during crises. By implementing modern trade facilitation measures such as electronic customs clearance systems, risk-based inspections, and advance rulings, customs administrations can significantly reduce clearance times and transaction costs for traders. Initiatives like the World Customs

Organization's (WCO) Revised Kyoto Convention (RKC) provide a valuable framework for harmonizing these procedures globally, further streamlining cross-border trade (Clark & Bernard, 2022).

Customs administrations remain key revenue-generating agencies for governments, collecting duties, taxes, and other levies on imported goods. Effective revenue collection strengthens a nation's fiscal health, creating a crucial buffer for economic shocks. Furthermore, customs play a significant role in combating illicit trade activities, such as smuggling, counterfeiting, and money laundering, which threaten national economies and social welfare (Basu, 2013; Mashiri & Sebele-Mpofu, 2015). By leveraging technology, data analytics, and training customs administrations can enhance their capacity to detect and deter these activities, safeguarding government revenues, protecting domestic industries, and contributing to a more stable economic environment.

Beyond trade facilitation and revenue generation, modern customs administrations can actively promote economic diversification and industrial development. Through the strategic use of trade policy measures such as tariff exemptions, duty drawbacks, and preferential trade agreements, customs can incentivize investment in strategic sectors and promote value-added exports (Hoekman & Nicita, 2018). Additionally, by simplifying procedures, providing trade facilitation assistance, and supporting capacity-building initiatives, customs can empower small and medium-sized enterprises (SMEs) to participate more actively in international trade (Lesser & Moise-Leeman, 2009). Aligning customs policies with national development objectives fosters economic diversification, creating sustainable livelihoods and enhancing a nation's resilience to external challenges in the long term (Pretorius et al., 2021).

While facilitating international trade, generating government revenue, and promoting economic diversification, customs administrations navigate an increasingly intricate landscape. The challenges for the future include:

- **Technological Advancements:** The rapid emergence of disruptive technologies such as blockchain, artificial intelligence (AI), and data analytics necessitates adaptation for customs administrations to maintain operational efficiency and effectiveness. Potential strategic solutions could include electronic customs clearance systems to streamline procedures, blockchain-based platforms for secure and transparent trade documentation, and AI-driven risk assessment tools for enhanced targeting and resource allocation (Chang et al., 2020).

- **Evolving Trade Dynamics:** The globalization of supply chains, the proliferation of free trade agreements, and the emergence of new trade routes demand agility from customs administrations to effectively regulate cross-border trade flows. From a strategy point of view, we could suggest proactive monitoring of trade patterns, coupled with strengthening partnerships with trade associations, industry stakeholders, and international organizations to foster knowledge exchange. Also, investment in trade facilitation initiatives like single window systems and mutual recognition arrangements could enhance efficiency and competitiveness (Grainger, 2008).
- **Resource Constraints:** Limited funding, inadequate infrastructure, and shortages of skilled personnel can hinder the implementation of modern customs practices and effective responses to emerging challenges. Trying to optimize resource allocation, customs administrations could prioritize investments in areas with the highest return on investment, such as technology upgrades, capacity building, and risk management systems (Kim & Kim, 2020). Further, investing in workforce development, training, and retention programs to build a skilled and adaptable customs workforce could be seen as a strategic sustainable capability for the future.
- **Security Threats:** The increasingly complex nature of security threats like terrorism, smuggling, and organized crime demands robust border security measures from customs administrations. A way forward could include the adoption of a risk-based approach to border security (Drobot et al., 2017), focusing on: a) enhancing collaboration with law enforcement agencies, intelligence organizations, and international partners, b) investing in advanced screening technologies like non-intrusive inspection systems and radiation detection equipment, and c) implementing robust customs enforcement measures, such as targeted inspections, intelligence-driven operations, and interagency cooperation.

Beyond overcoming immediate challenges, building long-term resilience is crucial for customs administrations (Valamalua et al., 2022). This involves:

- **Fostering a Culture of Innovation:** Encouraging continuous improvement and adaptation within the organization.
- **Investing in Disaster Preparedness:** Implementing business continuity planning and crisis management capabilities.
- **Promoting Transparency and Accountability:** Building trust with stakeholders through ethical operations.

By embracing these strategies, customs administrations can effectively navigate the complex landscape of the modern world. Their ability to overcome challenges and build resilience is essential for fostering economic development and social prosperity in the globalized era. This paper underscores the critical role of customs administrations in facilitating trade flows, generating revenue, and promoting economic diversification. Their continued success hinges on their ability to adapt, innovate, and build resilience in the face of a constantly evolving global landscape.

9.2.4 *Interplay Between Tax and Customs Administrations: Exploring Synergies and Collaborations in Bolstering Resilience*

Depending on the structure decided at a country level, Tax and Customs administrations are either separate or unified entities. Undoubtedly, they play a vital role in a country's financial health. As government agencies, they can achieve much more by working together. Closer cooperation between tax and customs can strengthen a country's ability to weather economic challenges and improve how it collects revenue (Yasui, 2009). When they combine their strengths and resources, tax and customs administrations become more effective, promote better compliance with regulations, and contribute to a more resilient economy overall.

Even though they have different jobs and ways of doing things, they ultimately share the same goals and face similar challenges. In today's fast-paced, globalized world, it's more important than ever for tax and customs to work together closely. This collaboration allows them to better address new threats, encourage businesses to follow the rules, and collect more revenue. Benefits of this synergy could take the form of:

- **Sharing Information:** Tax and customs can learn a lot from each other's data. By sharing information and using powerful data analysis tools, they can identify patterns of non-compliance, target enforcement efforts more effectively, and use their resources more wisely. They can also work together on investigations and take joint enforcement actions, leading to better results and higher compliance rates.
- **Simplifying Procedures:** Making things easier for businesses is another way tax and customs can collaborate. By aligning their procedures, regulations, and paperwork requirements, they can streamline the process of importing and exporting goods. This reduces the burden on businesses and makes international trade more efficient. Additionally, using common standards and electronic systems for sharing data can create a seamless connection between tax and customs, making it easier for businesses to operate and boosting economic growth.
- **Building Skills and Sharing Knowledge:** When tax and customs administrations work together to train their staff and share knowledge, everyone benefits. By combining resources and expertise, governments can provide training programs, technical assistance, and online platforms for information exchange. This strengthens the skills and abilities of tax and customs officials. Additionally, creating joint task forces and cross-functional teams encourages cooperation and innovation within both administrations.
- **Planning and Working Together Strategically:** Effective coordination and joint planning between tax and customs are crucial for aligning tax policies, trade regulations, and enforcement priorities. By talking to each other regularly and consulting on policies, tax and customs authorities can identify areas where they can work together, address new challenges, and develop clear strategies for collecting revenue and facilitating trade. Establishing joint working groups or interagency committees can further this cross-sectoral collaboration and ensure consistent implementation of policies across different government agencies.

However, for this collaboration to reach its full potential, there needs to be political will, a commitment from institutions, and ongoing investment in building skills and creating infrastructure for information sharing. By adopting a holistic approach to managing government finances and promoting cooperation between agencies, governments can create a more resilient, transparent, and efficient tax and customs administration system, ultimately contributing to inclusive growth and a stronger economy.

9.3 Building Institutional Capacity for Resilience

9.3.1 Strategies for Enhancing the Institutional Capacity of Tax and Customs Administrations

Underscoring the pivotal role of tax and customs administrations in effective fiscal governance through revenue collection, trade regulation, and enforcement of fiscal policies—directly influencing a nation's economic health—we should acknowledge that the effectiveness of these administrations hinges on their institutional capacity to adapt to evolving environments, leverage technology strategically, and engage stakeholders constructively (Junquera-Varela et al., 2022; Meyer & Peng, 2016). The imperative of institutional capacity dictates that the ability of tax and customs administrations to fulfill their targets effectively is contingent upon robust institutional capacity. The latter refers to the organization's ability to adapt to evolving contexts, leverage technology for efficiency gains, and engage stakeholders meaningfully. By strengthening institutional capacity, these administrations can enhance operational efficiency, promote taxpayer and trader compliance, and ultimately, bolster revenue mobilization efforts.

Drawing upon best practices from diverse contexts, we preconceive **organizational development** as a strategic way forward. Streamlining organizational structures by clearly defining roles and responsibilities, and reducing bureaucratic layers, can enhance efficiency and effectiveness. Flatter hierarchies and decentralized decision-making can foster agility, responsiveness, and a culture of innovation within the organization. Implementing performance management systems, such as key performance indicators (KPIs) and performance-based budgeting, can enhance accountability, transparency, and results orientation. By setting clear objectives, monitoring progress, and rewarding high performance, organizations can cultivate a culture of excellence and continuous improvement.

Investing in **capacity-building initiatives, training programs, and skills development workshops** equips tax and customs officials with the necessary technical expertise and professional competence. Specialized training in tax law, customs procedures, risk management, and technology adoption can improve operational effectiveness and regulatory compliance. Developing talent management strategies, career development pathways, and competitive incentive schemes can attract, motivate, and retain skilled personnel. Recognizing and rewarding excellence, providing opportunities for career advancement, and fostering a supportive work environment are crucial for retaining high-performing employees.

Modernizing information systems by adopting electronic filing systems, data analytics, and risk assessment tools can significantly improve the efficiency and accuracy of tax and customs operations. Investments in modern information systems, cloud computing platforms, and digital infrastructure can facilitate real-time data exchange, streamline processes, and enhance decision-making capabilities. **Leveraging technology for efficiency and innovation** is a promising way forward. Embracing automation, artificial intelligence (AI), and robotic process automation (RPA) can streamline routine tasks, reduce processing times, and minimize human error within tax and customs administrations. Furthermore, fostering a culture of innovation, experimentation, and knowledge sharing can stimulate creativity and drive continuous improvement in service delivery.

Strategic planning and stakeholder collaboration is another promising area for development in the future. Formulating strategic plans, roadmaps, and performance targets can provide a clear direction and sense of purpose for tax and customs administrations. Engaging stakeholders, including government agencies, business associations, civil society organizations, and international partners, in the strategic planning process fosters alignment with national development priorities and promotes ownership and accountability. Establishing stakeholder consultation mechanisms, public–private partnerships, and multi-stakeholder platforms can enhance collaboration, transparency, and trust between tax and customs administrations and their stakeholders. By involving stakeholders in policy formulation, implementation, and evaluation, organizations can build consensus, leverage resources, and promote inclusive decision-making.

By embracing a holistic approach to capacity building and institutional strengthening, governments can promote good governance, enhance public trust, and ultimately achieve their development objectives.

9.3.2 *Enhancing Institutional Resilience in Tax and Customs Administrations Through Capacity Building and Training*

Capacity building and training programs provide tax and customs officials with the specialized knowledge and skills necessary to execute their duties effectively, **enhancing their technical expertise**. Training initiatives can encompass a wide range of topics, including tax law, customs procedures, risk management, and technology adoption. By investing in targeted training and continuous skill development, tax and customs administrations can improve compliance rates, minimize errors, and enhance operational efficiency within the organization.

Robust capacity-building programs play a crucial role in **fostering compliance** with tax and customs regulations, and in **strengthening enforcement** efforts. Training initiatives can focus on enhancing officials' understanding of complex regulations, refining audit techniques, and effectively detecting fraudulent activities. Equipping officials with the necessary tools and knowledge to identify non-compliance and enforce regulations effectively allows capacity-building programs to contribute significantly to both revenue mobilization and trade facilitation endeavors.

In today's rapidly evolving landscape**, innovation and adaptability** are essential for Tax and Customs administrations to remain resilient and responsive to emerging challenges. Capacity-building programs can cultivate a culture of innovation by encouraging officials to explore new ideas, technologies, and approaches to service delivery. Additionally, training initiatives can equip officials with the skills and confidence needed to embrace change and adapt to evolving circumstances effectively.

Effective **leadership and management** are critical for driving organizational change and fostering a culture of excellence within Tax and Customs administrations. Capacity-building programs can target the development of leadership skills, strategic planning abilities, and performance management techniques. By investing in the development of future leaders and managers, Tax and Customs administrations can build resilience and ensure continuity in leadership amidst changing priorities and circumstances.

Highlighting best practices on capacity building, we could refer to:

- **World Customs Organization (WCO) Capacity Building Program:** The WCO offers a comprehensive suite of capacity-building initiatives, including training workshops, technical assistance missions, and e-learning platforms specifically designed to enhance the skills and capabilities of customs officials worldwide.

- **International Monetary Fund (IMF) Tax Administration Diagnostic Assessment Tool (TADAT):** TADAT serves as a diagnostic tool designed to assess the performance of tax administrations and pinpoint areas for capacity building and improvement. By leveraging TADAT assessments, countries can develop tailored capacity-building programs to address specific weaknesses and challenges within their tax administration systems.
- The Organization for Economic Co-operation and Development (OECD): The **OECD's Forum on Tax Administration (FTA)** fosters cooperation among tax authorities and promotes the exchange of best practices in tax policy and administration.

Capacity building and training are fundamental components of building institutional resilience within tax and customs administrations. By investing in the skills, knowledge, and capabilities of their officials, tax and customs administrations can enhance operational effectiveness, promote compliance, and adapt to evolving challenges and opportunities. Furthermore, fostering a culture of continuous learning, innovation, and leadership development is essential for building resilient and effective institutions capable of delivering on their mandates and contributing to sustainable development goals.

The complexities and rapid evolution of the modern tax and customs environment necessitate a paradigm shift in how administrations train their workforces. Traditional, siloed training methods struggle to equip staff with the comprehensive skillset and adaptability demanded by today's dynamic landscape. Thus, we suggest a transformative solution; i.e. the learning organization model. By fostering a culture of continuous learning, knowledge sharing, and adaptation, Tax and Customs administrations can cultivate a highly skilled and resilient workforce capable of thriving in an ever-changing environment.

Resource constraints and limited budgets often restrict the scope and frequency of traditional training programs. These siloed approaches, focusing on specific departments or tasks, impede the development of a holistic understanding of Tax and Customs administration processes. They also hinder collaboration and knowledge sharing across functional areas, hindering the development of critical competencies needed in today's environment.

To navigate the complexities of the contemporary landscape, Tax and Customs administrations require a workforce equipped with **a broader skillset**. This includes not only in-depth tax law knowledge and technical expertise, but also data analysis, critical thinking, problem-solving, and effective communication skills. Fostering collaboration across departments and with external stakeholders necessitates strong interpersonal skills as well.

Transforming Tax and Customs administrations into a learning organization requires a fundamental **shift in mindset from both staff and leadership**. Traditional views of training as a one-time event or a disruption to workflow must be replaced with a growth mindset that values continuous learning and adaptation as essential for success. Effective communication, leadership commitment, and demonstrating the clear benefits of a more comprehensive training approach are crucial in overcoming resistance to change.

Transforming into **a learning organization** fosters a sustainable environment for continuous adaptation and improvement. This model is characterized by the following core principles:

- **Learning as a Core Value:** Continuous professional development becomes a fundamental value embedded within the organization's ethos. Learning is no longer a peripheral activity, but an essential element for individual and organizational success.
- **Knowledge Democratization:** Collaboration and knowledge exchange are actively promoted, dismantling departmental silos and fostering a more collaborative environment. Best practices and expertise are readily shared across teams, cultivating collective intelligence that benefits the entire organization.
- **Diverse Learning Opportunities:** A variety of training methods cater to different learning styles and preferences. This may include traditional classroom courses, flexible and accessible online platforms, and peer-to-peer learning initiatives that leverage the collective expertise of the workforce.
- **Performance Measurement and Feedback Loop:** The impact of training programs is regularly evaluated through performance metrics and feedback mechanisms. This data is used to refine and adapt learning opportunities, ensuring they remain relevant, effective, and aligned with the organization's evolving strategic objectives.

By embracing the learning organization model, Tax and Customs administrations can cultivate a highly skilled and adaptable workforce. This translates to a more responsive and resilient administration, ultimately leading to a higher quality of service for stakeholders in a dynamic and ever-changing environment.

9.4 Conclusion

This chapter provides a comprehensive overview of the strategic significance of Tax and Customs administrations in fostering social and economic resilience, with a particular focus on the role of training in enhancing their effectiveness and impact. Tax and Customs administrations play a multifaceted role in promoting social and economic resilience. By effectively managing revenue collection, facilitating-promoting trade, and upholding a fair tax system (enhancing investment attractiveness), these administrations contribute to a more stable (mitigating financial risks), equitable (ensuring equitable distribution of resources), and prosperous society combating tax evasion and corruption and facilitating social security contributions. As the global landscape continues to evolve, Tax and Customs administrations must adapt their strategies to remain effective in the face of emerging challenges. The discussion made in the chapter suggests that the effectiveness of such organizations hinges on the competence and expertise of its workforce. Considering technological advancements, evolving legal frameworks, globalization and trade complexities, and shifting demographics (mainly retirement of experienced personnel), training and capacity-building initiatives should:

- Focus on soft skills apart from technical expertise.
- Blend learning approaches offering flexibility to cater for diverse learning styles.
- Utilize knowledge-sharing platforms to facilitate peer-to-peer learning and best practice sharing.
- Incorporate latest research and best practices, which are shared among administrations. This allows for access to expertise through the development of joint training programs.

By adopting a **learning organization** approach, Tax and Customs administrations can become more agile and better equipped to handle these challenges. Embracing a learning organization model equips them with the agility and capabilities necessary to navigate these complexities effectively. A learning organization fosters the development of resilient leadership, a critical element in navigating change and ensuring long-term success. By prioritizing continuous learning and improvement, Tax and Customs administrations can demonstrably enhance their effectiveness and efficiency.

Continuous Professional Development (CPD) is equally essential for tax professionals at all levels. Prioritizing CPD ensures that tax and customs professionals remain current in their knowledge and skillsets, adapt to evolving regulations, uphold ethical standards within the profession, foster innovation within their teams, and maintain their competitiveness. By prioritizing continuous learning and development at both the individual and organizational level, administrations can cultivate a skilled and knowledgeable workforce capable of addressing the evolving challenges and contemporary complexities.

Despite their potential benefits, tax and customs policies and administration strategies face significant challenges, including tax evasion, avoidance, and administrative capacity constraints. The evolving nature of the global economy, with trends like the rise of the gig economy and the challenges of taxing independent contractors and platform workers, necessitates innovative policy responses. Demographic shifts, such as aging populations in many developed countries, also pose challenges as they put pressure on social safety nets funded in part by tax revenue. Future research should focus on identifying effective tax policy reforms and administration strategies that promote economic stability, foster growth, and address emerging challenges such as digitalization, globalization, and environmental sustainability (e.g. exploring carbon taxes or tax breaks for investments in renewable energy as strategies to address environmental concerns).

References

Basu, G. (2013). The role of transnational smuggling operations in illicit supply chains. *Journal of Transportation Security, 6*, 315–328.

Baudisch, V., & Neuenkirch, M. (2023). Costly, but (relatively) ineffective? An assessment of Germany's temporary VAT rate reduction during the COVID-19 pandemic, *Cesifo Working Papers*. https://www.cesifo.org/DocDL/cesifo1_wp10417.pdf

Calabuig, V., & Olcina, G. (2023). The elite, inequality and the emergence of progressive taxation. *European Journal of Political Economy, 79*, 102433.

Chang, Y., Iakovou, E., & Shi, W. (2020). Blockchain in global supply chains and cross border trade: A critical synthesis of the state-of-the-art, challenges and opportunities. *International Journal of Production Research, 58*(7), 2082–2099.

Clark, J., & Bernard, D. (2022). Customs in a world of enhanced trade facilitation. *Customs Matters: Strengthening Customs Administration in a Changing World, 1*, 95.

Deshmukh, A. K., Mohan, A., & Mohan, I. (2022). Goods and services tax (GST) implementation in India: A SAP–LAP–Twitter analytic perspective. *Global Journal of Flexible Systems Management, 23*(2), 165–183.

Drobot, E. V., Klevleeva, A. R., Afonin, P. N., & Gamidullaev, S. N. (2017). Risk management in customs control. *Ekonomika Regiona = Economy of Regions*, (2), 550–558.

Fuest, C., Neumeier, F., & Stöhlker, D. (2024). The pass-through of temporary VAT rate cuts: Evidence from German supermarket retail. *International Tax and Public Finance*, 1–47.

Fung, M. (2020). Developing a robust system for upskilling and reskilling the workforce: Lessons from the SkillsFuture movement in Singapore. *Anticipating and Preparing for Emerging Skills and Jobs: Key Issues, Concerns, and Prospects*, 321–327.

Grainger, A. (2008). Customs and trade facilitation: From concepts to implementation. *World Customs Journal, 2*(1), 17–30.

Head, K., Mayer, T., and Melitz, M. (2024). The Laffer curve for rules of origin. *Journal of International Economics, 150* https://doi.org/10.1016/j.jinteco.2024.103911

Hoekman, B., & Nicita, A. (2018). Non-tariff measures and trade facilitation: WTO disciplines and policy space for development. *Non-Tariff Measures, 13.*

Hosie, P., (2006). *Human resource development: Proactive preparation to manage crises* (Working Paper Series: no. 2006-2), Curtin University of Technology, School of Management.

Junquera-Varela, R. F., Lucas-Mas, C. O., Krsul, I., Calderon Yksic, V. O., & Arce Rodriguez, P. (2022). *Digital transformation of tax and customs administrations.*

Kim, S. B., & Kim, D. (2020). ICT implementation and its effect on public organizations: The case of digital customs and risk management in Korea. *Sustainability, 12*(8), 3421.

Lesser, C., & Moisé-Leeman, E. (2009). *Informal cross-border trade and trade facilitation reform in Sub-Saharan Africa* (OECD Trade Policy Working Paper No. 86).

Mashiri, E., & Sebele-Mpofu, F. Y. (2015). Illicit trade, economic growth and the role of Customs: A literature review. *World Customs Journal, 9*(2), 38–50.

Meyer, K. E., & Peng, M. W. (2016). Theoretical foundations of emerging economy business research. *Journal of International Business Studies, 47*, 3–22.

Mezirow, J. (2009). Transformative learning theory. In J. Mezirow, & E. W. Taylor (Eds.), *Transformative Learning in Practice: Insights from Community Workplace, and Higher Education* (pp. 18–32). Jossey-Bass.

Pretorius, O., Drewes, E., Van Aswegen, M., & Malan, G. (2021). A policy approach towards achieving regional economic resilience in developing countries: Evidence from the SADC. *Sustainability, 13*(5), 2674.

Settembre-Blundo, D., González-Sánchez, R., Medina-Salgado, S., & García-Muiña, F. E. (2021). Flexibility and resilience in corporate decision making: A new sustainability-based risk management system in uncertain times. *Global Journal of Flexible Systems Management, 22*(Suppl 2), 107–132.

Schnepfleitner, F. M., & Ferreira, M. P. (2021). Transformative learning theory—Is it time to add a fourth core element? *Journal of Educational Studies and Multidisciplinary Approaches, 1*(1), 40–49.

Su, S., Qamruzzaman, M., & Karim, S. (2023). Charting a sustainable future: The impact of economic policy, environmental taxation, innovation, and natural resources on clean energy consumption. *Sustainability, 15*(18), 13585.

United Nations Department of Economic and Social Affairs. (2024, 4 10). Retrieved from https://sdgs.un.org/goals

Valamalua, A., Mohanakumar, S., Ranathunga, I., & Medonza, S. (2022). Bolstering resilience in Customs: The wellbeing of our people. *World Customs Journal, 16*(1).

Yasui, T. (2009). Cooperation between customs and tax administrations: Lessons learned from revenue authorities. *World Customs Organization Research Paper*, (5).

Zhou, Y., Yang, J., & Jia, Z. (2023). Optimizing energy efficiency investments in steel firms: A real options model considering carbon trading and tax cuts during challenging economic conditions. *Resources Policy, 85*, 104042.

CHAPTER 10

Development of State Infrastructure with the Involvement of the Private Sector

Ioannis Chatzopoulos, Andreas Kontos, and Christos Kallandranis

10.1 Introduction

Public–Private Partnerships (PPPs hereafter) do play a very important role in today's economic activities, aiming at giving an added value to the projects undertaken (European Investment Bank, 2022). They are crucial for the projects' completion, because both the private sector and the public sector are in need of one another to complete a project. That is why interest in PPPs is constantly growing today and more and more policymakers around the world choose this form of cooperation.

I. Chatzopoulos · A. Kontos
Democritus University of Thrace, Komotini, Greece
e-mail: ichatzop@econ.duth.gr

C. Kallandranis (✉)
University of West Attica, Athens, Greece
e-mail: chriskal@uniwa.gr

A. Hyz (ed.), *The Role of the Public Sector in Building Social and Economic Resilience*,
https://doi.org/10.1007/978-3-031-67702-1_10

The research aim of this paper is to present the PPP projects in Greece and their situation, while comparing them to other European countries. There is a significant gap in the literature, as not many researchers have previously tried to compare Greece with neighboring countries. The fact is that the public sector may not be able to undertake a capital-intensive project, because it may be indebted or it may not have the appropriate means or it may lack in well-educated human capital in order to be successful, and as a result, there is the need of the private sector (Ministry of Economy, Infrastructure, Shipping & Tourism, 2019). The private sector then offers its funds, human capital, expertise and means for the development and operation of a project, thus proving the need for cooperation (Aravosis, 2018). The structure of this chapter is as follows. Section 10.2 reviews the relevant literature. Section 10.3 analyzes the methodology that has been used to conduct empirical research on the topic, while it emphasizes on the main research areas and it covers the main expected results. The fourth section presents the main findings of the research. Finally, there will be concluding remarks on the whole research effort, and the author will try to interpret the results as well as provide recommendations for the coming years.

10.2 Literature Review

10.2.1 Definition

To begin with, it would be appropriate to present a widely accepted definition of the PPPs in order to make their subject more comprehensible. The Public–Private Partnerships are a kind of cooperation between a government agency and a privately held company that can be used to finance, build and operate projects. They are contracts and agreements, usually long-term, which are concluded between a public and a private body, for the purpose of executing projects and providing services (Ministry of Economy, Infrastructure, Shipping & Tourism, 2022).

Public & Private Sector Partnerships are an important reform in the field of infrastructure creation and the provision of public services, and as a pillar of a new development model, they contribute significantly to the development of the economy and society, improving the efficiency of Public Sector resources.

They relate to complex forms of public–private partnerships with long-term commitments, which, as proven by the worldwide experience, aim at improving the quality of services provided by the state to the citizen with different methods of the private sector to the public, in order to boost productive investment as well as to create new jobs (Aravosis, 2018).

10.2.2 Advantages

The PPCs have been gaining ground on economic activities, because they can offer some advantages which are unique and can help both sides, the public and the private sector. To begin with, the private equity which will be chosen for a specific project can provide finance, secure funds which will be allocated for the completion of the project (Rocca, 2017). This is the best case for a poor government which lacks money for public expenditure, while at the same time the very same government can save a significant amount of money, which could be used for other purposes on other industries (OECD, 2012). Furthermore, as the project goes on, more and more funds surely will be needed and the private sector seems more reliable and efficient to perform this kind of investment, rather than waiting the bureaucratic public procedures which will result in an underinvestment (Cuttaree & Mandri-Perrott, 2011).

A long-term contract like a PPP will require a more comprehensive, detailed and successful planning and management (Bregant & Dubovske, 2015). The private sector can adjust more easily and can have greater flexibility in adjusting its resources, such as capital, human resources, materials and equipment, to a constantly changing situation which can, notably, ensure timely performance (Grimsey & Cotter, 2020). Furthermore, the risk management will have greater performance, experience proves that PPP contracts are more efficient to meet deadlines, and cost predictions than any other form of conventional contracts (Corbacho & Schwartz, 2008). This will work again in favor of the public sector improving the efficiency of the project. The private equity will additionally bring a great form of innovation, as the long-term PPP contract will provide an incentive to find alternative solutions to meet excessive requirements. Research and development activities (R&D) will take place and will allow the improvement of quality and efficiency (World Bank, 2022).

In addition, a PPP contract can always act as an incentive for public sector reforms (OECD, 2010). Due to the PPP, the public sector will act as a regulator and will concentrate on service planning instead of being involved in day-to-day services (Marinelli, 2019). Furthermore, there will be more transparency, as a PPP will show the whole cost of the project, there will be no hidden costs and additionally there will be increased accountability as everyone involved in cost planning and fund expenditure will have to justify their choices (Marcelo et al., 2017).

10.3 Methodology

Relevant research on PPPs and their impact can be done by approaching a qualitative or a quantitative method. The quantitative method may include analyses of data, statistics and any other numerical information an author may choose to use. On the other hand, the qualitative method may include theory and political and economic considerations as well as the benefits and the outcome of any project an author wants to include in their research. For the purpose of this paper, a combination of these two methods will be used, with a primary focus on the qualitative method due to the nature of the subject of this paper. The quantitative method will be used mainly for the presentation and analysis of some statistics and to compare Greece with other major European Countries. The data collection will be done through reports from the European Institutions and from National Ministries.

A researcher or a scholar on the field should try to pursue a research and answers on some crucial questions, which could be regarded as follows. First of all, the first research question is about the literature review of the paper, which should include all the appropriate theory as far as the PPPs are concerned. Therefore, the definition of the PPP is included, as well as its typology and its advantages that it may bring to the overall economy of a country. Furthermore, the qualitative research will focus on the PPP projects in Greece from a historical point of view and today's projects as well. To further understand, the paper researches the sectors of the PPP in Greece and their funding. Finally, a comparison will be done in this paper, in order to identify where Greece stands compared to its neighboring emerging countries. To deepen, it is crucial that detailed sectors, which attract PPP, be presented as well as their funds.

The research is expected to show that on the one hand Greece has started to implement PPP projects relatively soon and it needs to further accelerate their implementation, but on the other hand Greece has achieved more than its neighboring countries with similar economic structure. As far as the sectors are concerned, transportation is expected to attract the most PPP projects and the most funds.

10.4 Results

10.4.1 History

The beginning of the PPP in Greece dates back to 1993, when the first regulatory framework was implemented (Ministry of Economy, Infrastructure, Shipping & Tourism, 2019). Since then, there have been many changes in the framework, which have introduced a number of significant legislative changes. For example, it was in 2004 that the first legislative introduction of incentives for the private sector took place. This was important, because until 2004, PPP was not widely accepted or performed and since that year there has been a shift toward that direction.

Greece has been using the form of Partnerships with the private sector since 1993, however the first significant projects were concluded in the years 2002–2004 (Roumboutsos, 2016). These were the bridge Rio–Antirio, the International Airport of Athens and the Highway Attiki Odos. These were the first successfully implemented projects and they were all supported and funded by the European Investment Bank (EIB), which provided significant and crucial aid for their completion (Ministry of Economy, Infrastructure, Shipping & Tourism, 2019). Today, all of these three projects are in total operation and they are properly functioning giving an added value to the Greek economy.

In addition, the second wave of projects that took place in the following years were regarding huge highway roads, which were completely underdeveloped in the country. As was the case before, with the three first projects, the highway projects were again receiving significant funds from the European Union (European Investment Bank, 2022).

It was in 2005 that the current law 3389/2005 was put into force, which further accelerated the processes. There were incentives introduced for the participation of private companies, auditing and licensing processes were reduced, while there were more funding possibilities put into place.

10.4.2 Overview

According to data taken from the European Investment Bank, the PPP projects in Greece until today are 25, implemented from 1993 to 2021. The total amount of these projects is 14.7 billion Euros and the most important and attractive sectors, as can be seen on Fig. 10.1, are transport, energy and environment, education, telecommunications and public order and safety (European Investment Bank, 2022).

Today there are efforts for 11 more PPP projects totally accounting for 1.5 billion Euros, which are expected to be finalized in the coming five years. They include highways in the Peloponnese and in Crete, telecommunications (broadband infrastructure) in Northern Greece, healthcare buildings in Athens and school buildings and waste management projects in the Dodecanese.

Figure 10.2 is important in order to understand where the funds came from and it is an important aspect because of the very indebted public sector in Greece. The funds come mainly from the European Union via its basic financing schemes, like National Strategic Reference Framework (NSRF), and from private funds, for example loans from the Greek banking system and the private companies themselves. Furthermore, an important amount comes from the European Investment Bank and the Joint European Support for Sustainable Investment in City Areas (JESSICA) of the European Commission, and the European Investment Bank (EIB), in cooperation with the Council of Europe Development Bank (CEB).

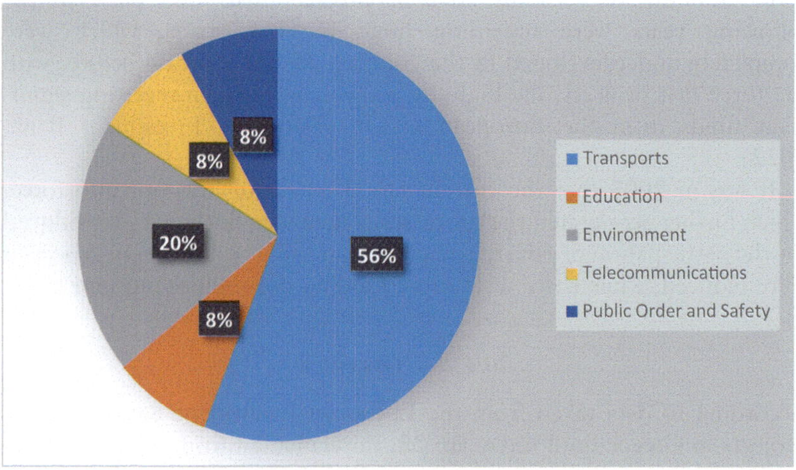

Fig. 10.1 Number of European PPP projects by sector in Greece (*Source* European Investment Bank [2022])

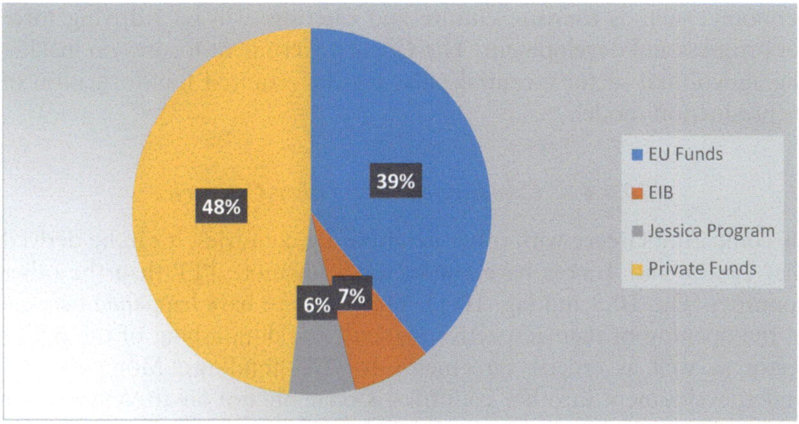

Fig. 10.2 Source of the funds used to finance the projects, since 2000 (*Source* Ministry of economy, infrastructure, shipping & tourism [2019])

10.4.3 A Hydroelectric PPP

As an example of a PPP, the project of Minagiotiko Pilou Dam can be presented in order to show how PPP is conducted in Greece. There has been an increased interest and major tenders totaling more than €1 billion related to the construction of dams and irrigation projects—water supply through PPP. If the "Water 2.0" program (Ministry of Rural Development) is to be added, the projects include an investment program of approximately 2.5 billion euros, as far as the construction sector is concerned, and more than 5 billion euros if the maintenance and operation costs for 25 years and the availability payments are taken into account.

Among others there is the Minagiotiko Pilou Dam, a project which will create a reservoir with a capacity of 11,000,000 cubic meters of water, from which 35,000 acres will be irrigated and 3,500 farmers will be served. It has an estimated cost of approximately 100 million euros and upon its completion, it is expected to grow the agricultural production in the region.

With this important infrastructure project, the Greek government aims to launch a dynamic development activity focusing on rural development. Thus, the necessary conditions for the primary sector to grow are being developed and the necessary synergies with other dynamic sectors of the economy, such as tourism, culture and catering, will be a driving force for progress and development. The Greek government focuses on making the agricultural sector a central pillar for the required transformation of its production model.

10.4.4 Comparison with Other Countries

By comparing Greece with other neighboring countries, it can be derived that Greece and Turkey have conducted a lot more PPP than the other countries (Fig. 10.3 and Fig. 10.4). This seems to have happened because of the opening of their respective markets, the diminishing of the public sector as well as crucial agreements for EU fundings. Moreover, the underdevelopment in other countries is certainly not an attractive factor for private investments. Greece has achieved more PPP in comparison to Turkey, especially for the smaller of its economy, due to the importance of the private industry in the Greek economy. As far as the sectors are concerned, transportations, healthcare and education are the most attractive sectors. Energy and environment are crucial for in the struggle against climate change, however they do not seem to be performing well. There needs to be a whole change in the energy landscape, especially in the production of electricity and to this manner, the Russia–Ukraine war could be a possibility, as European countries will try to diversify their resources and PPP could help build more environmentally friendly production means.

10.5 Concluding Remarks

The paper examines the overview of the PPP in Greece and compares them to other neighboring developing countries. The findings prove that the main sector is transport, and especially constructing highways, while serious projects are completed in waste management, buildings and telecommunications. In comparison with other countries, either EU members or not, Greece has achieved serious progress. For the present analysis, the choice included the neighboring developing countries, in order to show where Greece stands in comparison to them.

For the coming years, there is still a lot of work to be done, if Greece wants to fully take advantage of this scheme. For example, a major concern for not implementing PPP is the whole procedures which cost time and money. Moreover, the slow liberalization process does not create

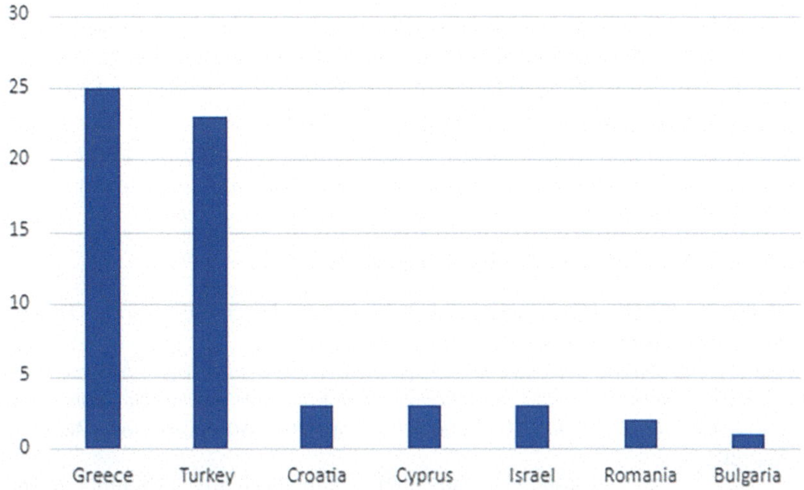

Fig. 10.3 Total number of PPP projects in selected countries (*Source* European Investment Bank [2022])

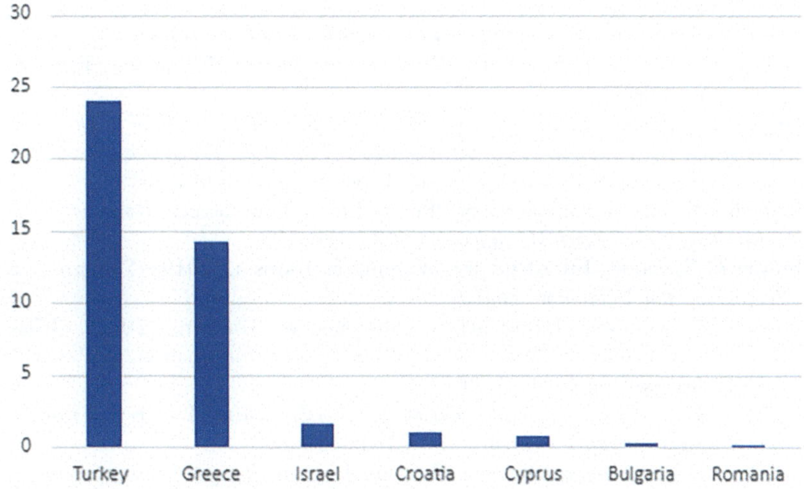

Fig. 10.4 Total amount of money used for PPP in selected countries (*Source* European Investment Bank [2022])

a private friendly investment environment to attract funds. Another major concern to be addressed is the financing problems, because banks are sort of funds, thus not being able to finance many projects. Lack of finance is a serious problem which affects many economic aspects and as a result PPPs do always find drawbacks in their final implementation. These three concerns must be solved to further accelerate PPP implementation.

References

Aravosis, K. (2018). Συμπράξεις Δημόσιου και Ιδιωτικού Τομέα. *Εθνικό Μετσόβιο Πολυτεχνείο.*

Bregant, L., & Dubovske, D. (2015). *Comparative analysis of lessons learned from recent development in implementation of public private partnership projects in the western Balkan region*. Regional School of Public Administration (ReSPA). WP 2015.

Corbacho, A., & Schwartz, G. (2008). PPPs and Fiscal risks: Should governments worry? In *Public investment and PPPs—Addressing infrastructure challenges and managing Fiscal Risks*. IMF Publication.

Cuttaree, V., & Mandri-Perrott, C. (2011). *Benefits and Risks of PPP*. Elibrary: World Bank.

European Investment Bank. (2022). *PPP statistics, EPEC data portal*.

Grimsey, D., & Cotter, S. (2020). *Where to now for the PPP Model?* Ernst & Young Australia.

Marcelo, D., House, S., Mandri-Perrott, C., & Schwartz, J. (2017). *Do countries learn from experience in infrastructure PPP? PPP practice and contract cancellation* (Policy Research Working Paper 8054). World Bank.

Marinelli, M. (2019). Evaluation of PPP road projects in Greece. *Built Environment Project and Asset Management, 9*(2), 186–198.

Ministry of Economy, Infrastructure, Shipping & Tourism. (2019). Συμπράξεις Δημοσίου και Ιδιωτικού Τομέα.

Ministry of Economy, Infrastructure, Shipping & Tourism. (2022). *What is PPP?* Available at http://www.sdit.gov.gr/en/information/PPP/what-is-PPP. Accessed on June 23, 2022.

OECD. (2010). *Dedicated public-private partnership units: A survey of institutional and governance structures*. OECD Publishing.

OECD. (2012). *Recommendation of the council on principles for public governance of public-private partnerships*. OECD Publishing.

Rocca, M. D. (2017). The rising advantage of public-private partnerships. *McKinsey*. Available at https://www.mckinsey.com/industries/private-equity-and-principal-investors/our-insights/the-rising-advantage-of-public-private-partnerships. Accessed on June 25, 2022.

Roumboutsos, A. (2016). Public private partnerships in transport infrastructure. *Transport Reviews*, 36(2), pp. 167–169.

World Bank. (2022). *Public-private partnerships*, overview. Available at https://www.worldbank.org/en/topic/publicprivatepartnerships/overview. Accessed on September 6, 2023.

CHAPTER 11

A Methodology for Measuring Job Satisfaction in the Public Sector

Andreas Alexopoulos and Evanthia Skliopidou

11.1 Introduction

Job satisfaction has been a subject of research since 1911 (Taylor, 1967). Many research studies in the past have attempted to demonstrate that job satisfaction influences the functioning of organizations and the behavior of employees as individuals. Higher levels of job satisfaction improve the everyday working life of the employees, positively affect their personal lives, and provide motivation to align with the organizational goals and adhere to culture and regulations (Hyz, 2010).

While previous discussions have focused on examining the link between job satisfaction and performance, the focus of contemporary studies is to

A. Alexopoulos (✉)
Department of Accounting and Finance,
University of West Attica, Athens, Greece
e-mail: a.alexopoulos@uniwa.gr

E. Skliopidou
Court of First Instance of Athens, Ministry of Justice, Athens, Greece
e-mail: e.skliopidou@protodikeio-athinon.gov.gr

A. Hyz (ed.), *The Role of the Public Sector in Building Social and Economic Resilience*,
https://doi.org/10.1007/978-3-031-67702-1_11

model and analyze the variables that influence the relationship between job satisfaction and performance. A question that the astute reader will inevitably pose is: What is the relationship between the resilience of an organization and job satisfaction? The most obvious way to define resilience is as the ability of an organization to withstand challenging conditions (Barasa et al., 2018). In fact, over the years there has been a plethora of definitions but a growing number of studies approach resilience as having multiple dimensions (Duit, 2016). In their paper Barasa et al. (2018) identify nine factors that shape the resilience of an organization. Among these factors human capital is recognized as one of the most important.

For the reasons stated above the main objective of the current research is to investigate the factors that affect job satisfaction in public institutions and more specifically in the Court of First Instance of Athens.

The chapter consists of seven sections. In the first section a theoretical context and a brief literature review are provided. The second section explains the data collection process and provides information about the content and the structure of the questionnaire. The third section presents the hypotheses that were identified in the survey and the theoretical model which links job satisfaction with the factors that are perceived to influence it directly or indirectly, positively or negatively. The fourth section begins with an exploratory and descriptive statistical analysis of the measurements followed by stepwise regressions to identify the important constituents of the factors. The fifth section discusses the results of the survey and presents a structural equation model the purpose of which is to test the formulated hypotheses. The chapter concludes with a summary of the findings and the limitations of the current research.

11.2 Theoretical Context

Numerous studies in the past indicate that there is a positive influence of job satisfaction on work performance (Albalá-Genol et al., 2023). Hence, organizations that embrace cultures to promote professional satisfaction and invest in human capital motivate employees to work under adverse conditions (FitzGerald et al., 2023).

Robbins and Judge (2021) group job satisfaction factors into four categories: working conditions, personality, pay, and corporate responsibility. With respect to working conditions, factors such as social interactions, feedback, interdependence, and interpersonal relationships are highlighted (Humphrey et al., 2007). At the same time, leadership plays an important role in employee job satisfaction, who feel more confident next to a competent leader (Fong & Snape, 2013) and are inspired by his commitment, support, and willingness to respond (Ronen & Mikulincer, 2012). According to Calvo-Salguero et al. (2011) the nature of the work is the most important factor with regard to job satisfaction. Employees who credit their intrinsic worth and competence (core self-evaluation) show higher levels of job satisfaction (Robbins & Judge, 2021). Additionally, employees with a high score of positive basic self-assessment and at the same time career dedication exhibit extremely high job satisfaction—according to Zheng et al. (2017). Rollinson (2008) concluded that an employee's attitudes and value system significantly influence job satisfaction factors, while Kreitner et al. (2006) reason that job satisfaction is linked to an employee's value system, based on expectations, experiences, beliefs, impact assessment, which is constantly evolving as it is shaped by individual socialization experiences, work experience, individual actions, and emotional reactions.

The relationship between salary and job satisfaction has been studied by many researchers in the past but the findings are complex to interpret and are often contradictory. It is reasonable to postulate that payment level has a positive and direct impact on job satisfaction, and this assumption has empirically been suggested by multiple models in the past (Judge et al., 2010). Meta-analysis conducted to estimate the correlation between pay level and job satisfaction verifies these findings, but the analysis indicates that this correlation is weak to modest (Judge et al., 2010). On the other hand, there is research in the field of psychology suggesting that payment satisfaction and job satisfaction are positively correlated, albeit very weakly (Ardabili et al., 2022) and the reason is there existing confounding variables originating from human psychology that mediate the effect of pay level to job satisfaction.

The relationship between salary and job satisfaction has not been clearly observed. It is very likely that the sector of work (private or public) as well as the relationship between expected—received salary or the relationship between received salary—salary of others in the same position determines the importance of the factor. According to Herzberg (1968), Zavlanos (1999), and Spector (1997), in the public sector, job satisfaction has a positive correlation with fair pay. Bright (2009), however, hypothesizes that if civil servants' pay were proportional to the employee's performance, they would show correlation. In contrast, McNeese and

Donna (1999) and, Appelbaum and Kamal (2000) consider that there is no correlation between salary and job satisfaction.

An important element related to job satisfactions is the level of Corporate Social Responsibility developed by the organization. Organizations and Services that take environmental sustainability initiatives, charity and non-profit work, and beneficence on a worldwide scale contribute to the benefit of society or the environment, beyond what is required by current legislation. Employees with personal values often support the organization's or agency's corporate social responsibility programs, feel that they contribute to the fulfillment of an important goal and are more satisfied with their work (Robbins & Judge, 2021).

By studying the public sector, which has not been sufficiently studied in contrast to the private sector, Perry and Wise (1990) identify different work characteristics, motivations, and employee behaviors in civil servants. More specifically, they argue that civil servants demonstrate altruism when defending the public interest, because they care personally, feel morally obliged, and emotionally bound.

Additional factors that influence job satisfaction are the demographic characteristics of employees. Spector (1997) and Crossman and Abou-Zaki (2003) report that women are more satisfied than men when it comes to salary. Women may expect less from their work. In addition, regarding age, older people hold higher salary bands and due to experience and self-confidence can maneuver easier and achieve their goals more comfortably. On the other hand, younger people experience frustration seeing how far their work is from their ideals (Riza et al., 2018).

Similarly, "working age" (work experience) is positively related to job satisfaction and education, as reported by Abraham and Medoff (1984). Educational level and job satisfaction according to Vila and Belen (2005) show a positive correlation, as higher-educated employees occupy more challenging positions and enjoy greater job satisfaction. Finally, the view that employees with lower-level degrees are less satisfied with their jobs is confirmed by Crossman and Abou-Zaki (2003) and Scott et al. (2005).

A correlation between work stress and job satisfaction has been pointed out in work by Kreitner et al. (2006). The effects of work dissatisfaction are also seen on employees' health both physical and/or mental. Specifically, symptoms such as fatigue, exhaustion, headaches, various physical discomforts as well as anxiety, melancholy, and mild depression are observed (Evans et al., 2007; Faragher et al., 2013; Fisher, 2010).

11.3 Data Collection Process

11.3.1 Sample Description

The participants in the survey are 331 employees (which is 79,59%) of the Court of First Instance of Athens—the total number of employees in the court is 416. More specifically, the sample selected from the population to be investigated went through five "filters": The respondents had to be (a) permanent staff, (b) with at least 6 months of work experience in the service. Before issuing the questionnaire, employees who (c) are absent on various leaves (such as postpartum, child-rearing, salary cut, pause payment), those (d) who have received a "departure report" (secondment), and those who (e) have received "teleworking" were removed from the survey sample (Hyz, 2010).

11.3.2 Survey Instrument

For the purposes of the survey, a questionnaire (of 12 factors and 11 demographic characteristics) was structured based on its content on the following four (4) existing standards questionnaires and three (3) set of research:

1. Job Satisfaction Survey_JSS (Spector, 1985),
2. Organizational Climate Measure_OCM (Smerek & Peterson, 2007),
3. The work design questionnaire_WDQ (Morgeson & Humphrey, 2006),
4. Minnesota Satisfaction Questionnaire -MSQ (Weiss et al., 1967), and
5. Lait and Wallace (2002),
6. Wright and Kim (2004),
7. Wright and Davis (2003).

The questionnaire, in terms of structure and form, was based on the finding of Robbins and Judge (2021) regarding approaches to measuring job satisfaction.

Analytically, the questionnaire consists of two parts. In the first part the questions are categorized into twelve sections and each section expresses a factor that affects job satisfaction. The second component of the questionnaire is devoted to demographics traits of the respondents.

The responders' demographics are: (1) Genter, (2) Marital status, (3) Age, (4) Educational level, (5) Working position/Chain of command, (6) Years of employment at the court of justice, (7) Years of employment in the private sector, (8) Years of employment in the same department, (9) Salary scale, (10) Number of children, and (11) Computer skills.

The answers were coded numerically using five-point Likert scale (Strongly disagree, Disagree, Neither agree nor disagree, Agree, Strongly agree).

The questionnaires were distributed face-to-face. In the first week, a pilot sample of twelve participants (eight females and four males) was selected to perform a quality control of the questionnaire. The participants were informed about the purpose of the research and were assured of the confidentiality of the data. The questionnaire was accompanied by a letter of appreciation and the option to subscribe to a mailing list in order to receive the results of the research study.

11.4 The Hypothesized Model

The hypothesized model is based on the theoretical work developed by Wright and Davis (2003_Causative Model of Job Satisfaction), Wright and Kim (2004), and Lait and Wallace (2002_Conceptual Model of Job Stress).

Twelve factors of job satisfaction have been identified and are included in the current study: (1) Nature/subject of work, (2) Environment/workplace, (3) Leadership/supervision, (4) Interpersonal—relationships/collaborations, (5) Salary, (6) Feedback/evaluation/, (7) Mobility/departure, (8) Absence/Commitment, (9) Work stress, (10) Training, (11) Work recognition, and (12) Targeting/job mission.

These factors are formulated as hypotheses which are interlinked together, and directly or indirectly influence job satisfaction to construct the Hypothesized Model that is depicted in Fig. 11.1. The hypotheses proposed and the corresponding section in the investigative tool are presented in the following list:

Hypothesis 1 *The work environment has a direct positive influence on job satisfaction.*

Hypothesis 2	*The nature/subject of work has direct positive influence on job satisfaction.*
Hypothesis 3	*The clear targeting/goal setting has a direct positive influence on job satisfaction.*
Hypothesis 4	*Work recognition has a direct positive influence on job satisfaction.*
Hypothesis 5	*Job training has a direct positive influence on job satisfaction.*
Hypothesis 6	*Salary has a direct positive influence on job satisfaction.*
Hypothesis 7	*Salary has a direct positive influence on feedback.*
Hypothesis 8	*Feedback has an indirect positive influence on job satisfaction via clear targeting/goal setting.*
Hypothesis 9	*Feedback has an indirect positive influence on job satisfaction via work recognition.*
Hypothesis 10	*Feedback has an indirect positive influence on job satisfaction via work training.*
Hypothesis 11	*Leadership has direct positive influence on job satisfaction.*
Hypothesis 12	*Interpersonal – relationships/collaborations have indirect positive influence on job satisfaction via nature/subject of work.*
Hypothesis 13	*Mobility has an indirect positive relationship on job satisfaction via nature/subject of work.*
Hypothesis 14	*Absence/commitment has an indirect positive influence on job satisfaction via nature/subject of work .*
Hypothesis 15	*The correlated responses to the questionnaire are associated with people with a similar demographic profile (network modeling).*

11.4.1 Measurement Validity and Reliability

As discussed in the theoretical section the authors have identified twelve factors that affect job satisfaction. One method to quantify how well the collected data fits the model is to examine the eigenvalues of the correlation matrix. It can be observed in the scree plot shown in Fig. 11.2 that twelve eigenvalues are larger than one, which corresponds to the number of factors in the theoretical model.

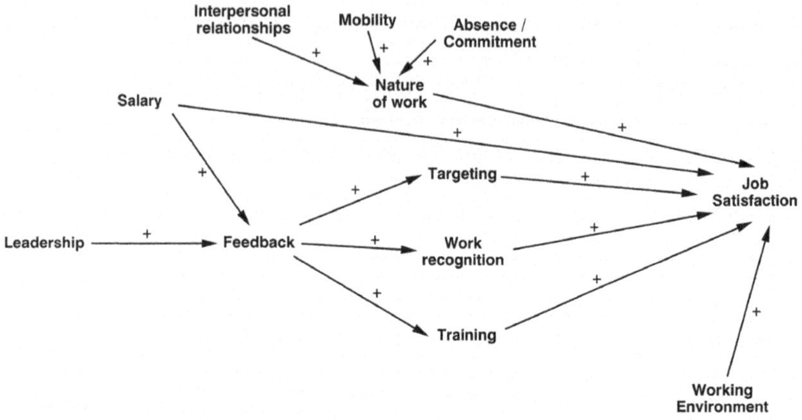

Fig. 11.1 Hypothesized model

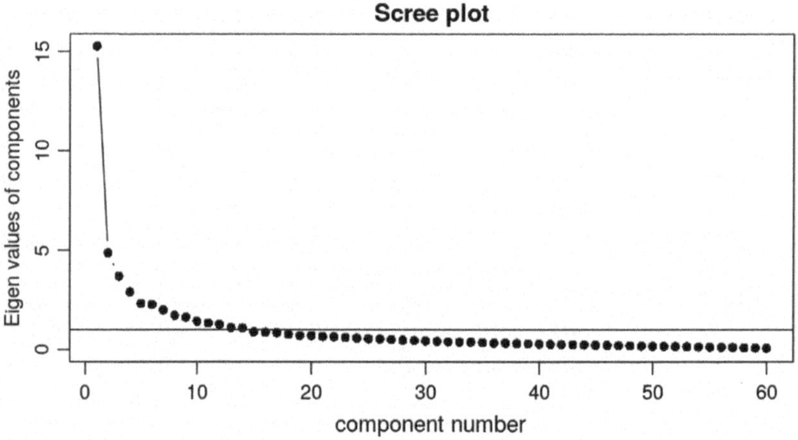

Fig. 11.2 Scree plot of eigenvalues of the correlation matrix

Reliability can be quantified using internal consistency methods. Internal consistency methods provide a measure of the degree of homogeneity among items in an instrument. One such statistic is the Cronbach's alpha coefficients (Tavakol & Dennick, 2011). Scores larger than 0.7 can be considered reliable and larger than 0.6 can be reported (Crick,

2023). The alpha was calculated by considering the individual measurement questions and was found to be equal to 0.91 with a 95% confidence interval of [0.9, 0.92], which indicates high reliability. The split-half reliability test is a second internal consistency reliability measure and reflects how well two halves of the test relate to each other. To increase the robustness of the estimate an implementation of split-half was used where many permutations of the halves of the data are created and for each permutation the Spearman-Brown correlation is applied (Parsons, 2021). The average split-half reliability was estimated to be equal to 0.95.

11.5 Methods and Tools

The analysis of the collected data is conducted in two dimensions: descriptive and inferential.

Descriptive analysis of the survey responses, in the first part of this section, is presented by providing frequency tables, statistical measures, and visual representations.

Inferential analysis is discussed in the second part of this section. Specifically, the analysis presented involves:

1. Statistical tools like *student's t-test, Spearman's rho correlation*, and *ANOVA* are performed on demographic variables.
2. *Multiple regression* analysis for each section of the questionnaire where the sixth, general question is used as the response variable and the first five questions as the covariates. A stepwise regression analysis was performed where at each step an additional covariate was introduced in the model and models were compared using the adjusted R-squared.
3. An investigation of positive or negative influence of each factor directly or indirectly on job satisfaction using *Structural Equation Model (SEM)*.

Where control is required, the level of statistical significance should be $\alpha = 0{,}05$.

For the needs of data analysis, (a) the *IBM SPSS* statistical package (version 28), (b) the variance analysis program, *LISREL 12*, and (c) the *neo4J* database were used.

11.6 Discussion of Results

11.6.1 Respondents' Demographic Characteristics

Tables 11.1 and 11.2 summarize demographic information from the respondents of the survey. The first table contains information related to the gender, the marital status, the age, the educational level, and the work position of the participants while the second table contains statistical information concerning employment information of the respondents, such as work experience and salary.

Regarding their demographic data, it was found that women constitute most of the sample (75%). Moreover, most of the employees belong to the middle age group (51–60 years), which means that the employees of the service in question have a great deal of work experience but at the same time confirms the rule of an aging workforce. Also, the educational level of the examined judicial employees is quite high with the majority having reported higher education.

Table 11.1 Demographic characteristics of participants (I)

		N	%
Gender	Male	80	25
	Female	240	75
Marital status	Single	85	26.6
	Married	200	62.5
	Divorced	31	9.7
	Widow	4	1.3
Age	31–40	34	10.6
	41–50	116	36.3
	51–60	139	43.4
	61–67	31	9.7
Education	Primary	10	3.1
	Secondary	104	32.5
	Higher education	8	2.5
	Technological	25	7.8
	University degree	117	36.6
	Masters	44	13.8
	PhD	12	3.8
Position	Secretary	281	87.8
	Typist	10	3.1
	Bailiff	11	3.4
	Supervisor/Director	18	5.6

Table 11.2 Demographic characteristics of participants (II)

	Scale	*N*	*%*
Number of years in the organization	0–2	30	9.4
	3–10	73	22.8
	11–20	60	18.8
	21–30	87	27.2
	More than 31	70	21.9
Number of years of experience in the private sector	0	36	11.3
	1–3	140	43.8
	4–10	84	26.3
	11–20	49	15.3
	21–30	10	3.1
	More than 31	1	0.3
Number of years of employment in the same department	1–5	165	51.6
	6–10	99	30.9
	11–20	48	15.0
	More than 21	8	2.5
Salary Scale	400–700€	11	3.4
	701–1.000€	98	30.6
	1.001–1.300€	172	53.8
	1.301–1.600€	28	8.8
	1.601–2.100€	11	3.4

Most respondents have several years of experience in the private sector (approximately 90%) and 67.9% have been employed for at least 10 years in the Court of First Instance of Athens.

Additionally, a permutation test was conducted to examine whether a statistically significant difference in the mean job satisfaction measured exists among the two genders. The null hypothesis is that the mean job satisfaction level is the same across genders and the alternative that the mean job satisfaction level is different between the two genders. This can be more formally expressed in the following way:

$$H_o : \mu_{male} - \mu_{female} = 0$$
$$H_A : \mu_{male} - \mu_{female} \neq 0$$

A significance level equal to 0.95 was chosen. The measured difference between males and females was equal to 0.154. The results of the test are shown in the Fig. 11.3. The vertical line represents the sample value, and it can be observed that it lies outside the statistically significant area.

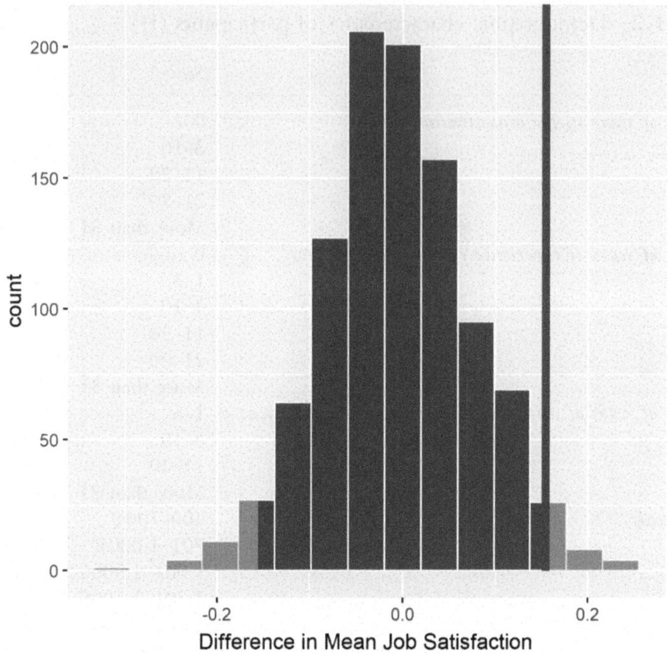

Fig. 11.3 Test for difference in the mean job satisfaction between genders

A p-value equal to 0.064 was obtained and thus there is no significant evidence to reject the null hypothesis that there is a difference in the mean job satisfaction level across the two genders.

11.6.2 Statistical Analysis of Measurements

Table 11.3 provides summary statistics for the overall questions of each factor. The results are ordered from the lowest to the highest overall average level of satisfaction.

It can be observed that salary has the lowest average satisfaction score with the lowest variance, indicating a high level of dissatisfaction with the salary among the employees. The distribution in Fig. 11.4 shows that approximately 85% of the employee's salary resides in the range 700 to 1300 euros and there is a prevalent range of salaries in which more than half of the survey respondents fall.

Table 11.3 Summary statistics of "overall" question per factor

Factor	*Mean*	*Median*	*Standard deviation*	*Confidence interval*
Salary	1.731	2	0.858	[1.64,1.83]
Training	1.841	2	0.935	[1.74,1.96]
Mobility	1.913	2	0.988	[1.81,2.02]
Work environment	2.394	2	1.051	[2.28,2.51]
Feedback	2.631	3	1.015	[2.52,2.74]
Commitment	2.747	3	1.095	[2.62,2.87]
Targeting	2.816	3	1.023	[2.7,2.93]
Work recognition	2.869	3	1.154	[2.75,2.99]
Work stress	3.075	3	1.193	[2.94,3.2]
Nature/Subject of work	3.150	3	1.015	[3.03,3.25]
Interpersonal relationships	3.241	3	0.934	[3.14,3.34]
Leadership	3.434	4	1.107	[3.32,3.56]

Low levels of satisfaction are also observed in training and mobility, which indicates that the employees perceive that there are low career development opportunities. In fact, it was in these three sets of questions (salary, training, and mobility) that the strongest negative responses were measured.

On the other end of the spectrum, the highest degree of average satisfaction (albeit with a relatively high level of variance) is observed in the leadership and supervision factor and interpersonal relationships.

The plots in Figs. 11.5 and 11.6 show the distribution of the response to each item of the set of questions per factor in the survey. Two separate plots are provided for improved visualization.

The Likert plots in Figs. 11.5 and 11.6 illustrate the proportion of responses to each individual question. Each horizontal bar graph corresponds to a specific question. The central response ("neither agree nor disagree") is placed in the middle of each plot and is accompanied by a percentage value that represents the proportion of the neutral responses. In colloquial terms, the neutral response partitions the x axis in two halves and the bar plots show the percentage of the replies that lie below or above it. The benefits of this visual representation become immediately apparent: with a single plot it is possible to identify tendencies (negative

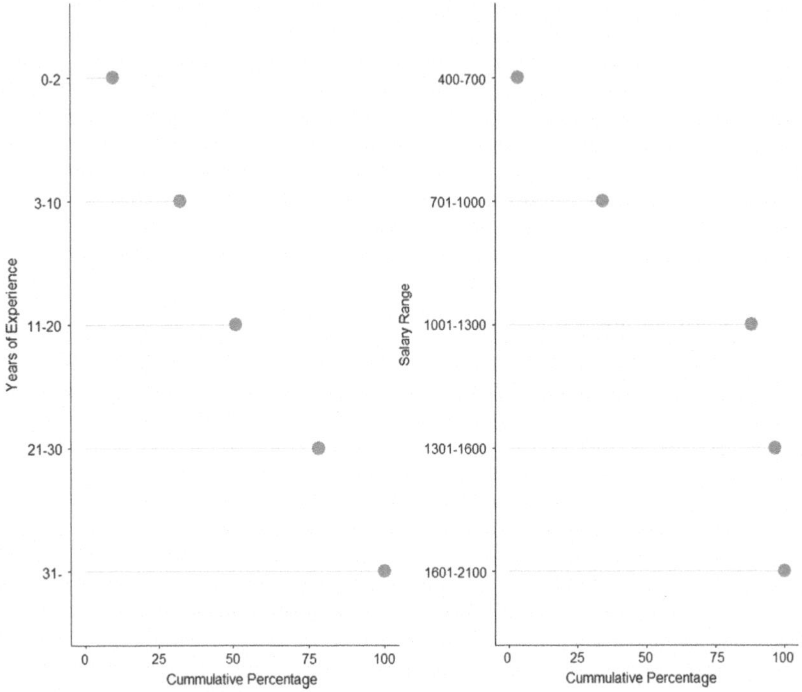

Fig. 11.4 Cumulative distribution of years of experience and Cumulative distribution of salary range

or positive) and simultaneously compare the responses across the different factors.

Questions related to the environment/workplace, salary, mobility/departure and training have been answered *negatively*, while the opposite is observed in the responses of leadership/supervision, interpersonal relationships, in which case the majority of respondents have answered *positively*. For other factors (nature/subject of work, feedback/evaluation, absence/commitment, job recognition, targeting, work stress) trends are *mixed*, in other words, the percentage of responses below the neutral is roughly equal to the number of responses above it.

A low level of satisfaction was reported in the question addressing bureaucracy and workload; however, a relatively high average level of satisfaction is observed when asked how important employees consider

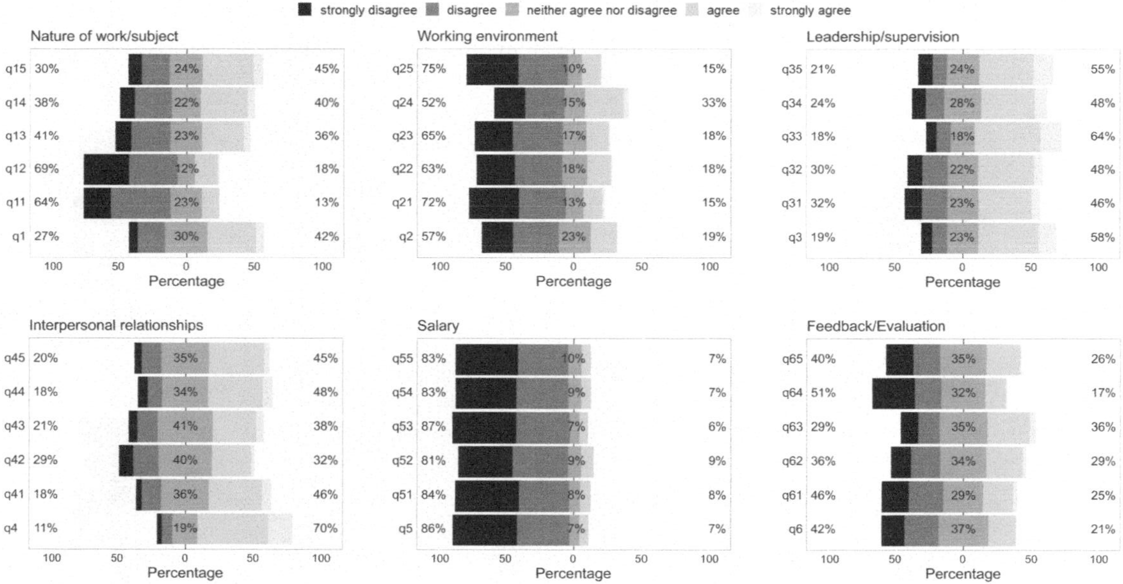

Fig. 11.5 Likert plot for the factors: nature of work, environment, leadership, relationships, salary, and feedback

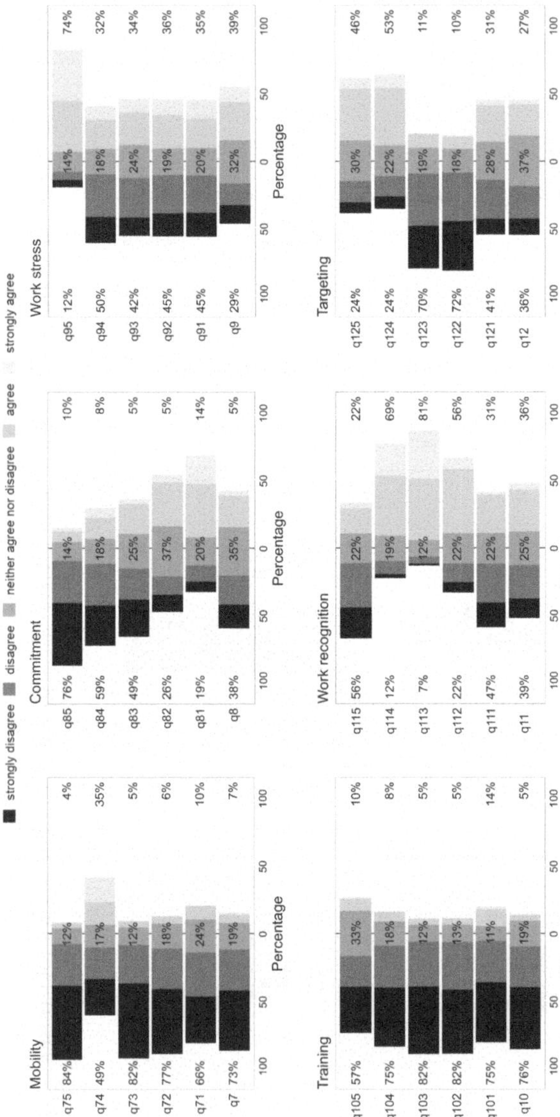

Fig. 11.6 Likert plot for the factors: mobility, commitment, work stress, training, work recognition, and targeting

their job, and in the "overall question" there are several individuals who report being satisfied with that aspect of their job.

In terms of the parameters that define the working environment, such as infrastructure and workplace safety, the plots reveal a low level of satisfaction. The opposite is observed for leadership/supervision in the workplace: the larger percentage of the participants respond positively when asked about the behavior of hierarchical superiors, their effectiveness in communicating work targeting and strategies as well as decision-making. Identical conclusions can be drawn for interpersonal relations in respect to their colleagues. Most of the participants are not satisfied with their salary related to their effort, their level of education, years of experience, work position, or working hours. Low satisfaction related to feedback and job evaluation is also measured—although a relatively satisfactory objectivity in evaluation by hierarchical supervisors is reported. The majority of the participants respond negatively when asked about mobility—the ability to move (temporarily or permanently) to another department within the organization and to another judicial or public organization.

An important cause of job stress appears to be the imbalance of job demands related to the available human resources and a significant percentage appears to report that they feel burnout, with no energy to work. The low level of satisfaction with the training provided to employees by their organization refers mainly to the opportunity to participate in training seminars. On the contrary, the average satisfaction of the participants' work recognition by their organization is relatively high and is mainly detected in the fields of productivity and completion of tasks.

The plot in Fig. 11.7 shows the correlation matrix for the item responses grouped per factor and the satisfaction level, which is typically calculated as the sum of the item responses per participant.

As expected, there is a positive correlation between the different factors and job satisfaction. The exception to this rule is work stress, which is negatively correlated to the rest of the variables.

11.6.3 Stepwise Regressions

A series of stepwise regressions were conducted for each of the twelve factors where the overall question was used as the dependent variable and the individual questions as the explanatory variables. The objective of

	1	2	3	4	5	6	7	8	9	10	11	12	13
1. Job satisfaction													
2. Nature of work	,66**	(,75)											
3. Work environment	,67**	,57**	(,87)										
4. Leadership	,52**	,25**	,29**	(,95)									
5. Relationships	,64**	,44**	,45**	,37**	(,81)								
6. Salary	,55**	,39**	,44**	,14*	,28**	(,94)							
7. Feedback	,66**	,35**	,43**	,52**	,50**	,33**	(,87)						
8. Mobility	,29**	,05	,05	,15**	,14**	,15**	,32**	(,62)					
9. Absence	,28**	,24**	,18**	,15**	,28**	,20**	,27**	,17**	(,70)				
10. Work Stress	-,46**	-,50**	-,36**	-,09**	-,35**	-,28**	-,28**	,00	-,00	(,87)			
11. Training	,60**	,33**	,35**	,28**	,29**	,36**	,36**	,33**	,14**	-,25**	(,87)		
12. Work recognition	,66**	,45**	,43**	,39**	,45**	,25**	,47**	,18**	,11**	-,36**	,42**	(,73)	
13. Targeting	,64**	,42**	,50**	,37**	,45**	,32**	,49**	,18**	,29**	-,30**	,46**	,61**	(,78)

Fig. 11.7 Response correlation matrix (*Note* in parenthesis Cronbach's alpha, $*p < 0{,}05$, $**p < 0.01$)

the regression models was to assess the importance of the measurements within the context of each factor. For the purposes of the current survey, the attention is directed to the relative strength and directionality (positive or negative) of the regression coefficients (Gelman, 2020).

Stepwise regression is used as a framework for comparison and is often used in social and behavioral analysis (Lewis, 2007). The process involves building several regression models by adding variables to the previous model in a sequential fashion. The linear models serve two purposes:

1. As inferential models to test the hypothesis that individual measurements explain the overall question (Overall, I am satisfied with...) in each factor and determine the strength of association of the predictors with the dependent variable.
2. To measure the contribution of each of the predictors to the proportion of variance explained by the model.

There are multiple practical benefits from this type of analysis:

(a) It provides a tool that can be conceived as a statistical lens to the organization to identify the job satisfaction facets that are most significant and focus its resources on improving those aspects.

(b) It allows the researcher to identify the measurements that are more important and thus provide a basis for refining the investigative tool.
(c) It can be used to understand which measurements are positively correlated and which negatively to the overall question.

The Fig. 11.8 reports, as an example, the stepwise regression for the "Salary" factor. All predictors are statistically significant and values of R^2 and adjusted R^2 indicate that the variability of dependent variable is sufficiently captured by the model.

As far as the dependent variable salary is concerned, the stepwise regression model is summarized as follows:

$$\begin{aligned} Salary = {} & 0.318 * \text{work experience} + 0.185 * \text{education} \\ & + 0.162 * \text{effort} + 0.158 * \text{position} \\ & + 0.145 * \text{working hours} \end{aligned}$$

In the factor depicted in Fig. 11.8 it appears that the most important variable is the "Years of experience".

	Dependent variable:				
	Salary				
	(1)	(2)	(3)	(4)	(5)
Work effort	0.758***	0.454***	0.264***	0.194***	0.162***
	(0.032)	(0.039)	(0.038)	(0.042)	(0.042)
Educational level		0.416***	0.249***	0.207***	0.185***
		(0.037)	(0.036)	(0.037)	(0.037)
Years of Experience			0.443***	0.331***	0.318***
			(0.043)	(0.051)	(0.050)
Position of work				0.218***	0.158***
				(0.056)	(0.057)
Hours of work					0.145***
					(0.039)
Constant	0.391***	0.143**	0.031	0.033	0.003
	(0.064)	(0.059)	(0.052)	(0.051)	(0.051)
Observations	320	320	320	320	320
R^2	0.632	0.736	0.802	0.811	0.819
Adjusted R^2	0.631	0.734	0.800	0.808	0.816
Residual Std. Error	0.521 (df = 318)	0.442 (df = 317)	0.384 (df = 316)	0.376 (df = 315)	0.368 (df = 314)
F Statistic	547.234*** (df = 1; 318)	441.548*** (df = 2; 317)	425.982*** (df = 3; 316)	337.526*** (df = 4; 315)	283.673*** (df = 5; 314)
Note:					*p<0.1; **p<0.05; ***p<0.01

Fig. 11.8 Multiple linear regression model for Salary

The complete list of stepwise regression models carried out is presented below:

$$\begin{aligned} \textit{Nature of work} &= 0.483 * \text{importance} + 0.198\,\text{variety} \\ &\quad + 0.153 * \text{load} + 0.086 * \text{balance} \end{aligned}$$

$$\begin{aligned} \textit{Environment} &= 0.231 * \text{equipment} + 0.220 * \text{safety} \\ &\quad + 0.215 * \text{infrastructure} + 0.208 * \text{space} \\ &\quad + 0.140 * \text{cleanliness} \end{aligned}$$

$$\begin{aligned} \textit{Leadership} &= 0.354 * \text{personal problems} + 0.283 * \text{receptive} \\ &\quad + 0.221 * \text{effective} + 0.111 * \text{ideas} \end{aligned}$$

$$\begin{aligned} \textit{Collaborations} &= 0.233 * \text{supervisors} + 0.223 * \text{colleagues} \\ &\quad + 0.213 * \text{lawyers} + 0.180 * \text{public} \\ &\quad + 0.180 * \text{judges} \end{aligned}$$

$$\begin{aligned} \textit{Feedback} &= 0.394 * \text{criteria} + 0.253 * \text{adequacy} \\ &\quad + 0.241 * \text{third parties} + 0.105 * \text{on time} \end{aligned}$$

$$\begin{aligned} \textit{Mobility} &= 0.324 * \text{judicial service} + 0.246 * \text{public service} \\ &\quad + 0.199 * \text{section} + 0.179 * \text{Delay} \end{aligned}$$

$$\begin{aligned} \textit{Absence} &= 0.365 * \text{recommend service} + 0.259 * \text{match} \\ &\quad - 0.109 * \text{early retirement} \end{aligned}$$

$$\begin{aligned} \textit{Work-related stress} &= 0.168 * \text{imbalance} - 0.232 * \text{expiration} \\ &\quad - 0.152 * \text{burnout} \end{aligned}$$

$$\begin{aligned} \textit{Education} &= 0.335 * \text{information systems} \\ &\quad + 0.299 * \text{educational leave} \\ &\quad + 0.163 * \text{integration} + 0.154 * \text{seminars} \end{aligned}$$

$$\begin{aligned} \textit{Recognition} &= 0.393 * \text{recognition} + 0.392 * \text{advancement} \\ &+ 0.256 * \text{success} + 0.184 * \text{confidence} \\ &- 0.129 * \text{productivity} \end{aligned}$$

$$\begin{aligned} \textit{Targeting} &= 0.302 * \text{approval} + 0.221 * \text{timely goals} \\ &+ 0.200 * \text{career} + 0.119 * \text{service delivery} \\ &+ 0.100 * \text{department objectives} \end{aligned}$$

11.6.4 Multivariate Analysis

Testing of the hypothesized relationships between the endogenous variables, and between endogenous and exogenous variables, was conducted using a single indicator structural equation model that incorporates measurement error (Hayduk, 1987).

The p-value for model convergence (0.13) was not statistically significant, indicating good model fit. RMSEA and RMR were 0.022 and 0.014, respectively, below the threshold considered necessary for a good model fit (0.08 and 0.05, respectively). The CFI is 0.714 and the GFI goodness of fit index is 0.90, which respectively indicate a good model fit. Of the six tests conducted for goodness of fit only the χ^2 (8) = 299.6, $p < 0.05$ maximum likelihood index does not confirm goodness of fit but according to James et al. (1982) this index is sensitive to the increase in sample size, which also increases the index value.

Most of the hypotheses were shown to be significant. Note that this does not mean the factors examined are not important (the descriptive analysis shows the contrary) but rather that they were not captured by the hypothesized causal model, which is not entirely surprising given the large number of hypotheses. The part of the hypothesized model with statistically important paths is depicted in Fig. 11.9.

It is interesting to note that salary does not significantly influence job satisfaction directly but rather through a distributed path via recognition, leadership, and mobility.

For job satisfaction, a relationship was found between the hypothesized factors that simultaneously explained 77.3% of the variance in job satisfaction.

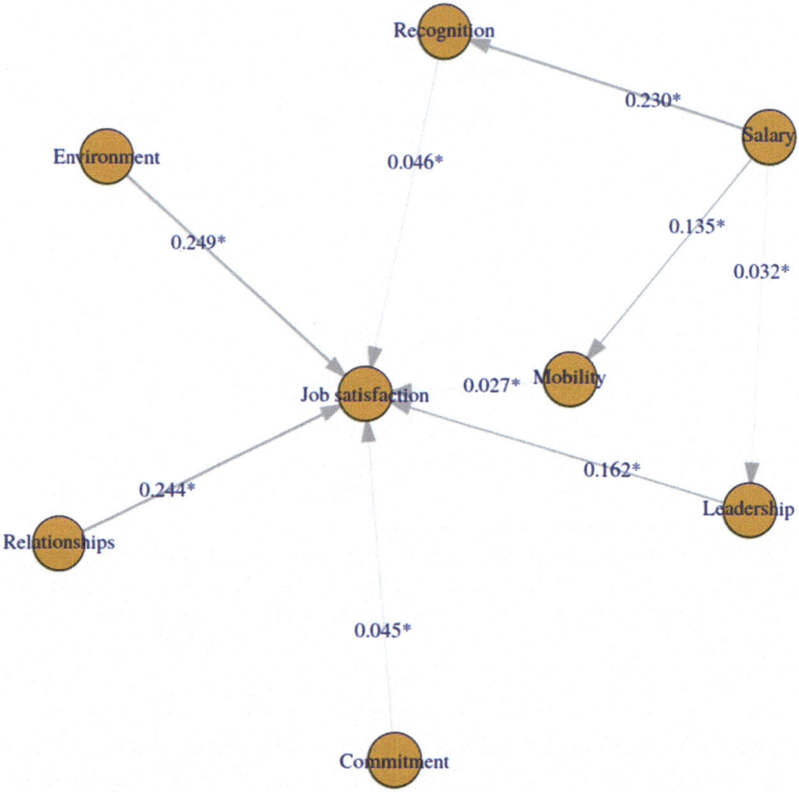

Fig. 11.9 Model results (*Note* in the structural path estimates are reported as standardized regression weights, and *path coefficients are statistically significant at $p < 0.05$)

All factors presented in the final model had a positive relationship with job satisfaction. The factors that have *direct* effect on job satisfaction are:

1. Environment/workplace (0.249) which includes safety, cleanliness, workspace, and infrastructure has a direct positive relationship with job satisfaction (explaining 57% of the variance).
2. Mobility/departure (0.027) which relates to the ability to move within and outside the organization.

3. Leadership/supervision (0.162) which relates to the promotion of ideas and effective communication between supervisors and subordinates.
4. Work recognition (0.046) which relates to confidence, productivity and effectiveness.
5. Interpersonal relationships (0.244) with colleagues and hierarchical superiors, as well as, with lawyers, judges, and citizens.
6. Absence (0.045) which relate commitment to organization's goals and desire to quit work.
7. On the contrary, salary has an *indirect* effect on job satisfaction via recognition, leadership, and mobility.

11.6.5 Network Modeling

From the correlation analysis of questionnaires and demographics, there is evidence that people who respond with a greater degree of correlation have, on average, more common demographics.

The analysis below examines whether the correlated responses are associated with people with a similar demographic profile. The questionnaire data were extracted from SPSS and uploaded to the graph database, Neo4j. Each respondent is modeled as a "node" uniquely identified by the index of the questionnaire and the properties of the node are the answers to the individual questions in points of the Likert scale. Nodes are connected to each other with edges and a complete graph structure is formed (Bratanic, 2019).

There are two main types of relationships: unidirectional and bidirectional. In this model the relationships are bidirectional, and the strength of the relationships is measured by the utilization of two weights (Pearson's correlation and Jaccard Distance). This results in a very dense network, as shown in Fig. 11.10.

The Pearson correlations are calculated using the questionnaire responses. Pearson takes values in the closed interval $[-1,1]$ where magnitude is a measure of strength, and the sign indicates the directionality (negative or positive).

Demographic information (salary category, level of education, gender, computer knowledge, etc.) are categorical variables. One method to measure the difference between vectors categorical variables is to use the

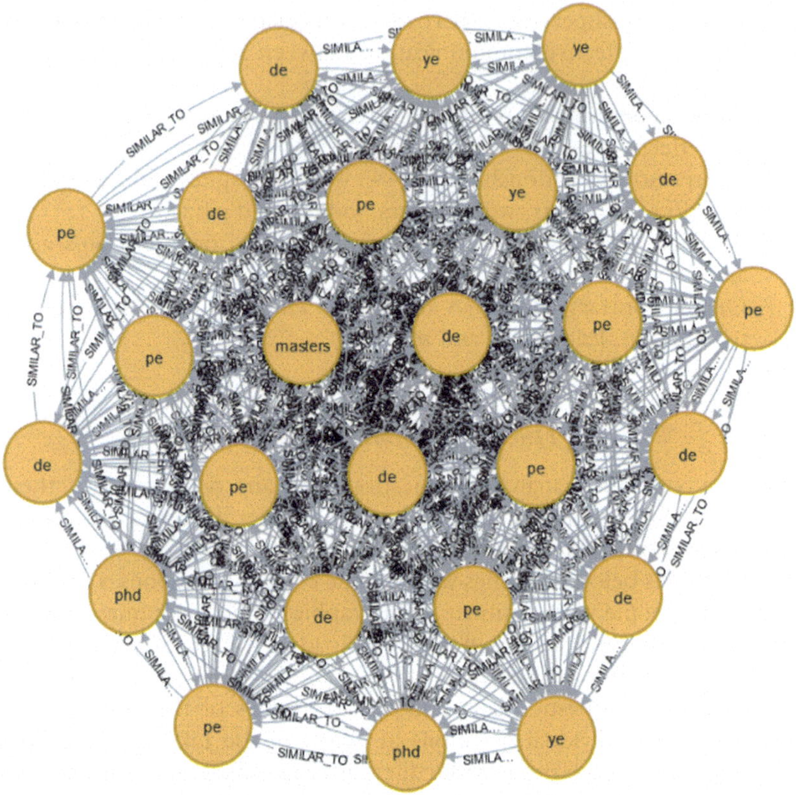

Fig. 11.10 The network of "nodes" (respondents to the questionnaire)

Jaccard distance, which is given by the following formula:

$$J(p_i, p_j) = \frac{|p_i \cap p_j|}{|p_i \cup p_j|}$$

The numerator is the cardinality of the intersection of two sets while the denominator yields the cardinality of the set resulting from the union of the two sets. The Jaccard distance takes values in the closed interval [0,1].

By calculating Pearson and Jaccard coefficients, it is possible to conduct a statistical analysis to study whether identical answers to questionnaires result from respondents with common demographics. For every node the database is queried to retrieve all connected nodes with which there is a Pearson is greater than 0.5 and for each the average Jaccard distance is calculated. The same calculations for nodes with a correlation rate of Pearson less than 0.4. Having collected the data, we can perform a 2-sample t-test as follows ($p < 0.01$):

H0 The difference between the average Jaccard distance for the subset with a correlation Pearson > 0.5 and that with Pearson < 0.4 equals zero.

HA The difference of the average Jaccard distance for the subset with a correlation Pearson > 0.5 from that with Pearson < 0.4 is greater than zero.

The result of the t-test returns p-value = 0.000003128 < 0.05. This means the null hypothesis is rejected in favor of the alternative. Hence, there is evidence that the identical responses to the questionnaire (measured by Pearson's correlation) were submitted by respondents with similar demographic characteristics (where similarity is quantified by Jaccard distance).

11.7 Conclusions

Systematic studies have attempted to derive and assert the importance of the factors influencing organizational resilience. In their paper Liu et al. (2021) identify twenty such factors that have direct or indirect influence. Among the most important are work passion, which is defined as the tendency and willingness of employees to invest time and energy in their work, organizational relationships, commitment, and leadership. All these constitute factors that significantly affect job satisfaction. It is, therefore, reasonable to postulate that there is a direct link between job satisfaction and organizational resilience. McCoy and Elwood (2009) view job satisfaction as a psychological contract between the individual and the organization. Should this contract be broken, there will be implications for organizational resilience.

The findings of the research, in such a large public body in Greece, despite its peculiarities, are connected to some important difficulties faced by the majority of public administration bodies in the Greek area, always to a different degree each and connected to the impossibility of implementation of results-oriented practices but also with phenomena such as fragmentation, the difficulty of managing change, and organizational culture issues (Sotiropoulos, 2021; Spanou, 2018; Tsekos, 2016). However, the methodological approach adopted regarding job satisfaction could be used, with any necessary adjustments, by any public institution in order all the involved (management, employees etc.) to be able to identify the most important factors to improve existing tools and techniques and thereby develop policies and strategies to enhance capacity and resilience of the organization.

11.8 Limitations

It is important to mention that even though the methodology and practices that were employed in this research are widely applicable, the results are confined to the Court of First Instance of Athens which has a specific organizational structure and culture. In effect, the investigative tool and the model developed are tailored to these idiosyncrasies and may not be applicable in the same form to a wide range of organizations.

References

Abraham, K. G., & Medoff, J. L. (1984). Length of service and layoffs in union and Nonunion Work Groups. *Industrial and Labor Relations Review, 38*(1), 87–97. https://doi.org/10.1177/001979398403800109

Albalá-Genol, J., Díaz-Fúnez, P. A., & Mañas-Rodríguez, M. Á. (2023). Resilience and job satisfaction: Effect of moderated mediation on the influence of interpersonal justice on the performance of public servants. *International Journal of Environmental Research and Public Health, 20*, 2957. https://doi.org/10.3390/ijerph200442

Appelbaum, S. H., & Kamal, R. (2000). An analysis of the utilization and effectiveness of non-financial incentives in small business. *Journal of Management Development, 19*, 733–763. https://doi.org/10.1108/02621710010378200

Ardabili, T., Chamorro-Premuzic, T., Grover, S., & Furnham, A. (2022). Neuroticism, materialism, pay and job satisfaction. *Psychology, 13*, 1697–1710. https://doi.org/10.4236/psych.2022.1312106

Barasa, E., Mbau, R., & Gilson, L. (2018). What is resilience and how can it be nurtured? A systematic review of empirical literature on organizational resilience. *International Journal of Health Policy and Management (IJHPM), 7*. https://doi.org/10.15171/ijhpm.2018.06

Bratanic, T. (2019). *Community detection of survey responses based on Pearson correlation coefficient with Neo4j*. Towards Data Science. Assigned 6 February 2023. https://towardsdatascience.com/community-detection-of-survey-responses-based-on-pearson-correlation-coefficient-with-neo4j-a522e2264c1c. Accessed on 16 February 2024.

Bright, L. (2009). Why do public employees desire intrinsic nonmonetary opportunities? *Public Personnel Management, 38*(3), 15–37. https://doi.org/10.1177/009102600903800302

Calvo-Salguero, A., Martinez, S., de Lecea, J. M., & Carrasco-Gonzalez, A. M. (2011). Work–family and family–work conflict: Does intrinsic–extrinsic satisfaction mediate the prediction of general job satisfaction? *The Journal of Psychology, 145*(5), 435–461. https://doi.org/10.1080/00223980.2011.584082

Crick, J. M. (2023, February). Analyzing survey data in marketing research: A guide for academics and postgraduate students. *Journal of Strategic Marketing, 32*(2), 203–215. https://doi.org/10.1080/0965254X.2023.2176533

Crossman, A., & Abou-Zaki, B. (2003). Job satisfaction and employee performance of Lebanese banking staff. *Journal of Managerial Psychology, 18*(4), 368–376. https://doi.org/10.1108/02683940310473118

Duit, A. (2016). Resilience thinking: Lessons for public administration. In *Special Issue: Symposium: Designing Resilient Institutions for Transboundary Crisis Management (e-book), 94*(2), 364–380. Preprint at 1-.1111/padm.12182

Evans, K., Hodkinson, P., Rainbird, H., & Unwin, L. (2007). *Improving workplace learning*. Routledge. https://doi.org/10.4324/9780203946947

Faragher, B. E., Cass, M., & Cooper, C. L. (2013). The relationship between job satisfaction and health: A meta-analysis. *From Stress to Wellbeing, 1*, 254–271. https://doi.org/10.1136/oem.2002.006734

Fisher, C. D. (2010). Happiness at work. *International Journal of Management Reviews, 12*(4), 384–412. https://doi.org/10.1111/j.1468-2370.2009.00270.x

FitzGerald, C., Hammed, T., Rosenbach, F., Macdonald, J. R., & Dixon, R. (2023). Resilience in public service partnerships: Evidence from the UK life chances fund. *Public Management Review, 25*(4), 787–807. Informa UK limited as Taylor & Francis Group. https://doi.org/10.1080/14719037.2021.2015186. Accessed 1 March 2024.

Fong, K. H., & Snape, E. (2013). Empowering leadership, psychological empowerment and employee outcomes: Testing a multi-level mediating model. *British Journal of Management*. Wiley online library. https://doi.org/10.1111/1467-8551.12048

Gelman, A. (2020). *Regression and other stories*. Cambridge University Press. https://doi.org/10.1017/9781139161879

Hayduk, L. A. (1987). *Structural equation modeling with LISREL: Essentials and advances*. Jhu Press.
Herzberg, F. (1968). One more time: How do you motivate employees. *Harvard Business Review*.
Humphrey, S., Nahrgang, J., & Morgeson, F. (2007). Integrating motivational, social, and contextual work design features: A meta-analytic summary and theoretical extension of the work design literature. *The Journal of Applied Psychology, 92*(1), 1332–1356.https://doi.org/10.1037/0021-9010.92.5.1332
Hyz, A. (2010). Job satisfaction and employee performance of Greek Banking Staff: An empirical investigation. https://www.researchgate.net/publication/263653444hdl.handle.net/11089/420
James, L. R., Mulaik, S. A., & Brett, J. M. (1982). Conditions for confirmatory analysis and causal inference. *Georgia Inst of Tech Atlanta School of Psychology*.
Judge, T. A., Piccolo, R. F., Podsakoff, N. P., Shaw, J. C., & Rich, B. L. (2010). The relationship between pay and job satisfaction: A meta-analysis of the literature. *Journal of Vocational Behavior, 77*(2), 157–167. https://doi.org/10.1016/j.jvb.2010.04.002
Kreitner, N. D., Kinicki, R., & Cole, A. (2006). *Fundamentals of organizational behavior*. McGraw-Hill Ryerson.
Lait, J., & Wallace, J. E. (2002). Stress at work: A study of organizational-professional conflict and unmet expectations. *Industrial Relations, 57*(3). https://doi.org/10.7202/006886ar
Lewis, M. (2007). *Stepwise vs hierarchical regression: Pros and cons*. Annual Meeting of the Southwest Educational Research Association.
Liu, Y., Chen, R., Zhou, F., Zhang, S., & Wang, J. (2021). Analysis of the influencing factors of organizational resilience in the ISM framework: An exploratory study based on multiple cases. *Sustainability, 13*(23), Article 13492. https://doi.org/10.3390/su13231349
McCoy, J. B., & Elwood, A. (2009). Human factors in organizational resilience—Implications of breaking the psychological contract. *Business Continuity Journal, 3*(4), 368–375.
McNeese, S., & Donna, K. (1999). A content analysis of staff nurse descriptions of job satisfaction and dissatisfaction. *Journal of Advanced Nursing, 29*(6), 1332–1341. https://doi.org/10.1046/j.1365-2648.1999.01018.x
Morgeson, F. P., & Humphrey, S. E. (2006). The work design questionnaire (WDQ): Developing and validating a comprehensive measure for assessing job design and the nature of work. *Journal of Applied Psychology, 91*(6), 1321–1339. https://doi.org/10.1037/0021-9010.91.6.1321
Parsons, S. (2021). Splithalf: Robust estimates of split half reliability. *Journal of Open-Source Software*. https://doi.org/10.21105/joss.03041

Perry, J. L., & Wise, L. R. (1990). The motivational bases of public service. *Public Administration Review, 50*(3), 367–373.

Riza, D., Shoshana, Y. S., & Yihao, L. (2018). Time and job satisfaction: A longitudinal study of the differential roles of age and tenure. *Journal of Management, 44*(7), 2558–2579. https://doi.org/10.1177/0149206315624962

Robbins, S., & Judge, T. (2021). *Organizational behavior* (18th ed.). Pearson Higher Edition.

Rollinson, D. (2008). *Organizational behaviour and analysis: An integrated approach* (4th Ed.). Pearson Edition Limited.

Ronen, S., & Mikulincer, M. (2012). Predicting employees' satisfaction and burnout from managers' attachment and caregiving orientations. *European Journal of Work and Organizational Psychology, 21*(6), 828–849. https://doi.org/10.1080/1359432X.2011.595561

Scott, M., Swortzel, K. A., & Taylor, W. (2005). The relationships between selected demographic factors and the level of job satisfaction of extension agents. *Journal of Southern Agricultural Education Research, 55*, 102–115. https://doi.org/10.5032/jae.2005.03002

Smerek, R. E., & Peterson M. (2007). Examining Herzberg's Theory: Improving job satisfaction among Non-academic employees at a university. *Research in Higher Education, 48*(2). https://doi.org/10.1007/s11162-006-9042-3

Sotiropoulos, D. (2021). *H Dimosia Dioikisi stin epohi meta ton koronoio* (Public Administration in the post-coronavirus era). Dianeosis. https://www.dianeosis.org/wp-content/uploads/2021/01/Sotiropoulos_final.pdf. Accessed on 13 January 2024.

Spanou, K. (Ed.). (2018). *Metarrythmiseis sth dimosia dioikisi sti diarkeia tis krisis (Public administration reforms during the crisis)*. ELIAMEP, Athens. https://www.eliamep.gr/wp-content/uploads/2018/11/metarrythmiseis-sth-dimosia-dioikisi-sti-diarkeia-tis-krisis.pdf. Accessed on 13 January 2024.

Spector, P. E. (1985). Measurement of human service staff satisfaction: Development of the job satisfaction survey. *American Journal of Community Psychology, 13*(6), 693–713. https://doi.org/10.1007/BF00929796

Spector, P. E. (1997). *Job satisfaction: Application, assessment, cause, and consequences*. Sage.

Tavakol, M., & Dennick, R. (2011). Making sense of Cronbach's alpha. *International Journal of Medical Education, 2*, 53. https://doi.org/10.5116/ijme.4dfb.8dfd

Taylor, F. W. (1967). *The Principles of Scientific Management*. The Norton library, N398. New York: Norton. ISBN 0393003981, 9780393003987.

Tsekos, T. (2016). Diarthrotikes allages kai Dioikitiki Metarythmisi (*Structural changes and administrative reform)*. In N. Georgarakis & N. Demertzis

(Eds.), *To politico Portraito tis Ellados* (The political portrait of Greece) (pp. 359–377). Gutenberg. https://www.academia.edu/21109558/Διαρθρωτικές_αλλαγές_και_διοικητική_μεταρρύθμιση_Structural_Changes_and_Administrative_Reform. Accessed on 7 January 2024.

Vila, L. E., & Belen, G.-M. (2005). Education and the determinants of job satisfaction. *Education Economics, 13*(4), 409–425. https://doi.org/10.1080/09645290500251730

Weiss, D. J., Dawis, R. V., & England, G. W. (1967). Manual for the Minnesota satisfaction questionnaire. *Minnesota Studies in Vocational Rehabilitation, 22*, 120. https://psycnet.apa.org/record/1968-08111-001. Accessed on 10 November 2023.

Wright, B. E., & Davis, B. S. (2003). Job satisfaction in the public sector the role of the work environment. *American Review of Public Administration, 33*(1), 70–90. https://doi.org/10.1177/0275074002250254

Wright, B. E., & Kim B. S. (2004). Participation's influence on job satisfaction. The importance of job characteristics. *Review of Public Personnel Administration, 24*(1), 18–40. https://doi.org/10.1177/0734371X03259860

Zavlanos, M. (1999). *Organosiaki Symperifora (Organizational behavior).* Ellin Publications.

Zheng, Z., Gangaram, P., Xie, H., Chua, S., Ong, S., & Koh, S. (2017). Job satisfaction and resilience in psychiatric nurses: A study at the Institute of Mental Health Singapore. *International Journal of Mental Health Nursing, 26*. https://doi.org/10.1111/inm.12286

CHAPTER 12

Fortifying Economic Foundations: Cybersecurity Imperatives for a Resilient Financial System

Alina Hyz and Grigorios Gikas

12.1 Introduction

During the recent years we observe extremely rapid technological changes taking place around us. This, so-called fourth industrial revolution caused changes in the system of work, education, production, consumption and provision of services.

As of January 2024, there were 5.35 billion Internet users worldwide, which amounted to 66.2% of the global population (Statista, 2024). At

A. Hyz (✉)
Department of Accounting and Finance,
University of West Attica, Athens, Greece
e-mail: alinahyz@uniwa.gr

G. Gikas
Department of Business Administration,
University of West Attica, Athens, Greece
e-mail: gikas@uniwa.gr

A. Hyz (ed.), *The Role of the Public Sector in Building Social and Economic Resilience*,
https://doi.org/10.1007/978-3-031-67702-1_12

the same time, there were almost 8.9 billion mobile phone subscriptions worldwide (2023) (Statista, 2023). The number of subscriptions exceeded eight billion for the first time in 2019. Over 62% of the world's population, were social media users. In these new circumstances it is difficult not to pay attention to the problem of security and the scale of threats associated with it. We can safely say that in the new reality, the broadly understood concept of security is one of the most frequently used and considered. Cybersecurity will thus be another key technology in the context of the 4th industrial revolution. Cybersecurity concerns actions to prevent and deal with digital attacks or otherwise cyberattacks. Existing definitions of cybersecurity focus on different aspects of this term. Some definitions focus on security and privacy, while others emphasize the need to define principles and policies regarding the integrity, confidentiality and availability of information. The Merriam-Webster Dictionary defines cybersecurity as measures taken to protect a computer or computer system against unauthorized access and attacks. According to Von Solms and Van Niekerk (Von Solms & Van Niekerk, 2013) cybersecurity is the collection of tools, policies, security concepts, security safeguards, guidelines, risk management approaches, actions, training, best practices, assurance and technologies that can be used to protect the cyber environment and organization and user's assets.

The transition of economies to remote and hybrid systems, accelerated during the pandemic and reaching previously unknown dynamics and dimensions, causes an increase in threats resulting from the activities of cybercriminals. The blurring of the boundaries between the so-called official sphere and the personal sphere also has a significant impact. Not so long ago it was easy to distinguish working hours from personal life, it was easy to distinguish the equipment used in the workplace from that used at home, the networks we connect to deal with our office matters and the networks we use for private matters. Over time, the boundaries and areas between the private and professional spheres in the emerging cyberspace are blurring. A cyberspace may be defined as interconnected networks, from IT infrastructures, communication networks, computer systems, embedded processors, vital industry controllers, information virtual environment and the interaction between this environment and human beings for the purpose of production, processing, storage, exchange, retrieval and exploitation of information (Jamal, 2023). Remote, hybrid, distance work, a general change in the organization of work using company equipment and encrypted connections, but also a change in the way of consumption and the use of e-services contribute to an increase in susceptibility to cyberattacks (Sahut et al., 2021). Therefore, the victims of cyberattacks can be both enterprises, organizations and private individuals (Rid & Buchanan, 2015).

When analyzing cyberthreats on the one hand and cybersecurity on the other, the fact that mobile devices are increasingly used in transactions, but not only, is also important. Mobile devices are becoming the target of sophisticated attacks carried out on a large scale, mainly due to the fact that mobile devices, especially smartphones, accompany their owners everywhere and each of them is a potential target, offering huge amounts of valuable information. Unlike computers on which the user can install a security suite, in the case of mobile devices such products are limited or simply do not exist, thus creating unique opportunities for cybercriminal groups. The advancement of technology and the development of the use of clouds and services outsourced through cloud computing increases the vulnerability to attacks by cybercriminals (Eddolls, 2016).

Cybersecurity Ventures expects global cybercrime costs to grow by 15% per year over the next five years, reaching $10.5 trillion USD annually by 2025, up from $3 trillion USD in 2015 (Morgan, 2020). Comparing the data over the years, there is a strong increase resulting, of course, from the development of technology, the increase in Internet connections, which leads to an increase in cybersecurity threats and vulnerabilities, and finally, an increase in expenditure on securing them. We live in a world where it is difficult to imagine any area of social life that functions entirely outside virtual reality. Interpersonal relations, health, transactions of sale and purchase and finally the whole financial system are subject to the development of digital technology and thus to the possibility of disruptions in business operations and loss of property, among others, through the public disclosure of personal data.

Cybercriminals use various hacking methods and techniques, such as phishing attacks, cryptography, data manipulation, malicious software, but often based on the so-called social engineering based on human feelings of fear, anxiety and curiosity, they organize cyberattacks causing losses and disruptions in smaller or larger social and economic subsystems. It is not uncommon for cyberattacks to undermine trust not so much in technology but in systems or institutions whose activities often combine these two aspects: trust and technology. A characteristic example is the financial system and its financial products and institutions. Its operation is based mainly on trust. The services they provide are estimated not only according to their costs, but mainly in terms of credibility and trust. So far, we have only had the opportunity to see the consequences of total cyberattacks in cinemas, but there is no doubt that the changes taking place around us will have a direct impact on the development of advanced attacks in the future. A characteristic example is the popular television series created by Sam Esmail, "Mr. Robot", in which the main character tries to overthrow corporate and government control of the world and which presents realistic consequences of actions in cyberspace, such as identity theft, loss of privacy, impact on financial and political systems. And in order for this not to become a reality, it is necessary to create security systems early, but also to develop and support people's knowledge and awareness both in their private lives and in the enterprises and institutions they create. The current weakness in cyber protection, resulting to some extent from the new reality, does not exempt us from the need to take all possible steps to counteract every cyber abuse and organize preventive actions. According to Garg et al. (2003) it could be considered that individual and business users need to take positive steps to reduce the risks and potential for financial losses (Garg et al., 2003). Therefore, the modern world faces a new challenge of organizing and implementing activities aimed at the security of data, end devices, but also employees and final consumers. A sense of security based on mutual trust is what we should look for when considering cybersecurity in the new technologically advanced world. According to Marshall and Tompsett (Marshall & Tompsett, 2005) security is meant to establish a relational trust between entities that supports safe business transactions and exchanges. A proactive approach is required, based on tightening cooperation between the public sector and financial structures, in response to dynamically changing cyberthreats on the part of political decision-makers, representatives of financial institutions and cybersecurity experts. Proactive action means preventive actions and initiatives before problems and events occur, focused on anticipating situations and taking steps to avoid potential problems, rather than reacting after they occur. This problem is not easy due to dozens of events that change the world of cyberspace every day. Tracking these changes, much less predicting them, is not easy. Referring to the earlier example from the film industry, we can say that we are looking for solutions that prevent movie plots from becoming reality. The opportunities for cybercrime to impact on stakeholders and damage communities continue to grow at an ever-expanding rate (Nigel & Rice, 2011). Since science is developing rapidly, technology runs at a frenzied pace, which is why man should catch up with developments and not let developments catch up with him. In the Greek version of the myth, Prometheus became a figure symbolizing human pursuits (especially the pursuit of scientific knowledge) and the risk of crossing boundaries or unintended consequences. In the Roman version, he was considered the epitome of a lonely genius whose efforts to improve human existence could also result in tragedy. Let's not forget that Mary Shelley, for example, subtitled her novel "Frankenstein" (1818) "The Modern Prometheus".

12.2 The Key Role of the Financial System: Maintaining Economic Stability and Supporting Economic Development

Looking globally at the world economy, private and public savings play a key role in the analysis of the financial system and one of the factors determining the development of national economies and the world economy. The amount of these savings determines investment opportunities, which in turn determines the pace and level of economic development. Four basic economic entities participate in the mechanism of transforming savings into investments. Let us briefly look at their role in this mechanism and in the financial system and try to understand why the loss of trust in this system has direct consequences for economic stability and economic development. Thus, we will be able to identify which entities and connections of this system are susceptible to cyberattacks. First, households that own the factors of production offer the use of these factors to enterprises. Firms use factors to produce goods and services. Households consume goods and services to meet their needs. In addition to the actual flow, there is also a cash flow resulting from remuneration for the services of factors of production on the one hand and products and services on the other. Some households and companies do not consume all of their income. The difference between income and expenses creates savings, and the economic entities that have them create surplus economic entities. These entities try to allocate these surpluses efficiently and effectively by making investments that are so important for economic growth. Part of the supply of domestic savings is placed in banks and other domestic and foreign financial institutions, in the form of deposits on current or term accounts, or for the purchase of securities or other products of the financial system. Confidence, stable economic situation, interest rate and tax policy are some of the factors that determine the level of savings and the effectiveness of the mechanism described above. With the internationalization of money and capital markets, savers have the opportunity to invest their money in the country or abroad, guided by the criterion of the highest efficiency and risk, one of the elements of which is technological risk. Enterprises are an important link in this process. Enterprises finance their investments from their own funds, as well as from the capitals they obtain from the capital and money markets. Enterprises play the most important role in the process of transforming capital into productive investments. Likewise the public sector, which may have surpluses of tax revenues. However, public sector revenues are often insufficient to finance ongoing investments and cover current expenses. In this case, they obtain funds from the domestic and international capital market and from external financial assistance. Therefore, in the process of transforming savings into investments, the public sector usually plays a dual role. On the one hand, it offers funds, and on the other, it creates demand for credit. The fourth important sector participating in the process of transforming savings into investments is the foreigners. Its participation and role are to create capital inflows and outflows. Its share is summed up in the balance of capital transactions. The inflow of capital into a country increases its savings, thus leading to a significant increase in the resources available for investment, while the outflow of capital from one country to another limits its domestic savings, which are the main source of financing for investments (Γκίκας & Χυζ, 2020).

The above-simplified classification of the economy into four main sectors briefly presents the role of participants in the process of converting savings into investments, but also the importance of risk, security, economic development and stabilization. The transformation of savings into loan capital takes place through the financial system, which is a set of financial markets in which people and institutions trading on these markets operate, as well as regulatory and supervisory bodies of this system. The financial system therefore consists of a set of institutions, organizations and markets that act as mediators between economic units with a surplus and a deficit. The role of the financial system is to collect surplus funds of business entities and direct them to deficit entities that need them for current or investment purposes. There is a positive relationship between the development of the financial system and economic growth. It can be said that the development of financial markets and institutions is an integral part of development processes. This means that the financial system is not just an observer of the economic development process, but positively contributes to its promotion. Financial system consists of three main subsystems: financial markets, financial products and financial institutions. The increasing internationalization of financial markets, technological progress and intense competition are the main reasons that have contributed to the complexity of the structure of the modern financial system. To sum up, it should be stated that the role of the effective and stable functioning of financial markets results from the fact that: they contribute to the financing of deficit economic entities, enable the conduct of monetary policy by controlling the amount of money in the economy, ensure the liquidity and marketability of securities, contribute to financing the state budget deficit through the issuance of securities and contribute to finding investment options for the surpluses of economic units. At the same time, the internationalization of money and capital markets and the accompanying technological progress force individual countries and economic areas to take actions aimed at increasing the speed, effectiveness and reliability of the individual elements creating these markets. At the same time, over the last thirty years, the role of the processes of financial liberalization of markets, securitization and disintermediation has become decisive. The reasons for the latter phenomenon are the lower cost of credit obtained through capital markets compared to the cost of bank loans, the increase in the costs of collecting savings by commercial banks resulting from a number of administrative and regulatory interventions, technological development and the dissemination of information through it. A new field combining technological innovations with financial services to improve the effectiveness, accessibility and efficiency of the financial sector, called FinTech (Financial Technology), adds a new aspect to the problem at hand. FinTech today includes technologies such as artificial intelligence, blockchain, data analysis and mobile applications. Examples of fintech services and products today include mobile payments, crowdfunding platforms, robo-investment advisory, online lending, digital currencies, insurtech (insurance technology) and many others. It is therefore easy to understand that fintech innovations have a huge impact on the financial industry, introducing new opportunities, but also posing challenges related to regulations, data security and the balance between innovation and consumer protection.

Financial security is inherently related to trust in the financial system, and its disruption has direct consequences for economic stability (Rodgers et al., 2020). Households, enterprises, the public sector and the foreign sector are the main participants in the process of transforming savings into investments, and their role is crucial for the effective functioning of the economy. In this context, there is also a need to take into account risk, especially in the context of cyberattacks, which may affect both entities participating in the financial system and its infrastructure. In this context, cyber-resilience poses a particular challenge for all stakeholders. This challenge concerns in designing cyber strategies that set standards and protocols but are not too restrictive in that they neglect the personal trust and relations with partners but are not too lax in technical terms and standards (Fisher et al., 2022).

12.3 Cyberthreats and Cyberattacks

The development of technology, as was emphasized at the beginning, contributes to increased prosperity and development. At the same time, it creates an additional source of threats, which in the case of this analysis takes the form of cyberthreats. In 2015, 25% of large firms and around 15% of smaller ones reported network penetration by unauthorized outsiders, while 90% of large firms experienced a security breach of some sort (the median number of breaches was 14) (PwC, 2015). A threat is an action that takes advantage of security weaknesses in a system and has a negative impact on it (Brauch, 2011). The latter can take many forms, which, when they occur, actually constitute cyberattacks. Attacks are actions taken to damage a system or disrupt its routine operation by exploiting security vulnerabilities using various tools and techniques. Attackers carry out these attacks to achieve their malicious goals, either for self-gratification or financial reward (Yuchong & Qinghui, 2021).

In recent years, the most common forms of cyberattacks were:

i. Phishing. The vast majority of cyberattacks begin with the so-called phishing. Phishing is a form of online attack in which fraudsters impersonate trusted institutions to obtain confidential information from users, such as passwords, login details or financial information. Phishing attacks are one of the oldest forms of hacking. They have existed since the very beginning of the Internet. In the early 1990s, they involved phishing for information related to credit cards and passwords. Nowadays, phishing takes various, sometimes very sophisticated forms. Some of them are:

a. Bulk phishing. This is a term used in the context of phishing attacks that are carried out on a large scale. Bulk phishing attacks involve mass sending fake emails, text messages or other forms of communication to a large number of people in order to trick them into gaining access to their confidential data. It is characteristic that the target of the attack is not a specific person or business entity, but access to as many people as possible, thus maximizing the number of potential victims.
b. Vishing is an abbreviation of the term "voice phishing", which means a phishing attack carried out via telephone calls. In the case of vishing, cybercriminals use phone calls to trick people into obtaining confidential information such as personal information, credit card numbers and passwords. Common vishing techniques include spoofed phone calls, where attackers may call victims impersonating financial institutions, telecommunications companies, government organizations or other trusted institutions. The attacker calls the victim's number and, by causing pressure, forces him to provide sensitive personal data, e.g. the user receives a call from the bank where he is informed about the hacking of his personal accounts. The fake bank employee asks him for his login password or user ID. Social engineering techniques where attackers can use psychological and social engineering manipulation to confuse victims and make them take desired actions.
c. Smishing is an abbreviation of the term SMS phishing and means an attack that uses text messages to deceive and extort information from victims. These messages may come from purported financial institutions and other organizations. The messages may contain links to websites where the victim is asked to provide sensitive information such as passwords, credit card numbers or other personal information. Smishing is similar to traditional phishing, but differs in that the attacker uses SMS communication instead of email or other online means.
d. Spear phishing is an advanced form of phishing attack that is more targeted and personalized than standard phishing attacks. In this

case, cybercriminals tailor their attacks to specific individuals, organizations or industries, using information obtained about potential victims.

e. Email phishing also known as "deception phishing". Hackers send emails to users impersonating a well-known brand (usually a bank). The goal is to get the recipient to click on a link in the message. The user is redirected to a fake website whose purpose is to steal credentials or install malicious software or code.
f. HTTPS phishing. A protocol considered secure is increasingly being used by hackers in email links that redirect to fake websites.
g. Spear phishing. A type of email phishing that is individual and personal in nature. Typically, this type of email contains personal information and is addressed to a specific person from an organization or company. The employee recognizes this internal message in which he is obliged to perform specific actions. A type of spear phishing is whaling/CEO fraud, in which the hacker impersonates the CEO or president of the company, forcing employees to perform specific actions.
h. Pharming is a dangerous type of phishing that is sometimes very difficult for the user to track down. In this case, visitors are redirected to a crafted page that is very similar to the original.
i. Evil twin. In this case, the phishing attack uses a fake Wi-Fi hotspot to capture data in transit.

As we can see, phishing can take various, often sophisticated forms, which is why it is often difficult to detect.

Other types of cyberthreats include malware. For example:

i. Malware (short for malicious software). It is most often a file or code that is intended to steal data, damage or destroy computers and computer systems. Malware is a general term that includes various types of malicious software such as viruses, worms, Trojans, spyware, adware and ransomware.
ii. Ransomware. This is malicious computer software that encrypts files on a computer or operating system and then demands a ransom (ransom) from the user to decrypt the data. Once the computer is infected, the ransomware blocks access to files or the operating system, and the victim receives a message from cybercriminals who ask for a certain amount of money in exchange for the key to

decrypt the data. A typical ransomware attack scenario involves infecting a computer by opening an infected email attachment, visiting an infected website or using another attack method. Cybercriminals often ask for payments in cryptocurrencies, which makes transactions more anonymous.

iii. Adware. Types of malware that install on computers and mobile devices and display unwanted ads. Adware can be a very intrusive attack. It usually takes the form of pop-up ads that appear on various sides of the screen. They seriously interfere with using the Internet and reading websites.

It is also worth mentioning such forms as:

i. Social media attacks. These are cyberattacks that target social media platforms. These attacks include various strategies and techniques that aim to harm users, organizations or the social platforms themselves. An example of such attacks is social media phishing, where attackers may use fake profiles or social media pages to conduct phishing campaigns. This is aimed at obtaining confidential information, such as passwords or personal data. Malware via links is when cybercriminals can place malicious links in posts, comments or private messages that lead to the infection of a user's computer or mobile device.
ii. USB Drop is a physical attack technique in which the attacker places a specially crafted USB device in a place where a potential victim can find it. The aim of the attack is to infect a computer system or network by manipulating an infected USB device.
iii. Business Email Compromise (BEC) is a type of cyber-attack in which cybercriminals gain unauthorized access to the email accounts of users or companies. The aim of the attack is often to extort confidential information, conduct financial fraud or obtain control over email communications in order to launch further attacks. These attacks can take many forms, such as email-based phishing, where cybercriminals can use fake emails that appear to be legitimate messages from trusted sources to convince victims to reveal confidential information. Password compromise, where attackers gain access to a mailbox by breaking a password. Email spoofing involves spoofing authentic email addresses to confuse

victims and convince them to take dangerous actions cybercriminals modify email messages regarding financial transactions in order to mislead the victim and transfer funds to a fake account.

iv. Sniffing. Sniffing attacks most often occur in local networks (LANs), where computers connect to a router through a switch or hub. Using the sniffing technique, hackers can take over, among others: email messages, passwords, data for router settings.

v. Skimming is a type of attack that primarily involves methods of intercepting and stealing cardholders' personal payment information. It usually involves illegally copying data on a magnetic card in order to obtain a duplicate card that will act as a real card. The most common type of skimming is ATM skimming. In such a case, special software is installed in the ATM, with which the hacker can obtain data from the cards' magnetic stripe and PIN codes.

vi. DoS, DDoS and DRDoS attacks. A group of cyberattacks aimed at preventing the operation of a network service or computer system. They largely involve overloading the system with data and files so that the system cannot accept further data and is blocked. In a more advanced version, DDoS (distributed denial of service), user computers (zombies) are used. DDoS is more difficult to locate because it is executed by a number of computers. It is difficult to determine the main source of the attack. DRDoS (distributed reflection denial of service) is an extended version of this technique that combines DoS and DDoS—it is called a reflection attack.

vii. Brute force also called brute force cracking is not so much a type of attack, but rather a cryptographic method. We see her very often in action movies. In brute force, hackers use special software to check various combinations of codes in order to gain access to the system.

viii. Cryptojacking, also called "malicious cryptocurrency mining", is a type of cybercrime in which the criminal secretly uses the computing power of victims' devices (computers, smartphones, tablets, etc.) to generate cryptocurrency. These types of programs are specifically designed to mine electronic money. In most cases, they are practically invisible to the user. They manifest themselves, among others: overloading the computer, slowing down its operation.

12.4 Financial Sector and Cyberattackers

The financial sector is one of the favorite targets of cyberattackers. Cybercrime causes the loss of billions of dollars for the global financial industry. The primary motivation for cybercriminals to organize cyberattacks is financial gain. Organizations worldwide don't only pay to get the lost data back; they also suffer from the disruption in operations caused by cybercrime. According to Statista, the average cost of a data breach worldwide is around 4.35 million U.S. dollars, but financial repercussions differ greatly depending on the region, organization size and industry. The attacks on the financial system can be classified into two main groups. The first one covers attacks on banking infrastructure, while the second one directly concerns banking clients, regardless of whether they are individuals or enterprises. Attacks on infrastructure mainly take the form of phishing campaigns in the form of emails aimed at stealing information, as well as smishing and vishing. Hackers send information containing messages such as "Change bank account details" using social engineering techniques and aim to take control of the computer of a person authorized to make bank transfers. Cyberattacks often involve the Society for Worldwide Interbank Financial Telecommunications, known as SWIFT. Protection against this type of attacks requires implementation of security protocols and security mechanisms. The next group of attacks includes those aimed at the functioning of ATMs. The physical presence of the hacker at the site of the attack is characteristic, regardless of whether the attack involves the use of a stolen card or monitoring the machine and its users by installing cameras, thus enabling the theft of data on the card. Of course, there are more sophisticated methods, such as the installation of a malicious components directly on the ATM, which orders to issue cash to the hackers. Observation of reality indicates an increasingly complex organization of attacks on ATMs around the world with the participation of various groups, starting from technicians and ending with criminals who are physically presented at the ATMs. The second group of attacks concerns a group of bank customers. There is great diversification and rapid development in this group. This is combined with the use of mobile terminals on an increasingly larger scale, such as smartphones and smartwatches. Most attacks here are based on social engineering techniques. One of them is offering fake banking applications that allow access to confidential data. These attacks are often aimed at e-commerce websites by stealing data at the time of transaction. The development of these attacks leads to an increase in the amount of loses that results from them. Protection against these attacks requires the cooperation of all interested parties: consumers, banks and suppliers.

12.5 Cybersecurity Culture in the Era of Artificial Intelligence: Investing in Human Competencies and Awareness

There are permanent rules in cybersecurity that, despite technological progress, do not lose their validity. These undoubtedly include resistance to social engineering. In the context of organizational security, we should not forget that people are the first line of defense, which is why it is worth investing in employee training. It can be expected that in response to the development of artificial intelligence, classic technical tools and anti-phishing and anti-spam policies will be improved. Artificial intelligence presents both threats and opportunities, so we should not forget that the same tools can be used to defend as well as attack (Hyz & Gikas, 2014). Therefore, we should not forget that criminals also learn. Therefore, attacks are becoming more and more sophisticated. SMSs, mails, etc., are becoming better prepared, free of inconsistencies and typos, obvious errors that not long ago allowed them to be easily exposed. Today, we should bear in mind that artificial intelligence is joining the fight and the use of tools based on it facilitates the generation and translation of texts. As a result, transmitted texts are increasingly similar to those created by humans. It can be expected that in the near future (we should probably write "tomorrow" here, bearing in mind the speed of changes taking place), phishing attacks will be prepared in such a way by artificial intelligence tools that they increase the danger of persuading the user to click on a link to a fake website and share data or clicking on an attachment containing infected files. Therefore, the educational aspect based on building awareness among employees and customers becomes valuable. This largely translates into the need to build a security culture in an organization with specialized services that, in the case of an incident, seal systems and processes, eliminating its weak points. It should not be forgotten that attacks targeting digital security cause not only financial losses, but mainly image losses. It is worth recalling here again the importance of trust for the functioning of the financial system. Every major failure is perceived by customers who may lose trust in institutions and companies. This indicates that regulatory requirements are still a key driver of cybersecurity procedures. However, everything indicates that the weakest element in cyber protection is still employees, who are often not aware of the required actions and precautions. Therefore, it is necessary, on the one hand, to invest in procedures related to cybersecurity and IT risk management, IT system security solutions, to invest in the protection of end devices (smartphones, laptops, desktop computers, printers, multifunctional devices) and, on the other hand, to invest in the competences of employees, creating a culture security and responsibility for online activity, but also the ability to identify and remove any breaches and their negative effects. Cybersecurity should be taken into account in every dimension of the functioning of public and private institutions. Existing international standards define criteria for assessing the security of IT systems, according to which the certification process includes, among other things, the determination of product security functionality, review of product architecture and development documentation, rigorous independent functionality testing and analysis of security gaps by an accredited, independent testing laboratory. The Common Criteria standard is recognized by many government bodies around the world, such as the National Cyber Security Center in the UK, the Criptologico Nacional in Spain, the Agence Nationale de la Securite des Systemes d'Information in France, the Bundesamt fur Sicherheit in der Informationstechnik in Germany and also the National Institute of Standards and Technology in the United States. Technical analysis of security goes beyond the scope of this chapter. However, behind each action there is a person who turns out to be the weakest link in the process of ensuring the protection of the data he manages and creates.

12.6 Final Remarks

Looking from the perspective of civilization development, we can see that, in principle, the whole world is moving in the same direction. The development of digitization, automation and artificial intelligence are just examples of technological tools to carry out civilizational changes. Globally, the financial sector has a very large share in this transformation. Cybersecurity is becoming a global topic. In the context of rapid changes, it is often difficult to say what is the effect and what is the cause—whether technology makes us behave differently, we live faster, exposing ourselves and the systems we create to attacks, or whether we live faster, change technology and, consequently, create opportunities for attacks. Probably both are true—we introduce new technologies that change our lives, and then we look for technologies that will continue to change our lives by keeping us safe.

In the new environment of rapid change, database systems, artificial intelligence or algorithms provide a competitive advantage. More directly, technology and artificial intelligence are changing the competitive landscape because now those with a lot of data can compete more effectively. On the other hand, collecting and possessing more data also brings greater regulatory or cybersecurity risks for companies. Is there a way to strike a balance between the need for development and maintaining data security and privacy policies? The moment we store data, we naturally create a security gap. Data is used to create value, but at the same time the value created becomes a target for attacks for the simple reason that data is valuable. The modern financial system uses data that it co-creates with its clients and uses it to train systems and develop technologies. The development of technology and the need for personal data protection on the one hand, and cybersecurity on the other, leads to the so-called federated learning. Federated learning, data ecosystems—this is something we will see more and more of in the next few years. Probably the concept that will dominate in the coming years is data ecosystems. And research must move in this direction, in which the participation of the private and public sectors is equally important and necessary.

References

Brauch, H. G. (2011). Concepts of security threats, challenges, vulnerabilities and risks. In *Coping with global environmental change, disasters and security* (pp. 61–106). Springer.

Eddolls, M. (2016). Making cybercrime prevention the highest priority. *Network Security, 16*(8), 5–8. https://doi.org/10.1016/S1353-4858(16)30075-7

Fisher, B., Meissner, D., Nyuur, R., & Sarpong, D. (2022). Guest editorial: Cyber-attacks, strategic cyber-foresight, and security. *IEEE Transactions on Engineering Management, 69*(6), 3660–3663.

Garg, A., Curtis, J., & Halper, H. (2003). Quantifying the financial impact of IT security breaches. *Information Management and Security, 11*(2), 74–83.

Hyz, A., & Gikas, G. (2014). Transition to industry 5.0. Is it possible to integrate environmental and social issues into technological innovation? In M. Baudry et al. (Eds.), *Financial stability, economic growth and sustainable development*. Routledge.

Jamal, A. (2023). A review on security analysis of cyber physical systems using machine learning. In *Materials today: Proceedings* (pp. 2302–2306).

Marshall, A., & Tompsett, B. (2005). Identity theft in an online world. *Computer Law and Security Report, 21*(2), 128–137.

Morgan, S. (2020). Cybercrime to cost the world $10.5 trillion annually by 2025. *Cybercrime Magazine.*

Nigel, M., & Rice, J. (2011). Understanding and addressing the concerns of stakeholders. *Computers & Security, 30*(8), 803–814.

PwC. (2015). *2015 information security breaches survey.* HM Government/PwC. www.pwc.co.uk/services/audit-assurance/insights/2015-information-securitybreaches-survey.html. Accessed August 2017.

Rid, T., & Buchanan, B. (2015). Attributing cyber-attacks. *Journal of Strategic Studies, 38*(1–2), 4–37.

Rodgers, W., Attah-Boakye, R., & Adams, K. (2020, September 16). Application of algorithmic cognitive decision trust modelling for cyber security within organisations. *IEEE Transactions on Engineering Management*. https://doi.org/10.1109/TEM.2020.3019218.

Sahut, J., Iandoli, L., & Teulon, F. (2021). The age of digital entrepreneurship. *Small Business Economics, 56*(3), 1159–1169. https://doi.org/10.1007/s11187-019-00260-8

Statista. (2023). *Number of mobile (cellular) subscriptions worldwide from 1993 to 2023.* https://www.statista.com/statistics/262950/global-mobile-subscriptions-since-1993/. Accessed 3 March 2024.

Statista. (2024). *Number of internet and social media users worldwide.* https://www.statista.com/statistics/617136/digital-population-worldwide/. Accessed 3 March 2024.

SWIFT. (2020). *The evolving cyber threat to the global banking community.* https://www.swift.com/news-events/news/evolving-cyber-threat-global-banking-community. Accessed 10 March 2024.

Von Solms, R., & Van Niekerk, J. (2013). From information security to cyber security. *Computers & Security, 38*, 97–102. https://www.sciencedirect.com/science/article/pii/S0167404813000801

Yuchong, L., & Qinghui, L. (2021). A comprehensive review study of cyber-attacks and cyber security. Emerging trends and recent developments. *Energy Reports* (pp. 2352–4847). https://www.sciencedirect.com/science/article/pii/S2352484721007289

Γκίκας, Γ., & Χυζ, Α. (2020). *Εγχειρίδιο Σύγχρονης Χρηματοοικονομικής*. 2η εκδ. Broken Hill.

CHAPTER 13

Innovation Districts as a Model of Sustainable Urban Economic Development

Argyro Paraskeva

13.1 Introduction

The future of humanity's ecosystem seems to be closely linked to the transformation of urban life. The number of people living in the cities around the globe is constantly increasing, making well-managed urbanization critical in order to achieve national and global goals for sustainable development. The need for deep and accelerated changes in urban patterns is emerging, as well as changes in processes in all areas of life, both locally and globally. *The present and future of humanity is urban.* Urbanization, as a way of developing and enlarging cities, plays a decisive role in shaping people's quality of life. Creating conditions for environmental sustainability and economic prosperity in the context of fair cities

A. Paraskeva (✉)
University of West Attica, Athens, Greece
e-mail: pep22007@uniwa.gr

A. Hyz (ed.), *The Role of the Public Sector in Building Social and Economic Resilience*,
https://doi.org/10.1007/978-3-031-67702-1_13

is of utmost importance for present and future generations (UN Habitat, 2023).

Rapid population concentration has been observed in the last century driven by the industrial revolution, which is associated with migration to urban areas and the development of urban-industrial economies (Satterthwaite, 2020). The 1st industrial revolution started from the United Kingdom in the eighteenth century whereas the 2nd industrial revolution started mainly from the USA and Europe at the beginning of the nineteenth century (Britannica 2023). From the same countries started the deindustrialization in the 1970s, with the phenomenon to be intensified in the 2008 when the financial crisis emerged followed by the Great Recession (Rowthorn & Ramaswamy, 1997). Nevertheless, manufacturing—which is at the core of the industrial revolution—continues to play an essential role in economic growth, enhanced by the capabilities of technology and the increasing contribution of services, leading to the 4th Industrial Revolution (4IR), which is expected to bring about substantial changes in the way of working (McKinsey & Co, 2022).

A key factor in the development and sustainability is the demographic characteristics on the planet, such as aging. Urbanization is intense in developed countries where population is aging, a phenomenon that is expected to intensify the competition of creating and attracting the talents that will cooperate toward sustainable development and resilience of the living environment in cities. While in developed countries the population is aging, the phenomenon is not yet observed in developing countries. But, as globalization progresses, the world is becoming increasingly interconnected, blurring the lines of borders and increasing the scope for mobility between countries. This interconnection allows the diffusion of knowledge in all directions, mainly through the possibilities offered by the technology. Diffused knowledge often prevails over the mobility of capital and labor due to digitization, opening horizons to the emergence of business opportunities, by exploiting this knowledge. Cities can act as hubs in this field of mobility, creating the environment for high-quality jobs with significant economic benefit (McKinsey & Co, 2018), with the necessary state/government support in a welfare state context, with regulation of the relations of the parties involved, as well as with the substantial presence of civil society. The interconnection of government-academia-business-citizen forces (Quadruple Helix Model) can act as a basis for innovation, which has driven human progress throughout the centuries (WIPO, 2021). The dominant global trend of urbanization highlights the need to strive for sustainability outcomes in cities, through the vision of sustainable cities and the continuous assessment of progress toward sustainable urban development (Cohen, 2017). There are researches showing that sustainability is the mother lode of technological and organizational innovations, environmentally friendly, which can lead to cost reduction because companies end up with reduced inputs (Nidumolu et al., 2009).

In this context of mobility and interaction, the complex and potentially contested model of innovation districts emerged (Drucker et al., 2019). Innovation districts are geographical places within cities where various institutions (universities, research centers, government agencies) meet with businesses and are getting connected to start-ups, incubators and accelerators with the aim of stimulating and developing an economy inextricably linked to innovation (Frattini, 2023). They are a relatively new form of urban development, within the existing urban fabric, reforming the areas in which they spread. In the relatively short period of the last twenty years, a large number of innovation districts, of different shapes and sizes, have been created in many cities around the world. In most cases, innovation districts are set up in the city and often in former industrial areas and/or areas with large-scale warehousing activity, which they radically transform by creating an interactive network between universities, large enterprises, research centers, leisure spaces, start-ups, residential, technological interfacing, food/retail and green spaces. At the heart of innovation districts' model lies the connection of economic growth with innovation in its relationships with productivity, investment, research and development. The form of innovation districts varies from region to region, as well as the purpose they serve. At the same time, the significant number of innovation districts operating today can be the starting point for exploring their sustainability in the medium-long term and the contribution of the public administration in this direction.

This paper approaches the model of innovation districts and their role in the context of urban economic development, on the occasion of the district's initiative to support the creation of the first innovation district in Athens (General Secretariat for Research and Innovation, 2023). Topics related to the relationship between innovation, urban sustainability and resilience, research and development, investments, the role of public administration in urban development issues linked to innovation are approached. The constantly changing climatic conditions, the swelling of cities, the need to review urban models of coexistence as cities mature, the examination of issues of smoothing inequalities, are factors that can contribute to the examination of the operation of innovative coexistence urban models in terms of economy and effectiveness.

In this context, the present approach is directed toward investigating the questions related to the form of innovation districts in different geographical areas and the purpose for which they are created. In addition, an attempt is made to investigate their sustainability in the medium-long-term perspective, and the contribution of the public administration to their creation, operation and sustainability, through the examination of some innovation districts, with different characteristics. Specifically, two cases are approached in more detail, using the existing literature as well as a multitude of online sources and analyses, and a concise approach to a wider network of innovation districts, in order to examine issues of urban economic development, sustainability and resilience, in an environment of instability and change. The study will continue with the approach of the designed innovation district in Athens. For the purpose of the analysis, three sources of data are used: case study analysis, secondary data and empirical observation analysis.

13.2 Urbanization and Industrialization

13.2.1 People in the City—Historical Review

The first cities appeared thousands of years ago, as a result of the agricultural revolution. The first cities appeared thousands of years ago, as a result of the agricultural revolution. Other cities took a long time to form and grow, while others appeared suddenly. Throughout history, cities have been operating as centers of commerce, education, cultural activity, and economic opportunity, and as a result they have experienced strong population fluctuations (The History of Cities, National Geographic, 2023). A large percentage of the population lived in rural areas. For example, 94% of the US population lived in rural areas around the eighteenth century (United States Census Bureau, 2023) and visited the cities mainly for commercial purposes.

The mass movement of population from the countryside to the cities first appeared in England. Much of the population began to concentrate around the big cities, from the end of the seventeenth century onward. It is likely that there are many reasons led to this demographic change, such as weather conditions that affected agricultural production and the increase in per capita income resulting from externalities (Voigtländer & Voth, 2006). The interest turned to the cities, where jobs were offered, mainly in manufacturing. Factories were created, production increased, the produced products were channeled to the new markets that England was opening. Solutions were sought to transport the products faster and more economically, leading to the use of coal for the movement of steam engines. The transport map changed with the advent of innovations in infrastructure and technology through vehicles such as wagons and ships powered by steam produced by burning coal. With the spread of the use of the steam engine, the 1st Industrial Revolution was a fact and has been rapidly transferred both to Europe and the Americas. Intense commercial activity brought economic growth that shaped and influenced the growth of cities, which tended to develop near coal and coal-related areas (Alvarez-Palau et al., 2020).

The change in the form of labor demanded, as a consequence of the industrial revolution, created migration flows from Europe to the USA in the mid-nineteenth century. The USA was just coming out of a civil war, in a time of re-organization and reconstruction of the country. Factories were created, which needed labor, leading to population growth in areas with rising industrial activity. The need for agricultural products increased, yet machines appeared which replaced much of the labor force in rural areas, contributing to the movement of the population to the cities. The need for agricultural products increased, yet machines appeared which replaced much of the labor force in rural areas, contributing to the movement of the population to the cities. Trade and labor mobility were enhanced by the development of the transport network. It was the period when the USA was implementing a project of enormous importance for its economic development, the creation of the railway network, with the aim of connecting the coasts of the country in the Atlantic with the coasts of the country in the Pacific. With the reduction of transportation costs, the creation and operation of factories for more mass production of goods were strengthened, which led to the concentration of manufacturing activity in specific areas, creating larger cities (Atack et al., 2021). The 2nd Industrial Revolution was a fact, at the beginning of the twentieth century (Yuko, 2021).

13.2.2 *Industrialization*

The industrial revolution brought about the transformation of human society gradually leading to industrialization, urbanization and globalization (Chen et al., 2014), phenomena that are interconnected. Industrialization led to economic growth, which gave impetus to an intense process of urbanization, both in developed and developing countries, mainly due to the specialization of labor and the development of non-agricultural sectors, which until before industrialization dominated. The relationship between urbanization and globalization is more complex. The relationship between urbanization and globalization is more complex. In the initial stages of globalization, large cities were created in powerful states. The complexity in the relationship between urbanization and globalization is intensified by the intense interconnection of businesses, cities and countries, brought about by technology, with the possible re-examination of economic theories in relation to the optimal size of a country, redirecting the interest to the sustainability of cities (McCann & Acs, 2010).

13.2.3 *Urbanization*

Urbanization is observed historically after the industrial revolution and refers to the increased number of people living in cities. In addition to the number of inhabitants, the term urbanization encompasses a series of changes resulting from the concentration of people in cities, in terms of industrial infrastructure, employment, living conditions and the provision of public services. For the first time in human history, there are more urban dwellers than rural dwellers. In the coming decades, population growth is expected to take place exclusively in cities. The total number of urban population is expected to increase to 6.7 billion in 2050, up from 4.4 billion in recent years (UN DESA, 2020).

Urbanization can work positively in the development of societies under conditions. When properly managed, urbanization can reduce poverty and inequality by providing equal opportunities for work, quality of life, education and health. However, when the necessary planning does not exist, it can lead to inequalities, crime increase, environmental pollution, social inequalities (UN DESA, 2020). Recording thoughts on urbanization in Rwanda, Somik Lall from the World Bank typically states that urbanization is a “messy” process—because it starts when countries are at low-income levels, without the possibility of investing in the necessary infrastructure, which will prepare the area to receive a large number of residents. Then, with the advent of prosperity, the cities that are created are called upon to manage the chaos that has arisen and to prioritize the necessary actions to maintain the institutional and financial capital that has already been created (Lall, 2014).

With the growth of cities, the complexity of their management also increases, introducing social inequality as a factor that needs special attention. Inclusive urban life and social inequalities require careful management of the spatial, economic and social aspects of the urban divide. The complexity in the process of urban development highlights the need to study multifaceted parameters, including urban infrastructure, which includes various types of functional infrastructure, such as water and energy supply infrastructure, transport infrastructure, wastewater management (Carrillo et al., 2014). The performance of operational infrastructure is expected to have at least a minimum degree of efficiency in order to serve urban development at the economic, social and environmental levels, in the context of ever-intensifying urbanization (Chen et al., 2019). Aiming at the economic, social and environmental resilience of cities, significant and substantial strengthening of urban infrastructure appears to be a fundamental component of a mix capable of supporting economic growth, in the trajectory of the planet's urbanization (Shen et al., 2011).

13.2.4 Urbanization and the Public Sector

The process of urban development involves several actors, both private and public, each of which pursues its own goals, and among which there is a need for cooperation (Faludi, 1987). Participants' cooperation in the urban planning process has worked in the form of the regulator from the side of the public administration, until around the 1980s (Verhage, 2003). A change is observed in relation to the role of the district in urban planning, moving from a hierarchic decision-making model to an "interactive policy network".[1] In the hierarchic model, government planning agencies have a central role and enforce the rules on everyone, for the common interest. In the interactive policy network model, local planning

[1] Verhage (2003).

authorities in particular and the state in general act as parts of a network of interdependent actors, for the implementation of urban planning aimed at facilitating and stimulating urban development. Placing the public sector in an active role within the process of urban regeneration in the sense of cooperation seems to remain at an initial stage. However, it is worthwhile to further investigate the regulatory role of the public sector in urban as a facilitator and enhancer of urban development (Verhage, 2003).

It seems that governments around the world will be called to manage intense pressures from the expected even greater concentration of people in cities, a fact that will lead to pressures the infrastructure and spatial management of cities to support the inevitably arising needs for dignified survival. Bearing in mind that urbanization is not only a challenge for the cities themselves but also for the wider geopolitical environment in which they are surrounded, managing the new urban reality will require closer cooperation at all levels of government (The World Bank, 2009). As developing countries are mainly experiencing the process of rapid urbanization, the effectiveness depends on the creation of multilateral cooperative mechanisms and cooperative interventions between the government and local administration to lead to economic development (Puga, 1996). Good management and information systems, combined with competent leadership, can be ineffective if accompanied by insufficient funding. Accordingly, a city without good governance and competent leadership will find it difficult to effectively manage tax revenues and finance the market. These elements remain at the center of the functional structure of the city systems for the years to come.[2]

13.3 Innovation and Urban Development

The term innovation, in economic theory, refers to the cultivation and application of technologies and ideas, which improve the goods and services produced, making their production more efficient (European Central Bank, 2017). Beyond its connection to economic theory, innovation is everywhere (Godin, 2008). It is discussed in the social sciences, management, economics, arts, public administration and is largely involved in the discussion to solve related issues, so it is a phenomenon to be studied. In this context, innovation can be a field

[2] The World Bank (2009).

of reference and research approach, since as a concept it can work on multiple levels. Innovation is a socio-economic process that can drive value growth exponentially, making understandable the divergence in innovation issues observed between different societies, with different social capital and different public policy (Branscomb, 2002).

13.3.1 Technological Innovation

Technological innovation, in particular, is an essential factor in economic development, enabling the production of more results, with the most intelligent and creative use of the same amount of resources. The role of technological innovations is increasingly strengthened in relation to the development of leading industrial economies, turning the attention of governments from science and technology policy to focusing on research and innovation policy (Branscomb, 2002). The search for new technologies or the improvement of the existing goes through a process of continuous uncertainty about the outcome. It is easy to assume, for example, that large US companies do not face such uncertainties in terms of searching for new technologies, and in general in terms of research and development (R&D). However, investment in research and technology, especially in OECD countries, seems to have become very expensive. Moreover, even if the necessary funds are available, the risk of investing in R&D is very high. The search for new technology can be faced with problems such as the failure to create the designed product, the creation of a product that is not marketable, the creation of a marketable product that is not economically beneficial, the longtime delay in the creation of the marketable and economically beneficial product, the lack of the necessary regulatory framework, etc. (Rosenberg, 2004).

13.3.2 Organizational Innovation

Another form of innovation is organizational innovation, which may include changes in business practices, changes in the organization of the workplace or changes in the company's external relations. Organizational innovation can have a significant impact on a firm's performance, in addition to its supporting role in product innovation. It can improve the quality and efficiency of work, stimulate the diffusion of information, as well as improve the firm's ability to acquire and use knowledge and technology (OECD, 2005).

The term organizational innovation is associated with the creation or adoption of an idea or practice new to the organization. However, it seems to remain unclear how organizations change their structural model and how innovation participates in the process of such changes. But it can be said with relative certainty that organizational and technological innovations are closely related. Furthermore, organizational innovation may be a prerequisite for technological innovation, which may be linked to internal organizational strengths such as the capacity to learn, values and the ability to shape organizational development and technological change (Lam, 2004).

13.3.3 Innovation Ecosystem

The foundation for the creation of innovation districts is the innovation ecosystem; for this reason, it is necessary to understand it in order to understand the value of innovation districts. Innovation ecosystems are networks of people and organizations that interact to nurture ideas that will turn into successful businesses. Innovation ecosystems include a range of different stakeholders, such as universities and research centers, human capital, information technology infrastructure, financial capital, the private sector and the public sector, which interact to create new products, services, technologies and policies. A healthy innovation ecosystem connects people with good ideas to training, funding, support and workers who want to turn ideas into action. A single ecosystem model to be implemented is not feasible, nor is a single model of innovation districts, as both reflect local culture and local habits (Lawrence et al., 2019).

13.3.4 Sustainability and Urban Development

Development that meets the needs of the present generation, without creating restrictions on the possibilities of future generations to meet their own needs, is considered sustainable (Vavouras & Vavoura, 2019). As the population is concentrated in cities at a rapid rate, reference to sustainable cities is widespread, but no clear answers to concerns about how cities and local governments can meet the challenges of sustainability appear (Bulkeley & Betsill, 2005). The use of indicators as a practice to measure the effectiveness of strategies toward sustainable development is observed. However, there are different practices in the creation and use of these indicators, depending on the policy applied, while at the same time there are actions toward the creation of international indicators to measure urban sustainable development (Shen et al., 2011).

Due to the concentration of economic activity and population, cities have an essential role in dealing with climate change. For a city to be considered sustainable there should be essential elements such as sustainable education, renewable energy, sustainable transport, sustainable buildings, waste management, which, if properly managed by willing and informed residents, can lead to sustainable development. By extension, a city can be considered sustainable when it is socio-environmentally regulated, integrates the elements of nature into the urban area and, in this context, provides the appropriate work and business environment. Looking for the elements of the concept of sustainability, one realizes the complexity involved in the analysis of the term. In anthropogenic tasks, the formation of environmental awareness through education for sustainable development is critical, an essential element for responsible societies, in order to preserve the environment for the survival of the human species (Sodiq et al., 2019).

13.3.5 Innovation Districts

Urban innovation districts have evolved into a tool for planning economic development in the field of public policy and economy, focusing on business opportunities around the context of interconnection and cooperation in order to develop their products and services and promote them to the market (Kayanan, 2021). As a new phenomenon, with a strong diffusion tendency, the spread of innovation districts has barely been recorded, in the form of systematic analysis, as a tool of neoliberal economic development. The success of the project in Barcelona in 2000 can be considered a starting point for the development of innovation districts. Katz and Wagner (2014) define innovation districts as "geographic areas where cutting-edge institutions and firms cluster and connect with start-ups, business incubators and accelerators. They are developed in a compact physical environment, with transport accessibility and offer technological connectivity and a mix of residential, office and retail space". Essentially, they combine entrepreneurship with investment in degraded or abandoned urban areas, in an attempt to bring together investment and economic development policy, through a neoliberal perspective. According to Julie Wagner of the Brookings Institute, an innovation district, in order to maximize its potential, combines a series of factors such as the creation of a critical mass of research and talent infrastructure, the design of systems and structures that create jobs with decent living wages, the design of equitable development strategies and the transformation of the environment to be inclusively accessible. All these factors, and obviously more, help to create an innovation district that will act as a force of growth.

The key feature of an innovation district is the existence of a complex interaction between business activities, urban planning, innovation and economic growth. A critical element of the urban regeneration process, with the aim of creating innovation districts, is the structure of the main actors involved, and these are: the public sector, the private sector and universities, which constitute of the Triple Helix approach. The creation of an institutional background among the involved actors can act as a mechanism to maintain the developing model of the innovation district (Gianoli & Henkes, 2020). In a competitive world where knowledge and information are major sources of innovation and economic growth, governments are looking for strategies to transform their current productive capabilities. Rapid urbanization and the need to create a more sustainable and efficient urban environment are driving cities to become smarter, with digital technologies playing an important role. A key strategy for the creation of smart cities is the creation of innovation areas as well as the development of productive ecosystems. Productive ecosystems emphasize economic and environmental sustainability and are a new way of dealing with urban development. According to them, the urban environment is designed as an integrated ecosystem that includes multiple sectors and functions such as energy production, waste management, agriculture, transport. All these sectors are interconnected in a productive ecosystem, to create a more sustainable and efficient urban environment (Castillo, 2023).

In that context, research searches around the innovation district model are increasing. An innovation district is a network of knowledge-based urban development where public and private actors work to promote, attract and retain both investment and talent, to revitalize urban areas and strengthen the knowledge-based economy and innovation in general (Esmaeilpoorarabi et al., 2020).

13.3.6 Public Administration and the Creation/Sustainability of an Innovation District

Cities around the world are becoming more and more "smart", as the urbanization of the last decades leads to the need of creating a more sustainable and efficient urban environment (Castillo, 2023), in which different sectors will be involved, such as research, production, workers, housing, waste management, recycling, energy self-sufficiency and public transport. The interaction and overall action can lead to the creation of innovation ecosystems, which will consist of companies, universities, research centers, public organizations, investors and other stakeholders. Together, the participants in these ecosystems will be able to create an environment closely linked to innovation. The public administration, through its mechanisms, could contribute to the creation of a culture of innovation, at many levels of the social network, most likely with a catalytic role in relation to the upgrading of living standards and coexistence in a society of balanced and fair development.

In that interconnected and complex environment, the development of an innovation district requires strong and long-term commitment from all key stakeholders involved. Uncertainty appears to be the new normal and, combined with the more complex structure of societies, implies the need for a degree of flexibility and adaptability in order to cope with possible severe shocks. There is a set of internal and external factors that influence the created urban complexity, such as internal change in the structure of organizations, economic crises, new technologies and policy changes. Therefore, the government system that will support the creation of an innovation district should have the ability to adapt to the ever-changing circumstances.

13.3.7 Adaptive Governance

The multiple crises, visible and invisible, of the last decades intensify the debates around the issues of reforms, so that societies are sufficiently capable of managing the crises that are expected, in terms of sustainability and resilience. Improving governance and public administration has been debated in recent years, as countries seem to recognize the role of public bodies and institutions in promoting economic efficiency combined with the effectiveness of policies implemented. Discussions have started in many countries, but they are not progressing at the same pace in all of them. An important role in the success of public administration reforms is played by the deep change in the culture of societies, often met with a strong resistance. This is why reformers are looking for practices from other countries, which have worked effectively in the direction of public administration reform. The process accelerates especially when financial resources are exhausted, so thinking and reflection deepen (Focus, OECD, 1996).

In this global changing field, a coordination between stakeholders, leadership and knowledge-based decision-making leads to an adaptive governance model as a framework to support the dynamic response required for the management of an innovation district. An innovation district relies, for its creation, on urban regeneration projects that are characterized by a high degree of uncertainty and complexity, as they develop in the long term with the possibility of situations of asymmetry in information and power between the participants. Adaptive governance can provide solutions to challenges that will appear in such complex urban regeneration projects as innovation districts (Gianoli & Henkes, 2020).

13.4 The Case of 22@Barcelona

A starting point for the innovation districts is considered @22 Barcelona, an iconic project that transformed a large area of the city, from an abandoned industrial zone into an innovation district, which offers modern activity spaces to skilled workers and talents, in order to face modern challenges (Intelligent Cities Challenge, EU, 2023). @22 Barcelona is a benchmark for innovation districts around the world and seems to be designed in this direction, combining urban planning with economic and social strategy, through public–private partnerships, as well as with the strategy of business cooperative formations (clusters), involving companies, universities and other factors.

13.4.1 22@Barcelona: The Implementation

The implementation of the 22@Barcelona project began in the 2000s and is one of the most ambitious urban regeneration projects in the world. It began as a government initiative to transform the historic but dilapidated industrial area of Poblenou into an innovative and dynamic district (Innovation Academy, 2023). Before the creation of 22@Barcelona, a group of the City Council of the Municipality of Barcelona (Ajuntament de Barcelona) asked the question: what measures should be taken to improve and increase interactions between the international community and local businesses and institutions in Barcelona? From the answers given, 22@Barcelona finally emerged, which was launched in 2000 to transform the historic abandoned textile area of Saint Marti into a growing knowledge center (Koven, ECPA, 2019). The aim of the project was to create an innovation area capable of developing economic activity and employment, emphasizing the economy of knowledge and new technologies (Gianoli & Henkes, 2020). In particular, the objectives from the operation of 22@Barcelona were linked to the transformation of the *physical*, *economic* and *social* dimension of the area, through the stimulation of economic activity, the creation of synergies and partnerships, the promotion of the image of the area and the development of new housing and green spaces. Regarding the *physical regeneration* of the area, emphasis was placed on the creation of a compact and flexible area, with modern infrastructure networks, mixed uses and enhanced density. Given the limited area, in order to achieve these specific goals, the effective use of available land resources was a necessary condition.[3] In terms of *economic* transformation, the creation of synergies and collaborations has been the main strategy to generate interest in bringing different stakeholders together in a common place, able and willing to support the pursuit of innovative ventures. The expected results from the cultivation of business partnerships and synergies—clusters—included both the integration of businesses based on the business rationale (more and better companies), as well as their contribution to the transformation of the city and the correlation of their activities with everyday life in the area. The expected *social* transformation is connected with the integration of this former industrial area into the main fabric of the city, with the improvement of the transport network, the increase in the supply of housing by the public sector, the creation of employment opportunities for the residents of the area and the promotion of the creation of business networks.

[3] Gianoli A. and Henkes R. (2020).

13.4.2 *The City of Barcelona*

The creation of 22@Barcelona in Poblenu is the result of wider collaborations involving different stakeholders of the city. Citizens, entrepreneurs, public bodies and especially the collaboration between the public sector, media and non-profit organizations were involved in one way or another in the project (Ali, 2021). In order for these collaborations to exist, in the previous years a culture of intense civic consciousness had been cultivated, which was manifested by the utilization of social capital, in the post-dictatorship era (after 1979). The opportunity given for the regeneration and reformation of the city, based on solidarity was perceived (Garcia-Ramon, 2000). After the end of the dictatorship period, from 1980 until the Olympics, Barcelona entered a period of reformation, led by a charismatic mayor. Infrastructure was built, the road and transport network was developed and beaches accessible to the population were expanded, actions that had already been planned much earlier (Garcia-Ramon, 2000). On the occasion of the hosting of the 1992 Olympic Games, the process of urban reformation of Barcelona began in 1980.

Poblenou area is located in the south-eastern part of Barcelona in the district of Sant Marti. Its boundary is a characteristic diagonal road, which crosses, among other things, an area with universities, technology incubators, companies and international organizations and is, today, an important part of Barcelona's identity. Before its upgrading, Poblenou was a run-down district, consisting of approximately 250 blocks of private land, with a high concentration of industrial units, mainly textiles. With the start of deindustrialization from the 1960s, the area experienced a process of abandonment and decline, which was reinforced by the creation of a railway center as well as changes in the urban plans of the city (Ali, 2020). Even earlier, Barcelona had entered a process of modernization, which was expressed by two important international exhibitions that took place in 1888 and 1929. Catalan artists influenced by Belgian and Parisian Art Nouveau, led the implementation of modernism in the city, and they succeeded in spreading the idea in the Catalan society of Barcelona. A new synthesis emerged in urban life, which included tradition and innovation, craft and industry, nationalism and internationalization, in a productive and not competitive way, aiming to create a better and more beautiful life (Bosch, 2005).

13.4.3 22@Barcelona—Planning for Change

Poblenou district was chosen for the creation of 22@Barcelona, a neighborhood where innovation, design, creativity and technology constitute the economic driving force in place of old factories (Meet Barcelona, Barcelona City Council). The industrial zone of the area was in the past the industrialized district of Barcelona and today hosts a cluster of knowledge. At the same time, the past coexists with the future through the use of old factories, which are transformed by the new companies into modern industrial complexes. For example, the old textile mill Ca l'Aranyó was transformed into the Pompeu Fabra University's Campus, and the Can Munné fabric warehouse today houses the Bau design school.

The area was chosen as it had reached a level of maturity for regeneration. In addition to conventional utilities, the area already had a fiber optic network, while creating a sophisticated waste management and facility air conditioning network. As the urban renewal process of Barcelona had started since the Olympic Games period, Poblenou area was chosen to develop a place for urban, economic and social innovation. The size of the selected area combined with its central location in the city and good transport connections offered significant potential for the international development of Barcelona, in terms of competitiveness, among metropolitan areas worldwide (Urban Sustainability Exchange 2024).

The first element of the 22@ integration process is spatial regeneration, which supports the concentration of businesses and institutions in closer geographic proximity. The design was based on four main clusters which were classified according to territorial location, typology, accessibility and spatial planning. These groups include: Media, Information and Communication Technologies (NTIC-New Technology of Information and Communication), Biotechnology and Design. This first element is linked to the effort and planning of the regeneration of areas in recession and decline, the inclusion in the planning of marginalized areas, the stimulation of regional competitiveness and, finally, their cooperation in a specific and clearly defined spatial framework (Battaglia & Tremblay, 2011). The model of restoration combined with the creation of modern architectural buildings coexists characteristically in 22@Barcelona. Palo Alto, an old industrial site, was restored and transformed into a center of creativity housing artists, exhibitions, events and at the same time television and film studios (Urban Next Lexicon, 2018) A characteristic building of 22@Barcelona is Torre Agbar, a small skyscraper, whose functionality and design are combined with environmentally friendly construction materials and elements, meeting energy efficiency requirements, with an external surface covered with photovoltaic panels and making use of underground waters. The building received the green building award from the European Commission in 2011 (Meet Barcelona, Barcelona City Council). Through the transformation of the landscape, which was based on the preparation and existence of the appropriate infrastructure, a new large "neighborhood" was created as well as an attractive environment for living and working. The implementation was based on the idea of the new territorial dimension of innovation, from its simple linear connection with the linear technopolis, to the wider dimension of functioning in an innovation cluster which will be based on relational proximity (Battaglia & Tremblay, 2011).

The second element in the 22@ integration process is institutional and relational integration, to promote and strengthen collaborations between universities, research and development (R&D) and businesses, acting on the basis of supporting a system of cultural values, shared codes and reflections, among local stakeholders, which are a foundation for the development of common governance spaces and common development strategies. And this is because, while the approach of creating an area in the form of a purely technopolis is somewhat limited, the model approached by 22@ includes more dimensions of relational connection and interaction (Battaglia & Tremblay, 2011). In this form of interaction, a conceptual connection is created between the concept of the smart city and an adaptive public governance (Gianoli & Henkes, 2020).

13.4.4 22@Barcelona—New Compact City Model

Barcelona, according to the Institute of Catalonia, had a population of approximately 1,620,000 inhabitants in 2018, in an area of 101.4km2, which corresponds to a population density of approximately 16,000 inhabitants per km2.

Population Composition: The population consists of approximately 52.5% women and 47.5% men. It is estimated that 62% have been born in the region (Catalonia), 24% come from other regions of Spain and 14% from other countries, a figure which has increased by 4% since 2001.

Main activities/industries: Barcelona is an economic, touristic, sports, cultural and commercial center with intense activity in the industry of fashion, science and the arts.

22@Barcelona district: Located in the Poblenou district of San Martins. The region seeks the strategic concentration of knowledge-intensive activities (Urban Sustainability Exchange, 22@Barcelona).

Implementation—Implementation stages of 22@: In 2000, the municipal organization 22 Arroba BCN, S.A.U., was created by the Barcelona Municipal Authority, which is responsible for the supervision, management and promotion of the project. The project implementation stages included:

2000: Master Plan
2001: Urban Planning
2003: 2004: Configuration of the infrastructure
2004: 2006: Construction
2004: Design and implementation of business partnerships and synergies
2008: Complete delivery of the project. Completion of a coherently structured area.

A total area of 4,000,000m^2 was planned, of which 3,200,000m^2 was allocated for production activities and 800,000m^2 for housing and services. In addition, an area of 114,000m^2 of green space has been planned (use.metropolis).

Financial & Technical Data—22@Barcelona District Innovation—2012

(*PEMB* 2014)

- Area size: 198.26 hectares, 115 building blocks, 1,159,626 m2 of land
- Floor space for productive use: approximately 3,200,000 m2
- 4,000 subsidized public housing (at least 25% for rent)
- 145,000 m2 of land for new facilities and 114,000 m2 for new green zones
- Companies established: 7,329 (December 2012)
- Employees: 85,000 (December 2012)

Infrastructures, wider and local, played a very important role in urban regeneration through 22@ implementation, based on the Special Infrastructure Plan (PEI) for Poblenou (Rius, 2011). In this text, the following urban infrastructures are analyzed: transportation, water supply, energy, waste and telecommunications.

22@ district extends over an area of 2 million square meters, of which approximately 600,000 sqm are *roads*, reconstructed to include the infrastructure necessary for the operation of the area and to organize the area (Rius, 2011).

In 2002, *a cooling-heating network* was designed, which started operating in 2004, providing heating, air conditioning and hot water to over 40 buildings with a coverage area of approximately 390,000 square meters, which corresponds to approximately 10,000 inhabitants, and with provision for coverage of over 2,500,000 sq.m., upon completion of the project (Districtlima, Ajuntament de Barcelona/Barcelona City Council). The project was based on the specifications of the European Union and the Kyoto Protocol and was implemented with the creation of a public–private partnership company, initially creating the main facility, which since then has been constantly evolving by adding substations, leading until 2011 to at least 40% saving energy compared to traditional means, and in a permanent reduction of CO2 emissions. The investment, up to 2011, was approximately €50 million, with an expected payback in 14 years, according to the 25-year business plan (Rius, 2011).

In *telecommunications*, since 1994, the Municipality of Barcelona already had optical fiber networks to connect its offices in the city, which were managed by different companies with annual contracts, in a public–private partnership (Salvator et al., 2017). As part of the infrastructure for 22@, telecommunications work focused on improving the existing infrastructure and creating an additional fiber optic network, which again belonged to the Municipality. As a wholesaler, the Municipality makes the network available to operators, providing services to businesses and individuals through enhanced broadband. From 2006 to 2011, a total of €3.5 million was invested in strengthening and reforming the telecommunications network by the Municipality of Barcelona, with an expected payback period in 2016. In the telecommunications industry, it is considered that every euro invested is converted into four in the long term. The investment in telecommunications by the Municipality of Barcelona can be considered to have had positive effects for the wider local community including the lower cost tariff policy, the attraction of businesses to areas with enhanced telecommunications services, the management of risk by the state through applied regulatory policies (Rius, 2011).

13.4.5 A Smart City Within the City

The 200 hectares of land in the Poblenou district of Barcelona, with the implementation of the 22@Barcelona project, was transformed into an innovation district that offers a modern environment for the strategic concentration of knowledge-intensive activities. The design of the project was based on the broader objective of attracting activities of knowledge and innovation, transforming the obsolete industrial area into a place of high urban and environmental quality (The European Commission's Intelligent Cities Challenge, 2023).

The design of the 22@ area, which was activated more systematically in the post-dictatorship Franco era, led to the development of the wider area of Barcelona centered on the 22@innovation district. According to research by Mobile World Capital Barcelona, the technology hubs of the greater Barcelona (Catalonia) region have created more than 15,000 jobs in technology companies in the region, with an economic footprint of more than 1.4 billion euros each year (Mobile World Capital Barcelona, 2023). Furthermore, according to the same research, in the last 5 years, the number of technology hubs in Barcelona and the wider region has doubled. At the same time, the number of jobs is expected to increase to 20,000 by 2025, with a turnover reaching 2 billion euros. About half of these businesses have chosen the narrowest region of the 22@ innovation district, with the region's ability to attract multidisciplinary talent, the high level of local talent, the already proven business and industrial ecosystem, and the most important criteria for their selection the geographical location. Four out of ten workers are foreigners of eighteen nationalities. 86% of the employees in the hubs are between 31 and 40 years old, while there are a significant number of employees with many years of work experience. 30% of the total employees are women, a percentage that can be considered satisfactory (Deloitte, 2023).

13.4.6 Planning the Next Phase for 22@Barcelona

Walking through and studying Barcelona's 22@innovation district, the collaborative culture that permeates all aspects of the city's life becomes apparent. It seems that the district is in constant discussion with its citizens, with strong voluntary participation, in discussions that include collective work in the direction of sustainable development with goals, data collection and indicators that reflect the social and economic reality of Barcelona. The collective effort appears widespread in the city, with constant reflection and actions toward the organization around the goals of sustainable development, with the municipal authority in the role of coordinator, which promotes the participation of the city's residents in the discussion. With the intention of aligning projects and uniting the efforts of all stakeholders in the common goals of ensuring decent living conditions for current and future generations, Barcelona expresses its commitment to creating a continuously better city in a sustainable world (Barcelona 2030 Agenda, UN Habitat, 2021). In the general planning of the city, the 22@ innovation district plays an important role, planning and redesigning the transformation of the urban environment, and creating a high-tech area, which at the same time is a pole of economic development, also participating in the creation of housing and entertainment spaces.

13.4.7 Public Sector and the Management of Innovation in 22@Barcelona

In times of economic prosperity, markets operate by the laws of supply and demand, often without the need for government support. In these periods, there is comfort in the implementation of measures to strengthen innovation (grants, financing, etc.). However, within the economic cycle there are periods of economic tightness that can dangerously deregulate economies, with possibly unforeseen consequences, without, however, eliminating the need to support innovation. In these times, one of the roles of governments is to act as driving forces and to support partnership processes between the public administration and the private sector and in matters of innovation.

In this context, an innovation laboratory, the 22@Urban Lab, was created in 22@, with the cooperation of the public and private sectors, to manage small innovation pilot projects. Through the operation of 22@Urban Lab, citizens benefit from receiving better products and services through processes in which the local administration such as the municipality is also involved. In addition, businesses benefit from testing their products in a real environment, while at the same time they can come into contact with customers, indirectly contributing to the strengthening of competitiveness. The process that has been initiated by cultivating a culture of innovation laboratories and implementing it at 22@ is difficult to be measured in terms of outcome. However, there are indications of the effectiveness of the initiative, which has created pilot units for the production of improved products, adapted to the needs of citizens (Majó, Barcelona City Council).

Another action taken by the public sector was the planning to create a public technical office that will gather all urban economic and socio-cultural information as a specialized information point for 22@. This office will function as a coordinating center for urban planning projects and will monitor issues of economic and socio-cultural development and as an information point for these projects. In addition, it will be the point of information, both locally and internationally, for the hours when the relevant public services are closed (Ajuntament de Barcelona, 2020).

13.4.8 The 22@ Barcelona in Brief

The planning for the creation of 22@ in Barcelona was based on a triple objective: the urban, economic and social renewal of the Poblenou area of Barcelona. The framework of the project is based on Barcelona's tradition of long-term strategic planning in terms of creating a city model. For Barcelona, the international recognition of the successful transformation of the city can be considered the modern manifestation of the long tradition of innovative and progressive city planning, which has started since the nineteenth century.

13.5 The Case of Boston's Innovation Ecosystem

An exemplary case of original connection of innovation policies with urban regeneration is the state of Boston, USA (Monardo, 2018). In Boston, the creation of innovation districts is combined with the regeneration of the city, through the implementation of a strategy centered on the interaction between urban regeneration initiatives and the dynamics of developing ecosystems related to innovation (European Commission, Joint Research Centre, 2019). The strategy followed to drive innovation in Boston can be interpreted within a three-level framework:

- On a financial and real estate level, as a promotion of a model of "excellence poles"—Boston Seaport Innovation District

- On a social level as connecting less privileged populations with employment and educational opportunities—Roxbury
- At the level of knowledge, with the interaction between recognized institutions of higher education, such as the Massachusetts Institute of Technology (MIT)—Kendall Square.

An essential role in the creation of the Boston-Cambridge innovation ecosystem is the interconnection of the four main institutions of higher education, namely Harvard, MIT, Northeastern University and Boston University.

13.5.1 Boston Seaport Innovation District

Boston Seaport is the first US region to be designated an innovation district. Prior to the declaration of construction of the Seaport, the state of Massachusetts and the city of Boston had allocated large funds to open the South Boston Waterfront peninsula and connect it to the airport (Kayanan, 2021).

An area of 1,000 acres located along the waterfront in Boston's South Side provided an excellent opportunity to redevelop the area, which was in transition. The South Boston Waterfront, which was to be transformed into an innovation district, began to attract growing technology and biotech companies, interested in using the existing industrial space as laboratories for research. Traditional office spaces have attracted the interest of start-ups and growing technology, digital design and e-commerce businesses. Adequate public transport infrastructure as well as proximity to the airport and a convention center also contributed positively (ECPA Urban Planning, 2017). However, the completion of the project was frozen due to the Global Financial Crisis (GFC). The restart of the project was announced in 2010 by the Mayor of Boston, who insisted that the project be managed by the Boston Redevelopment Authority (Kayanan, 2021) renamed Boston Planning & Development Agency (BPDA), which is a public agency with a vision of forever shaping Boston's future collectively (The Boston Planning Development Agency, 2024).

The Innovation Districts model is based on the belief that the creation of structures in a dense mixed-use context will lead to an environment consisting of the ideal mix of creatively talented people, who through collaboration and interaction will cultivate a culture of innovative activity and entrepreneurship. Despite the original planning in this direction, Boston Seaport seems to have moved away from its original pillars of creating an environment of equal opportunity, in relation to the supply of work and the possibility of accommodation. It seems that an area that lacks the sense of neighborhood has emerged, with expensive and relatively small houses, without schools, libraries, churches. The vision of Boston's Mayor Menino for 20 years, who aimed to create a vibrant neighborhood that would operate in these rhythms 24/7, is far from the final configuration in an area with expensive buildings, lack of greenery and public spaces, with jobs for the elite (Drucker et al., 2019).

Boston Mayor Menino's vision was to transform a large area of Boston into a hub for knowledge workers through a targeted, experimental approach. Referring to the creation of innovation clusters around biotechnology, green growth, health, technology and other sectors, he linked them to alternative models of worker housing. It seems that he envisioned the creation of a large neighborhood in which young entrepreneurs would be given the opportunity to test their ideas, while at the same time affordable housing solutions would be offered (Drucker et al., 2019). Within a few years, the area experienced unexpected construction activity and new job creation. By 2016 the number of new jobs was around 6,000 and further growth was expected. Technological incubators were installed in the area, co-working spaces and a college for entrepreneurs was created. Old warehouses were converted into modern housing complexes, and the Seaport's innovation district was perhaps the fastest-growing area in the state of Massachusetts from 2010 to 2015. However, Boston's Innovation District has, over the years, become more of a natural extension of Boston and less of an area of innovation and incubation of new ideas and business start-ups. The venture led to a renaissance of the area and ultimately contributed to the expansion of the city of Boston, with the construction of luxury housing, signs of widening the class gap and the support of a business model that excludes the less privileged. The creation of the Boston Innovation District highlighted the Mayor's contribution to the regeneration and development of an area, driven by innovation in a way that is accessible to more, as well as the possibility and ease of deviation from the original design (Bevilacqua et al., 2018).

13.5.2 *Roxbury*

In Boston, the City Council has adopted an additional strategic approach to creating an innovation ecosystem, the Neighborhood Innovation District (NID), with the primary goal of encouraging innovation in low-income areas of the city to support local economic development. The area chosen for the first pilot application of the NID strategy is in the Roxbury neighborhood of Boston (Rissola et al., 2019), an area that has traditionally experienced disproportionately high levels of poverty The idea to create the NID was championed by Menino's next mayor, with the belief that sustainability would be created by empowering the entrepreneurial talent that already exists throughout the Boston area and unemployment and has seen investment with optimistic signs of a recovery path.

Since the beginning of the implementation of the project in Roxbury, the area has attracted investment from mainly local stakeholders, such as the non-profit organization "Initiative for a Competitive Inner City" (ICIC). Research studies on the potential to strengthen the local market and proposed investments were supported. However, for several years after its operation, the Roxbury Innovation Center mainly offers educational activities for residents. The weak socio-economic environment of the region is the embankment in finding investors willing to invest with the existing conditions (Rissola et al., 2019).

13.5.3 *Kendall Square*

Since 2010, the Massachusetts Institute of Technology (MIT) has been working with the wider community to advance a proposal that will bring new dynamism to Kendall Square—the most innovative square mile on the planet (Kendall Square Initiative). Through a coordinated five-year process involving the MIT and Cambridge communities, the initiative to shape Kendall Square emerged. The plan for Kendall Square was the result of long-term planning, involving a significant number of stakeholders for the creation of an even more active and successful area, capitalizing on the successful course of recent years to create a center of innovation with a global reach, offering residences, shops and open spaces (City of Cambridge, 2013). The design was based on the idea of bringing together two nearby areas of Cambridge, an area that was at the center of the world in relation to biotechnology, entrepreneurship, high technology and the knowledge economy (Kendall Square) and an area with a rich cultural vitality, as well as the general economic benefits offered by the Cambridge, Massachusetts area. Both areas have good access to public transportation, have student housing neighborhoods and are close to MIT, while Kendall Square also has the advantage of having a significant number of property owners who are willing to work together for a common vision. Long before the final planning for the creation of the innovation ecosystem of Kendall Square, actions had been initiated to strengthen the infrastructure of the area.

In 2011–2012, a comprehensive planning study was carried out to reshape and develop an area around Kendall Square in the city of Cambridge. A number of consultants that included experts in land use planning and urban planning, commerce, housing, market analysis and transportation planning were selected after a large competition across North America. The group of consultants selected to work with the city of Boston were also tasked with evaluating proposals for further redevelopment in the wider area. Committees with various members, including local residents, property owners, representatives of businesses and foundations, participated in the process of drafting the study. The two committees worked for more than a year and held more than twenty meetings. In addition, there was a public consultation and comment period, as well as public meetings and discussions and workshops to seek input from the wider community. The process resulted in the final design text of Kendall Square in 2013 (Cambridge Community Development Department).

MIT's important role in Kendall Square's past and future

In the nineteenth century this area of Cambridge was an industrial center including a natural gas plant, a rubber factory and an oil refinery for soap production. Gradually the factories closed and the area was abandoned, until it was used by pioneering MIT researchers to create and establish biotechnology and IT companies. By 2009, the area had turned into what is often referred to as "the most innovative square mile on the planet". With the design plan complete, MIT proceeded to implement its own plan to transform the area by constructing buildings with research and development facilities, offices, residences, shops and restaurants. As they say at MIT, innovation is about human conflict, the power of the proximity of laboratories and those who can apply science. For this reason, they take care of their "backyard", the Kendall Square area (Mayfield, 2022).

The reshaping of the area has become an ongoing process, in which MIT is actively involved, by looking for places to develop new research, creating opportunities for research and innovation, looking for affordable housing for students, as well as housing for graduates who wish to remain in the area for work. Furthermore, MIT's intention is to contribute to the harmonious coexistence of its research activities with public urban life in a balanced framework for all. Innovation is created by people and people want great environments to live. By building infrastructure, improving public spaces, creating open spaces and retail in Kendall Square, it supports the competitive advantage innovative businesses need to attract and retain talent while creating an attractive environment for all (Kendall Square at MIT, MIT).

13.6 Innovation District in Athens–CHROPEI

The Greek government has announced the creation of the first Innovation District in Athens (CHROPEI), the design of which is based on the standards of Innovation Centers (Innovation District), and which will be a natural space where companies, institutions, start-ups and Incubators. The purpose of the first Innovation District in Athens will be to strengthen innovation and entrepreneurship, both at the national, European and international level [General Secretariat for Research and Innovation (GSRI), 2023].

Purpose—Design

According to the Special Town Plan that was drawn up, the area of the CHROPEI industrial complex was chosen for the establishment and installation of a Research and Technology Innovation Center, based on the business plan of the Ministry of Development and Investments and the GSRI. The planned Innovation Center, as an initiative called "Innovation District (CHROPEI)", will be based on the standards of the Innovation Districts that were created and operate in many cities around the world and its general objectives include: introduction of innovation in Greece in existing and new business schemes, entrepreneurship development, diffusion of innovation in society, skills development, proposals to change the business and development model, job creation.

Description of the Plan

The project is planned to be implemented on an area of 18 hectares of the wider Falirikos Bay area and is surrounded by various categories of land use such as residences, industries, recreational areas, free spaces, green spaces, parking spaces. The agency for managing the property and implementing the auction is designated by GSRI, and the purpose of its use is to develop it as a technological and scientific park, in which part of the activities should concern research and innovation in the health sciences. There are existing buildings on the site, some of which are listed and any interventions must respect their architectural character. According to the plan, the creation of the Innovation District in CHROPEI will be implemented, through a PPP scheme, by a Private Entity, which will finance the investment, having additional important responsibility for the planning of the project. The effects of the construction and operation of the proposed Innovation Center were studied, in relation to its climatic, bioclimatic, morphological and topological characteristics, effects related to the soil, the anthropogenic environment and the natural environment, socio-economic effects, effects on air quality and on water, effects from noise.

Attempt to evaluate the development footprint of the CHROPEI proposal

The proposed project to create an Innovation District in the existing industrial complex of the former CHROPEI in Piraeus is based on the reuse of the existing building stock in combination with the cultivation of innovation in Greece, strengthening entrepreneurship and job creation, according to the relevant strategic study. The combination of urbanization and sustainable urban development reinforces the idea of reusing abandoned urban land, helping to promote coherent development, reducing demand for long-distance commuting, upgrading urban functions, organizing metropolitan-level agencies to manage larger-scale projects. At the socio-economic level, the proposed functions of the project will be associated with a mix of start-ups, research and development departments of large enterprises, cooperation of academic institutions and enterprises, organization of events for innovation, aiming to create a live, work and play environment. CHROPEI is designed to host research centers, start-ups, research, technology and innovation companies, integrating scientists and knowledge workers into a continuous communication with the aim of developing innovative products for the benefit of society, through synergies and interaction (GSRI). The expected benefits for the citizen and society include the strengthening of innovation and development activities, the creation of jobs, the utilization of public property, the upgrading of the area which will be highlighted by the upgrading of a historical complex with a special historical character, which will contribute to the upgrading of the wider area which shows signs of abandonment and degradation. CHROPEI seems to have been planned of a basis of small-scale project with big prospects.

13.7 Development of Innovation Districts

13.7.1 Development of Innovation Districts in the Natural Urban Environment

The cases of the cities of Boston and Barcelona seem to rest on common assumptions about the decision to create innovation districts. The first common assumption is related to the belief that the nature of innovation today is based on collaboration, connecting disciplines, high technology and requires connectivity and density in the surrounding space. Therefore, a city can function as the ideal context for the creation of an innovation district, and at the same time as a pole of attraction for the migration of knowledge workers. The need was thus created to find free and available spaces in which to implement the plan. By choosing abandoned areas or areas in decline, the site was found and a process of attracting investors in construction was initiated. As a consequence of the first assumption, the role of the technological culture cultivated in the region emerges, which is cultivated by the design model applied and leads to the diffusion of innovation and enhancement of its productivity (Kayanan, 2021).

Innovation districts can breathe new life into old areas and beautify the streets of the surrounding urban area. With their regeneration and revitalization, the areas become a magnet for private investment, boosting tax revenues and creating economic vitality, while at the same time exuding safety, comfort, connectivity and a sense of welcoming. According to Lawrence, Hogan and Brown, a survey of real estate investment firms showed that, relative to offices scattered around the city, offices located in areas with concentrated business activity and similar organization have greater occupancy and attract more investors.

Reforms linked to the overall design of innovation districts, which emerge and evolve within the urban fabric, indirectly support resource savings, as there is no need to create the necessary transport infrastructure from scratch. The adaptation of transport networks to the new data is on a smaller scale, expanding or redesigning the existing network. The dense development model associated with the innovation districts can lead to targeted actions, such as the creation of more parks within the environment to be planned, the reduction of dependence on cars, in order to create a framework with better living conditions, taking into account the protection from potential risks, such as changes due to climate change (Lawrence et al., 2019). Barcelona's 22@ and Boston's Kendall Square also benefited from the existing transport infrastructure. 22@ used the existing telecommunications network and Kendall Square joined an already developed innovation grid that had been created in the greater Boston area, supported by the Boston Seaport Innovation District and the effort in Roxbury. The culture of dense urban structure had already been cultivated.

From natural resources, public ones such as parks, squares and streets are created or reconstructed so that they are digitally accessible, with high-speed internet, wireless networks, computers and digital signs with information. Roads also act as laboratories for testing new innovations in lighting, waste management, traffic regulation and new digital technologies.

Accordingly, from natural resources, private ones such as private buildings and offices are transformed into shared workspaces with laboratories, as well as smaller affordable solutions for start-ups. In addition, a new form of micro-housing is emerging, with small private apartments that have direct access to larger public spaces, such as co-working spaces, entertainment spaces and common dining areas (Katz & Wagner, 2014). 22@ has reformed and highlighted old, historical buildings, which gives it a tone of specificity, highlighting the design aesthetics of the past and connecting it with futuristic constructions. The city attracts knowledge workers all the time, and with its constant redesign, it has managed to remain attractive to workers, start-ups and businesses.

13.7.2 Development of the Urban Environment Based on Knowledge

The city can perhaps be compared to a living organism. Many factors contribute to its operation, and all of them are coordinated in a continuous interaction and cooperation with the aim of smooth operation. In this interactive context, resilience has been upgraded as a topic of discussion due to the unpredictable events of recent years such as economic crisis, extreme weather events and pandemic. The new conditions have led the discussion to create mechanisms with faster reflexes, with a view to improving resilience and creating sustainable economic development in the various regions (Hu et al., 2021).

A significant part of crisis management is transferred to the local level, with innovation playing an essential role in finding solutions on a new basis, which is defined by a large number of parameters and therefore involves complexity and is constantly changing. The concept of Knowledge-Based Urban Development (KBUD) is activated in the case of innovation districts, as shown by examining the two cases of Barcelona and Boston, in order to attract a significant number of talents and qualified professionals.

13.7.3 Resilience Approach of the Innovation Districts Model

While there seems to be a minimal amount of literature on innovation districts, the interest surrounding the subject is nevertheless intense, as its expansion can act as a driver of change in the urban way of living and being active. The economic crisis, the COVID-19 health crisis, the energy crisis are raising serious concerns about the sustainability of the urban fabric worldwide. The shielding of cities and their operation in a context where risks can be addressed through forms of activity quickly adaptable to change emerges as an important point for discussion and research. Innovation districts appear to be an instrumental model important and worthy of investigation.

In recent decades, mainly from the mid-1990s onward, a combination of many factors such as the rapid spread of the use of information and communication technologies, the consolidation of globalization as a new reality, the accelerated concentration of the population in cities, contributed to the strengthening of the phenomenon of innovation districts, resulting in their increasing spread across the planet. In March 2022, a global network of 23 innovation districts was created from 10 countries in Europe, North America, Latin America, the Middle East, Australia and Asia. The idea behind the creation of the global network of innovation districts seems to be based on the desire to create a strong group in order to improve their operation and support each other for further development. Furthermore, there seems to be a desire to interact as well as strengthen the model around the world, as well as an attempt to empirically analyze the various innovation districts in order to create an informative material for proposed investment actions. Through the creation of the network of the 23 innovation districts on the planet, signs of maturity in the operation of the model emerge. By creating networks, the idea and desire of prototyping sustainability and resilience of advanced urban models is strengthened, in a context of continuous cooperation, synergies, employment in knowledge, education and retraining, participatory action of the community, continuous renewal and reformation of infrastructures, so that the lasting urban growth to become sustainable and resilient.

13.7.4 Innovation Districts and Wider Regional Resilience

Starting from the assumption that regional resilience is difficult to capture in measurable quantities, it can be considered that resilience and economic development may not necessarily go hand in hand. And this is because resilience, since it cannot be measured, fails to satisfy the standard criteria of competitiveness for increasing wealth, business, income, employment. Moreover, it seems that issues of resilience are raised after some shock, some extraordinary event that highlights hitherto unnoticed problem areas, something that is not seen in issues of competitiveness and economic development. A possible broadening and perhaps shifting of policy debates from economic development to regional sustainability and resilience is apparent, extending research on the innovation environment to a broader approach to institutional adaptive capacities. At the same time, the use of physical systems, such as innovation districts, as frameworks for understanding contemporary forms of economic development is reexamined (Clark et al., 2010).

Innovation districts as models of urban regeneration, reshaping and development can act as platforms for analyzing and understanding the relationship between innovation capacity and regional resilience. The significant number of innovation districts operating in recent decades on the planet is capable for studying the sustainability, growth and resilience, at least at an empirical level. The dynamic phenomenon of innovation districts evolves from the initially closed model of innovation into a more open field in which organizations collaborate with ecosystems, networks and the physical space, forming unusual partnerships between previously unconnected disciplines (Little, 2014). Innovation districts appear to function as super-enhancers of the economy of innovation (Dews & Saxena, 2014), as for example happens in Kendall Square, where a wider area was redesigned in order to accept and join the necessary, perhaps, change of the operating model of the area, toward a "live, work and play" form of everyday life and interaction, based on sustainability and durability. In addition, both the financial crisis of 2008 and the crisis of the COVID-19 pandemic highlight more strongly the need for more collective action at all levels of human activity, in order to create useful interconnections. A case to mention is the case of New South Wales, Australia, where a wider ecosystem of innovation districts is being created to accelerate the economic recovery of a six-city region, which are expected to act as catalysts for the wider economic growth.

13.7.5 Innovation Districts and the Public Sector

Barcelona's 22@is considered the first innovation district, which was designed to upgrade an industrial area of the Spanish city in the post-Olympic period. A dynamic of renewal appears to have been cultivated in a concerted effort both formally and informally. Creativity and innovation characterize the development path of the city many years before the creation of the innovation district. A governance model influenced by the local culture was cultivated, and when the occasion of the Olympic Games was given, a dynamic of renewal, upgrading, creation and above all innovation emerged. With the continuous interaction over a long period of time between citizens, local government, people of the arts and creativity, as well as the business world, the conditions were ripe for the emergence of a new form of urban development, on a small scale, safe enough for non-disrupting the stability of the city and at the same time different enough to be considered innovative.

However, the success of 22@ is not a given for every new innovation district that is designed. The undertaking is multifaceted and complex, while its coordination starts from the vision for the development of the urban model and involves the government, local authorities, institutions such as universities and hospitals, businesses and stakeholders with different the culture at the different region (Wagner et al., 2019). Continuously strengthening the value proposition of an innovation district requires the implementation of a significant number of strategies and tactics continuously (Wagner, 2023). In addition, many of the innovation districts are located in degraded urban areas, with outdated infrastructure, which need physical renewal, so strategies for renovating old buildings, upgrading infrastructure, revitalizing green spaces, etc.

In Boston's Kendall Square, for example, the innovation ecosystem is supported by the airport access tunnel, the Roxbury upgrade, the Seaport area upgrade. The successful operation of Kendall Square's innovation district relies on the smooth functioning of a wider area, which includes underserved areas, as much as possible. The balances of the urban web require constant collaboration between both a set of local stakeholders and with other practices in the global web. The vision of the mayor of Boston, who knew very well the city, the possibilities and the needs, led to the creation of deeper structures, interconnected to support this project (Rissola et al., 2019), without complacency, however, as the preservation of balances requires constant cooperation.

13.7.6 The Contribution of Public Sector to the Sustainability of an Innovation District

An innovation district usually arises as a need either for development reasons or for risk management, crisis management, saving abandoned areas, building communities and a number of other reasons. In order for it to work, a plan is needed in which many stakeholders are involved. Implementation of the plan is primarily coordinated by local and state authorities. The sustainability of an undertaking of this size has elements of intense complexity and interconnectedness and requires orchestrated effort and dedication with constant review of plans and re-planning when necessary. The role of the state as a coordinator is certainly essential for its operation, while at the same time it needs to intervene by providing the appropriate infrastructure when needed. In addition, state institutions can create the appropriate structures to collaborate with innovation districts of other cities in a continuous interaction to exchange views, actions, trends, existence of risks and countermeasures. Innovation districts can emerge a new urban model of living over time, capable of managing crises such as natural disasters, economic policy failures, and challenges of ever-intensifying urbanization, through intense and sustained interaction and collaboration, to create inclusive, secure, resilient and sustainable human-made living environment (UN Habitat, 2017).

13.7.7 Existing Panning and Thoughts on CHROPEI's Project

Adopting the assumption that the key components of successful innovation districts are financial capital, physical capital and socially networked capital (Wagner et al., 2019), the question arises whether these have been taken into account in the case of CHROPEI. *Financial capital* includes the companies, institutions and organizations that support and cultivate an environment with an innovative character. *Natural capital* includes public and private spaces, such as buildings, open spaces, roads, technologies and other infrastructure, designed and organized to stimulate new and higher levels of connectivity, collaboration and innovation. *Socially networked capital* consists of the relationships between actors such as individuals, companies and institutions, which have the potential to create, shape and/or accelerate the promotion of ideas, with dynamics that differ significantly between different communities/societies.

A multifaceted approach of essential components is observed at the CHROPEI project in Athens, which correlate and connect innovation with structural components of the urban fabric. Beyond the analyses in relation to land uses, the plan of the project contains elements that relate the architectural design to international practices, references are made to the climate, the natural environment, the effects on topographic features and the anthropogenic environment, and measures are proposed for prevention, limiting and addressing environmental impacts. As the development of research infrastructure is a priority for the EU, CHROPEI has been planned toward the creation of a vibrant community where innovative ideas and projects will thrive, staring on a small scale basis, but with the possibility of creating an innovation district in the wider area where universities, hospitals, companies, the public sector and the local communities will be involved. The starting point of similar efforts in the international environment seems to have been the determination and dedication of the parties involved in the direction of sustainability and resilience. A successful launch is not guaranteed to ensure the viability of such a project. The planned innovation district of CHROPEI can be linked to the regeneration of the wider area of Falirikos Ormos in a holistic approach to the creation of a form of ecosystem reforming the urban tissue in terms of sustainability and resilience, with the cooperation of educational institutions, the state, entrepreneurs and local communities. The complex equation of the undertaking can be included, as a component, the need to create a critical mass of research infrastructure and talent, the design of equitable development strategies, as well as the design of systems and structures to create jobs with wages capable of providing a decent living.

13.8 Conclusion

Knowing that sustainability seems to be linked to resilience, by adopting the ESG criteria approach in an innovation environment with the contribution of the state as a guide and regulator of relations, an innovation district can be the start of a creative, productive course, with innovation prevailing in its microcosm, and gradually creating the conditions for the diffusion of the approach in the local and supra-local society, cultivating a pole of revitalization, restructuring and upgrading of the city. The need for changes in infrastructure, collaborations, synergies and planning considered in depth, taking into account global practices, can arise through coordinated action and people with visions. Of critical importance is the role of the coordinating body which will need to act as an initiator in the local and supra-local society. The environmental factor of ESGs is a given that should be taken into account in every action. At the same time, state authorities and businesses should include in their planning the social factor and how society will participate in the project. Information, awareness and participation of citizens in permanent actions need to be institutionalized. Finally, business and state governance should include transparency, the establishment of procedures and the control of their operation, the continuous information of citizens and workers. The collaboration between innovation districts around the world, mainly through networks, may be a subject for further research, in order to study and analyze the resilience of those districts in the recent crisis.

References

Ajuntament de Barcelona. (2020). *Government measure: A boost to 22@, 2020, Action lines and measures.* https://www.barcelonactiva.cat/documents/20124/259890/MG-Impulsem-22%40-EN-WEB_def.pdf/c969e58b-6989-1da7-9edf-621aa554a336?t=1607504071610

Ali, J. (2021). *22@Barcelona project, Barcelona*, © ISTE Ltd 2021. Published by ISTE Ltd and John Wiley & Sons, Inc., https://doi.org/10.1002/9781119821670.ch12

Alvarez-Palau, E., Bogart, D., Dunn, O., Satchell, M., & Taylor, L. (2020). *Transport and urban growth in the first industrial revolution*. The Cambridge Group for the History of Population and Social Structure

Atack, J., Margo, R., & Rhode, P. (2021). *Industrialization and urbanization in nineteenth century America*. National Bureau of Economic Research. Accessed on 24 September 2023.

Battaglia, A., & Tremblay, D. G. (2011). *22@ and the innovation district in Barcelona and Montreal: A process of clustering development between urban regeneration and economic competitiveness*, Urban Studies Research, Volume 2011 | Article ID 568159 | https://doi.org/10.1155/2011/568159

Bevilacqua, C., Parisi, L., & Biancuzzo, L. (2018). *Multi-stage strategic approach in spatial innovation: How innovation district matter?* Part of the Smart Innovation, Systems and Technologies book series (SIST,volume 100). New Metropolitan Perspectives

Bevilacqua, C., Rissola, G., Monardo, B. (2019). Place-based innovation ecosystems: Boston-Cambridge Innovation Districts (USA), In G. Rissola (Ed.), Publications Office. https://data.europa.eu/doi/10.2760/183238

Bosch Pascual L. (2005). *Modernisme and the 1888 Universal Exposition of Barcelona*. HISTORICAL LAB 1 BRUXELLES-BRUSSELS, Réseau Art Nouveau Network

Branscomb, L. M. (2002). *Technological innovation*. Harvard University. https://doi.org/10.1016/B0-08-043076-7/03208-3

Britannica, *Industrial Revolution*. Britannica-History & Society. Accessed on 17 September 2023.

Bulkeley, H., & Betsill, M. (2005). Rethinking sustainable cities: Multilevel governance and the "urban" politics of climate change. *Environmental Politics, 14*(1), 42–63. https://doi.org/10.1080/0964401042000310178

Carrillo, F. J., Yigitcanlar, T., García, B., & Lönnqvist, A. (2014). *Knowledge and the city: Concepts, applications and trends of knowledge-based urban development*. Routledge.

Castillo, R. (2023). *Productive ecosystems and innovation districts: Key drivers for sustainable smart cities*. https://illuminem.com/illuminemvoices/productive-ecosystems-and-innovation-districts-key-drivers-for-sustainable-smart-cities

Chen, M., Zhang, H., Liu, W., & Zhang, W. (2014). *The global pattern of urbanization and economic growth: evidence from the last three decades*. National Center of Biotechnology Information

City of Cambridge. (2013). *Kendall Square Final Report 2013*, www.cambridgema.gov/

Clark, J., Huang, H., & Walsh, J. (2010, March). A typology of 'innovation districts': what it means for regional resilience. *Cambridge Journal of Regions, Economy and Society, 3*(1). https://doi.org/10.1093/cjres/rsp034

Cohen, M. (2017). *A systematic review of urban sustainability assessment literature*, https://www.mdpi.com/2071-1050/9/11/2048

Deloitte (2023). *Women in the tech industry: Gaining ground, but facing new headwinds*, Deloitte Research—Women in the tech industry.

Dews F., & Saxena E. (2014). *Innovation districts are a clear path forward for cities and metros*, commentary at the Brookings.

Drucker J., Kayanan M., & Renski H. (2019). *Innovation districts as a strategy for urban economic development: A comparison of four cases*. Drucker et al - Innovation Districts

ECPA Urban Planning. (2017). *Case study: The Boston waterfront innovation district, smart cities dive*. SmartCities - The Boston Waterfront Innovation District

Esmaeilpoorarabi, N., Yigitcanlar, T., Kamruzzaman, M., & Guaralda, M. (2020). Conceptual frameworks of innovation district place quality: An opinion paper. *Land Use Policy, 90*. https://doi.org/10.1016/j.landusepol.2019.104166

European Central Bank. (2017). https://www.ecb.europa.eu/ecb-and-you/explainers/tell-memore/html/growth.en.html

European Commission, Intelligent Cities Challenge. (2023). *22@ Barcelona*. The 22@Barcelona project

European Commission, Joint Research Centre, Bevilacqua, C., Rissola, G., & Monardo, B. (2019). *Place-based innovation ecosystems : Boston-Cambridge Innovation Districts (USA)*, In G. Rissola (Ed.), Publications Office. https://data.europa.eu/doi/https://doi.org/10.2760/183238

Faludi, A. (1987). *A decision centred view of environmental planning*. Pergamon Press.

Focus, OECD. (1996). *Effective governance is crucial to national prosperity, Focus by PUMA of the OECD*. Accessed on 10 October 2023.

Frattini F. (2023). *Innovation Districts: where technology meets sustainable local development*, https://www.federatedinnovation-mind.com/en/custom/media/view/4134

Garcia-Ramon M. D. (2000). *Pre-Olympic and post-olympic Barcelona, a 'Model' for urban regeneration today?*. Barcelona and the Olympic Games

General Secretariat for Reaserch and Innovation (GSRI). (2023). https://gsri.gov.gr/en/protovoulies-draseis/athensinnovation-district-chropei/

Gianoli, A., & Henkes, R. P. (2020). The evolution and adaptive governance of the 22@ innovation district in Barcelona. *Urban Sci., 4*(2), 16. https://doi.org/10.3390/urbansci4020016

Godin, B. (2008). *Innovation: the History of a Category*, Working Paper No. 1, Project on the Intellectual History of Innovation, Montreal: INRS.

Hu, T., Pan, S., & Lin, H. (2021). Development, innovation, and circular stimulation for a knowledge-based city: Key thoughts. *Energies, 14*(23), 7999. https://doi.org/10.3390/en14237999

Katz, B., & Wagner J. (2014). *The rise of innovation districts: A new geography of innovation in America*. Katz & Wagner, Innovation Districts

Kayanan, C. (2021). A critique of innovation districts: Entrepreneurial living and the burden of shouldering urban development. *Environment and Planning*

A: Economy and Space, *54*(1), 50–66. https://doi.org/10.1177/0308518X211049445

Koven, Z., ECPA. (2019). *Case Study: 22@ Barcelona Innovation District*. Koven, Case Study, 22@

Lall Somik. (2014). Urbanisation and Economic Transformation, World Bank Blogs, World Bank.org. Accessed on 03 November 2023.

Lam, A. (2004). Organizational innovation, Chapter 5. In J. Fagerberg, D. Mowery, R.R. Nelson (Eds.), *The Oxford Handbook of Innovation*, Oxford University Press.

Lawrence, S., Hogan, M., & Brown, E. (2019). *Planning for an innovation district: Questions for Practitioners to Consider*, RTI. Planning Innovation District - RTI International

Little Arthur. (2014). The Future of Innovation Districts. https://www.adlittle.com/sites/default/files/prism/The%20future%20of%20innovation%20districts%20article.pdf

Majó, A. (2011). *22@Urban Lab, the example of Barcelona*, 'Barcelona City Council, 22@ Urban Lab.

Mayfield, M. (2022). *MIT Technology Review: The Past and Future of Kendall Square (2015)*, MIT Innovation HQ. MIT News Feature: A transformation in five acts

McCann, P., & Acs, Z. (2010). Globalization: Countries, cities and multinationals. *Taylor & Francis Online*. https://doi.org/10.1080/00343404.2010.505915

McKinsey & Company. (2018). *Thriving amid turbulence: Imagining the cities of the future*. https://www.mckinsey.com/industries/public-sector/our-insights/thriving-amid-turbulence-imagining-the-citiesof-the-future. Accessed on 04 August 2023.

McKinsey & Company. (2022). *What are Industry 4.0, the Fourth industrial revolution, and 4IR?*. www.mckinsey.com - 4th Industrial Revolution

Mobile World Capital Barcelona. (2023). *Catalonia's technology hubs generate more than 15,000 jobs*. Press Release.

Monardo, B. (2018). 'What Interpretations for 'Smart Specialization Strategies' in European Urban Regions? Lessons from Boston'. In A. Bisello, D. Vettorato, P. Laconte, & S. Costa (Eds.), *Smart and Sustainable Planning for Cities and Regions*. Results of SSPCR 2017. Springer, 2018.

National Geographic. (2023). *The History of Cities*. https://education.nationalgeographic.org/resource/history-cities/

Nidumolu R., Prahalad C. K., & Rangaswani, M. R. (2009). *Why sustainability is now the key driver of innovation*, https://hbr.org/2009/09/why-sustainability-is-now-the-key-driver-of-innovation

OECD. (2005). *Oslo Manual: Guidelines for collecting and interpreting innovation data. Oslo manual (3rd ed.)*, OECD and Development Statistical Office Of The European Communities, Paris, OECD.

PEMB. (2014). *Strategic projects—22@Barcelona, the innovation district*. https://pemb.cat/en/strategic-projects/22barcelona_the_innovation_district/23/

Puga D. (1996). *Urbanisation patterns: European vs. less developed countries*, Centre for Economic Performance, London School of Economics, Discussion Paper No. 305, https://diegopuga.org/papers/dp0305.pdf

Rius R. S. (2011). *The economic impact of infrastructures in 22@*, RACO (Catalan Journals in Open Access).

Rosenberg, N. (2004). *Innovation and economic growth*, OECD, https://www.oecd.org/cfe/tourism/34267902.pdf

Rowthorn, R., & Ramaswamy R. (1997). *Deindustrialization—Its causes and implications*. International Monetary Fund

Salvator, J., Ricart, J. E., Trillas, F., & Planas, M. R. (2017). *Barcelona gix: It network integration (SPAIN)*. University of Navarra, PPP FOR CITIES CASE STUDIES.

Satterthwaite, D. (2020). *The world's 100 largest cities from 1800 to 2020, and beyond*. International Institute for Environment and Development (IIED)

Shen L., Ochoa J., Shah M., & Zhang X. (2011). The application of urban sustainability indicators—A comparison between various practices. *Habitat International, 35*(1). https://doi.org/10.1016/j.habitatint.2010.03.006

Sodiq, A., Baloch, A., Khan, S., Sezer, N., Mahmoud, S., Jama, M., & Abdelaal, A. (2019). Towards modern sustainable cities: Review of sustainability principles and trends. *Journal of Cleaner Production, 227*, 972–1001.

The Boston Planning & Development Agency (BPDA) (2024). *About Us*. http://www.bostonplans.org/about-us/planning-boston-s-future

The World Bank. (2009). *Systems of cities : harnessing urbanization for growth and poverty alleviation*, Washington, D.C. : World Bank Group. The World Bank: Systems of cities

UN HABITAT. (2017). Trends in Urban Resilience 2017, United Nations Human Settlements Programme (UN-Habitat) 2017. www.unhabitat.org

UN HABITAT. (2021). *Annual monitoring and evaluation report on the Barcelona 2030 Agenda -Voluntary Local Review 2021*, UNHabitat, Barcelona Agenda 2030

UN HABITAT. (2023). *The world is failing to provide adequate housing*. unhabitat.org

United States Census Bureau. (2023). https://www.census.gov/. Accessed on 23 September 2023.

United Nations—Department of Economic and Social Affairs (DESA). (2020). *Urbanization: expanding opportunities, but deeper divides*, UN.org

Urban Next Lexicon (2018). *Palo Alto Barcelona: an Oasis of Creativity—A building with history.* https://urbannext.net/palo-alto-barcelona/
Urban Sustainability Exchange (2024). *22@Barcelona*, https://use.metropolis.org/case-studies/22-barcelona#casestudydetail
Vavouras, I. & Vavoura, C. (2019). *Economic Policy*, 3rd Improved Edn., Papazisis Publishers, Athens.
Verhage, R. (2003). The role of the public sector in urban development: Lessons from Leidsche Rijn Utrecht (The Netherlands). *Planning Theory & Practice, 4*(1), 29–44. https://doi.org/10.1080/1464935032000057191
Voigtländer, N. (2019, August). Voth Hans-Joachim, 2006, *Why England?. Demographic Factors, Structural Change, 227*, 1. https://doi.org/10.1016/j.jclepro.2019.04.106
Wagner J. (2023). *Why governance matters: An analysis on how innovation districts "Organize for Success"*, Research Brief, The Global Institute on Innovation Districts, GIID, Governance Matters
Wagner, J., Katz, B., & Osha, T. (2019). *The Evolution of Innovation Districts: The New Geography of Global Innovation.* The Global Institute on Innovation Districts, The Evolution of ID's - GIID. Accessed on 01 January 2024.
World Intellectual Property Organization. (2021). *Innovation driving human progress: WIPO and the Sustainable Development Goals, WIPO Innovation and SDG*, 06 September 2023.
Yuko E. (2021). *How the industrial revolution fueled the growth of cities.* https://www.history.com/news/industrial-revolution-cities

CHAPTER 14

The Implementation of Strategic Planning in Public Organizations in Greece: The Case of e-EFKA

Andreas Alexopoulos and George Makavelos

14.1 Introduction

The prevalence of neoliberal policies, after the 1973 oil crisis, according to which markets prevail in allocating resources and ensuring economic efficiency compared to governments (Goergen, 2012), led to the reshaping of the organizational and operational model of public entities as well. The new orientation, which was also seen as an attempt to mitigate public deficits and limit government expenses, emphasized the adoption

A. Alexopoulos (✉)
Department of Accounting and Finance,
University of West Attica, Athens, Greece
e-mail: a.alexopoulos@uniwa.gr

G. Makavelos
Ministry of Labour and Social Affairs, General Inspection
Directorate of e-EFKA, Athens, Greece
e-mail: gmakavelos@efka.gov.gr

A. Hyz (ed.), *The Role of the Public Sector in Building Social and Economic Resilience*,
https://doi.org/10.1007/978-3-031-67702-1_14

of private sector management practices such as size reduction, privatization, performance measurement and analysis (Hood, 1995). These policies were in fact the core of the New Public Management theory, which was introduced in the early 80s in the USA and the UK (Gruening, 2001). At the same time, various other events such as the globalization phenomenon and the intense interconnection of markets that entails, the economic development of the Asian continent countries and the competition framework that has been formed, issues related to climate change, as well as the rapid penetration of technology (Greek Special Secretariat of Foresight, 2023), created a highly fluid and at the same time demanding environment, making the adaption of the public sector to the new circumstances, a vital procedure.

These political and economic issues, which to a large extent affected the integration of the European Union, made imperative the reformation of the Greek public sector as well, based on the principles of the NPM and the implementation of Strategic Planning.

The effort to reform the social security system in Greece aims at the same above direction, especially with the establishment on 01/01/2017 of the electronic National Social Security Fund. Until then, the social security sector was dominated by an extensive fragmentation and complexity, characteristics that are more widely found in the field of Greek public administration (Spanou, 2018; Sotiropoulos, 2021). This was reflected by the presence of a plethora of social security organizations, operating simultaneously, but at the same time independently.

The establishment of e-EFKA was, due to its size, an unprecedented in scope and complexity, endeavor for the Greek reality, and had as its main objective the creation of a unified, efficient, flexible, sustainable, resilient and socially just provider of social security services (e-EFKA, 2024). It was quickly realized that the successful operation of the new organization would not be possible without the formation and the effective implementation of a strategic plan.

Taking into account the aforementioned factors and focusing on the case of one of the largest public organizations in Greece, the main purpose of this paper is to investigate the following questions related to the implementation of strategic planning in e-EFKA:

- What are the factors that affect the achievement of e-EFKA's objectives?

- In what extend are the employees involved in the shaping of the organization's strategy?
- Are employees aware of their participation in shaping the organization's strategy?
- Are there adequate mechanisms for diffusing strategic thinking to all hierarchical levels?

In order to investigate the importance of strategic planning and the degree of its adoption in Greek public administration, in addition to the relevant bibliographic review, a quantitative field survey was carried out in all the Regional Insurance Audit Centers (PEKA), which are the core of the audit mechanism for tackling undeclared and underd eclared work. PEKA are a newly established service consisting of 11 regional directorates, with an administrative organization and structure similar to that found in other public services in Greece.

In this section, we initially attempt to present the basic principles of strategic planning as they fit into the broader context shaped by the theory of New Public Management. Subsequently, the paper explores the prospects emerging from the implementation of strategic planning in public administration bodies. In this context is presented the framework for implementing strategic-operational planning in e-EFKA, specifically focusing on the Regional Insurance Audit Centers (PEKA). This is followed by the presentation and analysis of the research results, while at the end of the article, a synthesis of the conclusions is provided.

14.2 The Concept and Content of Strategic Planning

14.2.1 The Concept of Strategy

In the field of business administration, the concept of strategy was first introduced by Newman in the early 1950s (Papadakis, 2016), in an attempt to explain why companies competing in the same industry and using the same technology had different levels of performance. Since then, several definitions of the concept of strategy have been given. According to Bryson (2011) strategic planning is a discrete, disciplined approach to advancing fundamental decisions and actions that shape and guide what an organization or other entity is, what it does, how and why it does it. Osborne and Gaebler (1992) point out that strategic planning incorporates processes of objective analysis and subjective evaluation of organizational goals and priorities to chart the future course of action, ensuring organizational effectiveness and sustainability over the long term. Georgopoulos (2013) argues that with the formulation and implementation of strategy, each company is constantly aware of its position in relation to its main competitors in the present, but mainly it knows the directions it will take in the future, what opportunities to exploit, what threats to avoid, what strengths to improve and what weaknesses to overcome. According to Lawlor (2010), a successful strategy generates growth, profit and contributes to achieving the other goals set by managers. However, an inappropriate strategy can have disastrous results.

14.2.2 The Strategic Planning Process

The stages of the strategic planning process involve defining objectives, examining and assessing the current situation, designing the appropriate strategy, allocating resources, monitoring the program's progress and evaluating the results (Siomkos, 2013).

According to Hill et al. (2017) the process of strategic planning implementation includes six main steps:

1. Selection of corporate mission and primary corporate objectives.
2. Analysis of the external competitive environment of the organization in order to identify opportunities and threats.
3. Analysis of the internal operating environment of the organization in order to identify its strengths and weaknesses.
4. Selection of strategies that exploit the strengths of the organization and reduce weaknesses, aiming to exploit external opportunities and address external threats.
5. Implementation of the strategies.
6. Performance evaluation, structural measures, readjustment of vision, goals and strategies.

In addition to the above steps, the overall approach of the strategic plan preparation and implementation can be described as decisive. In this context, many scholars (David, 2011; Rothaermel, 2017, etc.) have highlighted the necessity of implementing bottom-up strategic processes as a means of early detection of impending changes, as well as mapping the needs and requirements of stakeholders. The latter are able to lead to a revision of strategic objectives, as well as the successful implementation of the strategy at the operational level. According to Kim et al. (2014), top-down action plans are formulated to support the strategic intentions of top management, while bottom-up action plans aim to pursue various improvement opportunities in operational, practical and procedural areas, which are significant for top management. Furthermore, relevant research by Parnell et al. (2002) demonstrated the link between the tendency toward participatory processes and the dissemination of strategy as a success factor. In particular, the results showed that greater participation in the strategic process can lead to more effective dissemination of strategy in the organization, which in turn leads to greater effectiveness of decisions.

14.3 New Public Management

14.3.1 The Impact of the New Public Management Theory

New Public Management (NPM) was the starting point for a different approach of the organization and operation of Public Services. Until the late 1970s, early 1980s, the organizational model of Public Administration, which dominated the European area, was based on the principles of Weberian theory with emphasis on the hierarchical model of public administration (Bourantas, 2015). The weaknesses of this model (Wollmann, Thurmaier, 2010) were mainly associated with rigidity, insistence on legal correctness, but also degradation of economic performance.

The basic principles of NPM could be originate in Henri Fayol (1949), who is considered the "father" of modern management theory. He described as basic functions of management: Planning, Organization, Leadership, Coordination and Control. The term New Public Management, according to Hood (1991), refers to the implementation of private sector practices in the public sector, with the main objectives of increasing efficiency and reducing operating costs. He describes NPM as a management philosophy for governments, oriented toward results and productivity. According to Borins (1995), the reasons for the establishment of NPM are the functional inadequacy of large bureaucratic organizations in conditions of economic tightness, the rapid development of information and communication technologies, the globalization of the economy, the demand for quality services and the search for work with growth potential. In general, NPM introduced more holistic management models of public and non-profit organizations, introducing the concepts of economy, efficiency and effectiveness, while helping to identify structural weaknesses in the management of these organizations (McLaughlin et al., 2005). Through the study of the relevant literature, the basic characteristics of NPM could be considered (Cohen, 2016; Gruening, 2001; Hood, 1991; Pollitt, 1995):

- Application of Private Management Techniques in the Public Sector.
- Privatization of Public Services and reduction of operating costs of public organizations, cutting budgets and seeking greater transparency in resources, implementation of improved accounting.
- Turning to results rather than processes.
- Definition of goals, objectives, success indicators expressed in quantitative terms to measure performance effectiveness.
- Emphasis on the "quality" of services.
- Setting standards and "responding to customers".
- Strengthening participatory processes and democratization in decision-making.
- Separation of the centralized management system and shift to decentralized units and division of responsibilities.
- Freedom of management (flexibility) and incentives.
- Accountability for performance and continuous performance auditing.
- Adoption of Strategic Planning and Strategic Management techniques.
- Intensify the penetration of information and communication technologies.
- Transition to greater competition in the public sector.
- Abolishing the permanency of civil servants and moving away from standardized national salaries. Establishment of performance-related pay.

The review of the basic principles of New Public Management reveals that the restructuring of the public sector toward reducing operating costs, improving performance and results, requires, among other things, long-term planning, targeting and dedication to the achievement of objectives, elements that compose the content of strategic planning.

14.3.2 Strategy Implementation in Public Organizations

In the previous section were presented the basic principles of strategic planning, which to a large extent can be considered to be incorporated in the theory of NPM. However, the question that arises is whether the theories, models and tools of business strategy find a suitable field of application in the public sector.

Regarding this issue, public and academic debate has been intense, particularly concerning the scope (Ellingson & Wambsganns, 2001), the content (Hatry, 2002), the stakeholders involved (Franklin, 2001) and the most effective practical approaches (Roberts, 2000). Though, the most important issue of strategic planning is its practical implementation. In this context, Donald et al. (2001) state that the implementation of strategic plans can be hindered by employees who feel threatened by organizational change or privatization, a point that is of particular importance for the public sector. To these could be added a series of factors that cause additional difficulties such as the lack of political will and leadership commitment, both in the adoption of strategic planning processes and in its implementation, in the lack of relevant know-how, but also in phenomena such as that of the "silo" that is encountered quite regularly within public administration organizations.

Much earlier, Vinzant and Vinzant (1996) characterized strategic planning in the public sector as the "cornerstone" of strategic management, pointing out that its successful implementation requires the evaluation of the organization's capabilities in areas such as managerial capacity, structures of power, organizational culture, leadership and organizational structure. Halachmi et al. (1993), in the same direction, stated that strategic planning is the main element but not the essence of strategic management, which includes other key features, the most important of which are implementation and evaluation. In general, it could be argued that these specific approaches fall within a broader understanding that more effective management is linked to stronger performance of public organizations (Boyne, 2003).

Although research on the degree of implementation and effects of strategic planning in the public sector seems to be relatively limited in most cases, exceptions include some studies in the USA and the UK (George & Desmidt, 2014), which suggest a positive correlation between the implementation of strategic planning and organizational efficiency (Poister et al., 2013; Walker & Andrews, 2015). Bryson et al.

(2010) argue that particular emphasis should be placed on measuring and managing the performance of public organizations, on expanding the methods and techniques used for identifying, analyzing and engaging stakeholders, as well as utilizing information and communication technology (ICT). According to Hansen and Ferlie (2014), the implementation of strategic planning in public organizations depends on their fundamental characteristics, which are determined on the basis of three conditions: (a) degree of administrative autonomy, (b) performance-based budgets, (c) conditions of private economy—competition.

Regarding the implementation process of strategic planning, Poister and Van Slyke (2002) state that public organizations should strive to ensure that their strategic plans guide the organization's decisions at all hierarchical levels, requiring all operational departments and subdepartments to develop their own strategic, annual and operational plans, supporting the strategic goals and objectives at an overall organizational level. Bryson (1995) argues that the implementation of strategic planning in public sector organizations is paramount, considering that strategic plans are implemented through the interconnection of corresponding processes, found at both higher and lower hierarchical administrative levels.

In this interactional context that unfolds within organizations, Poister et al. (2013) point out that managers are important in demonstrating adaptability during the strategic process, conducting experiments to promote learning associated with the mentality of achieving changes gradually.

However, many researchers focus on the fact that public organizations mostly differ from private sector enterprises, especially those providing services and non-profit organizations, as they do not aim for profit but for achieving public benefit. Consequently, their results are not easily measurable with quantitative methods (Matthews & Shulman, 2005). In many cases, public organizations intervene in the market by providing their services for free and sharing their specialized knowledge aiming to create new sectors or participating in high-risk, low-return investment programs (Hill et al., 2017). An important difference between the private and public sectors relates to the concept of value. As far as the private sector is concerned, the concept of value is synonymous with profitability. The concept of value in the public sector varies significantly, since public organizations aim to serve citizens individually, but at the same time to satisfy the collective interest. Public value incorporates the concepts of trust and legitimacy and relates to issues such as equity, ethics and accountability (Kelly et al., 2002). Williams and Lewis (2008), referring to the importance of stakeholders, argue that a decisive factor in the strategic management of the public sector is the complexity of relationships with stakeholders.

However, despite the significant differences between the private and public sectors, particularly regarding their fundamental objectives (e.g. profitability versus social justice), most views converge on the fact that, with appropriate adjustments (mutatis mutandis), the overall framework of strategic planning can also be applied with positive outcomes in public institutions.

14.3.3 Strategic Planning in the Public Sector in Greece

The significant economic and political crisis that Greece experienced at the end of the 80s, with the budget deficit and the debt exceeding the limits, acted as a burden for the public administration. According to the KEPE's report of 1988 (Michalopoulos et al., 2000), the absence of strategic planning was recorded as one of its main problems.

In the following years, in 90's in particular, with the influences of the New Public Management being particularly strong, successive governments attempted to reform and modernize the mechanisms of public administration.

The administrative modernization was pursued through a series of projects, aiming to address the documented structural problems of the Greek administrative system. The absence of coordination and planning, combined with the lack of relevant know-how and qualified personnel, made imperative the need for implementing strategic planning reforms, tailored to the circumstances and resources of each era. The aim was the gradual strengthening of the capacity of public services to operate strategically and implement programs based on valid environmental diagnosis processes (Michalopoulos, 2003).

Probably the first action in Greece that is part of these reform, can be considered article 80 of Law 1892/1990, according to which Strategic Planning and Policy Analysis Units were established in each Ministry. A series of legislative efforts followed in the next decades, with the most recent the enactment of L.4622/2019 regarding the "Executive State".

Despite this, the results in the strategic planning implementation in Greece during the previous decade can only be characterized as poor and fragmented. This is also the conclusion of the report drawn up by the OECD (2012), as an independent evaluator of the Greek public administration function. In this report, it was highlighted with rather unusually explicit wording, e.g. "abject failure" of reforms (OECD 2012), all those problems and dysfunctions had been identified by similar reports of the 80s and 90s (Michalopoulos & Makridimitris, 2000). Among them, the absence of strategic planning held a prominent position. Likewise, the absence of an appropriate center of governance, the lack of coordination of various policies and institutions, as well as poor legislation (OECD, 2012) were pointed out.

Generally, it is recognized that the Greek public administration has rarely been results-oriented and has remained distanced from modern organizational models (Sotiropoulos, 2021), with strong elements of administrative legalism that prioritizes rules rather than results (Tsekos, 2016). An additional problem is fragmentation, which seems to be favored by the inherent weaknesses that characterize the Greek public administration, such as the complexity of civil service regime, the introversion of administrative structures and the lack of civil service mechanisms for horizontal integration, coordination and control, as well as the lack of interconnection of electronic databases (Spanou, 2018).

14.4 The Case of e-EFKA

14.4.1 Brief General Description of the Organization

Among public organizations, Social Security Institutions can be considered a special case. The services they offer create multiplier benefits for society in general which, as mentioned above, are not easy to measure with quantitative data nor to be evaluated by cost-profit analysis methods. In particular, EFKA, provides mainly protection from risks such as illness, maternity, accident—occupational disease, old age, death and thereby contributing to the reduction of social inequalities, the improvement of life quality and the creation of a security and confidence climate in the labor market. Before the establishment of EFKA in 2017 (in application of the provisions of article 51—chapter E of L.4387/2016), the Greek social security system was characterized by fragmentation and complexity of procedures. The main social security institutions (about 6 main insurance institutions and multiple supplementary insurance funds) were incorporated into the new entity, resulting in the creation of a new unified organization that provides social security services to almost all employees of the country as well as to self-employed individuals and freelancers. In the funds that were merged, strategic planning was probably a relatively unknown concept.

Under these circumstances, the establishment of EFKA (with the L. 4670/20 it was renamed to Electronic-National Social Security Fund and briefly e-EFKA) was an extremely challenging and unprecedented project for Greek standards, marking the effort for a comprehensive reform of the social security system. The primary concern of the new endeavor was the merge of the aforementioned organizations, the unification of provisions and the simplification of procedures, with the main goals being the reduction of operational costs and the improvement of services provided to citizens.

With the Presidential Decree 8/23.01.2019, among other provisions, the establishment of the General Directorate of Strategy and Development was foreseen which was tasked with guiding, coordinating and supervising all involved General Directorates. According to article 53, par. 1 of the Presidential Decree, the strategic purpose of the above General Directorate is: (a) the operational planning of EFKA and (b) the development, implementation and updating of the Strategic and Operational Plan of EFKA.

14.4.2 Strategic Planning in e-EFKA

In implementation of the relevant provisions (L.4369/2016), the strategic planning of e-EFKA takes place through the preparation of Operational Programs by its General Directorates and follows the procedure presented in Table 14.1.

Table 14.1 Strategic planning process in e-EFKA

Central administration	*Defines its strategic objectives, which are then translated into operational plans per year*
General Directorates	– *They define the annual objectives, which should be linked to the Strategic Objectives* – *They submit to the Board of Directors of e-EFKA for approval, the final Business Plan of the year, then tables are prepared with Action Plans, timetables and Measurement Indicators*
Directorates	*They draw up the annual Operational Plan, where they should indicate their objectives, which should be linked to the objectives of the General Directorate to which they belong*

Source Ministry of Administrative Reconstruction (2018)

Along with the 826/56/27–12-2017 Decision of EFKA's Board of Directors, the Agency's Strategic Goals for the years 2018–2020 (which are still valid until today) were set, as follows (e-EFKA, 2024):

1. Improvement of service quality to enhance trust relationships with insured individuals.
2. Establishment of an administrative modernization system and strategic planning methods for better utilization of the Agency's resources for the benefit of citizens. Among other things, it was foreseen the creation of a new regional structure that consists of eleven (11) Regional Insurance Audit Centers (PEKA)—under the newly established General Directorate of Audits—distributed throughout the country. The mission of this new structure is to secure resources coming from insurance contributions as well as to tackle contribution evasion/avoidance and undeclared/underdeclared work. The creation, for the first time, of an effective audit service was considered to help ensure the sustainability of the social security system in the future.
3. Evaluation of the existing information systems of the EFKA and the implementation of advanced technological applications in all the services of the organization.

14.5 Research Methodology

For data collection, primary quantitative research was chosen. In addition, as can be seen from the previous sections, a review of the literature on strategic planning was conducted, while simultaneously examining the legislative framework supporting the strategic planning of public organizations in Greece and especially that of e-EFKA. The field research was conducted on the personnel of the eleven (11) Regional Insurance Audit Centers (PEKA).

In order to ascertain whether strategic thinking is disseminated to all members of the organization and to further investigate employees' perceptions regarding the process and implementation of strategic planning in the organization, a primary quantitative survey was conducted to collect the relevant data.

Taking into account the literature review, the following hypotheses emerge:

Hypothesis 1: The efficiency of e-EFKA is particularly affected by factors of the external and internal environment.
Hypothesis 2: There is a positive correlation between the level of information for strategic planning and the degree of participation in shaping strategic-operational objectives.
Hypothesis 3: There is a positive correlation between knowledge about strategic planning and the level of understanding of the objectives.
Hypothesis 4: There is a positive correlation between position in the administrative hierarchy and the extent to which objectives are considered realistic.
Hypothesis 5: There is a positive correlation between knowledge about strategic planning and position in the administrative hierarchy.

The survey was conducted using the census method on the entire population consisting of the employees staffing the audit mechanism of e-EFKA and specifically the Regional Insurance Audit Centers. It was carried out through postal delivery of a structured questionnaire for individual completion (Chalikias et al., 2015). During the period of questionnaire distribution, the human resources of PEKA amounted to 222 employees. A total of 164 questionnaires were completed, representing, participation rate of approximately 74%.

The questionnaire consisted of closed-ended questions structured based on the Likert scale. It consisted of two parts. The first part included questions regarding the demographic data of the participants (gender, age, level of education, position in the administrative hierarchy, etc.) The second part aimed primarily to investigate the factors that, according to the participants' estimation, affect the efficiency of e-EFKA and to capture the broader perceptions of staff regarding the formulation of the strategy and its implementation.

The interpretation of the survey results was conducted using descriptive statistical measures, including measures of central tendency (mean, mode, median, etc.) and measures of dispersion (such as standard deviation). Additionally, non-parametric tests were conducted to investigate the relationship of dependence between two or more variables.

Finally, a reliability test was performed based on the Cronbach alpha coefficient. The reliability test of the questions included in the survey questionnaire resulted in a strong reliability score of 0.881.

14.6 Analysis of the Results

14.6.1 *Demographics*

The survey sample consisted of 164 people, of which 54.88% (n = 90) were women, while 45.12% (n = 74) were men. The 20.73% of the participants were aged 30–45 years, while the majority, namely 72.56%, belonged to the age group of 46–60. The 6.71% were 61 years or older. A significant proportion of the participants, approximately 36.5%, were secondary school graduates. The 37.2% were tertiary education graduates. It is noteworthy that a significant percentage of 26.22% held a postgraduate degree. However, none of the participants had a PhD. Of those surveyed, 70.73% stated that they were employees, 24.4% that they held the position of Head of Department and 4.9% that they held the position of Head of Division (Directors).

14.6.2 *Elaboration of Strategic Planning*

The examination of the relevant literature (David, 2011; Greenlay, 1986; Hood, 1991; Pollitt, 1995; Rothaermel, 2017 etc.) revealed that among the success factors of an organization are, on the one hand the creation of mechanisms for diffusion of the strategic thinking from upper hierarchical levels to lower ones and on the other hand, the adoption of participatory processes at all stages of planning, implementation and evaluation of the strategy, to ensure everyone's commitment toward achieving the set goals. However, in the case of e-EFKA and specifically its audit mechanism, it emerged that a significant part of employees knows very little (or not at all) about the strategic planning of the Agency.

Specifically regarding the question to what extent you know about the mission, vision, strategic plan and strategic goals of e-EFKA, the results are presented in Table 14.2.

Regarding the first sub-query (about the mission), both the mode and the central value correspond to the option "very". This means that the most frequent answer given by the respondents is that they were well aware of the mission of e-EΦKA (see Table 14.3).

However, for the next three sub-questions, both the mode and the central value were the answer with the number three - "moderate". This indicates that the participants did not know enough about the vision, the strategic plan and the strategic goals of e-EΦKA.

Table 14.2 Level of knowledge about mission, vision, strategic plan and strategic objectives of e-EFKA

Level of Knowledge for:	*Mission*		*Vision*		*Strategic plan*		*Strategic objectives*	
Answers	*Frequency*	*Percent*	*Frequency*	*Percent*	*Frequency*	*Percent*	*Frequency*	*Percent*
Not at all	5	3	12	7.3	8	4.9	12	7.3
A little	13	7.9	28	17.1	32	19.5	34	20.7
Moderate	46	28	57	34,8	68	41.5	59	36
Much	71	43.3	45	27.4	40	24.4	46	28
Very much	29	17.7	22	13.4	16	9.8	12	7.3
Total:	164	100	164	100	164	100	163	99.4

Table 14.3 Statistics on central location and dispersion measures

		Mission of e-EFKA	*Vision of e-EFKA*	*Strategic plan of e-EFKA*	*Strategic objectives of e-EFKA*
N	Valid	164	164	164	163
	Missing	0	0	0	1
Mean		3,6463	3,2256	3,1463	3,0736
Median		4,0000	3,0000	3,0000	3,0000
Mode		4,00	3,00	3,00	3,00
Std. Deviation		0,96,404	1,10,950	1,00,455	1,03,970

Source Data processing of our own research

Next, the respondents were asked to answer the question about how they participate in shaping the operational goals of their department and the strategic goals of the Authority in general. The particular question consisted of four standardized answers. Respondents had the option to choose more than one answer. The results are described below:

The 25% answered that they participated in shaping the operational-strategic objectives by filling in a questionnaire or another form distributed by the Administration. 59% stated that their participation is ensured through departmental meetings where their opinions are gathered by the head of the Directorate. 28% indicated that they proactively

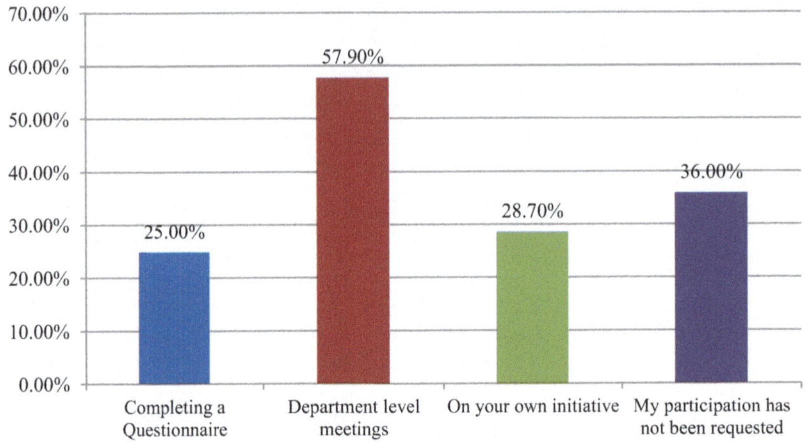

Fig. 14.1 Diagrammatic display of frequencies of PEKA employees' participation in the organization's operational-strategic planning (*Source* Data processing of our own research)

report their general concerns to their superior. However, a significant percentage around 36% of the participants stated that they had not been asked to participate (see Fig. 14.1).

Department-level meetings are the most common form of participation in strategic planning of e-EFKA, as indicated by the majority of responses. However, the lack of participation of a significant number of respondents, raises serious questions regarding the consequences for the effectiveness of strategic planning. The absence of a bottom-up approach may pose obstacles in terms of the degree of commitment, acceptance and knowledge regarding the strategic plan in the organization's human resources.

In response to the question "to what extent do you consider that the proposals or concerns you raise, are taken into account by senior management, in shaping the strategic plan of e-EFKA?", the results were as follows:

The 31.1% of the respondents consider that their proposals are not taken into account by the higher hierarchical levels. The 23.2% consider that they are taken into account minimally and 25% to a moderate extent.

Overall, 54.3% of the respondents expressed negative views, while 25% chose the moderate option. Only a small percentage of 7.9% believe that their proposals are taken into account to a satisfactory extent. The remaining 12.8% answered that they did not know.

Then, respondents were asked to determine the extent to which they understand the goals set by management. 7.98% of them stated that they do not understand the goals at all, 13.50% answered a little and 35.8% stated moderately.

Furthermore, respondents were also asked to determine the extent to which the goals set by management are perceived as realistic and achievable. 21.5% of them answered that they did not find it realistic at all, 21.5% answered a little and 40% to a moderate extent. Only 14.7% and 1.8% considered the goals as very and extremely realistic-achievable respectively. In fact, only 16.5% hold positive views regarding the feasibility of strategic planning in the organization.

Regarding the factors, at a strategic level, which were considered by the research participants to affect the efficiency of the organization, among the most significant were:

- Continuous training of auditors and further education: 83.6% (n:137)
- Interoperability of Information Systems: 83.5%, (n:137)
- Staffing of PEKAs with experienced and trained personnel: 83%, (n:136)
- Technological modernization: 79.9% (n:131)
- Reduction of bureaucratic procedures: 79.3% (n:130)

Finally, given the importance attributed to the organization's strategy regarding the process of digital transformation of the audit mechanism, an attempt was made to investigate the opinion of the employees on how digital transformation affects:

A. Simplification of audit procedures
B. Improvement of services provided to citizens
C. Tackling social security contributions evasion
D. Achieving goals

As shown in Table 14.4, the average of the responses fluctuated close to the value of 3.6 (that is, between moderate and very). Correspondingly, the mode was the fourth choice (a lot). From these data, it can be concluded that the respondents believed that the digital transformation of the audit mechanism would positively contribute to the simplifying audit

Table 14.4 Impact of digital transformation—measures of central tendency, measures of dispersion

		Simplification of audit procedures	*Improving services provided*	*Tackling contribution evasion*	*Achieving of individual goals*
N	Valid	164	164	164	164
	Missing	0	0	0	0
Mean		3,6768	3,6707	3,6890	3,7012
Median		4,0000	4,0000	4,0000	4,0000
Mode		4,00	4,00	4,00	4,00
Std. Deviation		1,11837	1,01588	1,03657	1,01025
Variance		1,251	1,032	1,074	1,021
Kurtosis		–,065	–,394	–,023	,027
Std. Error of Kurtosis		,377	,377	,377	,377
Range		4,00	4,00	4,00	4,00
Minimum		1,00	1,00	1,00	1,00
Maximum		5,00	5,00	5,00	5,00

Source Data processing of our own research

procedures, improving services provided to stakeholders, tackling social security contributions evasion and achieving the set goals. However, their support seems relatively moderate.

In the context of the inductive statistical analysis, it was found that there is a significant statistical correlation between the position held and the knowledge about the mission of e-EFKA, as $p = 0.019 < 0.05$.

In particular, it was observed that none of the managers or supervisors answered that they do not know at all or know a little, about the above concepts of strategic planning.

The p value regarding the dependency relationship between the position held and the degree to which the executives of the PEKA are aware of the strategic plan of e-EΦKA was calculated as $0.044 < 0.05$. In other words, there is a correlation between these two variables.

Specifically, none of the directors responded that they did not know at all or that they knew little, about the strategic plan of e-EFKA, while none of the department heads stated that they did not know at all. Regarding employees, forty out of a total of one hundred and sixteen participants in the survey (i.e., 30%) stated that they did not know at all or know little about the Strategic Plan of e-EFKA (see Table 14.5).

Table 14.5 Knowledge about e-EFKA's strategic plan* position held

Crosstab

			Not at all	*A little*	*Moderate*	*Much*	*Very much*	
Position	Director	Count	$0_{a, b}$	0_{b}	$2_{a, b}$	$4_{a, b}$	2_{a}	8
		Expected Count	,4	1,6	3,3	2,0	,8	8,0
		% within Position	0,0%	0,0%	25,0%	50,0%	25,0%	100,0%
	Head of Department	Count	0_{a}	5_{a}	$19_{a, b}$	$9_{a, b}$	7_{b}	40
		Expected Count	2,0	7,8	16,6	9,8	3,9	40,0
		% within Position	0,0%	12,5%	47,5%	22,5%	17,5%	100,0%
	Officer	Count	8_{a}	27_{a}	$47_{a, b}$	$27_{a, b}$	7_{b}	116
		Expected Count	5,7	22,6	48,1	28,3	11,3	116,0
		% within Position	6,9%	23,3%	40,5%	23,3%	6,0%	100,0%
Total		Count	8	32	68	40	16	164
		Expected Count	8,0	32,0	68,0	40,0	16,0	164,0
		% within Position	4,9%	19,5%	41,5%	24,4%	9,8%	100,0%

Each subscript letter denotes a subset of STRATEGIC PLAN OF e-EFKA categories whose column proportions do not differ significantly from each other at the, 05 level

Source Data processing of our own research

Chi-Square Tests

	Value	*df*	*Asymp. Sig. (2-sided)*
Pearson Chi-Square	15,901[a]	8	,044
Likelihood Ratio	18,567	8	,017
Linear-by-Linear Association	12,479	1	,000
N of Valid Cases	164		

a. 7 cells (46,7%) have expected count less than 5. The minimum expected count is, 39
Source Data processing of our own research

A significant correlation was also observed between the position held and the degree to which the objectives are considered realistic and achievable ($p = 0.042$). Specifically, those in higher positions tended to consider the objectives as more realistic and feasible compared to employees at other lower levels.

Furthermore, by conducting the non-parametric tests based on the Spearman coefficient (Table 14.6), a positive correlation emerged between the level of knowledge about the basic concepts of strategic planning and the extent to which the participants: (a) believe that their proposals are taken into account by the e-EΦKA's management, (b) understand and (c) consider the objectives realistic and achievable. In all cases the p value based on Spearman's coefficient was below $0.003 < 0.05$.

It is confirmed that the employees with a better knowledge of the vision, the mission, the strategic plan and the strategic goals of e-EFKA, consider to a satisfactory degree that their proposals are taken into account by management while at the same time perceiving goal setting as a process that is understandable, realistic and feasible.

It was also found that individuals who were more familiar with the basic concepts of strategic planning and the strategic objectives of the organization participated to a greater extent, primarily through department-level meetings, in shaping the operational goals. They also believed to a greater extent than other respondents that their proposals were taken into account by the management of the organization.

14.7 Conclusions

The process of strategic planning in organizations, both in the private and public sectors, is a vital function especially in the modern environment where the pace of changes is very rapid. Their ability to acquire resilience

Table 14.6 Calculation of statistical dependence based on the Spearman coefficient

		Mission of e-EFKA	*Vision of e-EFKA*	*Strategic plan of e-EFKA*	*Strategic objectives of e-EFKA*
Are the suggestions—problems report taken into account by the administration?	Correlation Coefficient	,227**	,361**	,363**	,343**
	Sig. (2-tailed)	**,003**	**,000**	**,000**	**,000**
	N	164	164	164	163
Do you find the goal setting understandable?	Correlation Coefficient	,284**	,351**	,371**	,365**
	Sig. (2-tailed)	**,000**	**,000**	**,000**	**,000**
	N	163	163	163	162
Do you consider the goal realistic and achievable?	Correlation Coefficient	,315**	,365**	,379**	,348**
	Sig. (2-tailed)	**,000**	**,000**	**,000**	**,000**
	N	163	163	163	162

**. Correlation is significant at the 0.01 level (1-tailed)

*. Correlation is significant at the 0.05 level (1-tailed)

Source Data processing of our own research

and adaptability in responding to the complex challenges of the environment largely depends on the formulated strategy and its implementation. In the Greek public administration, there is generally a reluctance to deeply adopt the processes of strategic planning and their substantial integration into the organizational culture (OECD 2012). This aspect is multifactorial and can be considered to be related to the deficit of trust between political leadership and managerial staff, the prevailing centralized logic, fragmentation, the difficulty in managing change, the lack of expertise in various cases and other factors encountered in the field of Greek public administration (Spanou, 2018; Sotiropoulos, 2021; Tsekos, 2016).

Regarding the case study examined in this article, namely that of e-EFKA, its establishment was the culmination of a complex but necessary effort, under the pressure of the severe problems faced by the Greek economy, the past fifteen years. This effort is part of a process of radical restructuring of the social security system in Greece.

However, the implementation of the strategic plan in e-EFKA would not have been possible without the creation of the appropriate organizational structure and the determination of the corresponding functions. From the study of the institutional framework, came up that the existing one in Greece, despite its fragmentary nature, provides relevant directions for the practical implementation of strategic and operational planning in Public Organizations (L.3463/2006; Ministerial Decision - Ministry of Administrative Reconstruction, (2018), L.4622/19 on "Executive State").

In the case of e-EFKA in particular, it is observed that both the adoption of the institutional framework's guidelines (specific procedures for planning, implementation and evaluation processes of the strategy were adopted and implemented) and the formation of the appropriate organizational framework (e.g., establishment of the General Directorate of Strategy and Development) were achieved to a satisfactory degree, forming the basis upon which the strategic process rests. Despite the aforementioned developments and taking into consideration that the achievement of an organization's goals depends largely on its ability to adapt timely to the constantly changing and unstable external environment, e-EFKA appeared to be affected by factors of the external environment and in particular by events which can be characterized as black swans (Taleb, 2007). An indicative example is the results of the primary survey, according to which 74% of the participants believe that the pandemic significantly affected the efficiency of the audit mechanism. This is also confirmed by the comparison of statistical data obtained by e-ΕΦΚΑ, for the time period of the pandemic, during which there was a sharp decline in the inspections carried out for the detection of undeclared and underdeclared work, as well as in the amount of fines assessed (Makavelos, 2022).

Nevertheless, significant progress has been observed in recent years regarding the integration of new technological capabilities within e-EFKA, a process that is part of the wider digital reform of Greek public administration. The importance of technological transformation was also highlighted by the results of the research. In response to the question about the factors contributing to the enhancement of the efficiency of the audit mechanism and e-EFKA, technological transformation, interoperability of information systems and reduction of bureaucratic procedures were among the options that gathered the most preferences.

Another significant aspect that should be highlighted and which also emerges from the examination of the relevant literature (David, 2011; Greenlay, 1986; Hood, 1991; Kim et al., 2014; Pollitt, 1995; Rothaermel, 2017. etc.) is that among the success factors regarding the implementation of an organization's strategic plan is, on the one hand the establishment of mechanisms for disseminating strategic objectives from the highest levels of management to the rest and, more broadly, to stakeholders of the organization. On the other hand, it involves the adoption of participatory processes at all stages of strategic planning, so that the final outcome arises as a product of interaction among the involved parties.

In the case of e-EFKA, however, it was found that a significant part of employees has little (or no knowledge at all) regarding the organization's strategic planning process. Inductive statistical analysis revealed that proportionally, employees in position of responsibility (directors, department heads) had a better understanding of the organization's vision and strategic goals, comprehended the objectives more and found them to be more realistic and achievable to a greater extent. These results collectively highlight the inadequate dissemination of strategic goals to other levels of the organization.

Similarly, 36% of respondents stated that they have not been asked to participate in shaping the organization's strategy, while approximately 29% indicated that they express their opinions to their head department, on their own initiative. In addition, 54% of respondents consider that their proposals are not taken into account by the management to a satisfactory extent, while 31.10% consider that they are not taken into account at all. Furthermore, 57.06% do not find the organization's objectives sufficiently understandable or understandable at all. This aspect raises questions about the extent to which members of the organization can contribute to achieving goals that they have not understood and have not made their own property.

Taking therefore into consideration that the successful formulation of an organization's strategic planning requires, among other things, the implementation of bottom-up approaches, in order to strengthen the sense of participation in shaping the organization's policies, the inadequate functioning of such mechanisms within e-EFKA, poses risks regarding the achievement of the set goals, while at the same time questioning their reliability and realism. Proposals and ideas coming from the lower executives of the organization could lead to a more rational planning of operational actions or to a revision and re-evaluation of the objectives.

Although in the case of public organizations the strategy is mostly formed on the basis of established political perceptions (Rothaermel, 2017), or logical "business as usual" approaches and therefore the implementation of bottom-up strategic methods is put on the back burner, the constantly changing external environment requires continuous feedback from lower hierarchical levels in order to identify more quickly upcoming changes and potential weaknesses.

This conclusion is further reinforced by the results of the inductive statistical analysis. It was specifically observed that individuals who had a better understanding of the basic concepts of strategic planning and the strategic goals of the organization participated more in shaping operational goals, had a better understanding of the direction and believed to a greater extent that their proposals were taken into account by the organization's management.

Therefore, the systematic and institutionalized dissemination of information to all employees regarding the strategic agenda could help enhance their sense of participation in shaping and implementing the strategy and in understanding goal setting.

In any case, the strategy of e-EFKA seems to be affected by the endogenous weaknesses that characterize the majority of public organizations in Greece, such as the low degree of administrative autonomy (since important decisions are taken with a top down-centralized manner by political leadership), the lack of relevant culture, the gap in necessary expertise and the limited financial resources, all of which pose obstacles to any effort to promote new initiatives and broader change.

A more holistic approach to strategic planning, focusing simultaneously on organizational culture and change management issues, in order to enable its acceptance and integration into the operation of public organizations, might contribute to ensuring that it does not remain merely a letter on paper and a formal operation for the majority of public bodies in Greece. Instead it could become a dynamic and continuously adaptive process that takes into account significant proposals from wherever they originate, for the benefit of all stakeholders involved.

References

Borins, S. (1995). The new public management is here to stay. *Canadian Public Administration, 38*, 122–132. https://doi.org/10.1111/j.1754-7121.1995.tb01133.x

Burandas, D. (2015). Manatzment, Plires Theoritiko Ypovathro - Sygchrones Prosegiseis kai Methodoi, Dioikitikes kai Igetikes Ikanotites. [Management, Full Theoretical Background - Modern Approaches and Methods, Management and Leadership Skills]. G. Benos Publications.

Boyne, G.A. (2003). Sources of public service improvement: A critical review and research agenda. *Journal of Public Administration Research and Theory, 13*(3), 367–394. ResearchGate. Accessed 02 Feb 2024.

Bryson, J. M. (1995). *Strategic planning for public and non-profit organizations: A guide to strengthening and sustaining organizational achievement*. Jossey-Bass.

Bryson, J. M., Berry, F. S., & Yang, K. (2010). The state of public strategic management research: A selective literature review and set of future directions. *The American Review of Public Administration, 40*(5), 495–521. https://doi.org/10.1177/0275074010370361

Bryson, J. M. (2011). *Strategic planning for nonprofit organizations*, 4th ed. Jossey-Bass, John Willey & Sons.

Chalikias, M., Manolessou, Al., & Lalou, P. (2015). Methodologia Erevnas kai Eisagogi sti Statistiki Analysi Dedomenon me to IBM SPSS STATISTICS, Ellinika Akadimaika Ilektronika Sygrammata kai Voithimata, (www.kalipos.gr).

Cohen, N. (2016). Forgoing New public management and adopting post-new public management principles: The on-going civil service reform in Israel. *Public Administration and Development., 36*(1), 20–34. https://doi.org/10.1002/pad.1751

David, R. Fr. (2011). *Strategic management: Concept and cases*, 13th ed. Prentice Hall. vdocument.in_strategic-management-fred-rdavid.pdf. Accessed 05 Dec 2023.

Donald, C. G., Lyons, T. S., & Tribbey, R. C. (2001). A partnership for strategic planning and management in a public organization. *Public Performance and Management Review, 25*(2), 176–193. https://doi.org/10.1080/15309576.2001.11643653

Electronic National Social Security Fund—e-EFKA. Mission of e-EΦΚΑ | (efka.gov.gr). Accessed 05 Apr 2024.

Electronic National Social Security Fund—e-EFKA. Strategic Plan of e- EFKA 2018–2020 | (efka.gov.gr). Accessed 05 Apr 2022.

Ellingson, D. A., & Wambsganss, J. R. (2001). Modifying the approach to planning and evaluation in governmental entities: A "Balanced Scorecard" approach. *Journal of Public Budgeting, Accounting and Financial Management, 13*(1), 103–20. Modifying the approach to planning and evaluation - ProQuest .. Accessed 15 Feb 2024.

Fayol, H. (1949). *General and industrial management*, Pitman and Sons Ltd. https://www.jstor.org/stable/258475. Accessed 23 Nov 2023.

Franklin, A. L. (2001). Serving the public interest? Federal experiences with participation in strategic planning. *American Review of Public Administration, 31*(2), 126–138. https://doi.org/10.1177/02750740122064884

George, B., Desmidt, S. (2014). A state of research on strategic management in the public sector: an analysis of the empirical evidence. In P. Joyce and A. Drumaux, (Eds.), *Strategic management in public organizations: European practices and perspectives*, 151–172. Routledge. Public Management Review 357. (PDF) A State of Research on Strategic Management in the Public Sector: An Analysis of the Empirical Evidence (researchgate.net). Accessed 07 Mar 2023.

Georgopoulos, V. N. (2013). *Stratigiko Manatzment [Strategic Management]*, 3rd ed. Benos Publications.

Goergen, M. (2012). *International corporate governance*, Pearson Education Limited. International Corporate Governance | Marc Goergen - Academia.edu. Accessed 12 Jan 2024.

Greenley, G. (1986). *Does strategic planning improve company performance? Long Range Planning, 19*(2), 101–109. Pergamon Press Ltd. https://doi.org/10.1016/0024-6301(86)90226-8

Gruening, G. (2001). Origin and theoretical basis of new public management. *International Public Management Journal, 4*, 1–25. https://doi.org/10.1016/S1096-7494(01)00041-1

Halachmi, A., Hardy W. P., & Rhoades B. L. (1993). Demographic data and strategic analysis. *Public Administration Quarterly, 17*(2), 159–74. Demographic Data and Strategic Analysis | Semantic Scholar. Accessed 15 Feb 2024.

Hansen, R. J., & Ferlie, Ew. (2014). *Applying strategic management theories in public sector organizations: Developing a typology*. article in public management review on May 2014. Applying Strategic Management Theories in Public Sector Organizations: Developing a typology: Public Management Review: Vol 18 , No 1 - Get Access (tandfonline.com). Accessed 29 Mar 2024.

Hatry, H. P. (2002). Performance measurement: Fashions and fallacies. *Public Performance and Management Review, 25*(4), 352–58. Performance Measurement: Fashions and Fallacies on JSTOR. Accessed 23 Feb 2024.

Hill, W. L.Ch., Schilling, A. M., & Gareth, R. J., (2017). *Strategic management: Theory: An integrated approach* (Theory and Cases), Broken Hill Publishers ltd.

Hood, C. (1991). *A public management for all seasons, public administration*, Vol. 69, Spring, pp. 3–19. https://doi.org/10.1111/j.1467-9299.1991.tb00779.x

Hood, C. (1995). *The "New Public Management" in the 1980s: variation on a theme accounting, organizations and society*, 20, 93–109. https://doi.org/10.1016/0361-3682(93)E0001-W

Kelly, G., Mulgan, G., & Muers, St. (2002). *Creating public value an analytical framework for public service reform*, Strategy Unit, Cabinet Office, UK. Creating Public Value An analytical framework for public service reform | Jesus Mejia - Academia.edu. Accessed 07 Jan 2024.

Kim, Y. H., Sting, F. J., & Loch, C. H. (2014). Top-down, bottom-up, or both? towards an integrative perspective on operations strategy formation. *Journal of Operations Management, 32*(2014), 462–474. https://doi.org/10.1016/j.jom.2014.09.005

Lawlor, J. E. (2010). The importance of strategic planning. *Observatory on Borderless Higher education Long Range Planning. 21*(1), 73–81. Page 7

L.1892/1990, art. 80. Systasi Monadon Stratigikou Schediasmou kai Analysis Politikis. [Establishment of strategic planning and policy analysis units]. et.gr/idocs-nph/search/pdf/L.1892/1990. Accessed 12 Mar 2024.

L.3463/2006, art. 206, § 4. Kodikas Dimon kai Koinotiton [Code of Municipalities and Communities]. et.gr/idocs-nph/search/pdf/L.3463/2006. Accessed 27 Mar 2024.

L.4387/2016, art. 51—Chapter E΄. Eniaios Foreas Koinonikis Asfalisis—Systasi Skopos [Unified Social Security Fund—Establishment Purpose]. et.gr/idocs-nph/search/pdf/L.4387/2016. Accessed 27 Mar 2024.

L.4622/2019. Epiteliko Kratos: Organosi, Leitourgia kai Diafaneia tis Kyvernisis, ton Kyvernitikon Organon kai tis Kentrikis Dimosias Dioikisis. [Executive State: Organization, Operation and Transparency of the Government, Government Bodies and Central Public Administration]. et.gr/idocs-nph/search/pdf/L.4622/2019. Accessed 27 Mar 2024.

L. 4670/20 Asfalistiki Metarrythmisi kai Psifiakos Metaschimatismos Ethnikou Forea Koinonikis Asfalisis (e-E.F.K.A.) kai Alles Diataxeis. [Insurance Reform and Digital Transformation of the National Social Security Fund (e-EFKA) and other Provisions]. et.gr/idocs-nph/search/pdf/L.4670/2020. Accessed 27 Mar 2024.

Makavelos, G. (2022). I symvoli tou Elegktikou Michanismou stin epitefxi ton stratigikon stochon tou e-EFKA: I periptosi ton Perifereiakon Elegktikon Kentron Asfalisis [The contribution of the Inspection Mechanism to the accomplishment of the strategic objectives of e-EFKA: The case of the Regional Insurance Audit Centres], University of West Attica, School of Administration, Economic and Social Sciences, Department of Accounting & Finance.

Matthews, J. H., & Shulman, A. D. (2005). Competitive advantage in public sector organizations: explaining the public good/sustainable competitive advantage paradox, *Journal of Business Research, 58*(2): 232–240. https://eprints.qut.edu.au/6977/1/6977.pdf. Accessed 10 Nov 2023.

McLaughlin, K., Osborne, P. S., Ew., & Ferlie. (2005). New public management current trends and future prospects. *Taylor & Francis e-Library*. https://doi.org/10.4324/9780203996362

Michalopoulos, N., & Makridimitris, A. (2000). *Ektheseis Empeirognomonon gia ti Dimosia Dioikisi [Reports of Experts on Public Administration]*. Papazisis Publications.

Michalopoulos, N. (2003). *Apo ti Dimosia Grafeiokratia sto Dimosio Management [From Public Bureaucracy to Public Management]*. Papazisis Publications.

Ministry of Administrative Reconstruction, (2018). Efarmogi tou Systimatos "Dioikisi meso Stochon" gia to etos 2019 [Implementation of the "Management through Objectives", System for the Year 2019], File No: DISSK/TPP/F.1/26898, Athens, 24 July 2018, ADA: 9ΨΞ3465ΧΘΨ-1ΒΔ. https://diavgeia.gov.gr/search?advanced. Accessed 27 Mar 2024.

Organisation for Economic Co-operation and Development—OECD (2012). Inspection of the Central Administration. translation of the ESDDA Alumni Association, Athens. OECD Public Governance Reviews: Greece: Review of the Central Administration (dianeosis.org). Accessed 14 Dec 2024.

Osborne, D., & Gaebler, T. (1992). *Reinventing government: How the entrepreneurial spirit is transforming the public sector*. Addison-Wesley. https://doi.org/10.1080/00222216.1995.11949751

Papadakis, V. (2016). *Stratigiki ton Epicheiriseon: Elliniki kai Diethnis Empeiria*, 7th ed. [Business Strategy: Greek and International Experience], Benos Publications.

Parnell, J. A., Carraher, S., Holt, K. (2002). Participative management's influence on effective strategic diffusion. *Journal of Business Strategies, 19*(2). https://doi.org/10.54155/jbs.19.2.161-179

Poister, T. H., & Van Slyke, D. M. (2002). Strategic management innovations in state transportation departments. *Public Performance and Management Review, 26*(1), 8–74. Strategic Management Innovations in State Transportation Departments on JSTOR. Accessed 16 Jan 2024.

Poister, T. H., Edwards, L. H., Pasha, O. Q., & Edwards, J. (2013). Strategy formulation and performance. *Public Performance & Management Review, 36*(4), 585–615.

Pollitt, C. (1995). Justification by works or by faith? *Evaluating the New Public Management, Evaluation, 9*, 133–154. https://doi.org/10.1177/135638909500100202

PD 8/2019. Organismos Eniaiou Forea Koinonikis Asfalisis (E.F.K.A.). [Organization of the Unified Social Security Agency (E.F.K.A.)]. et.gr/idocs-nph/search/pdf/PD.8/2019. Accessed 27 Mar 2024.

Roberts, N. (2000). The synoptic model of strategic planning and the GPRA: Lacking a good fit with the political context. *Public Productivity and Management Review, 23*(3), 297–311. (PDF) The Synoptic Model of Strategic Planning and the GPRA: Lacking a Good Fit with the Political Context (researchgate.net). Accessed 19 Feb 2024.

Rothaermel, T. Fr. (2017). *Strategic management*, Rosili Publications.

Siomkos, I. G. (2013). *Stratigiko Marketing [Strategic Marketing]*, 3th ed. Paschalidis BC .

Sotiropoulos, D. (2021). I Dimosia Dioikisi stin Epochi Meta ton Koronoio. [Public Administration in the Post-coronavirus Era], Dianeosis, https://www.dianeosis.org/wp-content/uploads/2021/01/Sotiropoulos_final.pdf

Spanou, K. (2018). Metarrythmiseis sti Dimosia Dioikisi sti Diarkeia tis Krisis: Episkopisi, Perigrafi, Apotimisi, [Reforms in Public Administration During the Crisis: Overview, Description, Evaluation], Hellenic Foundation for European and Foreign Policy, Papazisis Publications.

Special Secretariat of Foresight. (2023). Megatrends 2040: Volatility, Uncertainty, resourcefulness, https://foresight.gov.gr/en/studies/Megatrends-2040-Volatility-Uncertainty-Resourcefulness/. Accessed 18 Mar 2024.

Taleb, N. N. (2007). *A black Swan: The impact of the highly improbable*, Random House N.Y.

Tsekos, Th. N. (2016). Diarthrotikes Allages kai Dioikitiki Metarrythmisi [Structural Changes and Administrative Reform]. In Georgarakis N., Demertzis N. (Eds.), *The Political Portrait of Greece. Crisis and the deconstruction of the political* pp. 359–377, National Center of Social Research, Gutenberg Publications, Athens. Available at SSRN: https://ssrn.com/abstract=2724439 or http://dx.doi.org/10.2139/ssrn.2724439

Vinzant, D. H., & Vinzant, J. (1996). Strategy and organizational capacity: Finding a fit. *Public Productivity and Management Review, 20*(2), 139–57. https://www.jstor.org/stable/3380482. Accessed 17 Jan 2024.

Walker, R. M., & Andrews, R. (2015). Local government management and performance: A review of evidence. *Journal of Public Administration Research and Theory, 25*(1), 101–133. https://doi.org/10.1093/jopart/mut038

Williams, W., & Lewis, D. (2008). Strategic management tools and public sector management. *Public Management Review, 10*(5), 653–671. https://doi.org/10.1080/14719030802264382

Wollmann, H, & Thurmaier, K. (2010). *Reforming local government institutions and the new public management in Europe and the US* (p. 1). Oxford University Press. https://doi.org/10.1093/oxfordhb/9780195367867.013.0010

CHAPTER 15

Impact of Cost Accounting Models on Estimations in Adult Intensive Care Units (ICUs) and on Reimbursement System: A Case Study of a Public Hospital During the Covid-19 Pandemic

Maria Rodosthenous, Evangelos Roumeliotis, and Dimitrios Charamis

15.1 Introduction

The healthcare sector is one of the largest in the world, where changes are taking place at an incredibly fast pace, and this is reflected in the amounts spent for health services. According to the World Health Organization (2022a), global health expenditure, as a percentage of Gross

M. Rodosthenous · E. Roumeliotis (✉) · D. Charamis
Department of Accounting and Finance,
University of West Attica, Athens, Greece
e-mail: eroumeliotis@uniwa.gr

M. Rodosthenous
e-mail: mrod@uniwa.gr

A. Hyz (ed.), *The Role of the Public Sector in Building Social and Economic Resilience*,
https://doi.org/10.1007/978-3-031-67702-1_15

Domestic Product (GDP), rose from 8.63% in 2000, to 9.83% in 2019, while in 2020, following the outbreak of the covid-19 pandemic, it reached 10.8% or $9 trillion (World Health Organization-WHO, 2022b). In the United States of America, while health expenditure in 2019 reached 17.6%, in 2020, the first year of the pandemic, it reached the record level of 19.7% of GDP, while in 2021 decreased slightly, reaching 18.3%, which, according to Telesford et al. (2023) is due to the improvement of the US economy and the decrease in the growth rate of health expenditure. In Europe, the average health expenditure in 2019 was 8.3% of GDP, with Germany and France leading the way with 11.7% and 11.2%, respectively (Organization for Economic Cooperation and Development-OECD/European Union, 2020). With the emergence of the pandemic, the average health expenditure in Europe reached 10.9% of GDP, with Germany and France continuing to have the highest health expenditure, amounting to 12.8% and 12.2%, respectively (Eurostat & Statistics Explained, 2022). Greece's corresponding rates are 7.84% of GDP for 2019 (Organization for Economic Cooperation & Development-OECD, European Observatory on Health Systems & Policies., 2021) and 9.5% for the year 2020 (Eurostat & Statistics Explained, 2022), while according to the Hellenic Statistical Authority (Hellenic Statistical Authority, 2023) for 2021 health expenditure reached 9.17%.

The absorption of such a significant amount of financial resources by the health system creates the need for its proper management in order to ensure maximum efficiency (Cylus & Irwin, 2022; Polyzos et al., 2013). One of the most important tools for the proper management of health expenditure is the estimation of hospital costs, as this will lead to its control, more efficient allocation and the improvement of the quality of health services (Carey & Stefos, 2011; Jacobs et al., 2022; Tan et al., 2010). One of the most important segments of hospital resource absorption is the Intensive Care Units (ICUs), as due to their specificities, their costs largely exceed those of other clinics (Karabatsou et al., 2016; Oostenbrink et al., 2003).

The aim of the present study is to calculate the real cost of the adult ICU of a Greek public University hospital, in two different time periods,

D. Charamis
e-mail: dcharamis@uniwa.gr

before and during the occurrence of the Covid-19 pandemic, thus examining its possible impact on the cost of ICU operation. At the same time, a comparison will be made between the ICU costs and the amount of reimbursement, for the respective time periods, in order to investigate the reliability of the reimbursement/pricing system applied by the hospital, compared to its actual costs, especially in times of an extraordinary health crisis.

15.2 Literature Review

15.2.1 The Cost of ICUs

Intensive care management is the focus for many hospitals, worldwide, due to the high level of resource consumption. ICUs, because of their specificities, are one of the most expensive parts of inpatient care, with the ever-increasing demand for intensive care placing them at the top of the healthcare expenditure list. Although ICU beds represent a small percentage of total beds, they absorb about 20%-30% of a hospital's budget, and the total cost of critical care medicine in ICUs is about 0.5% to 1% of GDP (Decruyenaere, 2006; Halpern et al., 2016; Kilic et al., 2019).

Due to the critical, for the life of patients, work of ICUs, specific, minimum requirements for their operation within a hospital have been established such as the regulation of Greek Central Board of Health (Ministry of Health of Greece, 2019). The stipulated standards, which are highly detailed, regulate a wide range of parameters such as the specific construction of the ICU accommodation, the minimum number of beds and their construction specifications, the number of physician and nursing staff necessary for the safe and uninterrupted operation of the unit and the minimum medical-technological equipment. These conditions, combined with the high cost of the treatments provided by the ICU, raise its operating costs to levels much higher than those of other hospital departments.

The high cost of operating ICUs, combined with the economic crisis of the last decade and consequently, the reduction of health expenditure budgets, make the calculation of their costs a necessary procedure. Moreover, according to studies (Cambaro et al., 2023; Karboub & Tabaa, 2023), the calculation of ICU costs is important for optimizing the allocation of ICU beds among hospitals.

The estimation of ICU cost has been a matter of concern for many researchers. The findings of most studies do not coincide with each other, as the method of calculation applied and the amount of data available to each researcher differ (Hrifach et al., 2016; Tan et al., 2012). Negrini et al. (2006) conducted the first survey of costing ICUs among four countries by applying, the same costing method to all of them. Their findings showed significant differences in the average daily cost per ICU patient, $1,512 in hospitals in England, $934 in France, $726 in Germany and $280 in Hungary. Staff costs, absorbed most of their budgets, while in terms of pharmaceutical costs, Hungary and England appeared to consume more than Germany and France. Tan et al. (2012) carried out a similar survey among four countries, by developing a standardized costing methodology based on the data available. In line with the previous survey, the analysis revealed that the average daily cost of hospitalization per patient in the ICU varied significantly among the countries, with Italy having the lowest cost of €1,168, and England the highest at €2,025, while labor costs still accounted for the largest proportion of daily costs. McLaughlin et al. (2009) investigating the daily cost of ICU in a hospital in Ireland, estimated it at €2,205, while Kilic et al. (2019) in a similar study in Turkey, came to the same conclusion, that labor costs are the largest part of daily costs, with pharmaceutical costs being the next largest.

In Greece, there are not too many studies that have been conducted on the calculation of the cost of ICU. Kosmidis et al. (2021) studied the cost of ICU of a general (non-university) hospital in Northern Greece. The data were processed in two, annual, periods (2014–2015 and 2015–2016), and the average daily cost was €835.62 and €885.35, respectively. The most important cost element in the first period was the direct variable cost which amounted to 41.7%, while the second was the personnel cost at 40.4%, which as they point out, do not correspond to the global literature, as personnel costs usually absorb the largest costs. In the second period, however, there was a reversal of the above ratio, with personnel costs reaching 47.3% and direct variable costs 31.1%. They attribute the above change mainly to the large reduction in healthcare expenditure that the government made in the second period of the study, amounting to 38.2%. The variable cost was calculated at €334.06, which is considerably lower than the corresponding amount calculated by Karabatsou et al. (2016) studying the ICU of a general hospital, which amounted to €573.18. The difference, as explained by Kosmidis et al. (2021) is probably due to the different costing approach, the Average Length of

Stay (ALoS) and other factors that are not easy to identify. In 2010, Geitona et al. (2010) estimated the average daily cost of a Greek University ICU at €1,856. As in the majority of the other studies, labor costs absorbed the largest proportion of the costs, while pharmaceutical costs also accounted for a large proportion. The large discrepancy between Karabatsou et al. (2016) and Geitona et al. (2010) surveys is due to the significant economic changes that had been occurred in healthcare in Greece from 2006 onwards. In 2010, Greece entered the global economic crisis, which led to large reductions in the budgets of public hospitals, sometimes reaching 40%-50%, while the government proceeded to a significant reduction in salaries of public employees, and by extension, of medical and nursing staff, a reduction that reached an annual level of 30%. At the same time, in 2010 the Price Observatory was established at the Ministry of Health (Law No. 3846/2010, 2010), in order to control and contain the prices of all health material and services, and already, in the first year of implementation, a price reduction of 29.7% recorded. Another factor that contributed to the deviation in the daily cost of ICU from 2006 to 2011 is the successive reductions in pharmaceutical expenditure beginning from 2010. In particular, in the three-year period 2010–2012, the pharmaceutical expenditure decreased by 42% (Frouzis, 2013).

15.2.2 The Pricing/Costing System

The system of reimbursement/pricing of healthcare services has been of concern to many researchers, as it is the main factor in the financing of hospitals, worldwide. The healthcare reimbursement system, which has been adopted by most European and third countries, is the Diagnostic Related Groups (DRGs) (Leister & Stausberg, 2005). The USA, in 1983, was the first country to implement the DRGs reimbursement system, in an attempt to control the ever-increasing healthcare costs (Chilingerian, 2008; Davies & Westfall, 1983). The innovation of this system is the way the patient is treated. According to this, each patient is treated as a member of a group of patients with common characteristics (demographic, diagnostic, therapeutic, etc.) rather than as a unit. The amount of resources required for their treatment will be determined by their common characteristics. DRGs are therefore diagnostic categories, each with a specific level of health resource use, where patients with similar conditions are placed in one of these categories. Therefore, patients placed in the same diagnostic category (DRG) are expected to absorb the same amount of resources. The reimbursement provider is then required to pay the hospital the predetermined reimbursement price to which each diagnostic category is linked, without considering the resources absorbed by each patient. With this system, the health provider knows in advance the exact amount he will receive, while at the same time, through the coded diagnoses, more accurate pricing is achieved (Cylus & Irwin, 2022).

According to studies conducted in various countries, it seems that this reimbursement model has achieved its objectives, as it has achieved cost containment and increased hospital efficiency (Kaitelidou et al., 2020; Pirson et al., 2013; Tan et al., 2014). Nevertheless, this system, during its implementation, showed several weaknesses in the calculation of actual costs in different countries (Brannen, 1999; Kaitelidou et al., 2020), with the biggest problem occurring during the outbreak of the pandemic, where its failure in the calculation of the cost burden became apparent (Quentin et al., 2020). Many countries were forced to adjust their DRGs reimbursement system in order to calculate costs according to the new pandemic data (Quentin et al., 2020).

In Greece, in public hospitals until 2012, the reimbursement/pricing system was based on the daily hospital fee. According to this, the hospital invoiced each patient a fixed amount for each day of hospitalization, adding a certain amount for the tests performed. Since 2012, the daily hospital fee has been abolished and the Closed Consolidated Hospitalization model (KEN) was adopted, a variant of the Australian DRGs. The KENs include generalized hospital price lists, which define ALoS and its cost, for each category of hospitalization. The aim of this model was to simplify the pricing process and control health reimbursement, without considering the actual cost of the patient's hospitalization. However, KENs system has been raised strong criticisms, already from the first years of its operation. According to researches, the major weakness of the system in estimating the real cost of health services (Kaitelidou et al., 2020; Polyzos et al., 2013), especially during the pandemic where costs reached to high levels, was its inability to adapt the cost changes, as other countries (Quentin et al., 2020) did.

15.3 Methodology

The present study was conducted in the ICU of a Greek University Hospital during the pandemic, in early 2022. This hospital is the only purely university hospital in the capital city and its suburbs, while at the same time, it brings together all medical specialties. Moreover, as the subject of our research is also the impact of the pandemic on ICU costs, the hospital was one of the first six designated as main Covid-19 reference centers at the beginning of the pandemic, nationwide. Furthermore, it is the hospital with the largest budget and the highest percentage of reserved beds for Covid-19 cases out of its total bed capacity. Its main source of funding comes from the reimbursement of its health services by the country's social security fund, the National Organization for the Provision of Health Services (EOPYY), while cash flow difficulties are covered by government grants.

The methods of hospital cost calculation proposed by the world literature are mainly top-down and bottom-up cost analysis. The top-down methodology initially uses the annual costs to calculate the cost elements assigned to the costing department. Then, it determines the average cost per patient or per day of hospitalization, by dividing the amount of costs of the department by the number of patients or days of hospitalization. Alternatively, the bottom-up methodology details the resources absorbed by each individual patient, thus resulting in the determination of the actual, per patient cost (Jegers et al., 2002; Wordsworth et al., 2005). The bottom-up approach is reported as the most reliable method, as it provides the information of the actual cost per patient, thus allowing comparison and identification of cost differences between patients (Drummond et al., 2015; Wordsworth et al., 2005). However, the main drawback of this method is that the requirement for detailed data, at the patient level, makes the collection of such data costly and quite time-consuming (Reis Miranda & Jegers 2012; Tan et al., 2009), especially when the cost information available in the hospital is insufficient or difficult to extract from its information systems (Tan et al., 2009; Wordsworth et al., 2005). In contrast, the top-down approach does not provide costing information at the patient level, so comparisons cannot be made among them, as it calculates an identical, average cost for each one (Clement et al., 2009; Tan et al., 2008) and is not appropriate when the aim is to detail cost contributions among different patients (Reis

Miranda & Jegers 2012). On the other hand, this method is recommended when cost data per patient are not available or are too difficult and time-consuming to retrieve (Geitona et al., 2010; Kosmidis et al., 2021), or when the aim of the survey is not to compare costs among patients (Karabatsou et al., 2016; Reis Miranda & Jegers 2012). At the same time, previous research has shown that the top-down approach can lead to a reasonably satisfactory cost estimation (Tan et al., 2009, 2012; Wordsworth et al., 2005).

In our research, we adopted the top-down approach as our purpose was to calculate the real cost of the ICU, in order to compare it with the cost resulting from the costing system applied by the hospital. An additional purpose of our research was to compare the costs of the ICU with the amount reimbursed by the hospital. Our objective was to make these comparisons, of actual costs and reimbursement, for a time period before the pandemic and to compare them with the corresponding cost data during the pandemic period, in order to investigate the influence of the pandemic on ICU costs. Therefore, the time to complete the survey was very limited and the collection of data for bottom-up costing would delay the realization of research objectives.

In the cost calculation process the cost components were classified into fixed and variable costs. Fixed costs are those that remain almost unaffected by the production levels, i.e., they are not changed by the number of patients in the ICU, such as employee costs, depreciation of capital equipment, maintenance costs, etc. Variable costs are those that vary with the number of patients and their care procedures, such as drugs, diagnostic tests and consumable healthcare equipment (Tan et al., 2008). Previous studies have shown that fixed costs constitute the largest percentage of ICU costs (Karabatsou et al., 2016; Reis Miranda & Jegers 2012), a few the reverse (Kosmidis et al., 2021), while there are some that calculate only variable costs, as this is considered more important in rationalizing limited resources (Karabatsou et al., 2016). We proceeded with this distinction of costs in our study in order to compare it with similar researches. However, for the first time, in our study, we calculated the fixed regular salaries of medical and nursing staff, separately from their on-call and overtime compensation. The reason doing that was that while regular monthly salaries are a fixed cost, on-call and overtime are directly related to the number of patients or the severity of their illness, and for this reason, they were treated as variable costs when calculating costs.

Quantitative data collection was carried out by the departments of Finance, Procurement, IT, Revenue Invoicing and the hospital's ICU. Specifically, the calculation of personnel cost was performed according to the data provided by the hospital's payroll office and related to medical, nursing and other staff (pharmacist, physiotherapist, administrative, etc.). As other staff do not work exclusively in the ICU, their hours of work in the ICU were collected from the head of their respective departments and the cost was calculated on a pro rata basis. Apart from their regular salaries, data were also obtained on the amount of on-call time for physicians and overtime for nursing and other staff. Infrastructure and overhead costs (electricity, water, heating, cleaning services, building maintenance and repairs) were allocated to the ICU area according to the most appropriate per-expenditure apportionment key, applied by the financial department of hospital, such as square meters, kilowatt hours and cubic meters. The relevant cost allocation reports were provided by the hospital's finance department. Costs of capital assets and machinery depreciation of ICU were provided by the hospital's finance department and were calculated according to Greek Accounting Standards. On an annual basis, and not on a per patient basis, were the pharmaceutical costs received from the hospital's pharmacy, medical care materials and consumables cost, received from the hospital's supplies department and also the laboratory and diagnostic imaging costs, obtained from ICU's record files. The research protocol has been approved by the scientific board of the hospital after the opinion of the ethics committee (meeting 8th/2022).

15.4 Results

In 2019, the hospital had a total of 33 ICU beds, of which only 27 were operational. Table 15.1 depicts the breakdown of annual ICU real costs, into fixed and variable costs.

The total number of patients was 481, the total number of days of hospitalization was 6,565 and the Average LoS was 13.65 days. The total cost of the ICU was €5,758,551.78. Of this cost, €2,957,042.70 (51.35%) was fixed, while the remaining €2,801,511.08 was variable (48.65%). As for the personnel cost, it constituted 44.52% (€2,563,531.78) of the total cost. Nevertheless, due to the reduced medical and nursing staff and the large number of patients, the ICU physicians performed, in addition to the minimum required, on-call duties

Table 15.1 Total ICU hospitalization real cost 2019

Cost component	*Cost (€) per component*	*% of total cost*
Fixed cost		
Personnel cost:		
Physicians	1,077,658.66	18.71
Nursery	1,470,550.82	25.54
Other realized staff (pharmacist, physiotherapist, administrative)	15,322.30	0.27
Operational and general overhead costs (electricity, water, heating, cleaning services, maintenance and repair of existing equipment, etc.)	298,923.53	5.19
Depreciation of capital assets	94,587.39	1.64
Total fixed cost	**2,957,042.70**	**51.35**
Variable cost		
Physicians on call cost	151,883.41	2.64
Nursery overtime cost	136,468.82	2.37
Pharmaceutical cost	1,322,274.74	22.96
Medical care materials and consumables (gloves, etc.)	458,663.22	7.96
Laboratory cost (Hematology, Biochemistry and Microbiology)	221,887.38	3.85
Diagnostic imaging costs (X-ray, CT, U/S, MRI, etc.)	510,333.51	8.86
Total variable cost	**2,801,511.08**	**48.65**
Total cost	**5,758,553.78**	**100.00**

to ensure the smooth operation of the ICU, amounting to €151,883.41. For the same reasons, overtime worked by nursing staff amounted to €136,468.82. The average total cost of patient was €11,972.05, and the average daily cost was €877.16. The average fixed cost per patient was €6,147.70, and the average variable cost per patient was €5,824.35. In addition, the average fixed cost per day of hospitalization was €450.43, while the variable cost was €426.73. The analysis reveals that fixed costs represent the largest part of the ICU cost, and in particular the personnel cost bear the largest share, 44.52%, with a large difference from the second most burdensome cost element, which is medicine, at 22.96%. We also notice that the small difference between fixed and variable costs, amounting to 2.70%, would increase if the on-call and overtime of medical and nursing staff were counted as fixed costs. In this case, the difference would be 11.8%.

The following year, 2020, with the outbreak of the pandemic, the hospital increases the number of ICU beds with the six inactive beds of previous year, so the available ICU beds reached 33. The total number of patients was 443 (82 non-Covid-19 and 361 Covid-19 patients), the total number of days of hospitalization was 6,305 and the Average LoS was 13.10 days. The annual real cost reached €6,474,836.14, as shown in Table 15.2.

Comparing 2019 and 2020 ICU real costs (Table 15.2), we notice that the 2020 cost increased by €716,282.36 (12.44%). We notice that the average cost of the 82 non-Covid-19 patients increased this year by €516.58, reaching €12,488.63, which seems reasonable, as the hospital only proceeded to admit very serious non-Covid-19 patients to the ICU, since the ICU beds available for them were scarce throughout the year. Consequently, treatment of these very severe cases would probably be more expensive. The Covid-19 ICU patients amounted to 361 in 2020, with an average total cost per Covid-19 patient of €15,099.08, while in 2019 an ICU patient cost €11,972.05. Therefore, the additional burden of the pandemic on the cost of Covid-19 ICU patients reached €3,127.03, which is 26.12% higher than the corresponding cost in 2019. In total, Covid-19 patients absorbed 84.18% of the total annual ICU costs, with 46.86% of the costs absorbed by salaries, followed by pharmaceutical costs of 21.81%. We notice that there is a large increase of 19.59%, compared to 2019, in nursing and other staff overtime, which is justified by the fact that although the hospital recruited nursing staff (temporary), they were not enough to cover the great need. Also, noteworthy is the 15,2% increase in health equipment and consumables such as gloves, uniforms and footwear as the need for additional protection against Covid-19 within the ICU was fundamental in order to prevent the transmission of the virus initially to the ICU staff, and consequently to hospital.

In 2021, the dynamic of ICU beds changed from 33 to 55. The additional 22 ICU beds were donated by a private foundation. This resulted in 835 patients being treated, 132 non-Covid-19 and 703 Covid-19. The total number of days of hospitalization was 12,734, and the Average LoS was 15.25 days. The annual real cost reached €11,866,555.36, as shown in Table 15.3.

According to Table 15.3, ICU costs reached €11,866,555.36, an increase of 83.27% and 106.07% compared to 2020 and 2019, respectively. The average total non-Covid-19 patient costs reached €11,826.99,

Table 15.2 ICU hospitalization Covid-19 and non-Covid-19 real cost, 2020

2020			*Non-Covid-19*		*Covid-19*		
Cost component	*Cost (€) per component*	*% of total cost*	*Non-Covid-19 cost (€)*	*% of total 2020 cost*	*Covid-19 cost (€)*	*% of total 2020 cost*	*% difference compared to 2019*
Fixed cost							
Personnel Cost:							
Physicians	1,249,047.98	19.29	179,885.34	14.40	1,069,162.64	85.60	15.90
Nursery	1,726,494.00	26.66	255,686.36	14.81	1,470,807.64	85.19	17.40
Other realized staff (pharmacist, physiotherapist, administrative)	20,230.22	0.31	6,151.55	30.41	14,078.67	69.59	32.03
Operational and general overhead costs (electricity, water, heating, cleaning services, maintenance and repair of existing equipment, etc.)	294,184.62	4.54	49,889.69	16.96	244,294.93	83.04	(1.59)
Depreciation of capital assets	96,268.55	1.49	23,225.80	24.13	73,042.75	75.87	1.78
Total fixed cost	**3,386,225.37**	**52.30**	**514,838.74**	**15.20**	**2,871,386.63**	**84.80**	**14.51**
Variable cost							
Physicians on call cost	149,027.27	2.30	34,884.20	23.41	114,143.07	76.59	(1.88)
Nursery overtime cost	163,209.00	2.52	39,887.20	24.44	123,321.80	75.56	19.59
Pharmaceutical cost	1,414,895.00	21.85	225,888.52	15.97	1,189,006.48	84.03	7.00
Medical care materials and consumables (gloves, etc.)	528,366.44	8.16	80,225.63	15.18	448,140.81	84.82	15.20
Laboratory cost (Hematology, Biochemistry and Microbiology	243,554.65	3.76	40,118.30	16.47	203,436.35	83.53	9.76

2020			Non-Covid-19		Covid-19		
Cost component	*Cost (€) per component*	*% of total cost*	*Non-Covid-19 cost (€)*	*% of total 2020 cost*	*Covid-19 cost (€)*	*% of total 2020 cost*	*% difference compared to 2019*
Diagnostic imaging costs (X-ray, CT, U/S, MRI, etc.)	589,558.41	9.11	88,225.21	14.96	501,333.20	85.04	15.52
Total variable cost	**3,088,610.77**	**47.70**	**509,229.06**	**16.49**	**2,579,381.71**	**83.51**	**10.25**
Total cost	**6,474,836.14**	**100.00**	**1,024,067.80**	**15.82**	**5,450,768.34**	**84.18**	**12.44**

Table 15.3 ICU hospitalization Covid-19 and non-Covid-19 real cost, 2021

	2021		*Non-Covid-19*		*Covid-19*		
Cost component	*cost (€) per component*	*% of total cost*	*non-Covid-19 cost (€)*	*% of total 2021 cost*	*Covid-19 cost (€)*	*% of total 2021 cost*	*% difference compared to 2020*
Fixed cost							
Personnel cost:							
Physicians	2,081,824.63	17.54	261,558.50	12.56	1,820,266.13	87.44	66.67
Nursery	1,979,750.41	16.68	373,225.63	18.85	1,606,524.78	81.15	14.67
Other related staff (pharmacist, physiotherapist, administrative)	26,442.20	0.22	10,202.80	38.59	16,239.40	61.41	30.71
Operational and general overhead costs (electricity, water, heating, cleaning services, maintenance and repair of existing equipment, etc.)	503,249.63	4.24	78,852.24	15.67	424,397.39	84.33	71.07
Depreciation of capital assets	97,359.78	0.82	24,180.50	24.84	73,179.28	75.16	1.13
Total fixed cost	**4,688,626.65**	**39.51**	**748,019.67**	**15.95**	**3,940,606.98**	**84.05**	**38.46**
Variable cost							
Physicians on call cost	488,392.86	4.12	59,822.44	12.25	428,570.42	87.75	227.72
Nursery overtime cost	228,492.00	1.93	61,205.10	26.79	167,286.90	73.21	40.00
Pharmaceutical cost	3,318,403.49	27.96	352,778.20	10.63	2,965,625.29	89.37	134.53
Medical care materials and consumables (gloves, etc.)	1,524,185.43	12.84	138,532.33	9.09	1,385,653.10	90.91	188.47
Laboratory cost (Hematology, Biochemistry and Microbiology	467,888.63	3.94	62,252.22	13.30	405,636.41	86.70	92.11
Diagnostic imaging costs (X-ray, CT, U/S, MRI, etc.)	1,150,566.30	9.70	138,552.41	12.04	1,012,013.89	87.96	95.16

	2021		*Non-Covid-19*		*Covid-19*		
Cost component	*cost (€) per component*	*% of total cost*	*non-Covid-19 cost (€)*	*% of total 2021 cost*	*Covid-19 cost (€)*	*% of total 2021 cost*	*% difference compared to 2020*
Total variable cost	**7,177,928.71**	**60.49**	**813,142.70**	**11.33**	**6,364,786.01**	**88.67**	**132.40**
Total cost	**11,866,555.36**	**100.00**	**1,561,162.37**	**13.16**	**10,305,392.99**	**86.84**	**83.27**

and Covid-19 patient costs reached €14,659.16, slightly lower than last year's figures, while patients increased by 88.49%. For the first time, we observe that, in 2021, variable costs exceeded fixed costs, with 60.49% and 39.51%, respectively. In 2021, variable and fixed costs increased, by 132.40% and 38.46% respectively, compared to 2020. This disproportion is due to the fact that physicians cost increased by 66.67%, but this does not seem to have been enough to ensure smooth service to ICU patients judging by the large increase of 227.72% in their on-call costs. However, the same is true for nursing staff, as their regular salary costs increased by 14.67% in 2021, while their overtime costs by 40%, Nevertheless, as in previous years, salary costs continue to be the largest cost item in 2021, with pharmaceutical costs second in line, with 27.96%, the highest percentage of the three years.

Of great interest is the comparison of the real annual cost of ICU with the corresponding reimbursement, as shown in Table 15.4. The current ICU costing system applied by the hospital, that is the nominal cost, consists, on the one hand, of a fixed amount for each inpatient day, which varies according to the days of hospitalization (per diem payment) (Geitona et al., 2010), and on the other hand, by a number of clinical tests performed for the patient. The sum of these two cost elements is the amount that the hospital will invoice and consequently be reimbursed for, by the social security fund, EOPYY.

Financial data were obtained by hospital's Revenue Invoicing department, regarding the pricing of ICU cases for the three years. Regarding the year 2019, the real annual cost of the ICU was €5,758,553.78 (Table 15.1), but this includes an annual salary of permanent civil servants of €2,851,884.01, which is subsidized by the state and not

Table 15.4 ICU real cost and reimbursement comparison 2019–2021

Year	*Real cost*[a]	*Reimbursement*	*Difference between reimbursement and costs*	*% not reimbursed*	*Difference per day of hospitalization*
2019	3,255,319.84	2,867,722.91	**387,596.93**	11.91	59.04
2020	3,459,084.67	2,731,911.28	**727,173.39**	21.02	115.33
2021	7,280,685.67	5,847,672.90	**1,433,012.77**	19.68	112.53

[a] Exclude employee payroll which is paid directly by the central government (permanent civil servants) without burdening the hospital budget

charged to the hospital. Therefore, the amount of the reimbursement from the social security fund, EOPYY, should cover the remaining costs of €3,255,319.84. As can be seen in Table 15.4, the hospital was reimbursed for ICU services the amount of €2,867,722.91, which represented only 88.09% of the real cost. This means that the hospital was not reimbursed the amount of €387,596.93 (11.91%) or for every one day of hospitalization it lost €59.04.

Regarding the year 2020, we notice that the discrepancy between actual cost and reimbursement, compared to 2019, is more almost the double. The hospital was reimbursed by €727,173.39 less than its actual cost which was €3,459,084.67. [€6,474,836.14 (Table 15.2) minus €3,015,751.47 for the salaries of permanent civil servants]. The almost double rate of non-reimbursement in 2020 reveals the inability of the current costing system to monitor the changes caused by the pandemic in ICU costs and as a result the hospital cannot be reimbursed according to its real costs.

Finally, in 2021, we do not observe any significant change in the ratio between real cost and reimbursement, compared to previous year. The annual real cost of €11,866,555.36 (Table 15.3) includes the salary of permanent civil servants of €4,585,869.69; therefore, the hospital should be reimbursed for the rest of €7,280,685.67. Instead, it was reimbursed by €1,433,012.77 or 19.68% less than the real cost.

15.5 Discussion

This research tried to determine the real cost of the ICU of a Greek University hospital, one of the largest in Greece, during the period 2019–2021. Our aim initially was to compare the real cost with the cost resulting from the costing system applied by the hospital and following compare it with the corresponding reimbursement, received by the social security fund. The comparison of the data covered the years 2019–2021, in order to examine also the impact of the Covid-19 pandemic on ICU costs. During the costing process, the top-down microcosting approach was implemented, firstly because the aim was to find the total cost of the ICU and not the per patient cost, and secondly because the survey was conducted during the pandemic and the time to collect the data was limited. ICU costs were analyzed into fixed and variable costs, as this gives us a more complete picture of the costs, allowing to take better decisions

(Jacobs et al., 2022), compared to other surveys which give weight to variable cost only (Karabatsou et al., 2016).

The data analysis revealed that the ratio of fixed and variable costs for 2019 and 2020 seems to be in line with the international literature (Jegers et al., 2002; Kosmidis et al., 2021; McLaughlin et al., 2009; Negrini et al., 2006; Tan et al., 2012), as the findings show that the fixed is the main part of the costs, although it participates with a smaller percentage than in other surveys. The smaller participation may be due to several reasons, one of which is the separation of on-call and overtime costs from the rest of personnel costs. In contrast to other similar surveys (Kosmidis et al., 2021; Tan et al., 1007), where personnel cost is considered as a fixed cost, including on-call and overtime costs, in our survey this cost was treated as a variable, since it is directly related to the number of patients. In 2019, the per patient overtime cost was €599.48 for 481 patients, while in 2020, with 38 fewer patients than previous year, it increased by 17.71%. The reason is that with the outbreak of the pandemic, patients needed more medical and nursing care, which was mainly covered by the overtime work of physicians and nurses. In 2021, there was an increase of 22 ICU beds (66.67%), of 392 patients (88.49%), and an increase in personnel costs up to 36.41% due to new, but insufficient recruitment. Consequence of this insufficiency was the increase of on-call and overtime cost by 129.59%, compared to 2020. This great increase of overtime cost in 2021 led for the first time to the change in the ratio of fixed to variable costs, with the latter bearing more on total costs. This is a finding that differs from literature and similar research that want fixed costs to outweigh variable costs. A further reason why the fixed cost lagged behind the variable cost in 2021 is that the fixed equipment of the additional 22 beds was recorded in the hospital's accounting books with zero value, because it was a donation and not a purchase. This resulted in no depreciation being calculated, which otherwise would have greatly increased the fixed costs. The dominant cost element in all three years, similar to previous research (Kosmidis et al., 2021; Negrini et al., 2006; Reis Miranda & Jegers 2012), remained the personnel cost, which ranged between 34.23% and 45.96% of total costs, while the second most involved cost item was pharmaceutical, which ranged between 21.85% and 27.96%.

The average total cost per patient in 2019 was €11,972.05, the average total daily cost was €877.16, and the average daily variable cost was €426.73. Comparing these findings with other research, we can see that there are some differences. Negrini et al. (2006) in 2006, estimated the average daily cost per patient at $1,512 in England, $934 in France, $726 in Germany and $280 in Hungary. In 2009, McLaughlin et al. (2009) estimated the average total and average daily cost per patient of an ICU in Ireland at €16,850.63 and €2,513.84, respectively. In 2012, Tan et al. (2012) estimated the direct costs of seven ICUs in four European countries, Germany, Italy, the Netherlands and England. The average direct daily costs ranged between €1,1168 in Italy and €2,025 in Germany.

In Greece, the most recent survey was conducted by Platanias et al. (2022) where, by applying the bottom-up microcosting model, they estimated the total daily cost of an adult ICU, for 2019, at €827.30, a value that is quite close to our findings. Kosmidis et al. (2021) examining two years, 2015–2016, calculated the total cost per patient at €7,277.40 and the mean daily cost per patient at €860.49, while Geitona et al. (2010) in 2010 estimated the respective costs much higher, at €16,516 and €1,856. These high costs are justified as the large reductions in the prices of medicines, health materials and in salaries of medical staff had not been imposed until then. The following year Geitona et al. (2011) estimated the average daily cost per patient at €1,711.

The above discrepancies observed among different surveys may be due to many factors such as different costing methods, severity of patient's illness, age, physicians/patients ratio, costs included (total or variable only, direct or indirect), sample selection and size and other factors that are difficult to determine (Geitona et al., 2011; Karabatsou et al., 2016; Kosmidis et al., 2021; Moraru et al., 2022; Reis Miranda & Jegers 2012; Tan et al., 2012). The above reasons make the comparison of the findings difficult, and the process requires great care. In order to address the difficulty in interpreting the results between studies, De Araujo et al. (2019) propose the development of standardized guidelines for calculating the cost of healthcare services, especially regarding critical care.

In the years 2020 and 2021, the interest in the cost structure is monopolized by the pandemic. In 2019, the average total cost per patient was €11,972.05, while in 2020 the average total cost per Covid-19 patient reached €15,099.08 and €14,659.16 in 2021. In other words, we observe an increase in the average total cost per Covid-19 patient of 26.12% in 2020 and 22.44% in 2021, compared to 2019. According to our findings, the burden of the pandemic in the ICU therefore, appears to be higher than the 20% estimated by Cambaro et al. (2023) Moreover, in our previous research (Rodosthenous & Roumeliotis, 2021), at the same hospital, we found that Covid-19 costs of 2020 and 2021 burdened hospital's budget by about 10% annually, compared to 2019. In this research, we found that the Covid-19 ICU absorbed more than twice (26.12% and 22.44%) as much as other clinics (10%), evidence that confirms previous researches that suggest that although ICU beds represent a small percentage of the total hospital beds, they ultimately absorb a larger share of costs than other clinics with more beds (Decruyenaere, 2006; Halpern et al., 2016). The magnitude of the costs absorbed by the Covid-19 ICU, in 2020 and 2021, in relation to the total ICU costs (Covid-19 and non-Covid-19) is impressive. In 2020 it absorbed 84.18% and in 2021 86.84%, of the total ICU annual costs. These percentages reveal hospital's priority to serve Covid-19 cases, resulting in a large reduction of all other cases.

Regarding our second research question, we proceeded with the comparison of the real cost of ICU, which we estimated, with the cost resulting by the costing system applied by the hospital, i.e. nominal cost, and consequently, with its reimbursement from the social security fund. Our findings regarding 2019 do not seem to have great difference from those of other researches, which demonstrate a large deviation between the reimbursement of hospitals and their actual cost (Geitona & Hatzikou 2007; Kilic et al., 2019; Platanias et al., 2022; Polyzos et al., 2013). In 2019, the actual cost of ICU hospitalization was €3,255,319.84 (excluding the salaries of permanent civil servants), while the amount received as reimbursement was only €2,867,722.91, which indicates that the hospital was not reimbursed for 11.91% or for €59.04 per day of hospitalization. The next two years, where pandemic had begun, we found than the deviation largely increased, compared to 2019, more than doubled. The rate of non-reimbursement, relative to real cost, reached 21.02%, and 19.68% for the years 2020 and 2021.

In conclusion, the findings of our research highlighted the large discrepancy between the actual costs of the ICU and the costs resulting from the hospital's current costing system. Even more striking, however, is the fact that our research revealed the inability of the hospital's costing system to adapt to the costing changes caused by the pandemic. This resulted in even lower reimbursement during the pandemic years 2020 and 2021, compared to 2019. These findings make even more important the need for Greek public hospitals to abolish the current reimbursement model, which depends on an unreliable current costing system. As an alternative, each hospital should develop a modern and more sophisticated costing model, that will be able to adapt, in an immediate and reliably way, to the significant costing changes that may be occurred by extraordinary health crises, both now and inevitably in the future.

Restrictions

This study has some limitations. The most important is the adoption of top-down microcosting analysis which lacks in patient-level cost analysis. Also, as the study sample was the ICU of only one tertiary public hospital, the results cannot be generalized to the whole and great caution is required in their interpretation. On-call and overtime compensation of physicians and nursery staff was treated as variable cost.

Data Availability Statement The data that support the findings of this study are available from the corresponding author upon reasonable request.

Conflict of Interest Statement The authors of this paper declare no conflicts of interest.

Ethics Statement The authors confirm that all the research meets the ethical guidelines.

References

Brannen, J. T. (1999). DRG-based per diem payment system matches costs more accurately. *Healthcare Financial Management, 53*(4), 42–46. PMID:10557978.

Cambaro, M. A., Fusai, G., Sodhi, S. M., et al. (2023). ICU capacity expansion under uncertainty in the early stages of a pandemic. *Production and Operations Management*, 1–20. https://doi.org/10.1111/poms.13985

Carey, K., & Stefos, T. (2011). Controlling for quality in the hospital cost function. *Health Care Management Science., 14*(3), 125–134. https://doi.org/10.1007/s10729-010-9142-7

Chilingerian, J. (2008). Origins of DRGs in the United States: A technical, political and cultural story. In J. Kimberly, G. De Pouvourville, & T. D'Aunno (Eds.), *The globalization of managerial innovation in health care* (pp. 4–33). Cambridge University Press. https://doi.org/10.1017/CBO9780511620003.002

Clement, M. F., Ghali, A. W., Donaldson, C., et al. (2009). The impact of using different costing methods on the results of an economic evaluation

of cardiac care: Microcosting vs gross-costing approaches. *Health Economics, 18*(4), 377–388. https://doi.org/10.1002/hec.1363
Cylus, J., & Irwin, R. (2010). The challenges of hospital payment systems. *Euro Observer, 12*(3), 1–3. https://www.researchgate.net/publication/291592503_The_challenges_of_hospital_payment_systems. Accessed November 28, 2022.
Davies, R. H., & Westfall, G. (1983, Summer). Reimbursement under DRGs: Implementation in New Jersey. *Health Services Research, 18*(2 Pt1), 233–244. PMID: 6409841.
De Araujo, T. R., Papathanassoglou, E., Menegueti, G. M., et al. (2019). Urgent need for standardized guidelines for reporting healthcare costs in ICUs—Results of an integrative review of costing methodologies. *Intensive and Critical Care Nursing, 54*, 39–45. https://doi.org/10.1016/j.iccn.2019.07.005
Decruyenaere, J. (2006, May 1). *Cost-effectiveness analysis in the ICU*. Healthcre-in-europe.com. https://healthcare-in-europe.com/en/news/cost-effectiveness-analysis-in-the-icu.html. Accessed September 30, 2022.
Drummond, M. F., Sculpher, J. M., Claxton, K., et al. (2015). *Methods for the economic evaluation of health care programmes* (4th ed.). Oxford University Press. https://nibmehub.com/opac-service/pdf/read/Methods
Eurostat, Statistics Explained. (2022, November). *Healthcare expenditure statistics*. https://ec.europa.eu/eurostat/statistics-explained/index.php?title=Healthcare_expenditure_statistics. Accessed March 22, 2023.
Frouzis K. (2013, January). Διαιωνίζουν το φαύλο κύκλο, χωρίς να δίνουν λύση [They perpetuate the vicious circle without providing a solution]. Interview by H. Petropoulou (in Greek). *Economic Post*. https://sfee.gr/wp-content/uploads/2014/12/OE_40-41_K_F.pdf. Accessed September 18, 2022.
Geitona, M., & Hatzikou, M. (2007). Cost estimation of neonatal intensive care in Greece: The case of Athens maternity hospitals. *Journal of Medical Economics, 10*(3), 273–283. https://doi.org/10.3111/13696990701495975
Geitona, M., Androutsou, L., & Theodoratou, D. (2010). Cost estimation of patients admitted to the intensive care unit: A case study of the Teaching University Hospital of Thessaly. *Journal of Medical Economics, 13*(2), 179–184. https://doi.org/10.3111/13696991003684092
Geitona, M., Hatzikou, M., Steropoulos, P., et al. (2011). The cost of COPD exacerbations: A university hospital—Based study in Greece. *Respiratory Medicine., 105*(3), 402–409. https://doi.org/10.1016/j.rmed.2010.09.020
Halpern, N. A., Goldman, A. D., & Pastores, M. S. (2016). Trends in critical care beds and use among population groups and Medicare and Medicaid beneficiaries in the United States: 2000–2010. *Critical Care Medicine, 44*(8), 1490–1499. https://doi.org/10.1097/CCM.0000000000001722

Hellenic Statistical Authority. (2023, March 30). *System of Health Accounts (SHA) of year 2021.* https://www.statistics.gr/documents/20181/dd86dbea-fd0d-4243-8c5f-9f6fc0447038. Accessed April 16, 2023.

Hrifach, A., Brault, C., Couray-Targe, S., et al. (2016). Mixed method versus full top—Down microcosting for organ recovery cost assessment in a French hospital group. *Health Economic Review, 6*(53). https://doi.org/10.1186/s13561-016-0133-3

Jacobs, K., Roman, E., Lambert, J., et al. (2022). Variability drivers of treatment costs in hospitals: A systemic review. *Health Policy, 126*(2), 75–86. https://doi.org/10.1016/j.healthpol.2021.12.004

Jegers, M., Edbrooke, L. D., Hibbert, L. C., et al. (2002). Definitions and methods of cost assessment: An intensivist's guide. *Intensive Care Medicine, 28*(6), 80–685. https://doi.org/10.1007/s00134-002-1279-5

Kaitelidou, D., Galanis, P., Siskou, O., et al. (2020). *Μελέτη Εφαρμογής του συστήματος DRG διεθνώς: αποτελέσματα συστηματικής ανασκόπησης* [Study of the implementation of DRG internationally: Systematic review results] (in Greek). Center for Health Services Management and Evaluation, Department of Nursing, University of Athens, Greece. https://instdrg.gr/wp-content/uploads/ΜΕΛΕΤΗ-ΕΦΑΡΜΟΓΗΣ-ΤΟΥ-ΣΥΣΤΗΜΑΤΟΣ-DRG-ΔΙΕΘΝΩΣ.pdf. Accessed February 19, 2022.

Karabatsou, D., Tsironi, M., Tsigou, E., et al. (2016). Variable cost of ICU care, a micro-costing analysis. *Intensive and Critical Care Nursing., 35*(4), 66–73. https://doi.org/10.1016/j.iccn.2016.01.001

Karboub, K., & Tabaa, M. (2023). Bed Allocation optimization based on survival analysis, treatment trajectory and costs estimations. *IEEE Access, 11*, 31699–31715. https://doi.org/10.1109/ACCESS.2023.3260184

Kilic, M., Yüzkat, N., Soyalp, C., et al. (2019). Cost analysis on intensive care unit costs based on the length of stay. *Turk J Anaesthesiol Reanim., 47*(2), 142–145. https://doi.org/10.5152/TJAR.2019.80445

Kosmidis, D., Koutsoiki, S., Lampiri, K., et al. (2021). Cost evaluation in adult ICU: A two-year study in a Greek State Hospital. *Health and Research Journal, 7*(1), 39–54. https://doi.org/10.12681/healthresj.26097

Leister, J. E., & Stausberg, J. (2005). Comparison of cost accounting methods from different DRG systems and their effect on health care quality. *Health Policy, 74*(1), 46–55. https://doi.org/10.1016/j.healthpol.2004.12.001

Law No. 3846/2010. (2010, May 11). *Guarantees for occupational safety and other provisions.* Government Gazette A66. https://www.et.gr/api/DownloadFeksApi/?fek_pdf=20100100066. Accessed February 15, 2023.

McLaughlin, M. A., Hardt, J., & Canavan, B. J. (2009). Determining the economic cost of ICU treatment: A prospective "micro-costing" study. *Intensive Care Medicine, 35*, 2135–2140. https://doi.org/10.1007/s00134-009-1622-1

Ministry of Health of Greece. (2019, December 20). *Patient management in ICU in end-of-life situations*. Central Board of Health, Ministerial Decree No. 278. https://www.icu.gr/wp-content/uploads/2020/06/AP.pdf. Accessed January 26, 2023.

Moraru, A. C., Floria, M., Năfureanu, D. E., et al. (2022). Costs for a hospital day: Another lesson learned from the COVID-19 pandemic. *Romanian Journal of Military Medicine, CXXV*(3), 404–413. https://doi.org/10.55453/rjmm.2022.125.3.8

Negrini, D., Sheppard, L., Mills, H. G., et al. (2006). International programme for resource use in critical care (IPOC)—A methodology and initial results of cost and provision in four European countries. *Acta Anaesthesiol Scandinavica, 50*(1), 72–79. https://doi.org/10.1111/j.1399-6576.2006.00901.x

Oostenbrink, B. J., Van der Woude, B. T., Van Agthoven, et al. (2003). Unit costs of inpatient hospital days. *Pharmacoeconomics, 21*(4), 263–271. https://doi.org/10.2165/00019053-200321040-00004

Organization for Economic Cooperation and Development-OECD/European Observatory on Health Systems and Policies. (2021). *Greece: Country health profile 2021, State of health in the EU*. OECD Publishing. https://doi.org/10.1787/4ab8ea73-en. Accessed September 11, 2022.

Organization for Economic Cooperation and Development-OECD/European Union. (2020). *Health at a glance: Europe 2020. State of health in the EU cycle*. OECD Publishing. https://www.oecd-ilibrary.org/social-issues-migration-health/health-at-a-glance-europe-2020_82129230-en. Accessed September 11, 2022.

Pirson, M., Schenker, L., Martins, D., et al. (2013). What can we learn from international comparisons of costs by DRG? *The European Journal of Health Economics, 14*(1), 67–73. https://doi.org/10.1007/s10198-011-0373-4

Platanias, A., Mariolis-Sapsakos, T., Pavlopoulou, I. et al. (2022). Comparison of hospital compensation with actual costs in two Greek intensive care units: A retrospective observational study. *Archives of Hellenic Medicine, 39*(5), 662–668. https://www.researchgate.net/publication/363474595

Polyzos, N., Karanikas, H., Thireos, E., et al. (2013). Reforming reimbursement of public hospitals in Greece during the economic crisis: Implementation of a DRG system. *Health Policy, 109*(1), 14–22. https://doi.org/10.1016/j.healthpol.2012.09.011

Quentin, W., Albreht, T., Bezzina, A., et al. (2020). Adjusting hospital inpatient payment systems for covid-19. *Eurohealth, 26*(2), 88–93. https://eurohealthobservatory.who.int/publications. Accessed May 5, 2022.

Reis Miranda, D., & Jegers, M. (2012). Monitoring costs in the ICU: A search for a pertinent methodology. *Acta Anaesthesiologica Scandinavica, 56*(9), 1104–1113. https://doi.org/10.1111/j.1399-6576.2012.02735.x

Rodosthenous, M., & Roumeliotis, E. (2021). Adjusting the costing/pricing systems of public health units in times of emergency health crisis: The case of Greece. *KnE Social Sciences*, 294–307. https://doi.org/10.18502/kss.v5i9.9901

Tan, S. S., Bakker, J., Hoogendoor, E. M., et al. (2012). Direct cost analysis of intensive care Unite stay in four European countries: Applying a standardized costing methodology. *Value in Health, 15*(1), 81–86. https://doi.org/10.1016/j.jval.2011.09.007

Tan, S. S., Geissler, A., Serdén, L., et al. (2014). DRG systems in Europe: Variations in cost accounting systems among 12 countries. *European Journal of Public Health, 24*(6), 1023–1028. https://doi.org/10.1093/eurpub/cku025

Tan, S. S., Haakart-van Roijen, L., Maiwenn, J. Al, et al. (2008). A microcosting study of intensive care unit stay in the Netherlands. *Intensive Care Medicine, 23*, 250–257. https://doi.org/10.1177/0885066608318661

Tan, S. S., Rutten, F. F. H., Van Ineveld, M. B., et al. (2009). Comparing methodologies for the cost estimation of hospital services. *The European Journal of Health Economics, 10*(1), 39–45. https://doi.org/10.1007/s10198-008-0101-x

Tan, S. S., Van Ineveld, M., Redekop, K., et al. (2010). Structural reforms and hospital payment in the Netherlands. *Euro Observer, 12*(3), 7–9. https://www.aemh.org/aemh/Documents/2010. Accessed May 21, 2022.

Telesford, I., Rakshit, S., McGough, M., et al. (2023, February 7). *How has U.S. spending on healthcare changed over time?* Peterson-KFF, Health System Tracker. https://www.healthsystemtracker.org/chart-collection/u-s-spending-healthcare-changed-time/. Accessed May 20, 2023.

Wordsworth, S., Ludbrook, A., Caskey, F., et al. (2005). Collecting unit cost data in multicenter studies, Creating comparable methods. *The European Journal of Health Economics, 6*(1), 38–44. https://doi.org/10.1007/s10198-004-0259-9

World Health Organization-WHO. (2022a). *Global health expenditure database.* World Health Organization. https://apps.who.int/nha/database/Select/Indicators/en. Accessed May 25, 2023

World Health Organization-WHO. (2022b). *Global spending on health, rising to the pandemic's challenges*. World Health Organization. https://www.who.int/publications/i/item/9789240064911. Accessed June 9, 2023.

CHAPTER 16

Conclusions: Charting the Course Forward

Alina Hyz

Resilience is a crucial concept when evaluating and assessing a country's ability to withstand adverse shocks and maintain stable economic growth. To guarantee prosperity, economic systems should be sustainable, stable and resilient. Sustainability involves preserving the potential for future development. Stability refers to the short-term fluctuations of the system. Resilience, on the other hand, relates to the system's long-term robustness to preserve its fundamental functions.

Following the financial crisis and the pandemic, numerous studies have focused on examining the causes and effects of these events on the economic and social situation of individual economies, but also in the global arena. The results suggest that countries responded to these pressures differently. It leads to the conclusion that the distinct characteristics of individual economies are different enough to result in different resistance to the same shocks.

A. Hyz (✉)
Department of Accounting and Finance, University of West Attica, Athens, Greece
e-mail: alinahyz@uniwa.gr

A. Hyz (ed.), *The Role of the Public Sector in Building Social and Economic Resilience*,
https://doi.org/10.1007/978-3-031-67702-1_16

The research presented in this book seeks to determine the role of the public sector, from the perspective of public finances, in fostering social and economic resilience. It also examines the traits of a resilient social and economic system and the attributes it should possess to mitigate the negative social and economic impacts of future crises and shocks. The discussions presented consider strategies to bolster the resilience of economic and social structures.

The imperative to conduct and disseminate research is amplified by the internationalization, liberalization and globalization of economies, where issues in one nation can have a domino effect in other parts of the world. This is particularly important for smaller countries that are more open and at the same time vulnerable to external shocks.

Building economic and social resilience may become one of the priority goals of the functioning of economies and societies. It's crucial to distinguish resilience-building from economic protectionism or the imposition of constraints on economic liberty and openness.

Economic and social resilience can be interpreted as the ability of the economic and social system to protect itself against external shocks. Recalling the first chapter's analysis, resilience encompasses two fundamental aspects: one is the ability of each segment of the economic system to withstand shocks, and the other pertains to the system's capacity to foresee and adapt to changing conditions and potential future disturbances. Thus, resilience should be seen as a system's ability to adapt and transform over time. Formulating an effective resilience policy involves steering or influencing this evolution to attain specific objectives, essentially developing a strategy that encourages the system to self-organize toward these ends. This task is challenging, and there is no doubt that this task is difficult to accomplish because, unlike physical systems, prediction is difficult or even impossible in economic and social systems. In the physical sciences, resilience can be achieved at the design stage. In economics, research examines social and economic environments that are more complex than any other.

As mentioned earlier, both the recent crisis and the Covid-19 pandemic that recently shook the world have once again shown that individual countries have different degrees of resilience, and those that have been building it for many years are characterized by higher levels of resilience. The public sector undoubtedly plays an important role in building this resilience. But what capabilities support social and economic resilience?

In a broad sense, these are skills, production capabilities and experience that can be used to operate in any conditions. Resilience requires investment in strategic assets such as infrastructure, human capital and innovation. Essentially, it is a complex network of capabilities to prevent, withstand, resist, absorb, adapt and recover quickly, based on private and public sector factors, but also their mutual adaptation. Countries without this resilience are doomed to fall into a vicious circle in which one crisis leads to another.

Take business cycles as an example, which explain how short-term fluctuations occur around a medium-term growth trend. Although these cycles are unpredictable, the loses caused by economic downturns vary across economic systems. The actions taken so far to mitigate their effects are the so-called stabilization policy (exogenous), aimed at maintaining balance in the long term. The effects of its use appear after a long time. The time needed to implement such a policy is also long, and often even longer than the economic crisis itself. Structural effects are becoming more problematic as the deficit budget finances projects and ventures that are usually not profitable. The effects of stabilization policy are asymmetric. Therefore, introducing countercyclical fiscal policy in a procyclical or neutral form is also an important economic insight.

The question therefore arises: how to minimize the effects of shocks and how to create more resilient economic and social structures. Ideally, a development strategy should be developed that promotes economic stability, but also economic growth and structural and environmental change. This strategy must focus less on short-term goals and more on long-term opportunities.

Although, as emphasized earlier, for many years researchers have focused on counteracting the effects of economic crises, now more and more attention is being paid to examining ways to increase the resilience of economies to future shocks.

Let us briefly look at the main conclusions regarding the multifaceted issue of building social and economic resilience resulting from the research included in this study.

1. Fiscal discipline and management: Implementing fiscal rules to mitigate pre-election spending spikes and improving governance to support transparency and accountability are key steps highlighted by Petrakos et al. (Chapter 2) and Georgiou (Chapter 6), ensuring the productivity and sustainability of public spending.

2. Improved financial management: Aligning with standards and improving internal audits, as suggested by Papadeas and Tsamis (Chapter 3), promotes transparency in the management of public assets, improved financing conditions and long-term economic resilience. Promoting the adoption of a modern costing model in public services as indicated by Rodosthenous et al. (Chapter 15) in their research on the example of public hospitals. This is essential not only to ensure accurate cost management and reimbursement, but also to build resilience to future health crises, thereby strengthening the overall resilience of the health sector and contributing to broader social and economic stability, research shows.
3. Strategic public investments: Optimizing public–private partnerships (PPPs) as mentioned by Chatzopoulos et al. (Chapter 10), in key sectors such as transport and waste management, can strengthen infrastructure and economic stability if procedures are improved and financing challenges are resolved.
4. Human Resource Management: The integration of green human resource management (GHRM), highlighted by Gkikas et al. (Chapter 8), aligns HR practices with sustainability goals, increasing organizational and environmental resilience while promoting a culture of ecological responsibility.
5. Effective public administration: Dealing with job satisfaction and organizational challenges, as highlighted by Alexopoulos and Skliopidou (Chapter 11), through better leadership, commitment and participatory approaches can strengthen the capacity of public institutions to cope with crises and increase resilience.
6. Technological advancement and security: Balancing technological advancement with cybersecurity, as discussed by Hyz and Gikas (Chapter 12), through initiatives such as federated learning and data ecosystems, enables innovation while protecting against cyber threats, which is crucial for sustainable development.
7. Innovative public projects: Highlighting the IOC's approach to reducing reliance on public funds in Olympic bids by leveraging existing infrastructure, promoting collaboration and increasing the transparency of bidding processes promotes economic stability as Nicoliello (Chapter 4) points out, encourages innovation and contributes to the long-term social and economic resilience of communities hosts (Paraskeva's research, Chapter 13)).

8. Strengthened public budgeting and financial planning: Using crises as opportunities to improve public budgeting, as proposed by Grigoriadou (Chapter 7), through frameworks such as accrual and performance-based budgets, participatory budgeting and flexible public policies increase adaptive capacity and resilience. Research by Ioannidis et al. (Chapter 5) indicates that public sector wage spending plays a key role in maintaining labor force participation and reducing economic inequality, especially in times of crises. Higher wages for government workers are positively associated with reduced output gaps and the likelihood of recession, thus increasing social and economic resilience in Greece and the European Union.
9. Strategic tax and customs administration: Recognize the strategic importance of tax and customs administration, as highlighted by Ballas and Balla (Chapter 9), in promoting social and economic resilience through effective revenue collection, trade facilitation and fair tax systems.
10. Integrated Strategic Planning: Highlighting the role of strategic planning in public organizations, as highlighted by Alexopoulos and Makavelos (Chapter 14), shows the need to integrate strategic objectives at all levels of the organization in order to increase adaptability and responsiveness to external pressures and strengthen organizational resilience and goal convergence.

Involving the public sector in building socio-economic resilience is not intended to replace the role of the private sector, but on the contrary, to point to the necessary complementary role of this sector, especially after the period of belief that systems can self-regulate independently and without public sector intervention.

Correction to: Enhancing Social and Economic Resilience for a Changing World: The Strategic Role of Continuous Training and Capacity Building in Contemporary Tax and Customs Administrations

Panagiotis Ballas, *Alina Hyz*, *and Vassiliki-Maria Balla*

Correction to:
Chapter 9 in: A. Hyz (ed.), *The Role of the Public Sector in Building Social and Economic Resilience*, https://doi.org/10.1007/978-3-031-67702-1_9

The original version of the book was inadvertently published without the contributor name "Alina Hyz" in Chapter 9 which has now been added. The book and the chapter have been updated with the changes.

The updated version of this chapter can be found at
https://doi.org/10.1007/978-3-031-67702-1_9

A. Hyz (ed.), *The Role of the Public Sector in Building Social and Economic Resilience*,
https://doi.org/10.1007/978-3-031-67702-1_17

Index

A. Hyz (ed.), *The Role of the Public Sector in Building Social and Economic Resilience*,
https://doi.org/10.1007/978-3-031-67702-1

D

E

The manufacturer's authorised representative in the EU is Springer Nature Customer Service Centre GmbH, Europaplatz 3, 69115 Heidelberg, Germany. If you have any concerns regarding our products, please contact ProductSafety@springernature.com

Printed and bound by CPI Group (UK) Ltd, Croydon, CR0 4YY
01/10/2026
02225898-0009